Rhetorical Invention and Religious Inquiry

EDITED BY WALTER JOST
AND WENDY OLMSTED

Rhetorical Invention and Religious Inquiry

NEW PERSPECTIVES

Yale University Press
New Haven &
London

For David Smigelskis

Printed in the United States of America.

Library of Congress Cataloging-in-Publication Data
Rhetorical invention and religious inquiry : new perspectives / edited by
    Walter Jost and Wendy Olmsted.
        p.   cm.
    Includes bibliographical references and index.
    ISBN 0-300-08056-5 (hardcover : alk. paper) —
ISBN 0-300-08057-3 (pbk. : alk. paper)
    1. Rhetoric — Religious aspects — Christianity.   2. Rhetoric — Religious
aspects — Judaism.   I. Jost, Walter, 1951–   II. Olmsted, Wendy, 1943–
BR115.R55 R44 2000
230'.01 — dc21   90-089732

A catalogue record for this book is available from the British Library.

The paper in this book meets the guidelines for permanence and durability of the Committee on Production Guidelines for Book Longevity of the Council on Library Resources.

10 9 8 7 6 5 4 3 2 1

Contents

Introduction

WALTER JOST AND WENDY OLMSTED

Perhaps not since the Renaissance, when the rhetorical theologies and theological rhetorics of such figures as Thomas More, Desiderius Erasmus, and Philipp Melanchthon drew on the equally rhetorical Saint Augustine, the Church Fathers, and the Bible, have students of rhetoric and religion had so much to say to one another. Since the mid-1980s, primarily in journals but also in an increasing number of books, scholars in one field have been drawing out significant lines of inquiry and posing provocative questions to those in the other: Are rhetoric and religion in some sense "essentially" wedded? In general, what are the rhetorical warrants for religious belief? How might rhetoric mediate religion's ultimate commitments? How do rhetorical figures inform — or undermine — the movement of mind and heart to God? These and other questions, which are often not explicitly labeled "rhetorical" or "religious" but which are rhetorical and religious nonetheless, arise naturally in a time when language and communication are understood to be vital to thought, even as the meaning, the possibility, of "ultimate commitments" is impugned as hopelessly naive. Yet thoughtful and sensitive people still continue (the Enlightenment and postmodernist legacies notwithstanding) to articulate and practice their beliefs.

When firmly placed within religious, social, and intellectual history or located within the study of theology, the convergence of rhetoric and religion takes one to the most central issues of several fields—philosophy, psychology, literary history, and art—interpreting relations between self, language, and world that are central to past and present cultures as well as to their forms of life. In its exploration of the nature and scope of rhetoric and religion alike, this volume offers some of the best contemporary work being undertaken in these fields, in the hope of reinforcing these interdisciplinary efforts. Some of these essays are previously published works that are held in high esteem in their fields and deserve wider exposure; most were written for this volume. In religious terms, our aims are equally hopeful: we are convinced that these essays can speak to us not only as intellectuals or academics but as human beings. Whether we profess the Apostle's Creed or faithfully read the Torah or critically hold aloof from institutional religion altogether or patiently pursue (or are relentlessly pursued by) the divine or merely find ourselves alternately intrigued and bemused by public discussions of religion, each of us can learn something important about the possibilities of belief in our time. When, for example, James Fodor and Stanley Hauerwas analogize the practice of faith to rhetorical invention and musical performance, when Walter Ong or Marjorie O'Rourke Boyle explains that Christ speaks rhetorically and may himself be encountered as God's persuasive Word, when Mark Krupnick uncovers part of Americans' present-day philosemitism in their literary and rhetorical past, or when Stephen Webb or Thomas Carlson challenges standard academic dismissals that see religious language as irrational or impossible, they are illuminating important religious as well as academic issues. Although our volume confines itself chiefly to Christian and Jewish phenomena, we offer it as a point of departure for further rhetorical reflections and studies into even wider human possibilities.

Indeed, the religious issues examined in these essays can be taken as rhetorical models and resources for community- and self-invention, while the rhetorical approaches to religious matters illuminate ethical, emotional, and substantive dimensions of belief found in areas other than the religious. In this way *Rhetorical Invention and Religious Inquiry* departs from most other interdisciplinary studies of religion—philosophical, comparative, social or anthropological, historical—as well as from all other collections on rhetoric that we know. More specifically, in a companion volume to this book entitled *Rhetoric and Hermeneutics in Our Time,* "rhetoric" was broadly said to comprise "a family of questions about what is involved in influencing oneself and others regarding (the interpretation of) any indeterminate matter."[1] As the essays in this volume show, rhetoric necessarily overlaps with philosophical, historical, and other interests that inform the interdisciplinary study of religion. What is unique to the rhetorician's approach, however, as Manfred Hoffmann and

Victoria Kahn exhibit so well, is what may be called the "holistic" interest in the real, live, existing human being. As Renato Barilli puts it in his introduction to rhetoric, "Rhetoric is a comprehensive, total way of using discourse."[2] In the study of religion, accordingly, scholars taking a rhetorical approach locate its philosophical grounds as much in emotion as in reason (Shuger, Boyle), are concerned with practical problems of conversion or coming to faith (Olmsted, Eden), or understand its history as bound up with real-life "symbolic action" and its language as excessive as well as reasonable (Krupnick, Webb).

By contrast, rhetoricians with religious interests seem to be a rare breed, if not an endangered species, since the postmodern version of language holds that rhetoric *precludes* religious truth, which is typically cast as the final word in transcendental signifieds; or, at best, that negative theology alone has any plausibility. But this appearance — that "real" rhetoricians cannot care about religious truth or, formulated less personally, that rhetoric can have nothing to do with religious truth because it is philosophically impossible — is as misleading as the equally prevalent claim that religious belief defies the rhetorical commitment to human finitude and contingency. As Brian D. Ingraffia puts it in his *Postmodern Theory and Biblical Theology,* "What sets the biblical God apart from the god of ontotheology and negative theology is that the God of the Bible has revealed himself in human history. . . . The logos of biblical theology is radically different from the logos of Greek philosophy and modern rationalism."[3] Thus recent critical attacks on religion in the name of rhetoric may *not* be the last word after all, and fuller versions of "rhetoric" may have much to say that illuminates if not the "rationality" of belief then the sort of considerations a rational person might consider in coming to belief, and that illuminates what otherwise reasonable people do when they practice their faith. Conversely, even the scientific commitments of nonbelievers may be understood to exhibit fundamentally religious cares and concerns in ways that people may not even notice.

The present study of rhetoric and religion is meant to resist and correct the contemporary tendency to consider a particular version of rhetoric (often a badly reduced version) as the chosen "alternative to the West's philosophical logocentrism."[4] In this well-worn narrative, rhetoric is equated with subversive tropes that undermine tradition, authority, and interpretation itself, all of which are said to be most fully embodied in the metaphysics of presence that is thought to be "religion" proper.[5] By contrast, more-informed approaches relating rhetoric and religion to philosophy, psychology, history, and art liberate rhetoric and religion from the effects of those progressively narrower and more desiccating definitions of these subjects, definitions that historically had marginalized rhetoric, in particular, before it was revived in contemporary thought and scholarship. This rejuvenation has made possible newer inquiries into our two subjects, in which theories of language, reasoning, and figurative speech illuminate faith and its justification and expression. Without serving to underwrite logocentrism, and although also capable of exposing ideology, contemporary rhetoric nevertheless proves to be something other than exclusively an instrument of suspicion.

The present moment opens still further possibilities for recovering both rhetoric and religion. For too long such rhetorical figures as symbol, analogy, and hyperbole have seemed foolish or dangerously "irrational" when considered from the point of view of rationalistic theories of language or methods of proof. But in fact these theories risk "losing a dimension to language which stretches the imagination, challenges reader-made assumptions, and forces unusual perspectives."[6] Pursued in the light of contemporary understandings of reason, language, and history, rhetorical approaches to religion are capable of revitalizing our language and experience alike, by suggesting, for example, how rhetorical figures constitute forms of language that say what cannot be said any other way, or how rhetorical modes of argument are second to none because *all* argument is more or less rhetorical.

More specifically, what kinds of problems does this book address? First, by relating rhetorical theories of argument, persuasion, and language primarily to classic Judeo-Christian religious texts, traditions, and theological problems, the contributors seek to demonstrate that rhetorical means — including the "acknowledgments" made possible by story, adage, metaphor, analogy, and paradox, among others — point to some greater reality that they cannot adequately express. Our scholars disagree, to be sure, about whether such a reality can be genuinely encountered in the language and dispositions of belief. Wayne Booth argues, for example, that rhetorical language, argument, and figuration, though necessarily inadequate to the higher reality which the individual or community seeks, nevertheless partially "re-present" or "show forth" that reality to human beings. In this way rhetoric itself can be understood to lead us toward religious belief — or, said otherwise, rhetoric itself is incipiently religious. Thomas Carlson, Stephen Webb, David Tracy, and Susan Shapiro, however, wish to distinguish between paradoxical language as representing on the one hand an experience of what is unimaginable or unrepresentable and therefore "empty" (as in much modernist and postmodernist art and literature) and as intimating on the other a God who cannot be fully known because of our human limits. In further ways, Paul Ricoeur argues that some forms of language — metaphor, analogy, commandment, and kerygma — manage to accommodate their mutual tensions, while other forms, like parable, create Dostoevskian improbabilities of plot that confront readers with something puzzling, even scandalous, or in any case altogether "other," thus provoking them to question what is disclosed through models and analogies.

Other contributors are preoccupied less with tropes than with topics and rhetorical deliberation in coming to, justifying, or even making possible religious belief. Wendy Olmsted, for example, analyzes Saint Augustine's account of his conversion as a slow, sometimes halting, ever-thoughtful struggle to find his way by sensitive reading and listening, weighing commonplaces and their various probabilities. Debora Shuger generalizes this struggle in terms of reason and emotion imaginatively fused, while Walter Jost investigates three overlapping models of commitment, showing how rhetorical deliberation is first made possible by our human need to acknowledge other persons and be acknowledged by them. These studies, in turn, can be related to the essays we have grouped under the rubric "Rhetoric and Community." Kathy Eden meditates on *koina*, the term that Aristotle and others used to characterize topics "that are held in common," as a way to explain the bonds between rhetoric and religion, bonds (commonalities) which are implicitly thematized in the essays by Mark Krupnick, by James Fodor and Stanley Hauerwas, and by Stephen Happel, and which provide a structure for our book as a whole. The organization of this volume, in fact, might be thought of in rhetorical terms as the interrelation of commonplaces (topics) and their orientations (tropes) — that is, of recurring and variously interpretable positions for inquiry and thought, and of the multiple, often conflicting ways thought can be turned to contradictory purposes, practices, and forms of life.

Although all the chapters embody both topics and tropes, Parts 1 and 4 particularly stress commonly held "places" for debate and deliberation, ranging from philosophical and theological foundations of rhetoric in Part 1 to rhetorical strategies for thinking about and practicing religious belief in Part 4. We begin and end the book this way to highlight the centrality that we award to topics in rhetoric — in Kenneth Burke's language, our chosen "God-term" that focuses attention on where, what "places" (which is to say *who*) we human beings are as historical and contingent creatures.

Parts 2 and 3 share a rhetorical stress on the sometimes nonargumentative tropes and other linguistic and artistic means of figuring both the human and the divine and our relation to it. Here the questions are, Within what narrative and toward what beginning and end shall our topics be turned? and What kind of "mind-bending" should metaphor, analogy, or hyperbole be praised, or blamed, for? Indeed, at times topics can be thought of as tropes and tropes as topics, when any "place" presupposes a larger metaphor or narrative within which it makes sense, just as tropes like metaphor or irony can open up new ways to think about where (who) we are.[7] As a whole the book should thus help readers appreciate how human beings are at once religious and rhetorical creatures.

At the same time that we have sought to exhibit interrelations of commonplace topics and tropes, we have tried to place the essays so as to suggest various lines of inquiry. Although our main goal was to assemble provocative essays on important but neglected matters, in the process we discovered that the whole may be greater than its parts. We placed Walter Ong's seminal essay "The Word as History" first in the book, for example, because it has largely defined the boundaries of later debates on rhetoric and religion. Ong views the development of the word as a human coming-to-awareness that parallels the coming of humanity to the Logos or Word of God. His simultaneously historical and ontological approach provides a frame for rhetoric and religion as they work together. Booth's essay extends Ong's insight by examining rhetoric more fully as a disciplinary practice that leads to and implicates religious belief. Booth uses the thought of Kenneth Burke to argue that logology, the study of language and especially of the term "God," has theological as well as linguistic consequences. Shuger carries the inquiry into the relations between rhetoric, belief, and truth further by demonstrating how a new critical rhetoric has emerged that is not the opposite of reason or philosophy. In her analysis of Renaissance rhetoric, she shows how historical and contemporary critical rhetoric overcomes misleading disjunctions between reason and rhetoric, re-situating terms in ways that set up arguments for later essays in the volume.

Thus in these and other ways the book presents religion as a quest and rhetoric as the evocation of that quest, even as it describes a passage in which ideas and arguments regarding what it might mean "to believe" develop. Our first section (to indicate one way such a passage might be undertaken), thus confronts several fashionable dismissals of both rhetoric and religion but provides positive considerations for belief, while the following sections unfold inquiries into the possibilities of religious language and its rhetorical and historical range. As editors we hope that the present collection stimulates further studies of these possibilities.

We wish to express our gratitude to Susan Laity, our manuscript editor, for her dependable tact and sense of style.

Notes

1. Walter Jost and Michael J. Hyde, *Rhetoric and Hermeneutics in Our Time* (New Haven: Yale University Press, 1997), xviii. For an interesting addition to rhetorical stud-

ies, see George A. Kennedy, *Comparative Rhetoric: An Historical and Cross-Cultural Introduction* (New York: Oxford University Press, 1998). Kennedy's venture beyond strictly Western models of rhetoric will considerably inform and enrich rhetorical studies in comparative religion of the sort that we have not pursued in the present volume. To our knowledge no work of this kind has yet been done.

2. Renato Barilli, *Rhetoric* (Minneapolis: University of Minnesota Press, 1989), vii.

3. Brian D. Ingraffia, *Postmodern Theory and Biblical Theology* (Cambridge: Cambridge University Press, 1995), 227, 237.

4. Debora K. Shuger, *Sacred Rhetoric: The Christian Grand Style in the English Renaissance* (Princeton: Princeton University Press, 1988), 12.

5. For one of the more sophisticated accounts, see Mark C. Taylor, *Altarity* (Chicago: University of Chicago Press, 1987).

6. Stephen Webb, *Blessed Excess: Religion and the Hyperbolic Imagination* (New York: State University of New York Press, 1993), xii.

7. Cf. Wayne C. Booth, *A Rhetoric of Irony* (Chicago: University of Chicago Press, 1974); for an account, see Walter Jost, "Teaching the Topics: Character, Rhetoric and Liberal Education," in Fred Antczak, ed., *Pluralism and Rhetoric: Legacies of Wayne Booth* (Columbus: Ohio State University Press, 1994), 19–39.

PART I

Coming to Faith in Rhetoric

Part 1 explores relations among persuasion, discovery (*inventio*), and religious faith, investigating how words serve as a place where divine power may intersect with the embodied, temporal lives of human beings. Hence the ambiguity of our title, "Coming to Faith in Rhetoric," which is intended to suggest that rhetoric involves a faith of its own even as it mediates and may entail religious faith. Indeed, these two faiths may be one and the same. Several of our contributors inquire into how human beings use the rhetorical power of discovery to find warrantable religious beliefs and to improve those beliefs through discourse and argument. Behind some of these inquiries lies the question of whether rhetoric, as an art of generating as well as evaluating the reasons for our beliefs, inextricably implicates itself in religion, understood as a universal human need and practice. These concerns with persuasion and discovery take our contributors into further questions of how appeals to emotion and human character work with argument to change people's minds and move them toward the divine.

If rhetoric and religion are to work together to change minds, these chapters suggest, rhetoric must be capable of affecting both the will and the intellect, while religion must be conceived of not as a revelation of an unalterable, fully known truth but rather as an idea mediated by discourse and the human attempt to evaluate and improve our religious commitments through discourse.

Religion can be understood as open to inquiry and evaluation through the intellectual, emotional, and ethical means available to rhetoric. At the same time, in order to be useful to religion, rhetoric must not be reduced to sophistry, capable only of promoting or subverting ideology. Certain truths and goals must be conceivable as truer and higher than others.

It is not by accident that we begin this book with a chapter from Walter J. Ong's pathbreaking *The Presence of the Word* (1967), which is still in print and still as provocative and profound a rhetorical approach to religious matters as when it first appeared. The chapter we have chosen, "The Word as History: Sacred and Profane," addresses the intersection between God's communication of himself and the strategic point in human history when this communication took place. Ong argues that although the historical moment when interior human awareness met an external event was crucial, it does not follow that "the Hebrew and Christian revelation" is "no more than a projection of the human psyche at one of its stages of development." Instead, "the word of God fits the psychological structures of the milieu in which it acquires its biblical currency." "The question is thus not whether one's views or beliefs or knowledge reflect one's psychological structures or even psychological needs (if they do not, they are useless for representing objective truth) but whether they do so in the right way or not — whether in doing so they relate to actuality."

In spite of Kenneth Burke's demurs that his own interest in religion encompassed not the study of God (theology) but only the study of language (logology), Wayne Booth argues that "Kenneth Burke is a modern prophet engaging in a postmodernist, postpositive revival of religious inquiry." In defending this claim, Booth advances the challenging notion that all expressions of value imply hierarchy and that once we accept the belief that some hierarchies are "superior to others," we find ourselves on an ontological ladder leading to a belief in a value at the top (what Burke calls a God-term). In Booth's version, rhetoric both presupposes and leads to religion.

Debora Shuger approaches the quarrel between the philosophical validity of religious belief and its rhetorical power in a different way, arguing that too often the persuasive power of rhetoric to move the emotions has been devalued by modern and postmodern thinkers who overemphasize the "quarrel between philosophy and rhetoric." These thinkers believe that rhetoric lacks "responsibility to the Truth or to the Good" and that it seeks "victory rather than understanding." Shuger's groundbreaking work on the history of the grand style demonstrates to the contrary that Renaissance rhetorics articulated an emotionally powerful and distinctly religious *inventio* that is accountable to both the true and the good. Erasmus, for example, believed that rhetoric could be serious and vehement, evoking a sense of urgency and involvement in religious issues in speakers and audiences alike. As Shuger notes, Bartholomew Keckerman argued in the seventeenth century that "since both moral and spiritual life are less a matter of theoretical knowledge than of rightly ordered will, the preacher . . . must concentrate his endeavours on 'moving the emotions rather than [on] teaching the minds of hearers.'" For these thinkers, invention of matter, not form or tropes alone, was the source of rhetoric's moving power. Shuger notes that the "standard postmodern understanding of the rhetorical . . . does not work here."

Chapters by Wendy Olmsted and Walter Jost investigate how rhetorical discovery and prudence function in the religious inquiry into God and into what is to be sought and what avoided in a religious life. According to Olmsted, Augustine's youthful rhetoric (as distinct from the mature rhetoric of the *Confessions*) includes many of the elements that eventually led him to discovery, "but they are isolated from one another and used for narrow, preestablished purposes rather than for the sake of inquiry." The mature Augustine, on the other hand, posits a "*distance* between human and divine judgment" that "constitutes a space for ongoing inquiry." Her essay, like Booth's Anselmian troping of Burke's logology, entertains the question of *why* those who practice rhetorical inquiry (technically *heuresis* or *inventio*) are led to religion. Her essay also suggests, however, that the full inventive power of Augustine's rhetoric tends to remain "elusive for us . . . because of the modern tendency to oppose dialectic and philosophy to rhetoric rather than to sophistic eloquence." (See Shuger on this same point.) Augustine's practice implies, instead, that substance and arguments, not style, have the most profound effects on character and emotions.

Referring to a number of the central thinkers in the history of rhetoric, religion, and theology, Marjorie O'Rourke Boyle argues that rhetoric can be used to move hearers and adapt the soul to the word of God. She demonstrates the importance for the humanists of the power of rhetorical language to move the will and accommodate theology to "the subject and audience of the discourse. Since theology was speech about God by and to mortals, a creaturely measure was to be observed." The language that converts is also rhetorical: "Christ spoke rhetorically because rhetoric is the language of the Holy Spirit, which he possessed in his mission. He breathed this Spirit upon persons in exhorting, consoling, instructing, admonishing, convicting, exciting their wills toward assent."

Finally, Walter Jost brings together three ostensibly different thinkers—John Henry Newman, Michael Novak, and Stanley Cavell—each in his way a pragmatist and rhetorician who attempts to stabilize human thought and activity in the criterial measure or standard of "conscience," variously defined. By juxtaposing their views and extending several lines of their arguments, Jost contributes to the contemporary revival of thinking about conscience by giving the inquiry a rhetorical turn, indicating as well that rhetorical theory and philosophy can gain from these religious thinkers. Novak, for example, engages in another version of the ontological argument that Booth detects in Burke, while Cavell's analysis of acknowledgments "recalls and extends" Newman's and Novak's inquiry "while itself being recalled (called back and corrected) by it."

The Word as History: Sacred and Profane

WALTER J. ONG, S.J.

The Word and the Interiorizing of History

The history of what was originally the spoken word cannot be considered merely as a chain of events, a series of phenomena strung out in a neutral field of time, but rather must be taken as a succession of difficult, and often traumatic, reorientations of the human psyche. As the word moves from sound into space (without ever fully departing from sound) and then restructures itself electronically into sound in a new way, the sensorium is reorganized, and man's relationship to the physical world around him, to his fellow men, to his own thought, and to himself radically changes.

The transformations of the word affect the total situation of man in the world to such a degree as to suggest new kinds of answers, though still only partial ones, to the old questions that lie at the root of history — What is going on in the world? What is the succession of events in human existence about? Answers to such questions provided by historians of the past have tended to focus on successions of external events. From antiquity through the eighteenth century, secular history, insofar as it was distinguished from religious history, tended to be thought of chiefly as political history, the story of external events in externally constituted realms. Even among religiously oriented historians, when Christian salvation history was either distinguished from secular history (as in Augustine's *City of God*) or amalgamated with it (as in Joachim de Floris), secular history was taken to be constituted largely of widely known external happenings. But by the time of Giambattista Vico, the historical mind had taken a noteworthy, Descartes-like interiorizing turn. In *The New Science,* Vico starts with his own "truth beyond question," namely that "this world of civil society has certainly been made by men, and that its principles can and must therefore be found within the modifications of our own human mind." History here somehow comes out of man: to this extent, as Karl Löwith has suggested in *Meaning in History,* attention is focused on the human interior. Georg Wilhelm Friedrich Hegel goes further. For him the history of external events merges with the development of an absolute (interior) Spirit; and for Auguste Comte, history has become the history of civilization and knowledge. From Hegel on, political and other external history has been more and more overlaid, or underpinned, by what might be called psychological history, with the work of Löwith and that of H. Stuart Hughes in *Consciousness and Society* and comparable work by others.

A further step in the same direction is taken by Freud, who in *Civilization and Its Discontents* and elsewhere relates the existence and operation of historical institutions to the structure and restructurings of the psyche itself. The story of social and even political institutions is now told (in part) in terms of what individuals do to survive: they repress the "pleasure principle," followed initially by the id, in favor of the "reality principle," which is sponsored by the ego. The reality principle calls for postponement of immediate gratification in order to secure subsequent real gratification, and demands for its operation a sense of guilt developed under a third sector of the psyche, the superego. At this point, external and public institutions such as kingship and democracy and war can be at least partly accounted for in terms of the individuals' interior reactions to their own fathers and mothers and to themselves. External institutions can be seen to depend upon complicated interior restructurings of the psyche (and vice versa). Not just "ways of looking at things" but the entire personality structure, from abstract heights to uttermost subconscious depths, is quite different in men coming from different civilizations. Both Monarchy and democracy arise from and create differently organized interior personality structures. Insistent awareness of the interaction of interior consciousness and external institutions inspires some of the best historical work of today, such as that of H. Stuart Hughes or Löwith in the books just mentioned. The absence or feebleness of this awareness is probably Arnold Toynbee's most central weakness.

In *Eros and Civilization,* Herbert Marcuse develops these ideas further and suggests that each individual's "autonomous personality appears as the frozen manifestation of the general repression of mankind." In less specialized perspectives, we could say that history is deposited in all of us as personality structure. The framework of awareness out of which I face actuality is the past of mankind, which I acquire as structure in my consciousness of myself and of my life-world by growing into consciousness in the culture that has bred me.

The work of the phenomenologists, from Edmund Husserl on, is of a piece with the development of historiography and with the work of Freud insofar as it intensifies man's sense of interiorized history by making more accessible to descriptive treatment the inner world of consciousness in its "intentionality" or other-directedness. And in an even more sweeping fashion, Pierre Teilhard de Chardin has undertaken in *The Phenomenon of Man* and elsewhere to relate the interior consciousness of individual human beings to the external history of the cosmos. This he does by showing that human consciousness itself, as "interiority," is not an entirely isolated phenomenon but rather constitutes the definitive breakthrough following on a series of preparatory breakthroughs into interiority, achieved as inorganic matter, and then organic matter, have become more and more "interiorized" or organized from within through the stages of cosmic and biological evolution.

Our present concern with the history of the word and of the media of communication, verbal and other, is patently part of man's larger present concern with history as an interior as well as an exterior reality. The word itself is both interior and exterior: it is, as we have seen, a partial exteriorization of an interior seeking another interior. The primary physical medium of the word — sound — is itself an exteriorization of a physical interior, setting up reverberations in other physical interiors.

The Word of God in Hebrew and Christian Tradition

Hebrew and Christian theology has to a degree felt the effects of what we have here called the interiorization of history. It has registered these effects chiefly through existentialist and phenomenological concerns. Thus far, however, it has done little to understand the word of God in terms of the relationship of word to sound. The patristic age and even the scholastic age were far more oral than our own, and yet neither reflected on the oral to the degree that it reflected on the visual, as in the well-known and indubitably valuable exploitation of light imagery in treating of the generation of the Son or Word by the Father.

There is, of course, a vast and rich literature of the Word. Literature about preaching will obviously be concerned with the spoken word as such. But it is informative to note how much of the literature concerned with the Word as the

Person of Jesus, from patristic times on, has veered away from considering the Word in terms of sound to consider the Word in terms of knowledge-by-vision—the Word (or Son) as the "image" of the Father is interpreted all but inevitably as some kind of visual image. What might be a complementary treatment, and a more direct one, of the Word in terms of voice and sound has been rather thoroughly neglected.

An oral-aural theology of revelation through the Word of God would entail an oral-aural theology of the Trinity, which could explicate the "intersubjectivity" of the three Persons in terms of communication conceived of as focused (analogously) in a world of sound rather than in a world of space and light. Such a theology is still so underdeveloped as to be virtually nonexistent. In the Catholic tradition, certainly, instead of a theology of shared consciousness and personal presence (as examination of theological manuals such as Tanqueray's makes clear), we have thus far principally a theology of "relations" (a concept visually based: *referre, relatus,* to carry back, carried back). The communication of the Persons with one another is typically treated in terms of *circumincessio,* a "walking-around-in" (one another). This latter is patently a concept based on a visual analogy with strong tactile and kinesthetic components. These concepts, with others like them, have profoundly aided understanding and should certainly be respected, but their awkwardness shows the strain under which visual analogies must operate when one is speaking of conscious awareness or of presence as such.

A theology of the Word of God as word will not, of course, explicate everything, if only because the history of the word of God among men is not identical with the history of the human word. For the history of the human word is not the history of salvation, as the history of God's word is. But because the human word is uttered at the juncture where interior awareness and external event meet and where, moreover, encounter between person and person occurs at its most human depths, the history of the word and thus of verbal media have rather more immediate religious relevance than the history of kingdoms and principalities. Study of man in terms of the changes in the verbal media establishes new grounds for the relation of sacred and secular history.

The Christian should, however, be under no illusion that the history of the word will enable him to explain either profane history in terms of salvation history (as Jacques-Bénigne Bossuet and others have attempted to do) or the history of salvation—the Incarnation and its consequences as known to the man of faith—in terms of secular history (as Voltaire and others have undertaken to do). But the Christian will consider that, although sacred and profane history are neither the same nor varieties of each other, they are mysteriously related, casting on each other reciprocating, if mysterious, light.

Any understanding of the word of God as word must of course take cognizance of the fact that "word of God" is used in a number of senses within the Hebrew and the Christian traditions, senses not any the less bewildering because of the fact that all of them are related to one another. It would be impossible here to explicate all the details of the various senses, but we can survey some main centers of meaning for the term as found in the Scriptures and basic Church documents from antiquity to the present, such as are collected in Denziger's *Enchiridion symbolorum* and in Leith's handy *Creeds of the Churches*. Details of the various meanings are further discussed by the Catholic theologian Hans Urs von Balthasar in his *Word and Revelation* and by the Protestant theologian Gerhard Ebeling in his *Word and Faith*, to cite only two sources.

In the Bible, as in some other religious traditions, the word of God often refers to an exercise of divine power. God's word is efficacious. "By the word of the Lord the heavens were made," reads Psalm 32 (33), which continues, "He spoke, and it was made; he commanded, and it stood forth." In Isaiah 55:10–11, the word implements God's will: "For just as from the heavens the rain and snow come down and do not return there till they have watered the earth, making it fertile and fruitful, giving seed to him who sows and bread to him who eats, so shall my word be that goes forth from my mouth; it shall not return to me void, but shall do my will, achieving the end for which I sent it." More particularly, the word of God refers to communication from God to man. Such communication can range from something private and humanly inexpressible within the quiet of the individual soul out to the communication implied by the mere existence of the universe itself as either created or controlled by God. With the propensity for auditory models common to highly oral cultures, the Bible often refers to the universe as "speaking" of God or as speaking God. "The heavens declare the glory of God," proclaims Psalm 18 (19).

The word of God can also mean God's communication to the Prophets or others who are to speak out for him (a prophet is first an utterer of God's word, only secondarily a seer). From this sense another readily derives, that of the utterance of the Prophets or others speaking what God has given them to speak as from him. The prophet would ordinarily know that his message came from God, but in biblical accounts he also might not. Balaam (Num. 23:7–24:25) and Caiphas (John 12:49–52) prophesied in spite of themselves, Caiphas without knowing that he was prophesying. Further extended, the word of God is what is heard by Christians in sermons. Speaking for a group of

Reformers in 1566, the Second Helvetic Confession makes explicit and strategic use of this meaning to advertise the high value Protestants generally put on preaching: the Confession states that the preaching of the word of God *is* the word of God.

God's word can also mean his communication to the inspired writers of the Bible. These writers of God's word were not necessarily the utterers of God's word, for the prophets who received and spoke God's word or those who composed songs such as the Psalms were not necessarily the ones who wrote the prophetic books or the Psalter. Catholic theology, which is probably the most elaborately detailed in its theoretical treatment of inspiration, does not commonly consider it necessary that the writer of Sacred Scripture even be aware that what he is writing is God's inspired word. Inspiration is not necessarily conscious. It is recognized by its acceptance in the church, not by its writer's assertion, gratuitous or even accompanied by proofs, that he writes under divine inspiration.

The word of God can also mean what was actually written down in the original texts of the Bible and, by indefinite extension, in copies of these texts and in translations and copies of translations and translations of translations, and so on. This is one of the commonest meanings of the word of God in actual popular usage. "It is in the Bible" — "it" being the translated, written utterance. The history of the biblical text is intricate beyond belief, since the Bible often incorporates into itself lengthy passages that were previously pretty well shaped up elsewhere either by formalized oral tradition or in writing. At what point such preexisting portions become the word of God is not easy for the most adept theologians to say. Catholic theology, which here again has probably developed its theoretical structures most elaborately, is in a state of active evolution at this point, especially since modern scholarship has uncovered not only the complications of the textual history of the Bible but also the intricate and frequently very sophisticated oral substratum, often a formal catechesis, passed on from generation to generation. Some theologians speak of parts even of this oral substratum also as the word of God in the sense that they would accord to it some sort of divine inspiration.

Finally, there is the Word of God who is Jesus Christ. Once Christ comes, this sense of the Word of God becomes for the Christian more central than any other sense. In classic Trinitarian theology, developed by reflection on the Scriptures in the light of both biblical and extrabiblical knowledge and forming the permanent core of Catholic thought and liturgy, the Word or Son, the Second Person of the Trinity, is the primary "utterance" of the Father, equally eternal. "In the beginning was the word, and the Word was with God, and the Word was God" (John 1:1). The Father's Word, which God the Father "speaks," is a substantial Word, a Person, God like the Father, but a different Person from the Father—another "I," who even to the Father is "Thou," to put it in present-day personalist terminology (a terminology which makes rather more accessible than formerly the meaning of much in Trinitarian theology). Although human concepts can never apply adequately to God, but only imperfectly, no matter how they are refined, nevertheless the human terms "Word" and "Son" apply to the Second Person with a directness enjoyed by no other terms. The Second Person is the Word, although he is so in a transhuman sense, a fuller sense, a sense of which the most penetrating human concept of *word* is only a poor echo. Thus it is true to say that the Second Person is the Word, although doing so strains the human concept beyond its normal limits. The assertion has its full meaning only in faith, as is the case with other assertions regarding Jesus—"No one can say 'Jesus is Lord' except by the Holy Spirit" (1 Cor. 12:3). The Word, the Son, himself God, is, in classic Trinitarian theology, the one who takes to his person a human nature so that thenceforward the "Thou" which is addressed to the man Jesus Christ is addressed necessarily to God himself, in the Second Person, for there is only one "Thou" here, a single "Thou" with a divine and a human mode of existence or nature, a divine and human actuality and "resonance" (one might also say a divine and a human "face," but this visually based concept necessarily suggests superficiality if not indeed two individuals).

Jesus Christ was, of course, visible during his life on earth, but to say he was "visible" or "manifest" or that he "showed himself" does not restrict his sensible presence to the field of vision but rather takes vision as the surrogate or paradigm for all the senses. Thus "visible" does for "sensible." Nevertheless, despite this assertiveness of vision in descriptions of the Word Incarnate, his incarnation maintains for the believer a special rapport with sound, for he who is manifest is the Word. One of Jesus' disciples can say that what he has seen with his eyes and touched with his hands (as well as heard), what has "appeared" to man, is the Word of Life (1 John 1:1). The Christian hierophany is in this sense oral-aural. Indeed, as applied to the Word of God the very concept of "hierophany" bogs down insofar as it is rooted exclusively in visual apprehension: the second part of the term "hierophany" echoes the meaning of the Greek *phainein*, to bring to light, to show, to make clear (with primary reference to vision). For if God manifests or shows himself here in the Word (as there is, of course, ample scriptural warrant for the believer to say he does), he more fundamentally communicates himself. Communication peaks in sound.

At this point, the "word of God" becomes more than ever a kaleidoscope of interwoven meanings, for the Word of God, Jesus Christ, himself actually speaks, using human words but manifesting through these words more than they usually manifest precisely because he is the Word. We are faced further with the fact that the Word of God in his sensible human nature is at first, like other men, an infant, who does not speak (*infans* is Latin for nonspeaker). A long-standing heritage of profound meditation on this theme of the "unspeaking Word," the *Verbum infans,* runs from Augustine and other patristic sources through the medieval theologians and a nativity sermon by Lancelot Andrewes in the year 1611 to T. S. Eliot's lines in *Gerontion,* "The word within a word, unable to speak a word, / Swaddled with darkness." When the Word does speak, the words of the Word, the sayings of Jesus, themselves become the core of the good news, the Gospel, part of the Bible — which is as a whole the word of God already. Acceptance of God's kingdom, which these sayings of Jesus announce, is dependent upon hearing, directly or indirectly: "Fides ex auditu" — Faith comes through hearing — Paul declares (Rom. 10:17).

God's word, in all its senses, is for the believer, of course, not entirely like man's word. For it is also like the opposite of man's word, silence. Man's word is fleeting precisely because of the way it not only flows through time but depends on time, vanishing successively with each instance in which it comes into existence. But "the word of our God stands forever" (Isa. 40:8). It occupies time without disappearing with time. It is also like silence, for silence endures; and silence, moreover, in a real way is for man even more communicative than words. It is, as we have seen, of a piece with sound, for it is sound's polar opposite: sound and silence define each other. Words must be interspersed with pauses, silences, to be understood. Indeed, the deepest understanding, especially as between persons, comes often in the silence that follows an utterance, as the effects of the words reverberate without sound in the auditor's (and the speaker's) mind. For sound itself is defective in accomplishing its own aims. Silence makes up for what sound lacks. There has perhaps never been an asceticism, and certainly never a Christian asceticism, which has not made much of silence as a way of life and a mode of communication and presence.

The term "word of God" can be explored endlessly, and a halt must be called here. Through the entire web of meaning, it will be noted, the sense of the spoken word is everywhere utterly basic. To this sense is tied, as has been seen, the feeling for the word as effective, real, powerful, eventful. For truly conceived as sound, word, like all sound, signals the present use of power. When the Son is conceived of as the Word of God, he is certainly not conceived of as a written word, either in the Father's thought or in our own. The Father "utters" the Word. And the Third Person of the Trinity, significantly, is thought of in the Scriptures and subsequently in classical Christian theology as breath (Latin, *spiritus*), the Holy Spirit — connection with oral utterance is patent here. The spoken word is inseparable from the breath, though it is not the breath. Even in the Scriptures as written documents, indeed especially in the Scriptures, the word of God is the work of the Spirit: the biblical writers are "inspired," that is, "breathed into by the Holy Spirit" (2 Pet. 121). Without the Spirit, the "breath" of life, the written letter itself is a threat: "For the letter kills, but the spirit gives life" (2 Cor. 3:6).

The centrality of the spoken word as a point of reference for the various senses of the word of God is due not only to the fact that the spoken word is always primary (writing and print always refer directly or remotely to the word as sound) but also to the fact that the Bible, from Genesis through the entire New Testament including its epistolary parts, registers the oral culture still so dominant when the Bible came into being. Typographic man, unreflective until recently concerning the oral structures of all early human culture, has tended to interpret the oral state of mind as simply "oriental." Thus in *La Parole et l'écriture*, Louis Lavelle echoes a tradition widespread even among scholars when he writes that "all Orientals think that in addition to physical forces there is a magic force which is that of language." We have seen earlier how the attribution of "force" to language derives not from some unaccountable geographico-cultural situation but from the habit of thinking of language in auditory terms (as Lavelle's own culture had also once done) rather than in visualist-typographic terms, and how there is as much truth as magic in the persuasion that language has real force. The oral state of mind and psychological structures so evident in the Bible are strange to us, as we now know, not because we are "Western" but because we are typographic folk, more intensely alphabetized than were the ancient Hebrews.

At the same time, however, despite this firm oral-aural grounding of the various scriptural and traditional meanings of the word of God, God's word in all its senses within the Hebrew and Christian traditions was definitively conveyed to man through a chirographic culture — indeed, through one of the first alphabetized cultures. The word of God centered in the Hebrew and Christian heritage thus came to man at a strategic point in history, which is to say, as we have seen, at a strategic point in the development of the human psyche, when the oral-aural world was being reshaped toward visualism by the force of alphabetic writing.

For the unbeliever, this is an invitation to explain the Hebrew and Christian revelation as no more than a projection of the human psyche at one of its stages of development. The notion of the word of God fits the psychological structures of the milieu in which it acquires its biblical currency. Such association of the word of God, of course, is hardly an embarrassment to the believer unless he is unconscionably naive. All man's concepts always fit the psychological structures of the milieu in which they develop, today just as well as in the past. This does not disqualify them from representing truth but rather orients them historically and helps validate them. The thinking that constitutes our highly quantified modern physical science fits our visualist psychological structures today. True though it is, such science could come into being only in a sensorium organized as ours is, relating itself to man's life-world (of which science is now a part) as ours does, and such science will doubtless be altered (which is not to say disqualified) as the sensorium changes in generations to come. Primitive man could not have known modern science without restructuring his personality in the process—something in his own day quite impossible for him. The question is thus not whether one's views or beliefs or knowledge reflect one's psychological structures or even psychological needs (if they do not, they are useless for representing objective truth) but whether they do so in the right way or not—whether in doing so they relate to actuality. Believers have found that their notions of the word of God do so relate.

Indeed, the fact that the focal point of Hebrew and, even more, of Christian belief is found in a culture which for historical reasons makes so much of the word should be thoroughly reassuring for the believer: God entered into human history in a special fashion at the precise time when psychological structures assured that his entrance would have the greatest opportunity to endure and flower. To assure maximum presence through history, the Word came in the ripeness of time, when a sense of the oral was still dominant and when at the same time the alphabet could give divine revelation among men a new kind of endurance and stability. The believer finds it providential that divine revelation let down its roots into human culture and consciousness after the alphabet was devised but before print had overgrown major oral structures and before our electronic culture further obscured the oral nature of the originally nontechnologized spoken word.

2

Kenneth Burke's Religious Rhetoric: "God-Terms" and the Ontological Proof

WAYNE C. BOOTH

Speculation about Kenneth Burke's actual religion, in the face of his claims to be an unbeliever, has increased over recent decades.[1] Almost everyone who digs into his *Rhetoric of Religion* emerges with some sense that it is a work exhibiting genuine religious inquiry. But we all are plagued by Burke's repeated and aggressive claims that his "religious" interest is only in logology, the study of language, and not in theology: in the word "God" and not in God himself. Thus as I pursue the claim of this essay — that Burke is best thought of as a theologian, or even a prophet — I am haunted by an imagined voice echoing the voice of the Lord at the end of his book, repeatedly answering Satan's speculation with the caution: "It's more complicated than that."

This is actually my second search for the center of this dodgy polymath. My first effort followed decades of shameful neglect — even downgrading of Burke's importance. I had been taught by my mentors, whom outsiders mistakenly called Chicago-School Neo-Aristotelians but who were really a new kind of pluralist, that Burke, like the New Critics, did not really deserve prolonged attention; he was just another instance of the movement trapped in the prison house of language-centered dogmas. What's more, we were taught never to honor anyone who reveled in his kind of parataxis; our intellectual heroes — "syntactic" laborers like Aristotle, Spinoza, Hume, even Matthew

Arnold — never committed Burke's kind of mysteriously clueless drift from one topic to another.

When I finally began in the 1960s to read him seriously, probing behind what too often seemed his airy non sequiturs, I became increasingly — inevitably — impressed. I reviewed his new book on religious language, itself a revelation to me, and I then taught several graduate courses that centered entirely on him and Ronald Crane as complementary, perhaps contradictory, pluralists. Finally, I wrote what I intended to be the first fully empathic, fully *comprehending* account of his whole project. I was even tempted to call it — so confident did I feel — "Kenneth Burke from the Perspective of Kenneth Burke." In what I finally called "Kenneth Burke's Way of Knowing," I celebrated his dramatistic "dancing" according to his pentad (purpose/act/agent/agency/scene) — the five causes that he had developed from Aristotle's four — and I was certain that he would say to himself, "At last I have found one reader who has really understood me."

As it happened, my account offended him, partly because I had placed his "pentad" at the center instead of what he would have put there: his logology, his half-religion. His unhappy response, both in letters and in the article "Dancing with Tears in My Eyes," almost drew tears from mine. Addressing me as "Dear Ever-Wax" in January 1979 (sometimes it was "Dear Ever-Waxing Wayne"), he lashed out with an unequivocal demonstration that I had simply got him wrong: "Your mistake in starting from the dramatistic pentad rather than from the principles of form in the "Lexicon Rhetoricae" was due to a hangover from Ronald Crane's brain-washing of you before you had a brain!" Then, after a bit more nasty-but-witty remonstration, he wrote: "Peace, peace! While I call Crane the Stalin of pluralism."

Was I devastated by his "friendly," no doubt half-jesting, attack? I was. But I went on reading him, teaching his works, quoting him in many a public talk, attempting to probe more deeply into what continued to feel a bit mysterious, unfathomable, shifting under my feet.

A few years later, when I was attempting a pluralism of my own, I felt that the way to honor the validity of Burke's objections would be to print them in the book along with an effort at "placement": not a pinning down but an interrelating of pluralists who honored his "perspectivalism."[2] As I should have predicted, the response, friendly as could be, was clearly that of one who felt grossly misunderstood and mistreated. I had done him wrong again; honoring him as one of three major pluralists, I had misleadingly placed him *between* R. S. Crane and M. H. Abrams, instead of at the beginning or at the climactic end where he belonged. "Maybe it's this way: as a logological pluralist [placed by you] in the middle, I couldn't deserve [from you] an adequate statement of my case at intra, for it wd. look too much like a brand of 'dualistic monism.' So I'm caught in the middle, not like our savior between two thieves, nor like my intermediate section on "perspectives by incongruity" in *Permanence and Change,* but like my adopted and adoptive state of New Jersey, which gets trampeled on by the traffic to and from New York."

What his response demonstrates, even when we catch its jesting tone, is just how much he resented being reduced, as he saw it, to a modified Aristotelian, rather than being seen as a true "logologist" — the student of the deepest implications of our use of language. I had failed to do justice to the rhetorician/dialectician revealed not just in the "Lexicon Rhetoricae" and other passages in earlier works but most aggressively in *The Rhetoric of Religion.* A true logologist studies the word — not the Word as God, but the God-terms that all human languages necessarily implicate. Though he will of course find analytical uses for schemata like the pentad that I had placed as his center, the logologist pursues the "principles of form" that underlie all efforts at analysis. The logologist, in other words, goes deeper than anybody else.

Just where the center of this particular logologist is to be found can never be easily determined. The invitation to write about him once again led me to the first full re-reading of his letters to me, and I have been even more strongly impressed there than in his published work by how many different "Kenneth Burkes" he presented; many of them were "voices" never encountered in his publications. Before turning to my attempt to reunify the explosive Kenneth Burke, I should summarize the longer account I give of a selection of eight of them in "The Many Voices of Kenneth Burke, Theologian and Prophet, as Revealed in His Letters to Me."[3] One must hear the threatening, contrapuntal variety in order to savor any attempt to discern not just a coherent logologist, in his transformed definition of the ancient term, but a disguised theologian.

- Voice One: the self-reproaching egotist who is never fully satisfied not just with my efforts but with anyone's to sum him up: as if to say that those he calls "the assholes" — Frank Lentricchia, Fredric Jameson, Wayne Booth — haven't bothered to read all or most or any of his work.
- Voice Two: a man who, while still suffering from competitive angers, turns the blame upon himself — what he once called his "sickly sylph"; the man who feels guilty about making his professional vexations "his home." "I feel guilty (heck, I always feel guilty in some way . . .)"[4]
- Voice Three: the witty, genuinely humble comedian who simply enjoys joking about everything, whether putting down other critics, putting down himself, or inventing new versions of his own schemata, Christianity, or

just about anything. Some of it is just plain irresistible wordplay, as in his "Thanks one whole lot for thy promptitudinosity" or his occasional reference to his book *Attiturds Towards History*.

- Voice Four: an old man lamenting his aging and thinking about death but still usually keeping alive the wit of Voice Three. He often sounds much like the kind of preacher one would like to attend to on a Sunday morning after a bad week in one's later decades. The echoes of biblical language pour out, but with never a hint of any sort of literal theism.
- Voice Five: a voice that sometimes harmonizes the others by sounding like the publishing scholar pursuing his universalizing attempt to understand everything. I can think of no modern scholar whose letters contain as much genuine critical thinking (and of course controversy; Ronald Crane is a close rival).

This voice exhibits two quite different tones that might be labeled "the rhetoric of suspicion" and "the rhetoric of affirmation."

- Voice Five-A: the skeptical prober who sees humanity primarily as inventor-discoverer of the skeptical negative, and thus as a creature inevitably caught up in misguided, sacrificial, competitive, destructive entelechial warfare salvageable only by — well, by the efforts of dialecticians like Kenneth Burke. This KB can be seen as a man who uses the negative as what knocks down every aspiration toward perfection, even though the aspiration toward perfection is irresistibly built into our natures. He can often sound like a forerunner of the deconstructionists: as if every statement (except of course some of his own) can be deconstructed to show how it can lead to aporias.[5]
- Voice Five-B: still the relentless scholar but one who would be troubled by the comparison I just made. This is the voice not of the system-smasher but of the confident system-builder, the voice of a man who believed not just that there is indeed some truth worth pursuing but that he was really pursuing it in the one proper way: a voice that could jokingly say he wanted to live a long time because he always wanted the last word.[6] This voice he himself even called the "absolutist," when he was seeking to divorce himself from what he saw as deconstructionist relativism or the reductionism of behaviorists.

It is the clash between these two voices that proves most interesting when we think of him as doing theology: everybody got everything wrong, because everybody latched onto only one fragment, whereas the true KB was attempting the noble, if impossible, task of putting it all together.

But that gets me ahead of my story.

- Voice Six: the poet, the man attempting not to pin down the world with speculation but to evoke wittily or feelingly a lived piece of that world, with all its resistance to any formulation in prose. His letters would often include poems cooked up on the spot or copies of poems that he later published. Some of them are a bit prosaic, even windy, but some are as lovely as—and as pertinent to my thesis here as—the one he sent me on the death of his wife:

> Postlude
> When something goes, some other takes its place.
> Maybe a thistle where had been a rose;
> Or where lace was, next time a churchman's missal.
> "Erase, efface," Life says, "when something goes."
>
> Her death leaves such a tangled aftergrowth,
> By God I fear I have outlived us both.

I could go on adding voices—Burke the physician, curing the world's ills; Burke the ecologist (his ecological explorations have by now produced a large following: in the thirty-six dissertations I've located relating him and religion, a large proportion emphasize ecology as if it were his center). But the point is not to add to the chaos but to face the question, Can I find any one voice that might unify the huge chorus? Though all of these voices, these roles, are audible, does the full coherent drama ever get written, with any kind of discernible center?

Naturally I did not hope for the kind of coherence that postmodern theory, the early pragmatists, and the ancient rhetorical tradition have rightly ruled impossible. Our "selves," our "centers," are all essentially social—more or less multiple even at our most coherent. But the more I read Burke the less he seems to be to be torn apart in his manifold roles: the question, Does the chorus harmonize? makes more and more sense.

To face that question adequately requires a close look at two more voices, those that interest me most at this stage of my life: Seven and Eight.

Voice Seven is that of a man who I claim employs Voice Three, the wit, to play with religious phrasing and terminology, rarely with so much as a hint of any actual religious belief—indeed, usually with no admission that he's coming even close to addressing religious questions religiously. Burke again and again claims that his logology can neither prove nor disprove religion or the existence of God, and I have nowhere found any statement in which he admits to being anything other than an agnostic who was raised as a Christian Scientist. But if you read his work with religion in mind, you find from the beginning an astonishing amount of subtle allusion. Some of this is perhaps merely a verbal echoing of his religious upbringing, no more meaningful than his use of the word "orange" or the phrase "to cash in." But the religious allusions are impressive. The letters are my prime source of this voice, though it can also be found in any careful reading of most of his poems. The letters are laden with biblical phrasings. Of course, that is true of the writing of most good writers, even professed nonbelievers like Joyce and Beckett. But there's an astonishing amount of direct reference to God, some of it obviously only playful, some of it ambiguous.

As you read the following, help me decide whether Burke is addressing God, in your definition, however obliquely:

> February 7, 1976
> Only God can know how much I may be sacrificing when I fail to cash in on this sure thing for myself.
>
> May 13, 1977
> And you phoned me on my God-luck day of all days (Wow! I thought I meant "good." Give me enough Friday the thirteenths, and I'd own the world.)
> Forgive me for being so superstitious.
>
> May 31, 1977
> The makings of "please" are in the infant which, as it develops from speech-lessness into talk and even talk-about-talk, learns to transform its spontane-ous cry into a mode of communication. It began by crying because it had a bellyache, and it learned to cry as a way of summoning mamma. Thus I would see religion as grounded in prayer, supplication — an infant experience that confronts the basic "speaker/speech/spoken-to" design. . . .
> Ennihow, such considerations may indicate why I felt that it wd. be spec-ulatively relevant to start my hymnal deductions from "we in our weakness cry unto thee." Proceeding thence to the Latin amplifying of thee, and thence to the "mediatory" stage of Christ as the transition from topics of power to topics of weakness. Viewed thus, at least the chorale is well-formed.
>
> January 16, 1978
> Would C[ritical] I[nquiry] want this companion piece (which I have re-cently revised)? 'Tis but three sentences, a bit longish, but designed as an invocation for a meeting of logologers, and intended to indicate how deeply pious we are, after all. And sure you'll agree: if a guy aint pious enough to scare himself, he . . . well, what the heck?
>
> January 29, 1978
> Meanwhile, here's what makes me feel that Big Shot may still be on my side: Were I not down here [in Florida] now, the chawnstes are that by now some or-gan of mine would have been expertly excised in the light of my symptoms. . . .
> Ennihow, 'tis a sunny Sunday morning, and I wish the same even to [you]

Mormans; and may we all be enterprising, as one thing leads to another. I write you as an ex-Christian-Scientist, with love to all.

January 2, 1979

Ennyhow, apparently there is a God—for youenz guys, and not us, are getting the worst of the bad weather.

I find that whenever he is worrying about aging, ill health, or dying, he moves quickly to religion.

April 12, 1980

Gad, is it a brain-lesion? I can imagine how an unwanted x-ray of the brain (circa 3 ½ years ago) could have begun what now attains fulfillment (Ah! most glorious word: "Teteletai," I think the Greek is, but I can't check on it, for someone seems to have "borrowed" my Greek N.T.; consummatum est, before our legendary savior mythically bowed his head and died; es ist vollbracht, as per one of Bach's passions—the Greek, I think, wd. be a reduplicated future perfect). But heck, a guy like I'm could be excused for feeling a bit "sacrificial" if he proves to be the victim of unwanted scientific prowess, e'en as he now welcomes the powers of applied science to check on these matters of its own excesses.

I feel so damn-tangled, I'm almost ready to welcome a sugar-augury that would settle for incipient diabetes. And in any case, we're dealing with a physiological condition, regardless of its source. . . .

KB.

"Source" is not capitalized. Source is not at this point discussed. And when it appears, in any context even vaguely religious, it is usually surrounded with "if"s or scare quotes.

February 8, 1973

Even if there be a heaven, and I were able to get there (two tremendous if's indeed!), even with infinity in which to catch up on my required reading, I could neer catch up with Dick [Richard McKeon].

In my view, even those "if's" demonstrate that what we've seen him call the "Big Boss" or "Whomever" is always in the wings.

That leads us to Voice Eight, the one that I claim at least comes close to harmonizing them all—though still of course in an irreducibly complex chorus. This is the voice that becomes most prominent in *The Rhetoric of Religion,* the voice that openly and systematically probes into religious questions. It is that of the man who revived and transformed the word "logology." It is used by a man who increasingly in his later years unites questions about religious language with questions about other perfectionist quests and worries about the triumphs of technology, about ecological decline, about aging and death—and always about the incompleteness of his corpus. The Kenneth Burke we meet in that book, wrestling with Genesis and the works of Saint Augustine, daring to create the cleverest dialogue between God and Satan since Milton—*that* Burke is "doing theology."

Dealing with this voice we come to that grand unanswerable question, What were Burke's deepest unspoken beliefs about God and creation? Obviously I cannot hope to answer that question firmly, but what I cannot doubt is that genuinely religious questions—according to my own conception of genuine religion—were at the center of his later thinking. In his youth, the miracle-flaunting gods of his religious training had been killed off by science and modernism. Then in the early thirties he embraced for a time what might be called the god of aestheticians, Beauty or Symbolic Richness. Some of his essays then sound almost like a defense of art for art's sake. The young aesthetician was a man who thought he had found a new, superior religion—beauty, form. But he then soon discovered that this was not enough, and turned briefly to left-wing politics, as if the replacement for religion should be Human Progress. When that also proved insufficient, he took up what I now call the lifetime project of disguised theology.

It is still true that Burke remained "irreligious," if to be religious requires that one embrace some sort of church. If religion requires unambivalent belief in an intervening providential Lord, Burke is again out—most of the time, even though, as you've heard, the question is often on his mind. To call someone religious, one must have some sort of clarity about what religious belief is.

To me, as I am sure it would have been to Burke, the answer must be "rhetorical": not that one literally accepts any single verbal formulation of a dogma but that one exhibits, verbally or practically, commitment to certain crucial "marks" or "signs" of belief. These necessarily ambiguous, not to say vague, marks of the believer can be thought of under the traditional notion of topoi—the almost-empty places-of-agreement where those who think they disagree can stand as they hammer out their disagreements.

A truncated version of the religious marks that I shall discuss more fully elsewhere can be superficially applied to Burke like this:

1. Belief in a "cosmos" or "order" or "set of principles" that is/are superior to the tangible world that we think of as the "everyday" or "quotidian" world. Burke's language is always loaded with a sense of the "order" that is just out of reach, awaiting but defying his final formulation.

2. Belief that we live in a lesser version of that larger system; what we see around us is self-evidently inferior to the cosmos we can imagine. My everyday world is obviously maimed; my "cosmos," in fact, suggests standards by

which I come to see that something is radically wrong with my everyday world. The times are out of joint. We live lives that are at least partially broken, in need of fixing. (In other words, Genesis got it right: there was a Fall.) No preacher has ever dwelt more aggressively than Burke on what is wrong with the world — including what is wrong with blockheaded criticism like Booth's.

3. Belief that I, the believer in the existence of that order, that cosmos that somehow got maimed, am also partially out of joint, in need of being repaired: made better than I am at this moment. Perfection is beyond me, yet I long for it. Again his work reveals this throughout — but it is much more explicit in his letters than in his published works.

4. Belief that I have a responsibility to do whatever fixing I can of what is wrong not just with myself but with the tangible world. Has any critic or philosopher ever worked more aggressively than Burke to cure the world of its ills — even while echoing Hamlet's "Oh cursed spite, That ever I was born to set it right"?

5. Belief that whenever my immediate impulses conflict with the standards my cosmos or God implies (or pronounces), I have a duty to abide by or pursue the standards. It is this belief that leads so many overt believers to talk about feeling guilty all the time, as we find Burke the nonbeliever talking in his letters: nobody can fully live up to the standards implicit in any fully articulated view of the creation — of the totality of things.

. In short, if we choose to define religion not according to this or that particular denomination's formulation but as an elusive, always ambiguous *belief in an ineffable, mysterious but real cosmic creative power — not just nature in the pantheistic sense but the creating and ordering of nature that somehow keeps getting "broken"*; or if it is *belief in the power that confusingly but genuinely commands us to pursue its inner nature and the relation of that nature to ours — dictating, for example, hard honest thought, decent treatment of our fellows, and so on to a long list of Burkean virtues*; or if it is *belief in what Matthew Arnold calls "something eternal not ourselves that makes for righteousness"*; or if it is, in more current terms, *belief in whatever center in the so-called scientific universe gave us the gift of life and along with it the irresistible urge to improve life*; or if — and now I ask you to fill in your favorite ecumenical, pluralistic, nonparticularist belief that you employ when deciding whether this or that ostensibly religious belief is religious, but not when you are deciding whether it is finally the one right belief — if, if, if religion is *that*, then Kenneth Burke is a modern prophet engaging in a postmodernist, postpositivist revival of religious inquiry.[7] His probing of our origins in "nature" and our ways of transcending the world of motion; his defense of free agency against the behaviorists; his probing of our satanic commitments to victimization and sacrifice and our manifold efforts to escape them; his marvelous grappling with the central issues of Genesis and Augustine's work; his many other intellectual moves that traditionally had been made only by theologians, particularly when they constructed the ontological proof for the existence of God—*all* these drives show that religious questions and cautiously labeled "religious" answers were in his bones, aching to come out into the open. It was not just that he perpetually raised interesting religious questions. It was that he was steadily committed to the affirmation: genuine meaning, genuine value, genuine principles are built into our cosmos, however we define it, and our lives have meaning only in relation to that cosmos.

The ache, the commitment, expressed itself most fully in his frequent echoing of the ancient ontological proof of the existence of God. Burke knew, indeed was obsessed with, the knowledge

— that once we speak, we express value,

— that once we express value—a distinction between the good and the not good—we imply a hierarchy of values according to which that judgment makes sense,

— and that any hierarchy of values necessarily entails a supreme value term at the top, a God-term validating the steps in the hierarchy.

This pyramid, he shows again and again, works for any value system, defensible or indefensible. What is more, it always implies that the principles on which a pyramid works have always been there, from the "beginning," and that those who build the pyramid should be aware, as they play naively with their symbolic orders, of the parallel with traditional religion.

His grappling with the parallel is so original that it justifies lengthy quotation:

> The design [any design using language to make distinctions between the "natural world" and the "socio-political world"] must be "mythically" duplicated by the postulating of an analogous arrangement whereby there is a supernatural (or super-sociopolitical) order, with its corresponding hierarchy. This formal "perfecting" of the design, ideally duplicating the human sociopolitical order in "higher" terms, was "prior," was "there from the start," to the extent that it sums up all the principles felt to have been guiding the sociopolitical order. The vision says in effect, "Only if the socio-political order is on such-and-such relations with the principles of all order, can the order be reasonable."
>
> And thus, the "perfecting myth" becomes like the originator of the order it perfects. It also has so rounded out the pattern that the human state of sov-

ereignty over nature can itself be seen as servitude to the superhuman powers or principles by which it is implicitly guided. . . .

Note that we here come upon the logological equivalent of the theological definition of God as "pure act." In principle, the consistency that prevails "eternally" among the terms of a nomenclature is "at rest." The relations are all symmetrically there "in advance," before being "made manifest" in the "history" of an analytic procession from one to another. (*Rhetoric of Religion*, 240–41)

As Burke thus explores the various perfectionist pyramids and God-terms that the secular world has substituted for the Genesis world, he often sounds as if his main point is to convince the scientific-minded (often lumped with "technologists") that they are living in fact in the world of "symbolism": "A logological calculus inclines to look . . . for the continuities in the development from Western theology to the order of modern accountancy and modern technology, particularly since such a calculus helps keep us ever on the alert to spot the role of symbolism as the motivating genius of secular enterprise. Otherwise, our world looks too purely 'pragmatic,' whereas its recently much-accelerated dreams of unlimited power and interplanetary empire become so hard to distinguish from paranoia — we should do best to watch for purely symbolic motivations here, despite the undeniable material reality and might of the technologist's engines" (*Rhetoric of Religion*, 170).

As I make my way through the qualifications and the multiplied scare-quotes in such passages, I simply cannot resist seeing a Kenneth Burke who is combating, as best he can, the scientism or "enlightenment" that discards what I would call religion. Note how he concludes that passage: "Insofar as 'technologism' is a 'religion' (and it is a 'religion' to the extent that technology is viewed as an intrinsic good, so that its underlying unspoken assumption is: 'The more technology, the higher the culture'), we had better favor a calculus that keeps us always aware of technology's possible relation to theology's vast motivational Cathedrals, and particularly such as Augustine's, which is so tirelessly concerned with problems of words and The Word" (*Rhetoric of Religion*, 170–71).

Reading such passages, I never can resist asking, "*Why* had we 'better favor a calculus' of your kind, O master? Where does your authorization to use that word 'better' come from?" By now I think we know the answer: it comes from Burke's notion of what is "intrinsically good," as discovered in his picture of how our worlds are ordered.

Through all such talk Burke is always careful to dissociate himself from any claim that he embraces any one pyramid or hierarchy — except the one implicit in his own pursuit of what is true about the world. Such theories, he says, do not "dispose of the possibility that one such 'myth' may be 'true' while the others are 'false.' It merely explains the verbal mechanisms by which such myths can arise, regardless of whether they are true or false."

But though he sees the many ways in which such inescapable hierarchy-building can lead to a perfectionism that destroys and to God-terms or "entelechies" that are absurd, I see him as driven by the conviction that if we are ever to achieve loving peace, if we are ever to destroy war, if we are ever to pursue a proper ecology — indeed if we are ever even to formulate a defensible way of talking about the world — we must not just ask the questions about that hierarchy that the best religious questioners have always been asking, while translating them into a mere study of how language works: we must ask them religiously. We must, that is, commit ourselves to the belief that some value-pyramids are superior to others, a belief that lands us back on the onto-logical ladder. "According to what value judgment is my ladder (KB's) superior to that of the technologists?" Answer: according to value X — and in his practice KB reveals in thousands of places that he sees his central endeavors as superior to many another. "Just where does that value reside?" Well, KB always implies, it has been present "in principle" from the beginning: horizontal, temporal questions can always be translated into "ladders," and vice versa. "Is the 'top' real — does it have genuine existence or is it only an idea?" (This is the question that has led many a critic of Saint Anselm and Descartes, like Kant, to get off the boat: merely to think about a top doesn't show that it's there.) Why yes, my KB always implies about his "top": it must be real, from the beginning — real in the sense of existing, of being, of acting from top to bottom of the pyramid.

Although it is true that the "tops" of most pyramids, like the notion of technological perfection, are likely to prove illusory, the top of my pyramid — the truth about what is good for humankind and how we should pursue it — is actively working in the very moment of our questioning. To talk of any non-illusory hierarchy, for example, the difference between honest dialogical inquiry of my kind and scientific cheating, as if it were merely invented, willfully imposed, by language users, would be absurd. As Anselm put it (making the same point about the inescapably real existence of supreme being), and as the later Burke often almost put it, only a fool can deny not just the radical distinction, say, between the world of motion and the symbolic world of action but also the distinction between genuinely good actions and bad actions, along with the hierarchy of values that that distinction introduces and finally, the existence of "good" at the top, from the beginning.[8]

In sum, Burke joined, always in a sense reluctantly, usually surrounding his deepest affirmations with quotation marks, the community of religious believers. Here is how he concludes *The Rhetoric of Religion* (before he added the "Prologue in Heaven"): "But what of 'providence'? What of 'divine fore-knowledge'? Is there an empirical equivalent of that? As regards the infinity of particulars that will make up tomorrow, no. But 'in principle,' formally, tauto-logically, most decidedly yes. For language is just made that way. And in its will is our (definition of) peace."

I would sometimes push him, as I've tried to do here, into openly fusing the two grand ontological pyramids, the substantive hierarchy of good versus not-so-good, leading to "the philosopher's God," and the linguistic hierarchy of value-laden terms, leading only to diverse God-terms. I would argue that some versions of his ontological proof for the inescapable triumph of God-terms could be inserted into Anselm or Descartes without disrupting their texts. "What keeps you from making the leap," I would ask, "from one pyramid to the other? You always imply and often assert that the values underlying your symbolic ordering are superior to those dominant in the technological age. You don't think that difference was just invented by modern man. Aren't you thus just a disguised but true believer — not in this or that God-term but in an untraditional philosopher's god who fits your notion of how the world works and what we ought to do about it?" (We never discussed the question of an intervening, miracle-producing god, since that had nothing to do with my point.)

He always rejected the full affirmation, though he sometimes would equivo-cate. "Oh, sure," I remember his saying, "You can cook up a definition of God-as-One-Part-of-Nature that I might embrace." But he would usually turn to that other question, about whether his logology is too tightly tied to Christian thinking. For example:

> Somewhere . . . (I seem to have lost the reference) you seem to feel that my logologizing of theology is too local to Christianity. Though the stress upon the motif of "original sin" as "inherited" from the "first" man is a major "strategic" device in "rationalizing" the grandest case of infanticide conceiv-able (much grander than its O.T. forerunner in Abraham's willingness to sacrifice Isaac for the good of the cause), I don't see that my way of interpret-ing the story of the integral relationship between the "creation" and the "fall" should be any different if I were a pre-Christian rather than a post-Christian interpreter of the relation btw. "narrative" and "logical" terms for motiva-tional "priority." (Yet it is true that, as the OED tells us, "logology" first meant the doctrine of Christ as "the Word," then later got its analogical secularization as a synonym for "philology.")
>
> One thing is certain here. The Hellenic stress upon the divinity of "the Word" (as per the Book of John, and the sectarian haggles around the role of

the "Judaizers" as to whether that book should be admitted into the canon), the specifically Christian emphasis upon "the Word" did sharpen our awareness of "the Word" as motive. But I can't see how, given any logologizing of any myth in any theological structure, my essential point about temporal and logical priority would be any different. Smattera fack, the issue is discussed in gm [*Grammar of Motives*], written long before my essay on "the first three chapters of Genesis." True, I had been engrossed with Augustine's Latin as early as my days as a masturbating adolescent. And to them as knows . . .

In 1981 Burke submitted to *Critical Inquiry* a brief, somewhat carelessly assembled article called "Sensation/Memory/Imitation/Story," in which he repeated his strong case against the behaviorist's reduction to body, but moved more aggressively to rebut those language-centered critics who claim that there is nothing before language. (See the appendix to this chapter for the full unpublished article). We editors at the journal, supported by Burke specialist William Rueckert, turned it down. As I see it now, we made a mistake: we should have been smart enough to see that Burke was in fact grappling with the very issues I am raising, moving beyond the rhetoric of religious *talk* to the rhetoric of religion. In short, we should have helped him produce a revised version of "Sensation/Memory/Imitation/Story."

We could have gone further, urging him to combine what he had written about individual literary works into that third step in his trilogy, the book he struggled with over the years but never completed: the "symbolic of motives," in which literature as literature, story as story, would have revealed its religious nature.[9]

In the rejected piece, he accompanied each of the four stages of our experience with a dramatic "gong," the last one ringing more and more like what I see as a religious hymn. What he wrote went like this:

> gong gong   gong   ### gong
> sensation memory   imitation /// story
> and — the most musical gong of all — gong: story.

The "gong" of story (like the gong of music that filled his nonpublishing life) resonated with religious tones. It thus seems to me inescapable that Burke moved closer and closer, as the years went by, to an open profession of a replacement for his lost Christian Science, the childhood orthodoxies he had rejected.

My claim, then, is not just that *The Rhetoric of Religion* belongs on every genuine religious inquirer's bedside shelf as an inquiry into religious language. Rather, the book must be seen as one major step in a lifetime of disguised inquiry into genuine religious belief—and thus of a supreme demonstration of how serious rhetorical inquiry is inevitably wedded to genuine religion.[10] Indeed, if I were in charge of the next printing of this matchless book, I would add some polite elaborations about its true point, after the last page of Burke's unequivocally/equivocally agnostic foreword, which ends like this: "In this book we are to be concerned not directly with religion, but rather with the *terminology* of religion; not directly with man's relationship to God, but rather with his relationship to the *word* God. . . . Whatever else it may be, and wholly regardless of whether it be true or false, theology [like logology] is preeminently *verbal*. It is '*words* about "God"' " (vi).

My new foreword would add, in italics or boldface, the following, signed by "Waxing Wane":

> Actually, in contrast to this assertion, Burke was distressed, more and more openly as the years went by, when any thinker reduced all reality to language. Consider, for example, his annoyance about deconstructionists like Derrida who, in Burke's reading, deny the plain fact, the hard substantive reality, that a child learns to distinguish real tastes before he or she learns any words for distinguishing tastes. Any careful reader of the whole of what he called boikswoiks will discover that in his gut, as in his heart, KB knew that he was grappling not just with language about reality but with the reality of value distinctions and their mysterious source at the top. His reality was permeated with the presence of a mysteriously shifting, unfixable totality so complex, so full of conflicts between what look to us like both affirmations and negations, that no human language can ever encompass Him/Her/It/Them.
>
> What you will find if you read this volume carefully, ignoring his warning that it has nothing to do with God or actual religion, are profound reasons for being skeptical about everyone's totalizing enterprise—except, of course, his own: the theorizing of the dialectician/logologist/theologian.
>
> Burke's kind of totalizing is not arrogant but humble; even as he tries to harmonize all his competing voices, he knows, as the Lord says again and again in the great "Prologue" that concludes the book, the dialogue between God and Satan: "No, it's more complicated than that." "It's" more complicated even than "It" seems throughout this book.
>
> What even a careful reading here may obscure is a further distinction that dominated more and more of his thought in later years. Once we move from body/motion to mind/action, from the brute world to the symbolic world, once we take seriously the distinction between "taste of the orange" and words about the taste of the orange, we encounter a further step: the difference between merely pointing with words to something not "present" and telling a story with those words, still about what is not present. Burke sometimes actually calls the symbolic world of words about the "taste of the

orange" the world of spirit. Is not the world of story even more obviously a world of the spirit?

I would save words like "spirit" and "spiritual" for this third world we enter when not just naming oranges but telling stories, or sharing a painting, or composing or listening to music, or worshiping or engaging in genuine prayer, or writing a book like this one, with its elaborate story of life's meaning. In stories, in any medium, we escape from both the body world and the word-bound symbolic-action world into a new world freed from our ties to ordinary time. We move up and out of the temporal order into a new order that many have called transcendence of ordinary time but that may require a new term, perhaps something like "virtual symbolic action." In other words, there are, as Burke always implies but too rarely notes here, two domains within his domain of symbolic action: symbolic naming, "the taste of the orange," and symbolic story making that uses the words "Yesterday I peeled an orange, hoping for the usual wonderful taste, and out popped a geni with a magic wand and . . ."

Well, I must leave it to readers to speculate about the motives of the grand rhetorologist who at one point replied to my religious naggings like this:

June, 5 1979
> Dear Web-ster — and wadda stir!
> Naw, I'm still hangin on. . . .
> No need to [try to] convert a nonbeliever like I'm. St. Paul tells us that there would be no theology without language. And my theories tell me that theology is the "perfect design of grace." Why, then, should a shrewd logologer frustrate the "natural" rites of speech? Why just talk to himself when he could address "Big Shot"? And when he hears himself talk, that would be the equivalent of Paul's pronouncement that "faith comes from hearing."
> As ever, towards freedom,
> KB

Does not the subtle shift in tone within that paragraph show Prophet Burke saying that there's no need for a missionary type like Waxing Wane to try to convert a nonbeliever because KB is already converted? — converted, that is, to his religion, the true religion, not to any standard version? Is he not saying that beneath and beyond the dark inhospitable sky which masked his loneliness lived a rhetorician who saw that sky as divinely, gloriously attuned to rhetorical inquiry?

Appendix

The following is a literal transcription of KB's typescript, with a few corrections of typos and occasional additions in brackets of his original version.

Sensation/Memory/Imitation/Story
Kenneth Burke

A reference [by Brown] to "Kant's notion of knowledge as mediated by the categories of mind" involves Kant's distinction between "percepts," or "intuitions of sensibility" (as per his "transcendental aesthetic") and the "categories," or "concepts of the understanding" (as per his "transcendental analytic"). The body's senses in themselves are a primary medium of awareness, giving us, in our nature sheerly as animals, reports of external conditions. But such sensory "percepts" could be called "immediate," in contrast with the kind of "mediation" that comes to fulfillment in the "conceptual" objectifications of scientific knowledge. Kant also has a third stage, a "dialectic" that deals with "ideas" of "reason." Unlike the "concepts" of the understanding that are "constitutive," these terms have no "objective" counterparts; [they say "What do" rather than "What is]; they involve "regulative" beliefs which cannot be scientifically proved or disproved; yet one should act "as if" they are true. His top ones of this sort are: God, the soul, freedom, and immortality.

Logology of secular cast would somewhat resemble yet depart from that lineup thus: In keeping with the distinction between non-symbolic motion and symbolic action, along with the "principle of individuation" implicit in the centrality of the nervous system, we take it that as regards the body's contact with its environment, it is aware of impressions, as recorded by the senses, in terms of sound, sight, taste, "here" rather than "there," "before-after," heavy, light, moments sometimes painful, sometimes pleasurable, etc. These are a *medium* of "appearances" which could be called (our style) a kind of translation, the figurative use of the term referring to the fact that certain kinds of goings-on "out there" can be experienced ("interpreted" by the senses in terms of sight or sound or as at a particular location, etc.), but only if the organism that "naturally" sees and hears ["from within itself"] does not suffer sensory privation whereby it is blind or deaf, etc. (We need not be concerned with Zen-like quandaries as to whether thunder is noising when there is no ear thereabouts to hear it. Given the centrality of the nervous system, regardless of how everything merges into everything else, a physical sensation is "immediately" the experience of one organism and no other's, as my toothache is mine not yours.)

But besides being *immediately* experienced, sensations may be remembered; besides *seeing* an "appearance," an "image" of something, we may remember such an experience. And the corresponding *duplications* of all sensations could be called "images." (A Platonist would say that a word for such a duplication is the duplication of a duplication.) Hume called such remembrances "less lively impressions," in an empiricist philosophy the attempt to dodge which drove Kant to the ingeniously intricate weavings of a "transcendental" epistemology such that even stylistic challengers like Nietzsche and Marx could be classed as offshoots of Kant, via offshoots of Schopenhauer and Hegel respectively.

To sensation and memory, add imitation. And since humans are the kind of organism that lives by locomotion, we should also include here the kind of response to others that may counter the motions of others. This view of imitation includes both doing exactly what others are doing and, for instance, fleeing because some other is attacking. Mead would have called it "taking the attitude of the other," and "acting accordingly." (Some Zen tricks are possible here, too. If the proverb, "the burnt child dreads the fire" implies a "memory" of the sensation, might it then follow that Pope's proverbial proposition, "Just as the twig is bent the tree's inclined," implies that the tree's inclination is a "behavioral" form of memory? And since his line rhymes with "'Tis education forms the common mind," might we go on to observe that, inasmuch as education is a form of conditioning, if a stick is broken, it has been conditioned to respond in a way it will never forget? But we must hurry on.)

The main point is that sensation and memory as here considered differ in one notable respect from imitation as a form of physiological motion. Such sensation and memory are in the nature of "reports" about the individual body's relation to the conditions of the environment in which, on the basis of its sensory reports, it finds its way about. The term "imitation," as extended to cover the field of locomotive response in general, implies not just a way of swimming with the current, but also a way of going against it—for as Bergson taught us to realize, our *sympathy* with where things *hurt* (or taste good?) can guide our choice of *where* to hurt some other (and thus what to eat, at the edible's expense?).

Logology inclines to assume that, if our primordial ancestors had but gone on thus, sans words, *we'd* still not be any farther from *their* natural responses to a natural environment than *they* were; and there would be no other kind of environment for us, their descendants, to live in now (in contrast with the technologically formed equivalent of exceptional genius which the stupidest of us now is, when going to a supermarket with some money to "freely" buy some "goods"—and in a long, industrious life one could not remotely chart the great complexity of "unnatural" processes and relationships that come to a focus in a sales transaction at the check-out counter).

This all had its beginnings when the primitive powers of imitation could be expended in a direction not possible to sheerly physiological modes of awareness (sensation, memory) and corresponding modes of imitation. The human animal's *departure* from nature (in the purely physiological dimension) owes its origin to the fact that a so-called "natural" language (developed largely by imitation as the child learns the idiom of its tribe) introduces a wholly different kind of duplication. It is the difference, say, between the immediately physiological experience that something *feels hot* and an expression such as "that feels hot," as conveyed in one or another conventional, arbitrary symbol-system.

At that point enter the resources of *story,* resources constituting a realm of motivation in their own right, involving transformations local to any one medium, and in the large developed by modes of analogical extension, itself an aspect of imitation that Bentham called "fictions."

"Immediately" our range of experience (and corresponding knowledge) is confined to the order of "appearances" as reported by the body's senses and memories of such. But the peculiar symbolic medium of communication which, apparently, no other animal on earth "naturally" masters, *mediates* a vast world of accumulated knowledge, fragments of which largely constitute our "orientation," our "adjustments," our notions of "reality," our "taking the attitude of the other," though none of it has the *immediacy* of sensation. It comes from the world of *story,* the realm of *entitlements.*

The *taste* of an orange is a sensation. The *words* "the taste of an orange" tell a story. They are in the realm of symbolic action, a realm that duplicates the realm of non-symbolic motion, but is not reducible to it (though not possible without it). By this resource, which adds narration to speechless nature, there arise in time stories of the Supernatural, or astrology, astronomy, alchemy, chemistry, geology, biology, geography, history, myths and rituals, ideologies and routines, etc. (beginning with gossip and the news; all animals, and even inanimate things, have modes of communication, in purely physical ways; but only human animals can gossip, tell one another stories).

In brief the *wordless* "universe" which can tell no stories gets fragmentarily translated in countless "universes of discourse" made possible by the *public* nature of the medium which the individual wordless human body is born with, the ability to learn by imitation. And the human powers of imitation in this mode of *mediation* are such that many members of the human kind are now monkeying around with things like atom bombs and recombinant DNA — and what a story! . . . and though the day will come when, as was before human speech got started on this planet, things will again go on and on, as processes unmentioned, wholly devoid of story, the resources of story are such that we can say: "What is now going on will forever go on having gone on exactly as it is now going on — and so throughout all eternity [having gone on as they once did go on in a line with whatever we mean or think we mean by "eternity"] (a storytelling word which has grammatical dimensions of its own, with a corresponding range of personal attitudes involving in our idiom first person, second, third, singular, and plural; and be they right or wrong, all attitudes are real so far as concerns their grounding in the constitution of the body).

Notes

Parts of this essay are taken from a talk given at the Kenneth Burke Society meeting in Pittsburgh, 1996. A revised version of that talk will also appear in a forthcoming book edited by Greig Henderson.

1. See, for example, Appel, Burks, Carter, Duerden, Durham, Freccero, Gunn, Gusfield, Jay, Wess.

2. Booth, *Critical Understanding,* chap. 3.

3. This essay is forthcoming in a book edited by Greig Henderson. For a more detailed tracing of a slightly different list of "six Burkes," see Rueckert, who traces Burke the aphorist, the comedian, the dialectician, the logologer, the dramatist, and the poet.

4. Ellipses in original.

5. Several critics have noted how prescient Burke was in "predicting" postmodernism. See Lentricchia and Wess. But others have emphasized differences, some on Burke's side (Henderson, *Kenneth Burke,* p. 99), some on Derrida's.

6. See *Burke Newsletter,* December 1993, p. 6.

7. For a quick sample of language found almost everywhere in his later work, see his "Above the Over-Towering Babble," a review of George Steiner's *After Babel.*

8. A more sophisticated version of the ontological proof for "goodness" is performed by Iris Murdoch in *The Sovereignty of Good.* See also Chapter 6, in this volume, by Walter Jost.

9. *Language as Symbolic Action* was the closest he came to doing that third volume.

10. See my "Rhetoric and Religion: Are They Essentially Wedded?"

References

This listing assumes that readers are aware of Burke's chief publications. Wess provides a full bibliography of his works and works about him.

Anselm, Saint. "Dialogue on Truth." In McKeon.

Appel, Edward C. "Kenneth Burke: Coy Theologian." *Journal of Communication and Religion* 16 (Sept. 1993): 99–110.

Bygrave, Stephen. *Kenneth Burke: Rhetoric and Ideology.* London: Routledge, 1993.

Booth, Wayne C. "Kenneth Burke's Comedy: The Multiplication of Perspectives." In *Critical Understanding: The Powers and Limits of Pluralism.* Chicago: University of Chicago Press, 1988.

———. "Kenneth Burke's Way of Knowing." *Critical Inquiry* 1 (1974): 1–22.

———. "Rhetoric and Religion: Are They Essentially Wedded?" In *Radical Pluralism and Truth: David Tracy and the Hermeneutics of Religion,* 62–80. Ed. Werner G. Jeanrond and Jennifer L. Rike. New York: Crossroad, 1991.

———. "Systematic Wonder: The Rhetoric of Secular Religions." *Journal of the American*

Academy of Religion 53:3 (1985): 677–702. (Contains a "scientific" version of the ontological proof.)

——. "The Transformation of Semantics." Review of *The Rhetoric of Religion: Studies in Logology,* by Kenneth Burke. *Modern Age* 6 (1962): 329–30.

Burke, Kenneth. "Above the Over-Towering Babble." *Michigan Quarterly Review* (Winter 1976): 88–102.

——. "In Response to Booth: Dancing with Tears in My Eyes." *Critical Inquiry* 1 (1974): 23–32.

——. "Letter from a Gentile." *Dialectical Anthropology* 8 (1983): 161–71.

——. "Mysticism as a Solution to the Poet's Dilemma." In *Spiritual Problems in Contemporary Literature: A Series of Addresses and Discussions,* 105–15. Ed. S. R. Hopper. New York: Institute for Religious and Social Studies, 1952.

——. "(Nonsymbolic) Motion/(Symbolic) Action." *Critical Inquiry* 4 (1978): 809–38.

——. *The Rhetoric of Religion: Studies in Logology.* Boston: Beacon, 1961.

——. "The Study of Symbolic Action." *Chimera* 1 (1942): 7–16.

——. "Theology and Logology." *Kenyon Review* 1 (1979): 151–85.

Burks, Don M. "Kenneth Burke: The Agro-Bohemian 'Marxoid.'" *Communication Studies* 42 (Fall 1991): 219–23. (Mainly about KB and Marxism but concludes with interesting speculation about KB's religion.)

Carter, C. Allen. *Kenneth Burke and the Scapegoat Process.* Norman: University of Oklahoma Press, 1996.

——. "Logology and Religion: Kenneth Burke on the Metalinguistic Dimensions of Language." *Journal of Religion* 72 (1992): 1–18.

Descartes, René. *Meditations,* vol. 5. (Other versions of the ontological proof are found in Spinoza, *Ethics,* part 1, props. 7–11, Leibniz, *New Essays Concerning Human Understanding,* book 4, chap. 10; *Monadology, 1* secs. 44–45.) See Hick.

Duerden, Richard Y. "Kenneth Burke's Systemless System: Using Pepper to Pigeonhole an Elusive Thinker." *Journal of Mind and Behavior* 3 (Summer and Autumn 1982): 323–36.

Durham, Weldon R. "Kenneth Burke's Concept of Substance." *Quarterly Journal of Speech* 65 (1980): 351–64.

Freccero, John. "Logology: Burke on St. Augustine." In White and Brose.

Gunn, Giles. *The Culture of Criticism and the Criticism of Culture.* New York: Oxford University Press, 1987.

Gusfield, Joseph R., ed. *Kenneth Burke: On Symbols and Society.* Chicago: University of Chicago Press, 1989.

Henderson, Greig E. *Kenneth Burke: Literature and Language as Symbolic Action.* Athens: University of Georgia Press, 1988.

Hick, John. "Ontological Argument for the Existence of God." In *The Encyclopedia of Philosophy,* vol. 5. Ed. Paul Edwards. New York: Macmillan, 1972.

Jay, Paul. "Modernism, Postmodernism, and Critical Style: The Case of Burke and Derrida." *Genre* 21 (1988): 339–58.

Lentricchia, Frank. *Criticism and Social Change.* Chicago: University of Chicago Press, 1983.

McKeon, Richard. "St. Anselm." Introduction to Anselm's "Dialogue on Truth." *Selections from Medieval Philosophers,* 1:142–84. New York: Scribner's, 1929.

McWhorter, Ladella, and David Cratis Williams. Review of *Kenneth Burke and Martin Heidegger, with a Note against Deconstruction,* by Samuel Southwell. *Philosophy and Rhetoric* 23 (1990): 75–80.

Murdoch, Iris. *The Sovereignty of Good.* London: Routledge and Kegan Paul, 1970.

Rueckert, William. *Encounters with Kenneth Burke.* Urbana: University of Illinois Press, 1994.

Wess, Robert. *Kenneth Burke: Rhetoric, Subjectivity, Postmodernism.* Cambridge: Cambridge University Press, 1996.

White, Hayden, and Margaret Brose, eds. *Representing Kenneth Burke.* Selected papers from the English Institute, new series no. 6. Baltimore: Johns Hopkins University Press, 1982.

3

The Philosophical Foundations
of Sacred Rhetoric

DEBORA K. SHUGER

In a 1990 essay, Stanley Fish suggested that the history of Western thought from Plato through postmodernism could best be understood as a protracted debate between those who seek the truth and the sophists, or as what he terms the "quarrel between philosophy and rhetoric" ("Rhetoric," 206, 209).[1] According to Fish, rhetoric is thus sophistic discourse, at once partisan and playful, and hence doubly "unconstrained by any sense of responsibility either to the Truth or to the Good"; it appeals to the emotions rather than the intellect and strives for victory rather than understanding. Philosophy, conversely, pursues "what is absolutely and objectively true" — real knowledge, "which is knowledge as it exists apart from any and all systems of belief," "knowledge free from doubt, free from metaphysics, morals, and personal conviction." Philosophy is thus serious business, and "from serious premises, all rhetorical language is suspect" (204–5, 208–9). Moreover, Fish adds, "Although the transition from classical to Christian thought is marked by many changes, one thing that does not change is the status of rhetoric . . . [as] the force that pulls us away from . . . a foundational vision of truth," whether secular or religious, "and into its own world of ever-shifting shapes and shimmering surfaces. The quarrel between philosophy and rhetoric survives every sea change in the history of Western thought" (205–6).

This is an old, familiar story. Yet it cannot be the whole story. One need only

skim J. J. Murphy's *Renaissance Rhetoric: A Short Title Catalogue* to sense
that there must be something wrong with Fish's paradigm. If rhetoric is inherently unserious, amoral, and irreligious, how can we account for the scores of
sacred rhetorics — on my count (and Murphy's list is by no means complete)
504 of them, including reprints and reeditions, between 1500 and 1700? Examination of the texts themselves only compounds the problem. The majority
of Renaissance sacred rhetorics, both Catholic and Protestant, do not favor
a dispassionate, unadorned, "philosophic" language but, quite startlingly, advocate a deeply emotional and richly figured style.[2] In his *Theologia prophetica,* Johann-Heinrich Alsted demands that a sermon "be powerful and
strong . . . composed partly of emphatic, weighty epithets and antitheses, partly
of passionate figures" (8).[3] Bartholomew Keckermann, like Alsted an early
seventeenth-century Protestant, recommends that the preacher dramatize biblical scenes "as in a theater," using prosopopoeia, dialogue, and hypotyposis to
place the subject before our eyes "surrounded with various striking details and
circumstances, as if we were painting with living colors, so that the listener,
carried outside himself, seems to behold the event as if placed in its midst"
(*Rhetoricae ecclesiasticae,* 27, 44). The great Spanish preacher and theologian
Luis de Granada advocates the grand style because of its "sublimity and power
to move souls," this being "the special and distinctive duty of a preacher"
(*Ecclesiasticae rhetoricae,* 328). These texts unequivocally sanction the emotional power and shimmering surfaces of rhetoric, yet one could scarcely accuse them of being "unconstrained by any sense of responsibility either to the
Truth or to the Good." They are simultaneously rhetorical and serious.

Fish's paradigm, which summarizes the standard postmodern understanding of the rhetorical, clearly does not work here. Whatever its overall validity,
it cannot account for the ethical and epistemic bases of early modern sacred
rhetoric. Yet given the current unimportance of sacred rhetoric, to investigate
its premises might be thought a rather specialized project. I am not sure,
however, that this is a fatal objection. At least, I shall argue in what follows
that these sacred rhetorics point to key difficulties in postmodernism's "platonic" historiography. In particular, these texts suggest that its central narrative — the quarrel between rhetoric and philosophy — hinges on three deeply
problematic claims about what Fish calls "Western thought": that it viewed
rhetoric as basically another name for sophistry; that it considered the emotions to be *sub*rational; and that it identified dispassionate, objective inquiry
with the pursuit of both Truth and Goodness. I would not for a moment deny
that numerous thinkers, from Plato on, make these claims, but not all of
them — not even all the important ones. If Renaissance sacred rhetorics retain
significance now and for us, it is because they complicate the postmodern

account of Western thought and do so in ways that allow the possibility of disavowing Plato without falling into the clutches of Protagoras.

Rhetoric and Sophistic

The contrast between seriousness and play is central to both ancient and Renaissance thought; in each period, however, this contrast does not distinguish philosophy from rhetoric but rather rhetoric from sophistry. Although *sophistic* has more than one sense—humanists tend to use it as a pejorative synonym for scholastic philosophy—both ancient and early modern usage principally associate it with aesthetic pleasure (*delectatio*), playfulness, and the desire for praise. The sophist uses a highly wrought style to impress audiences with his own artistic virtuosity. Ludovico Carbo thus defines *elegantia* as "a harmonious and ornate style of speaking, designed to delight, as was once popular among the sophists." But he immediately proceeds to differentiate this style from that appropriate to rhetoric: "In *elegantia* is a certain power of delighting, in eloquence the power of persuasion. The former shines and sparkles, occupying the senses with trifles; the latter burns and flames in order to move souls" (23; see also Sturm, 665). The opposite of sophistic prose in most Renaissance discussions is not an unadorned, "philosophical" style but the conjunction of power and luminosity. Although Christ did not use "sophistic elegance and a vain rouge of words and delicate harmony," nevertheless his words were "sinewy and splendid... suited for teaching and moving, which are the two principal gifts of an orator" (Carbo, 18). Rhetoric is not sophistry precisely because the former is passionate, and hence serious *rather than* playful.

The bifurcation of rhetoric and sophistic rests on the premise that visible art inhibits emotional response. As soon as the audience notices how well something is said, it assumes a position of critical detachment. The delight in language for its own sake thus produces a playful, distanced appreciation that is at odds with the commitment and unselfconscious absorption of strong emotion. The sophist excites applause; the orator, passion.[4] Both ancient and Renaissance rhetorics thus typically render the distinction between sophistic and rhetoric via the paired metaphors of game and battle. Criticizing the sophists of his own day, Erasmus writes that such teachers train their students "more for the gymnasium than for battle. . . . When they come to serious matters they seem inept rather than instructed: wherefore scarcely any others are more unprepared for real fighting than those whose whole lives have been spent teaching and learning the art of sword fighting. In their games they know how to slice with a sword the arrow hurled at them before it reaches its goal. But in war the archer does not warn his victim in advance nor abide by the rules of the swordsman's game" (5:849f.). This military imagery can be easily misunderstood. The comparison between the soldier and the orator highlights the vehemence of forensic oratory. More important, however, it picks out the urgency and involvement of all true rhetoric. In this latter sense, rhetoric is not primarily a form of aggression but a kind of commitment to the real issues of human existence, whether political or spiritual. Oratory resembles a battle because both are serious and therefore impatient of virtuoso flourishes and the other self-pleasing refinements of art.[5]

In Renaissance rhetorics, the classical metaphors of oratory as warfare undergo specifically Christian transformations. The contrast between play and commitment, between the shade of the declamatory schools and the sun of the forum, between games and battles, familiar from the ancients, reappears in sacred guise in Nicholas Caussin's attack on florid, "sophistic" preaching: "The Hebrew women are not as the Egyptian; whereas the latter bore children on ivory couches among vain luxuries; the former lightened their womb in the sun and dust, even among their burdens. . . . But we by whom the heat of the day and its weight must be borne, we who must preach the cross, the cross, who must arouse, prick, thunder against all sinners sunk in perfidy by their crimes, what have we in common with these luxuries? . . . Who could fight against sins if tied and bound by the laws of rhythmic speech? What energy and vehemence will he have who plays with circular periods? . . . He does not come to fight, he comes to show off. Do you expect him to contend? He plans to dance" (945).

Christian urgency opposes the refinements of sophistic eloquence — but it does so under the banner of rhetoric. Caussin's martial imagery associates verbal power with spiritual combat, with the agon of Christian existence, not with the speaker's own aggressive designs on his audience. The sacred orator, unlike the sophist, does not fight for victory but against sin. As a late sixteenth-century rhetoric explains, "Because our internal enemies, who treacherously attack us . . . are most strong and fierce, we must move [men's] souls and arouse them to this inevitable battle, lest careless and asleep they be conquered" (Valiero, 45).

As Fish observes, the aesthetic of conversion "is finally an anti-aesthetic. . . . It is surely anti-art-for-art's-sake because it is concerned less with the making of better poems than with the making of better persons" (*Self-Consuming*, 3–4). But although Fish regards this attitude as fundamentally unrhetorical, the same anti-aesthetic suffuses Renaissance sacred rhetoric, which everywhere juxtaposes the language of ornamental, gratifying self-display with passionate and redemptive discourse. The two are incompatible because insofar as language calls attention to itself as art, it undercuts the possibility of emotional involvement, which depends on at least the illusion of sincerity and spontaneity. Since sincerity is a necessary condition for passion, the evident playfulness of conspicuous art defeats the psychagogic and serious aims of Christian rhetoric. Those whose sermons are "so garnished with quibbles and trifles," the Restoration Anglican churchman Robert South complains, act "as if they played with truth and immortality. . . . For is it possible that a man in his senses should be merry and jocose with eternal life and eternal death?" (2:81).

The Revaluation of the Emotions

The sacred rhetorics associate conversion with eloquence rather than dialectic because the former touches not only the intellect but the heart. Since both moral and spiritual life are less a matter of theoretical knowledge than of rightly ordered will, the preacher, Keckermann argues, must concentrate his endeavors on "moving the emotions rather than [on] teaching the minds of his hearers, for men sin more from corrupt emotions than ignorance of the truth" (*Systema*, 2:1392). In his magisterial biblical rhetoric, the early Lutheran theologian, polemicist, and scholar Flacius Illyricus likewise comments, "Emotion or the movements of the heart govern practical knowledge and choice. . . [and] Holy Scripture deals not with speculative but practical knowledge, which God wishes to be, above all else, living, ardent, and active" (1:179). Sacred rhetoric presupposes an audience at least nominally Christian and therefore less in need of being intellectually convinced than of being moved to embrace what it already believes true.

But these arguments for the efficacy of emotional suasion do not address the problem of its epistemic value; as Fish notes, philosophy mistrusts rhetoric precisely because it muddies objectivity with emotion, or, as John Locke memorably put it, "If we would speak of things as they are, we must allow that all the art of rhetoric, besides order and clearness . . . [is] for nothing else but to insinuate wrong ideas, move the passions, and thereby mislead the judgement" (3.10.34). In antiquity, as in the Enlightenment and thereafter, the pursuit of truth was typically (although not invariably) held to require dispassionate, rational inquiry, so that rhetoric's power to move the emotions seemed little else than the power to distort reality and deceive reason.

The polarization of reason and passion, and hence of philosophy and rhetoric, does not seem, however, to have been central to Renaissance thought. Into the seventeenth century, the distinction between rhetoric and philosophy centered on decorum rather than epistemology. Sacred orators and scholastic philosophers shared the same basic doctrines and beliefs. Rhetoric differed from philosophy in being a popular and practical art, more concerned with right action than speculative inquiry,[6] but both disciplines, in the still largely Christian cultures of the Renaissance, assumed and expounded the same Truth. Thus, in contrast to virtually all classical thinkers, Cicero as well as Plato (both of whom took for granted that philosophic wisdom differed in substance from popular belief; Seigel, 9–10, 19–25), Saint Augustine repeatedly insists that although a Christian "may be unacquainted with the writings of the philosophers[,] . . . [this] does not mean that he is ignorant of the teaching thanks to which we acquire knowledge of God and ourselves"; rather, Christianity is a "universal way," given "not to a few sages, but to the whole nation, an immense people" (*City,* 8.10, 10.32, 10.13). George Herbert's "Faith" makes the same point:

> A peasant may believe, as much
> As a great clerk, and reach the highest stature.
> Thus dost thou make proud knowledge bend and crouch,
> While grace fills up uneven nature.

Because Christianity subordinates knowledge to faith and love, it weakened the classical link between the philosophic quest and the summum bonum. Once gnosis no longer leads to the fulfillment of human existence, it sinks from a divinizing power to a technical specialty. For the mid-seventeenth century Protestant Johannis Ursinus, in contrast, preaching aims not merely "to arouse a probable opinion but rather divine faith . . . to the glory of God and their own salvation" (Ursinus, 9; see also Fenelon, 89). Insofar as saving faith is more valuable than systematic argument, the superiority of philosophy to rhetoric with respect to either its methods or its ends seemed less evident to early modern Christians than it had to Plato.

The deeply favorable view of the emotions that is characteristic of the sacred rhetorics depends in part on denying reason's exclusive proprietary rights to truth. The emotions present a threat to rational objectivity but not to faith, particularly if one understands faith in the Protestant sense of *fiducia,* or trust. But the principal factor in the legitimation of affect, and hence of rhetoric, was Augustine's sweeping and massively influential rejection in *The City of God* of the classical intellectualist tradition with its hierarchical faculty psychology in favor of a more unified picture of mental activity, one in which feeling, willing, and loving become tightly intertwined. The emotions, Augustine thus argues, "are all essentially acts of the will," for as the will is attracted or repelled by different objects, "so it changes and turns into feelings of various kinds." Volition, subjectively experienced, is emotion, and Augustine uses the term "love" to denote this orientation of the self toward the desired object (14.6–7). Affectivity, instead of being an irrational perturbation, thus moves into the center of spiritual experience.

The Renaissance appropriates Augustine's psychology for rhetorical theory, restoring the connection between the emotions and rhetoric that is fundamental to Aristotle but thereafter largely abandoned. This is particularly true for the sacred rhetorics, since Renaissance Augustinianism belongs to the history of the religious renewal, both Catholic and Protestant, that took place in the sixteenth and seventeenth centuries. Many of these texts, especially the more scholarly ones, contain detailed lists of emotions as part of their emphasis on *movere* and passionate discourse. Almost always the list begins with the love of God and includes hope and sometimes even faith—the Pauline theological virtues—along with spiritual joy, contrition, and desire for God, as well as "secular" emotions like shame and anger. Only the nature of their object differentiates secular from sacred, evil from good emotion. "For the sake of example," Carbo writes, "if desire (*concupiscendi vis*) is directed toward the heavens, it brings forth praiseworthy emotions which move us toward perfect virtues: as weariness of this life, fear of future punishment, desire of eternal beatitude, love of God, contempt of self, and others of this sort" (204).[7] The sacred rhetorics can advocate an intensely emotional style because the whole view of the passions has changed and broadened to include the upper reaches of distinctively human experience. As Philipp Melanchthon writes, "Human emotions—love, hate, joy, sadness, envy, ambition, and the like—pertain to the will. . . . For what is the will if not the fount of the affections? And why do we not use the word 'heart' instead of 'will.' . . . For since God judges hearts, the heart must be the highest and most powerful part of man" (*Loci*, 27–29).

The distance between ancient and Renaissance views of emotion can be measured by looking at a revision of the Platonic tripartite soul found in Alsted's *Orator*. Alsted starts out like Plato, dividing the soul into intellective, irascible, and concupiscible components—Plato's charioteer, white horse, and black horse (*Phaedrus*, 253–54). The passage begins normally enough: the intellective faculty is the mind itself, to which Alsted attributes wisdom, prudence, and eloquence. But then the analysis takes a surprising turn. Plato's appetitive horse had been "crooked of frame, a massive jumble of a creature, with thick short neck, snub nose, black skin, and grey eyes; hot-blooded, consorting with wantonness and vainglory; shaggy of ear, deaf, and hard to control with whip and goad." But for Alsted the concupiscible part of the soul contains the love of God and man, love of virtue, zeal for divine glory and the salvation of all men, and so forth. In the irascible part, which Plato associates with courage and a sense of personal honor, Alsted places hope and faith (*fiducia*), fear of God, fortitude, magnanimity, and outspokenness (208–9). In the process of Christianizing Plato's model of the soul, Alsted has completely disregarded Plato's rationalism and mind-body dualism, although in some sense Alsted's concupiscible faculty is not unrelated to the Platonic eros, the daimon in the middle space (*metaxy*) between gods and men. But this eros never appears in Plato's analyses of the parts or faculties of the soul; in these the model for appetite is physiological desire (food, sex), which Plato generally perceives as irrational and dangerous. If we might call Plato's model of the psyche, with its internal hierarchical subordinations, polytheistic, then Alsted's is Trinitarian — three coequal faculties subsisting in a single nature.

The evaluation of passionate discourse in Renaissance rhetoric follows from this assimilation of spiritual and affective experience. *Movere* is no longer thought of as subrational obfuscation. Rather, emotional persuasion aims at the transformation of moral and spiritual life by awakening a rightly ordered love, by redirecting the self from corporeal objects to spiritual ones. But it turns the heart toward spiritual reality by fulfilling, not subverting, the human need for the sensible and corporeal. It gives invisible truth a local habitation and a name through metaphor, symbol, prosopopoeia, and all the figures that create drama, vividness, and force. The criticism of passionate rhetoric as either sophistic play or sophistic deception fails because it ignores the Renaissance's unplatonic view of the seriousness of rhetoric, based on its unplatonic psychology of the emotions and their relation to the *iter mentis ad Deum*.

Passionate Knowledge

The sacred rhetorics (and, in general, Augustinian Christianity) set affective inwardness over dispassionate intellection. Yet — and this is the crucial point — they do so in a way that links rather than opposes emotion and reason. That is, they do not treat rhetoric's power to move the heart and will as separate, or even separable, from the procedures of rational inquiry, as though rhetoric concerned the pursuit of the Good, while philosophy alone directed the search for Truth. Rather, these texts typically insist on the ineluctable "interwovenness" of cognitive and emotional experience. This claim partly derives from the Aristotelian position that emotion is not an irrational perturbation but the offspring of belief (Fortenbaugh, 17, 83). We feel fear, for example, because we judge that danger is imminent. Emotion is therefore bound up with argument; the orator moves by giving reasons. As early modern rhetorics and logics endlessly remark, the loci of dialectic and pathos are identical.[8] Obviously, not all arguments arouse emotion because some subjects have no affective valence, being too abstract, trivial, or logically intricate. Nevertheless, in principle, passion flows from proof, and thus discussions of *movere* often occur under invention rather than (or as well as) under *elocutio*.

But the link between intellection and affect found throughout the sacred rhetorics has deeper and more complex epistemic premises. These are worth tracing in some detail, for they imply that with respect to the Christian cultures of the Middle Ages and Renaissance, Fish's paradigm rather profoundly misrepresents the fundamental nature of "Western thought": that for these cultures, the distinctive features of rhetorical discourse had an *essential* role in the pursuit of truth and goodness.

Here again, Augustinian theology proves crucial. For Augustine, love and knowledge are tightly interconnected, since the noetic quest begins from and is propelled by love, yet we can only love that which, in some sense, we already know. Rather than undermining rational judgment, love wings the mind's search for God and truth. As Augustine writes in the *Confessions,* "My weight is my love; wherever I am carried, it is my love that carries me there. By your gift we are set on fire and are carried upward; we are red hot and we go" (13.9).

This erotic epistemology pervades early modern thought. In his *De anima,* Juan Luis Vives writes, "The object is known so that it may be loved, but the knowledge need only be so much as is sufficient to elicit love. Yet when we are connected to the desired object we know it better and more intimately, and then we enjoy it. Our first knowledge leads us to believe the object is good; in the latter knowledge we feel that it is so. . . . Thus love is the middle point between inchoate knowledge and the full knowledge of union, in which desire always disappears but not love. This rather burns more fiercely, the more and greater the goods found in that union" (178).

The noetic quest begins in inchoate knowledge, in a dim and partially realized faith, which awakens in turn a desire for this faintly glimpsed object. Impelled by desire, the quester strives to apprehend what he loves, which achieved, creates the ardent love of full union. As Edward Reynolds's *A Treatise of the Passions* (1650) explains, "Love and Knowledge have mutuall sharpening and causalitie each on other: for as Knowledge doth generate Love, so Love doth nourish and exercise Knowledge. The reason whereof is that unseparable union which is in all things between the Truth and Good of them. . . . The more Appetite enjoyeth of [the Good], the deeper inquiry doth it make and the more compleat union doth it seek with [the Truth]" (103–4). In the sixteenth century, this epistemology enters the rhetorical tradition — as, significantly, a defense of *movere.* Erasmus's *Ecclesiastes,* the earliest full-scale sacred rhetoric, makes the debt to Augustine explicit: "what Augustine, following Plato, said is true: nothing is loved unless known at least to some degree and again nothing is known unless loved in some respect. . . . In the *Hortensius* Cicero praised philosophy and aroused love for it before he taught it. And those who undertake to teach a subject first inflame their students, showing through amplification how noble it is . . . what great things it promises and how useful it will be" (5:952b).

The *Hortensius* was the book that first stirred Augustine to embrace philosophy. For Erasmus, it was not Cicero's arguments but his encomiastic rhetoric that led Augustine to love a subject he barely knew. Eloquence is not philosophy; but both, like Dante's Virgil and Beatrice, direct the *viator* into the ways of truth. The connection between love and knowledge appears again in Keckermann's *Systema rhetoricae:* "Reason and will should be implicit in emotion, and emotions resolve into knowledge and understanding. . . . Will and emotion derive from reason and knowledge" (2:1612). Here again emotion is bound up in the larger cognitive process. Our emotions spring from belief and lead us to further insight.

This sense of the inseparability of love and knowledge found support in the biblical anthropology of the Renaissance. Both Flacius's *Clavis Scripturae Sacrae* (1562) and Glassius's *Philologia sacra* (1623) point out that the Bible does not differentiate between knowing and feeling, as classical philosophy did. Glassius thus comments that in Hebrew, "to know or to think does not denote simply gnosis but also emotion and affect, . . . or what is the same, it signifies a living and efficacious knowledge. . . . Thus [in Hebrew] to know is the same as to love, to care for" (1053–54). Flacius makes the same point: "The Hebrews attribute the whole psychic life of man to the heart and appear to place the rational soul completely in the heart, . . . ascribing to the heart the power of both thought and choice, of wishing and doing. . . . On the other hand, the philosophers locate the rational soul . . . in the head or brain, leaving only emotion in the heart" (1:178). Both classical and biblical anthropology coexist up through the Renaissance, sometimes causing no small inconsistencies. The biblical, however, dominates what William Bouwsma has called the Augustinian Renaissance, to which belongs most of the period's rhetorical theory and whose ideal was not Jonathan Swift's stoical horses but a passionate and unitive knowledge. Rhetoric on this view participates in the noetic quest; its emotional power does not subvert reason but animates it, drawing heart and mind toward union with the desired object. As Adam says in his conversation with Raphael, "Love thou say'st / Leads up to heav'n, is both the way and guide" (Milton, *Paradise Lost*, 8.612–13).

The claim that the emotions, particularly love, span the distance between confused intimation and full apprehension addresses what may be *the* fundamental problem in premodern epistemology: How and to what extent can human minds gain access to that which cannot be perceived by the senses? This is, obviously, a theological matter. But it is also a rhetorical one — as can be seen from Francis Bacon's well-known declaration: "The duty and office of Rhetoric is to apply reason to imagination for the better moving of the will[,] . . . for the affections themselves carry ever an appetite to good, as reason doth. The difference is, that the affection beholdeth merely the present, reason beholdeth the future and sum of time. And therefore the present filling the imagination more, reason is commonly vanquished; but after the force of eloquence and persuasion hath made things future and remote appear as present, then upon the revolt of the imagination reason prevaileth" (1:153–54). That is, for Bacon rhetoric brings the distant objects of reason imaginatively close enough to seem visible, to seem real. Or as John Donne remarks in the course of a sermon, "Rhetorique will make absent and remote things present to your understanding" (4:87).

But this contrast between the remote objects of reason and close-at-hand sensible particulars derives, as Wesley Trimpi has shown, from Aristotle's crucial distinction between two types of knowability (87–129). For Aristotle things can be knowable either to us or in themselves: the concrete objects of sense are most knowable to us; that which lies farthest from perception (that is, universals), most knowable in themselves. Since all knowledge derives from sense experience, cognition always involves a movement from that which is knowable to us toward that which is knowable in itself but harder for us to know—a movement from, in Bacon's terms, things present toward things remote (Aristotle, *Post. An.* 1.2.71b–72a; *Meta.* 7.4.2–3).

What is at stake is not merely knowability, inasmuch as those things most distant from us are also more excellent than what we can perceive close-up. As Aristotle explains in a remarkable passage from *The Parts of Animals:*

> Of substances constituted by nature some are ungenerated, imperishable, and eternal, while others are subject to generation and decay. The former are excellent and divine, but less accessible to knowledge. The evidence that might throw light on them . . . is furnished but scantily by sensation; whereas respecting perishable plants and animals we have abundant information, living as we do in their midst. . . . [Yet] the scanty conceptions to which we can attain of celestial things give us, from their excellence, more pleasure than all our knowledge of the world in which we live; just as a half-glimpse of persons that we love is more delightful than an accurate view of other things, whatever their number and dimensions (1.5.644b; see also *De anima,* 1.1.402a).

The objects least accessible to knowledge are also the most valuable (and vice versa). There thus exists an *inverse* proportion between the excellence of an object and our knowledge of it: an epistemic state of affairs that Trimpi labels the ancient dilemma of knowledge and representation. The issue then becomes finding a way to bring what is remote and yet most worth knowing into some kind of relation with what we can more accurately grasp. Rhetoric, Bacon suggests, does just that by making the distant and remote present to the imagination.

Whereas Bacon would appear to be thinking mainly of secular oratory, the ancient dilemma had perhaps greater significance for the sacred rhetorics. But in the sacred rhetorics, the terms of the dilemma have been reshaped by specifically Christian (and profoundly un-Aristotelian) modes of spanning the distance between the divine and the humanly knowable. To get some idea of these theological solutions, which turn out to be identical to the rhetorical ones, we might look briefly at two early modern English divines, Richard Hooker and John Donne.

Hooker's account of the grounds of faith begins by restating the Aristotelian distinction between two kinds of knowability: "*Certainty of Evidence* we call that, when the mind doth assent unto this or that, not because it is true in itself, but because the truth is clear, because it is manifest to us." The truths of logic and perception are certain because evident to us; we find ourselves, however, painfully unsure concerning the more excellent objects of faith precisely because clear evidence for these is unavailable. Hooker resolves the ancient dilemma by arguing for a second type of certainty, the "certainty of adherence," whereby the person who has once tasted God's "heavenly sweetness" hopes "against all reason of believing." For Hooker faith grasps its object by love, not evidence (3:470–71). Hooker, that is, not only accepts the terms of the dilemma as those relevant to Christian belief but assigns emotion a central role in the act of faith—the same role that the sacred rhetorics attribute to *movere* in the art of persuasion.

In a somewhat different way, the ancient dilemma also structures Donne's treatment of the Incarnation and sacraments. Here too, the theological attempt to make that which is remote near and hence knowable has rhetorical implications. The parallel is apparent from Donne's phraseology: as rhetoric makes "absent and remote things present to your understanding," so the sacraments bring Christ "nearer [to us] in visible and sensible things." Similarly, the Incarnation brings "*the glory of God* . . . within a convenient distance to be seen *in the face of Jesus Christ*," for Christ "could not have come nearer, than in taking this nature upon him"; he is the "image of the invisible God, and so more proportionall unto us, more apprehensible by us" (5:144, 4:90–91, 125, 2:320). As "visible and sensible things," image and sacrament thus negotiate the poles of the ancient dilemma, enabling us to bridge the epistemic and ontological distance between the invisible God and the sensory objects knowable to us.

As ways of negotiating the terms of the ancient dilemma, the routes laid down by Hooker and Donne of love and images are fundamental for Renaissance sacred rhetorics. These affirm that the emotions are moved by the conjunction of *magnitudo* and *praesentia,* by the union, that is, of the excellent object with sensuous immediacy. *Magnitudo* and *praesentia* thus represent the polarities that must be brought into relation for the most excellent objects to penetrate our thought and feeling, for as Edward Reynolds notes, the emotions are moved only by the presence of their object (97). In his *Ecclesiasticae rhetoricae*, de Granada writes, "Emotions are quickened (as philosophers say) both by the excellence of the objects [*magnitudo rerum*] and by placing them vividly before the eyes of the audience [*praesentia oculis subiecta*]" (158).[9] For the most valuable things or truths to become objects of men's love, they must be brought "near" through the figural techniques for rendering things both large and luminous.

Hence the sacred rhetorics insist on the value of images, whether literal or metaphoric. Since the "deep things of God," according to a late seventeenth-century Protestant, "lye remote from our Understandings (as all Spiritual Objects do)," they need to be "represented under some obvious and sensible Image . . . that so the disproportion between them and our faculties, being qualified and reduced, we may the better . . . converse with them. . . . For as we are more affected when the things of God are brought down to us, under sensible representations, so likewise the things themselves become more intelligible" (Ferguson, 320–23). Images make what is unseen accessible to both feeling *and* thought. Nor are affect and intelligibility unrelated; as we have seen, the sacred rhetorics presuppose the Augustinian dialectic of love and knowledge. Their mutual dependence is likewise implicit in Hooker's claim that love — our love of God's "heavenly sweetness" — creates the certainty of adherence. Love bridges the poles of the ancient dilemma precisely because, as Thomas Aquinas states, it brings its object nearer (*propinquius*) to the lover (*Summa*, 1a.2ae.66.6). But love requires the presence of its object, and hence requires images.

The correspondences between religious and rhetorical techniques arise from their common basis in the ancient dilemma. As rhetoric, in Bacon's formulation, makes "things future and remote appear as present," so for Reynolds, "Divine love hath the same kinde of vertue with Divine Faith; that as this is the being and subsisting of things to come and distant in Time; so that is the Union and knitting of things absent, and distant in Place" (96). Whereas in the classical tradition the ancient dilemma is negotiated by *scientia* or discursive reasoning, in Christianity only faith working by love can traverse the distance between God and humans. Saint Thomas thus writes, "By faith we know certain things about God which are so sublime that reason cannot reach them by means of demonstration" (*Introduction,* 459). This is also Hooker's point: in matters of faith, love outstrips evidence. Renaissance sacred rhetorics build on this theological (that is, philosophic) foundation in their claim that passionate vividness can carry the mind to God while reason flounders in its inevitable limitations. The language of images, which overcomes the distance of both time and place, knits the soul to God, while no amount of argument can enable the intellect to know him. The sacred rhetorics lay so much weight on imaginative vividness because it creates both love and faith. In his discussion of hypotyposis, Flacius thus comments that "the Bible employs pictorial language not only to move the stony heart of man more strongly . . . but also to strengthen [it] with greater certitude" (2:310). Rhetoric in this sense, then, is not below but beyond reason.

Absolute and Objective Truth

Early modern sacred rhetorics thus raise serious doubts about the historical, and hence theoretical, validity of the standard postmodern account of rhetoric. These texts oppose rather than equate rhetoric to sophistic play and skeptical relativism; they do not treat the emotions as subrational; they do not view rhetoric as antithetic — or even as unrelated — to the pursuit of the True and the Good. This much seems fairly obvious; its significance, however, depends on the significance one is willing to accord these obscure, if numerous, works, by no means a clear-cut issue. But the fact that the sacred rhetorics repeatedly and explicitly base their project on philosophic (including theological) axioms points to a further conclusion, on which a good deal hinges. If philosophy is the unvarnished language of objective and absolute rational certitude, as Fish claims, it would seem inherently hostile to rhetoric. And yet the sacred rhetorics defend the use of passionate, figured language on philosophic grounds. That they would — that they could — do this suggests that Fish's notion of philosophy may be seriously inaccurate and hence that the postmodern narrative of the quarrel between rhetoric and philosophy fails not simply because it ignores one subcategory of rhetoric but also because it misrepresents the nature of Western thought *totaliter*.

It is not, first of all, self-evident that philosophy pursues "objective and absolute" truths untainted by "metaphysics, morals, and personal conviction" (this latter category including, one presumes, religious belief). Metaphysics, ethics, and theology have usually been regarded as philosophic concerns, and it seems both likely and proper that what philosophers write on these matters expresses their personal conviction. And although numerous philosophers have held that one truth or another was objective and absolute — the law of noncontradiction, the *cogito*-few claimed that philosophy deals exclusively, or even primarily, with objectively demonstrable certainties.[10] Aristotle's methodological preface to the *Nicomachean Ethics* has particular interest in this regard: a philosophical analysis, he begins, "will be adequate if it has as much clearness as the subject matter admits of; for precision is not to be sought for alike in all discussions." Ethical and political goods, in particular, "exhibit much variety and fluctuation . . . for before now men have been undone by reason of their wealth, and others by reason of their courage. We must be content, then, in speaking of such subjects . . . to indicate the truth roughly and in outline . . . for it is the mark of an educated man to look for precision in each class of things just so far as the nature of the subject admits: it is evidently equally foolish to accept probable reasoning from a mathematician and to demand from a rhetorician demonstrative proofs" (1.4.1094b). Moral and political inquiry, that is, seeks to formulate approximate rather than absolute truths; its arguments are probable, which is to say that they are rhetorical. Yet for Aristotle the fact that these subjects use probable (rhetorical) reasoning does not render them unphilosophic.

A second, perhaps equally important, problem with Fish's definition of philosophy is that a great deal of Western philosophy — nearly all of it for the thirteen centuries separating Origen from Descartes — is religious. This returns us to the sacred rhetorics. These draw on central philosophic traditions in which the pursuit of goodness is inseparable from love and therefore never wholly objective, in which truth is apprehended by faith and therefore never known with absolute evidential or logical certainty. The same traditions likewise argue that one can only "speak about God" in the language of "figures, tropes, metaplasms and allegories" (Trinkaus, 1:62–63; see also Ferguson, 279–80). Aquinas thus defends the radical metaphoricity of the Bible by invoking the Aristotelian postulate that human beings "attain to intellectual truths through sensible things, because all our knowledge originates from sense" (*Introduction*, 16). Before the Enlightenment, that is, a good deal of Western philosophy makes belief, affect, and nonliteral, nontransparent language central to the pursuit of the Good and the True, and consequently has no quarrel with rhetoric, which is simply language that relies on probable argument, emotional power, and figurative heightening. *"Rhetoricatur igitur Spiritus sanctus,"* as Luther puts it: "and therefore the Holy Ghost," although most certainly not a sophist, "is a rhetorician."[11]

Notes

1. Considerable portions of this essay offer a revised version of chapters 3 and 5 of my *Sacred Rhetoric: The Christian Grand Style in the English Renaissance* (Princeton: Princeton University Press, 1988). All translations are mine unless otherwise indicated.

2. The distrust of artistic language found in most English vernacular sacred rhetorics,

especially those of a Puritan stripe, is atypical; see Shuger, *Sacred Rhetoric*, pp. 50–53, 69–70, 93–95.

3. For a general overview of Renaissance sacred rhetoric, including brief summaries of the major texts and information concerning their availability in Tudor and Stuart England, see chapter 2 of Shuger, *Sacred Rhetoric*.

4. See, for example, Dionysius of Halicarnassus, "Demosthenes," 40; Quintilian, 12.10.62; St. Augustine, *On Christian Doctrine*, 4.53; Valades, p. 85; Lamy, 1.145, 2.40; Erasmus, 5:959b, 922d; de Granada, pp. 306–7; Keckermann, *Rhetoricae ecclesiasticae*, p. 110; Alsted, *Theologica*, p. 8.

5. See, for example, Strebaeus, p. 323; Caussin, pp. 70, 360; Lamy, 1.99, 145.

6. See, for example, Valiero, p. 95; de Granada, pp. 41–43; Carbo, p. 187; Keckermann, *Systema*, 2:1391–92; Caussin, p. 12; Hemmingsen, p. 14; Hyperius, pp. 1–2; Alsted, *Orator*, p. 148.

7. See also Caussin, pp. 459–512; Keckermann, *Systema*, 2:1615–31, and *Rhetoricae ecclesiasticae*, p. 43; de Granada, pp. 83–87; Melanchthon, *Elementorum rhetorices*, 13:425–27, 434.

8. Agricola, pp. 199–200; de Granada, pp. 110–11; Alsted, *Orator*, p. 91; Carbo, pp. 124–25, 188; Keckermann, *Systema*, 2:1610; Caussin, p. 552.

9. The formula likewise appears in Keckermann, *Rhetoricae ecclesiasticae*, pp. 53, 85; Alsted, *Theologia*, p. 20; Carbo, p. 208; Valades, p. 159.

10. The only philosophers to do so who come to mind are the logical positivists and Spinoza, Wittgenstein, and Russell in their early writings.

11. Martin Luther, *D. Martin Luther's Werke*, 66 vols. (Weimar: Boehlaus, 1883–   ), vol 40, pt. 3, 59–60; quoted in Dockhorn, p. 28.

References

Agricola, Rudolph. *De inventione dialectica libri tres* [ca. 1480]. Frankfurt: Minerva, 1967.

Alsted, Johann-Heinrich. *Orator, sex libris informatus* [1612]. Herborn, 1616.

——. *Theologia prophetica*. Hanover, 1622.

Aquinas, Saint Thomas. *Introduction to Saint Thomas Aquinas*. Ed. Anton Pegis. New York: Modern Library, 1945.

——. *Summa theologiae*. 5 vols. Ottawa: Commissio Diana, 1953.

Aristotle. *The Complete Works of Aristotle: The Revised Oxford Translation*. Ed. Jonathan Barnes. 2 vols. Princeton: Princeton University Press, 1984.

Augustine, Saint. *On Christian Doctrine*. Trans. D. W. Robertson. Indianapolis: Bobbs-Merrill, 1958.

——. *The Confessions of St. Augustine*. Trans. Rex Warner. New York: New American Library, 1963.

——. *The City of God*. Ed. David Knowles. Trans. Henry Bettenson. Harmondsworth, Eng.: Penguin, 1972.

Bacon, Francis. *The Works of Francis Bacon*. 7 vols. London, 1826.

Bouwsma, William. "The Two Faces of Humanism: Stoicism and Augustinianism in Renaissance Thought." *Itinerarium Italicum: The Profile of the Italian Renaissance in the Mirror of Its European Transformations,* 3–60. Ed. Heiko Oberman with Thomas Brady, Jr. Leiden: Brill, 1975.

Brown, Peter. *Society and the Holy in Late Antiquity.* Berkeley: University of California Press, 1982.

Caussin, Nicholas. *De eloquentia sacra et humana, libri XVI* [1617?]. Paris, 1630.

Carbo, Ludovicus. *Divinus orator, vel de rhetorica divina libri septem.* Venice, 1595.

Dionysius of Halicarnassus. "Demosthenes." *The Critical Essays,* vol. 1. Trans. Stephen Usher. Cambridge: Harvard University Press, 1974.

Dockhorn, Klaus. "Rhetorica movet: Protestantischer Humanismus und karolingische Renaissance." *Rhetorik: Beitrage zu ihrer Geschichte in Deutschland vom 16.–20. Jahrhundert,* 17–41. Ed. Helmut Schanze. Frankfurt: Athenaion, 1974.

Donne, John. *The Sermons of John Donne.* 10 vols. Ed. Evelyn Simpson and George Potter. Berkeley: University of California Press, 1953–62.

Erasmus, Desiderius. *Ecclesiastes sive concionator evangelicus* [1535]. Ed. J. LeClerc. Vol. 5 of *Opera omnia emendatiora et auctiora.* 10 vols. Leiden, 1703–6.

Fenelon, François. *Fenelon's Dialogues on Eloquence* [1717]. Trans. Wilbur Samuel Howell. Princeton: Princeton University Press, 1951.

Ferguson, Robert. *The Interest of Reason in Religion; With the Import and Use of Scripture Metaphors.* London, 1675.

Fish, Stanley. "Rhetoric." In *Critical Terms for Literary Study,* 203–22. Ed. Frank Lentricchia and Thomas McLaughlin. Chicago: University of Chicago Press, 1990.

———. *Self-Consuming Artifacts: The Experience of Seventeenth-Century Literature.* Berkeley: University of California Press, 1972.

Flacius Illyricus, Matthias. *Clavis Scripturae Sacrae, seu de sermone sacrarum literarum, in duas partes divisae* [1562]. Leipzig, 1695.

Fortenbaugh, W. W. *Aristotle on Emotion.* London: Duckworth, 1975.

Glassius, Salomon. *Philologia sacra liber quintus, qua rhetorica sacra comprensa* [1623]. Frankfurt, 1653.

Granada, Luis de. *Ecclesiasticae rhetoricae, sive, de ratione concionandi, libri sex* [1576?]. Cologne, 1582.

Hemmingsen, Niel. *The Preacher or Method of Preaching.* Trans. John Horsfall. London, 1574.

Herbert, George. *The Temple: Sacred Poems and Private Ejaculations. George Herbert and Henry Vaughan,* 3–180. Ed. Louis Martz. Oxford: Oxford University Press, 1986.

Hooker, Richard. "Of the Certainty and Perpetuity of Faith in the Elect" [1586]. Vol. 3 of *The Works of Mr. Richard Hooker,* 469–81. Ed. John Keble. 7th ed. 3 vols. Oxford, 1888; repr. New York: Burt Franklin, 1970.

Hyperius, Andreas. *The Practis of Preaching.* Trans. John Ludham. London, 1577.

Keckermann, Bartholomew. *Rhetoricae ecclesiasticae sive artis formandi et habendi conciones sacras, libri duo* [1600]. Hanover, 1616.

———. *Systema rhetoricae in quo artis praecepta plene et methodice traduntur* [1606]. Vol. 2 of *Opera omnia quae extant.* 2 vols. Geneva, 1614.

Lamy, Bernard. *The Art of Speaking: Written in French by Messieurs du Port Royal: In Pursuance of a former Treatise, Intituled "The Art of Thinking."* London, 1676.

Locke, John. *Essay Concerning Human Understanding*. Ed. John Yolton. 2 vols. London: Dent, 1961.

Melanchthon, Philipp. *Elementorum rhetorices libri duo* [1519], 414–506. Vol 13 of *Opera quae supersunt omnia*. 28 vols. Ed. Carolus Gottlieb Bretschneider. Brunswick and Halle, 1834–1860.

——. *Loci communes theologici*. Ed. Wilhelm Pauk. Trans. Lowell Satre. In *Melanchthon and Bucer*, 18–152. London: SCM Press, 1969.

Milton, John. *Paradise Lost*. Ed. Merritt Hughes. New York: Odyssey, 1935.

Murphy, James J. *Renaissance Rhetoric: A Short-Title Catalogue*. New York: Garland, 1981.

Plato, *The Collected Dialogues*. Ed. Edith Hamilton and Huntington Cairns. Princeton: Princeton University Press, 1961.

Quintilian. *Institutio oratoria*. Trans. H. E. Butler. 4 vols. Cambridge: Harvard University Press, 1920.

Reynolds, Edward. *A Treatise of the Passions and Faculties of the Soul of Man*. London, 1650.

Seigel, Jerrold. *Rhetoric and Philosophy in Renaissance Humanism: The Union of Eloquence and Wisdom, Petrarch to Valla*. Princeton: Princeton University Press, 1968.

Shuger, Debora. *Sacred Rhetoric: The Christian Grand Style in the English Renaissance*. Princeton: Princeton University Press, 1988.

South, Robert. *Sermons Preached upon Several Occasions*. 4 vols. Philadelphia, 1845.

Strebaeus, Iacobus Lodovicus. *De verborum electione et collocatione oratoria . . . libri duo* [1538]. Basel, 1539.

Sturm, Johannis. *De universa ratione elocutionis rhetoricae, libri IV* [1575]. Strassburg, 1576.

Trimpi, Wesley. *Muses of One Mind: The Literary Analysis of Experience and Its Continuity*. Princeton: Princeton University Press, 1983.

Trinkaus, Charles. *In Our Image and Likeness: Humanity and Divinity in Italian Humanist Thought*. 2 vols. Chicago: University of Chicago Press, 1970.

Ursinus, Johann-Henricus. *Ecclesiastes, sive de sacris concionibus libri sex*. Frankfurt, 1659.

Valades, Didacus. *Rhetorica Christiana ad concionandi, et orandi usum accommodata* [1574]. Perugia, 1579.

Valiero, Agostino. *De ecclesiastica rhetorica libri tres* [1575]. Vol. 1 of *Ecclesiasticae rhetoricae*. 2 vols. Verona, 1732.

Vives, Juan Luis. *De anima et vita* [1538]. Turin: Bottega d'Erasmo, 1959.

4

Invention, Emotion, and Conversion in *Augustine's* Confessions

WENDY OLMSTED

Saint Augustine's *Confessions* offers a telling site in which to investigate the relation between religious belief and rhetorical invention because it rejects both the sophistic version of rhetoric as mere eloquence and the notion that argument should depend on subject matter alone—what James J. Murphy calls the "Platonic rhetorical heresy."[1] Indeed, the *Confessions* anatomizes the partial, distorted rhetorics that impeded Augustine's own search for God in order to define the rhetoric through which he was converted to his new belief, to a better idea of God, and, ultimately, to a new *ethos* and a new Christian life. The understanding of the full inventive power of this better rhetoric remains elusive for us, however, because of the modern tendency to oppose dialectic and philosophy to rhetoric rather than to sophistic eloquence.[2] Because for Augustine "truth comes before the statement of truth," scholars have focused on dialectic as prior to rhetoric considered as a mode of presentation, rather than stressing the importance of rhetorical inquiry into particular questions for Augustine's conversion.[3]

The distance between rhetoric and the inquiry into truth seems to increase even farther when we realize that unlike the rhetoric of Cicero, Augustine's inquiry often seeks truth as distinguished from mere verisimilitude or probability.[4] Augustine exhorts his reader to "learn the source of the [mathematical] truths which he had somehow perceived and to know whence those things are not only true but immutable," a learning that makes use of dialectic and philosophy.[5] Moreover, in commenting on the use of the word *verisimiliter* in *De doctrina Christiana* (*DDC*), Ernest Fortin notes that the term "appears only in connection with teachers of false doctrines" and argues that Augustine's whole discussion plays on "the contrast between the eminently truthful character of the Christian faith and the apparent truths or merely plausible teachings of the promoters of erroneous doctrines."[6] In addition, if we consider the fact that one of Augustine's greatest achievements was to develop a Christian rhetoric to replace the Ciceronian probable or likely truth with doctrine, so that teaching (*docere*) thus comes to the fore as the most important rhetorical function, we are led inexorably to a rhetoric that is ancillary to the knowledge it imparts.[7] Rhetoric then becomes for Augustine mostly a matter of presentation (*modus proferendi*) and style, as set forth in book IV of *DDC*, rather than a matter of inquiry or *inventio*. As in the case of many modern thinkers, Augustine is understood to relate rhetoric and religion "as handmaid to master: serious study of religion or theology or plain faith yields the truths that rhetoric then must propagate."[8]

On the other hand, if we interpret the *Confessions* in light of ancient understandings of prudence as "the practical knowledge of things to be sought for and things to be avoided," and if we consider that a central power of rhetoric consists in the discovery of arguments (*inventio*) that inform prudence, we grasp how rhetoric, when rightly understood, enables an intellectual activity generative of substance, not style alone.[9] This inventive rhetoric discovers arguments, shapes character, and touches hearts.[10] When the full range of classical sources of persuasion (*logos, ethos,* and *pathos*) is brought into play to understand how these effects are produced in the *Confessions,* we discover "why . . . the student of rhetoric is led, inescapably led — provided that he or she pushes the inquiry with full rigor — to religion" and how an inadequate rhetoric confines understanding to inadequate, because partial, beliefs.[11] Only the invention made possible by a full range of pathetic topoi allows Augustine to inquire fully into the grounds of his emotional responses. He represents himself in infancy and childhood as dogmatic, as it were, and driven to short-range pleasures; but only because emotion can be linked to signs and argument can the child inquire, grow, and be converted. Augustine's conversion from eloquence to philosophy transforms his religious and rhetorical resources by introducing him to arguments that reorient his character and move his emotions. All three persuasive resources are at work in a conversion that may achieve a reorientation toward philosophy but which, more importantly for our inquiry, is also represented as a rhetorical and religious event. The *Con-*

fessions delineates how the resources of rhetoric work together with divine *caritas* to bring about this event.

The importance of the full range of rhetorical discovery in Augustine's search for God as represented in the *Confessions* manifests itself in the expressive theory of the sign that informs Augustine's description of his attempts to learn language as an infant.[12] Although some believe that the infant is impoverished because language begins in desire and lacks an orientation to truth, I propose that Augustine's descriptions of childhood language acquisition and youthful studies of grammar and eloquence provide elements of a rhetorical framework in terms of which wisdom and happiness are eventually sought.[13] The elements are, however, partial, distorted, and flawed. As we shall see, signs mediate between desires and things, but a child has few signs, and his desires are too shortsighted. Education makes his situation worse by over-emphasizing the coercive power of signs. So the young Augustine has the elements of a fuller insight but does not have the freedom or the knowledge to put the elements together to achieve the sort of fuller rhetoric we find in his mature thought.

The problem with infancy, then, is not that the infant's signs begin in desire (for all signs express desire or purpose) or that he lacks any understanding of a *res* to which his *verba* might refer but that he cannot produce the emotions and meanings (*sensa*) of his heart because he lacks the signs with which to do so (*Confessions*, I.viii.9). He is thus unable to make the connection between inner desire and outer thing, between his wishes and the people who might help him obtain them.[14] The senses of the adults are unable to "enter into [his infant] mind" (*introire in animam meam,* I.vi.26). He attempts to bring forth or publish the meanings or emotions (*sensa*) of his heart (I.viii.9) but cannot do so until he remembers how when adults name a thing (*rem*), they move their bodies toward it; these gestures and motions indicate the inclinations of the mind either to desire or to avoid a thing. Once the child understands the connection between signs, things, and expressions of desires, he is able to assemble bits of language and communicate his wishes.

This description of the child's language acquisition fits the expressive theory of the sign enunciated in *DDC;* in this sense, Augustine's rhetoric and sign theory are presented "in little" in the account of infancy and are not abandoned, even in the shift from pagan to Christian rhetoric.[15] In *DDC* conventional signs are distinguished from natural signs on the grounds that living beings show them to one another in order to convey the "motion of their spirits or something which they have sensed or understood. Nor is there any other reason for signifying, or for giving signs, except for bringing forth and transferring to another mind the action of the mind in the person who makes the sign" (II.ii.3).[16] Augustine's sign theory, like John Searle's theory of language, is intentional, and it is designed to have an effect: in the infant Augustine's case that of causing adults to give him what he desires. In these senses, the sign theory is fundamentally rhetorical.[17]

The language of a child is truncated and distorted not only by his lack of a mediating sign to relate his inner desires to outer persons and things but by the blindness of his desires. If, as Aristotle first suggested and Cicero affirmed, rhetoric is the art of discovering what is advantageous and beneficial to the happiness of human beings, then the infant's rhetoric lacks inventive power because it does not allow him to discover whether, far from leading him to happiness, what he seeks will injure him or other people.[18] In time the search for wisdom and happiness requires Augustine to refine his understanding of ends and to change his purposes and desires — in a word, to become more prudent.[19]

In the *Confessions,* however, before he is represented as reaching a point at which discovery in the classical sense becomes possible for him, Augustine receives an education in oratory that increases his power over the word even as his elders impel him, by the physical and rhetorical violence of his education, toward a narrow range of emotional and intellectual responses. The text tells how Augustine becomes fully able to express himself and to make others respond as he wishes, but he does so only because he received an education that taught by means of "shattering rituals of pain," which obliterated the will at the same time that they socialized him into fallen society.[20] Urged on by beatings, which Augustine compares to the torment of martyrs by the rack and the strappado, he acquired learning (I.ix); moved by the fear of cruel punishment with which his elders threatened him, he strove to understand Greek (I.xiv). But the mature Augustine comments that a free curiosity has more force (*vim*) to teach language than does a rigorous compulsion. *Vim* and *vehementer* suggest the rhetorical force that rhetoricians strove to cultivate, following Quintilian's insistence that the power to move a judge by the force of eloquence is superior to the ability to discover arguments for a case.[21] Even when Augustine was still very young, the teaching of rhetoric he received stressed compulsion and force, seeing the sign strictly as a means of coercion or its opposite, seduction.

Augustine appears to reject the inherited view of the supreme power of eloquence as one that compels the audience to feel and respond as the speaker wishes them to. Whereas Quintilian and the educators who followed him had believed that a good man could use the force of eloquence to promote wise actions that might not otherwise be embraced, the *Confessions,* in its treatment of grammatical and rhetorical education, implies that eloquence can never serve as a mere means, that when words are used to compel or seduce the will even for good ends, injury occurs. This injury does not spring from the words themselves; Augustine writes that he does not "accuse the words, which are like precious vessels." But he accuses the turpitude they express (I.xvi.29–30). When young scholars are told to read Terence or to declaim Virgil in order to learn words and arouse emotions in their audiences, their imitations bind them in their own desires and emotions, making them focus on imaginative self-stimulation rather than leading desire beyond itself.[22] The use of literature to teach eloquence calls to Augustine's mind Terence, who represents the process of imitation with a man exhorting himself to lust by gazing at a picture in which Jove showers gold on Danaë. Declamations, in teaching students of oratory to arouse the emotions of others by feeling the emotions themselves, made use of the advice of such classical orators as Cicero and Quintilian.[23] In dwelling upon their own emotions, however, the students inadvertently became infected by a sort of disease.

A similar distrust of delectation in emotion informs Augustine's critique of stage plays. Although his treatment of literature may seem harsh, it is important to notice that he approaches the subject from a distinct point of view that emphasizes how rhetorical imitation, by leading performers and spectators to feel emotion vividly, aestheticizes feelings that would serve better as a source of action. Whereas in classical eloquence and in *DDC,* speeches were fashioned to delight audiences (so that audiences would be more attentive to what they heard) and to move audiences so that they might be persuaded to a decision or action, the *Confessions* represents emotion as isolated from persuasion and action and turned into an object to be dwelt on, delighted in, and reproduced for the sake of stimulation.[24] The *Confessions* criticizes the compassion that theatrical spectacles produce, not on the grounds that compassion must be rejected, but on the grounds that it leads nowhere (III.ii).

Augustine's youthful eloquence, then, includes many of the elements that eventually lead him to discovery, but they are isolated from one another and used for narrow, preestablished purposes rather than for the sake of inquiry. Delectation is cultivated apart from moving and teaching in order to promote a pleasurable or painful response in the audience in accordance with the will of the speaker. Signs and speeches are used to express desires for things or people, but speakers and audiences are trapped within short-sighted conceptions of those things and desires. In sum, the text represents the young Augustine as a man who was taught the elements of a fuller rhetoric but who does not know how to put them together and use them in a search for greater wisdom and happiness.

If I am correct that Augustine's accounts of language acquisition, declamation, and theatrical shows represent his rhetoric as closed in upon itself, then *Confessions* III.iv, on his experience of reading Cicero's *Hortensius,* can be seen to break into this self-absorption of language and passion. According to Augustine, "In truth, this book changed my affections, and shifted my prayers to you yourself, Lord, and transformed my desires and purposes" (*Ille vero liber mutavit affectum meum, et ad te ipsum, domine, mutavit preces meas, et vota ac desideria mea fecit alia,* III.iv.6–8.) The arguments of the *Hortensius* are transformative in every respect, introducing Augustine to a new object (logos or *res*), to new passions, and to a new character capable of altered purposes and desires. Here then we see the first evidence in Augustine's youthful life as he describes it of the power of the full range of rhetoric and *inventio,* of arguments and exhortations that convert Augustine, and the reader, to something new, and that lead him beyond himself to a search for wisdom.

However, when we ask ourselves what the arguments were that so persuaded, moved, and changed Augustine's character, we are somewhat at a loss because no text of the *Hortensius* survives. The extant fragments suggest that it offered both ethical and intellectual guidance and aimed to affect manners and practice as well as the thought of the reader.[25] Thus, when Augustine is converted to "philosophy," he is converted to a kind of prudent philosophy "whose cultivation is [probably] due to the studies commended by Crassus in the *De oratore.*"[26] *Humanitas,* the term that expresses this ideal, implies a way of acting and relating to other people, as well as an educational program that goes beyond the study of philosophy as we might understand it.

Augustine's conversion from eloquence to philosophy represents a reorientation in his whole way of life, one that changed his ideas, his character, and his passions. "It was by that discourse that I was roused and stirred and inflamed" (*excitabar sermone illo et accendebar et ardebam,* III.iv.31–32). Even when discussing the grand style in *DDC,* that style that beyond all others converts and persuades, Augustine asserts that it does so through the force of the matter, following the ardor of the heart. Substance and arguments, not style, have the greatest effect on character and emotions. Logos and *pathos* are the strongest sources of fire.[27]

If we attend to the rhetorical terms in which the *Confessions* describes the effect of Augustine's conversion and not just the fact of that conversion, we find that the change is incomplete — incomplete, I would suggest, because it is both religiously and rhetorically inadequate. Although Augustine has been struck by the possibility of discovering a wisdom beyond what he can presently conceive, he (the young Augustine described by the text) does not seem to realize the ambiguity of the term "wisdom," nor that "wisdom" could adequately serve him at this juncture more as a topos to point the way toward further discovery than as something that can be fully known in a short time. As a thing worthy of further inquiry, "wisdom" could have been understood as an indeterminate intellectual term susceptible of many different probable (persuasive) instantiations. As things stood, Augustine took the term for granted as having a single, unambiguous meaning; as a result, it is small wonder that he was seduced by the chattering of the Manicheans who mouthed the word *Truth* and took their *phantasmata* to be objects of certain knowledge. Yet the question continues to nag: Why was Augustine's conversion to philosophy unable to keep him from the sect of Mani? After all, part of what delighted him in Cicero's exhortation was that it "did not bind him to a particular sect, but that he could 'love and seek Wisdom itself' " (III.iv.29–30).

The text suggests that although Augustine glimpses something of what the search for wisdom might entail, he continues to function in terms of the rhetoric to which he has been educated and acculturated. Even after he writes the philosophical treatise *De pulchro et apto*, he dedicates it to Hierius, the Roman orator, whom he loves because of other men's praise (*Confessions*, IV.xiv.4–9). As a young man he does not seem to have questioned the potential difference between the character conveyed by the words of praise and the actual character of Hierius. Rather, he seems to have possessed an unreflective enthusiasm for Hierius similar to his enthusiasm for the "truth" of Mani. In reflecting upon the effects of laudatory rhetoric and the kind of love it produces, the *Confessions* suggests a perverse relation between the human praise of this eloquent Latinist and Augustine's own celebration of God, intended to rouse the hearts of his readers to love of God. Augustine puzzles over how praise can cause people to love Hierius in his absence, wondering whether love can move directly from the mouth to the heart. He resolves the issue by asserting that one lover is inflamed (*accenditur*) by another when the one who praises is believed to truly commend and love the other (IV.xiv.11); in other words, a representation conveys a human judgment that is believed to be true to the audience. Augustine, the mature narrator, contrasts this human judgment (which rests on common opinion at best) with the divine judgment that later in his life will serve as an undeceptive standard of truth (X.xxvi). The *distance* between human and divine judgment constitutes a space for ongoing inquiry which the young Augustine does not yet apprehend. Only the mature Augustine understands that the celebrated qualities of Hierius might have had no reference to his actions or character. Augustine as a young rhetorician does not seem to exercise the critical function one finds in classical rhetoric, a function that would have allowed him to evaluate the probability or plausibility of the rhetorical constructions which he was so adept at creating and to which he responded so passionately. This naïveté has, by implication, important consequences for his praise of truth and God. Is God like Hierius, an image present in human celebrations of purely human ideals that are taken to be God while God himself is absent and unknown? Is the divine, as in Augustine's version of Manicheanism, a fiction of the human mind, which is unconsciously using imagined properties of the physical universe as its inspiration? Is "divinity" what emerges when the human mind reifies its own fantasies in a conception of that cosmos? Augustine promotes a fuller understanding of these issues by delineating steps in his process of discovery as he moves from uncritical adherence to a logos ("wisdom") to the Manicheans' inadequate model of this logos (the *verbum* "truth") to his youthful recognition of the misleading nature of this model and finally to his turn to Saint Ambrose's better model.

Augustine's adherence to Manicheanism exhibits a rhetorical naïveté similar to that which he reveals in dedicating his treatise to Hierius. As Augustine tells it, rather than taking words as instruments for discovery, the Manicheans dwell upon their materiality, repeating "Truth, truth" and objectifying their fantasies, collapsing the difference between their *phantasmata* and the physical universe they claim to know absolutely (III.vi.46ff.). They err, according to the mature Augustine, not because their language fails to correspond to a referential world, but because rhetorical distortion affects both language, reduced to mere names, and the knowable, mistakenly located in *phantasmata* (III.vi.27–43). According to Augustine's account, truth is not found in the relation of language to its referent (language only indicates things); it lodges in the thoughts and perceptions themselves. The Manicheans offered up the sun and moon for aesthetic enjoyment: *phantasmata splendida* (III.vi.28), they were also, alas, false bodies because the Manicheans actually knew nothing about them. Augustine may have been excessively literal in his reading of these beliefs, but he was hungry for truth, not beautiful images. That he associated Manicheanism with pleasure is shown by the way he uses words referring to the rhetorical office of delighting in his descriptions of the sect, and especially with Faustus: Faustus's words are apt, his delivery delightful, his disputation full of feeling, his words smooth and jocund (V.iii.4 and vi.7ff.). Stimulated by his dissatisfaction with pleasant words and images that now cloy his ears, Augustine begins to make distinctions between a wise soul (*sapiens anima*, V.vi.12) and one whose language achieves an eloquent decorum, between prudent judges of things and those whose speech is delightful.

The rhetorical danger of delight, as Augustine conceives it, lies in the way it invites the mind to dwell on rhetorical expression rather than on learning or on being moved to right action. In *DDC* he cautions his readers in their use of delight, the effect associated with the moderate style, to gain the attention of their audiences: "That which the moderate style urges, that is, that the eloquence itself be pleasing, *is not to be taken up for its own sake,* but in order that things which may be usefully and virtuously spoken, if they require neither a teaching nor a moving eloquence, may have a knowing and sympathetic audience."[28] In accordance with the distinction between *uti* and *frui* (what is to be used and what is to be enjoyed), only God should be enjoyed for his own sake; everything else must be used in the service of the love of God. The dangers of delight, then, are both rhetorical and religious. They are rhetorical inasmuch as delight, engaged in for its own sake, distorts rhetorical speech and argument by focusing attention upon language itself rather than upon some area of inquiry that would lead in time to truth. The dangers are religious in that delight may cause human beings to cleave to the transient rather than to the divine author of the whole.

Given Augustine's distrust of the delightful and his subsequent turn to allegorical reading and to Neoplatonism as a remedy for Manichean linguistic literalism and materialistic sensualism, we may well understand why modern treatments of the *Confessions* have argued that the crucial changes in Augustine's beliefs are the move from rhetoric to philosophy, from the delight in an eloquent pleasing "religion" (Manicheanism) to the contemplation of truth (Neoplatonism), and, finally, from a secular rhetoric to a Christian rhetoric distinguishable by its new content (eternal things). These differentiations, however, are too broad for our purposes; they may be seriously misleading, as we have seen in the case of Augustine's conversion to the search for wisdom.

Although in *DDC* book IV and in his attack on rhetorical training early in the *Confessions* Augustine clearly rejects sophistic oratory (with its emphasis on the supreme power of pure eloquence and style at the expense of the invention of argument and matter), he does not envision truth as separate from a speaker or teacher and an audience. The audience's attention and intentions play a crucial role in reading, hearing, and learning about truth. When Augustine hears Ambrose expound the spiritual, allegorical interpretation of Scripture, for example, he changes the direction of his attention from Ambrose's eloquence to his arguments and, as a result, the rhetorical discipline by which he evaluates Ambrose's words.

Instead of directly apprehending a truth expressed by Ambrose, Augustine first approaches him as a professional rhetorician. After Augustine has spoken on behalf of the city and been received approvingly by Ambrose, he fixes his interest on judging Ambrose's words in order to determine whether they measure up to their author's fame. Shortly, however, as has been widely noted, Augustine's delight in eloquence is replaced not with *res* but with a new union of *res* and *verba*. Equally important, Augustine discerns that Ambrose can meet the challenges of the Manicheans with his allegorical reading of Scripture.[29] Ambrose's refutations stimulate Augustine to challenge the arguments of the Manicheans, and he begins to consider and compare arguments, seeking out the most probable and deciding that the philosophers' accounts of these issues come nearer the truth than the Manicheans'. A degree of skepticism finally introduces a salutary doubt into Augustine's thinking.

Rhetorically probable arguments, then, play a legitimate and central role in the opening up of the Manichean aporia to Augustine's long inquiry; probability is not associated with fallacy in the *Confessions*. Though Augustine becomes trapped in unfruitful skepticism for a while, this aporia is introduced in part by his own desire for a knowledge of God that is as certain as the knowledge of mathematics (VI.iv) and by his fear of believing anything that cannot be proven. Earlier in the text, when considering the *Hortensius* he expressed admiration for the way it provided grounds for refuting beliefs rather than seducing its reader under the name of philosophy (III.iv).

The fundamental rhetorical and religious inadequacies of Augustine's belief in Manicheanism (V.xiv) are addressed by Ambrose's use of argument and his exposition of the allegorical reading of the Bible. First, through argument and refutation Augustine learns that he can evaluate and reject improbable beliefs. Second, tropological reading insists on the need for interpretation of signs. Augustine need not take naive imaginings (*phantasmata*) as truth. This insistence on the importance of a hermeneutics is also an insistence on the need for rhetoric, that is, for a tropological reading that acknowledges a gap between sign and signified. Augustine discovers that difficult passages in Scripture offer a space of indeterminacy where argument, allegory, and other modes of invention or discovery can work. In the *Confessions'* reading of Genesis, Augustine insists that one word can be understood in many ways (XII.xviii.8–9). The looseness of the relation between word and truth allows multiple readings; because people read the text in terms of their own lives, they will discover different insights about how to change. These discoveries make up the activity of *inventio* through which people seek a wise and blessed life.[30]

Manicheanism, understood in light of Augustine's discoveries on hearing Ambrose, proves to be rhetorically inadequate because it eschews argument, doubt, and self-conscious tropological interpretation. It is religiously inadequate because it does not risk faith in an expression of the meaning of life "as related to, indeed as both participating in *and distanced from,* what is sensed as the whole of reality."[31] Instead of attending to the distance between their own cosmological images and truth, the Manicheans accept their imaginings and metaphors as reality. Their inability to read spiritually is a rhetorical incapacity because it ignores the tropological dimension of language, but it is also a religious incapacity because it reduces a truth accessible only to the intelligence to a corporeal image.

Although Ambrose enlightens Augustine concerning important relations between language and truth, he does not resolve Augustine's problems of belief. Augustine is convinced that the Bible need not be interpreted as teaching perversely, yet he remains ignorant about whether the things Ambrose teaches are true (VI.i). Fearful of falling into illusion, he keeps his heart from assenting to anything; but having suspended his judgment, he is unable to trust and be healed. Only when he accepts the credibility of probable arguments and witnesses does he become able to affirm a belief: the belief in the Bible as an authoritative text. Thus, the obscurities and tropological indeterminacies of Scripture do not block inquiry or disappear in deferrals of judgment; instead, they stimulate consideration of how interpretation may lead to a wiser and happier life.

Deliberation and consideration are pivotal for Augustine's discovery of religious faith in the authority of Scripture. Through deliberation, Augustine discovers that he already believes many things he has never seen — the history of nations, accounts of places and cities, reports of friends and physicians "which unless we believe them, we would be unable to do anything" (VI.v). He reflects that he has a fixed faith in reports of his parentage, which he would otherwise never be able to know. These considerations and others like them convince him that that those who believe in the Bible as a work of the Holy Spirit are correct.

Rhetorical persuasion becomes an important instrument for Augustine in thinking through what can be believed and what cannot. Equally critical, Augustine here recognizes what his narrative technique repeatedly implies and what studies of that technique have stressed, namely, that he must rely on the testimony of others even to understand himself, beginning with his own activities as an infant (which, again, are forever hidden from him by time and the absence of memories).[32] Before Augustine's Christian conversion can take place, however, another series of critical steps takes place in the alteration of his religious and rhetorical discipline. First, though he continues to struggle with the heritage of his Manicheanism, try as he may to conceive of an immaterial God, he is unable to shift his awareness from images (*imagines*) to his own endeavor (*intention*) in forming them (VII.i.1–2). He is also tormented by the question of evil; if God is uncorruptible, he wonders, whence comes evil. As he eventually concludes, because he seeks outside himself for the answer his questions remain unanswerable.

Much as Ambrose's preaching had freed Augustine from literalism by intro-

ducing a distinction between the literal and the figurative, Neoplatonism liberates him from his reification of God and evil by introducing the distinction
between the soul of man that gives testimony to the light of truth and the light
itself. Through the justly famous inward turn, Augustine discovers over the
eye of his soul (his mind) the incommutable light of truth. He moves from
objects of thought to activity of mind to a truth that illuminates the mind.
Here dialectic plays a crucial role in liberating Augustine from his notion of
God as a kind of matter and in leading him to an understanding of God as
incorruptible and nonspatial.[33]

At the same time, Augustine gives Neoplatonic contemplation a highly rhetorical reading. Brian Stock notes that in book VII, chapter ix, where we find
an account of Neoplatonist ideas, Augustine "shifts the reader's interest away
from charismatic teachers such as Ambrose and toward the written page (or,
more precisely, toward the inward experience for which the page is an 'ad-
monishment')."[34] Moreover, conversion for Augustine always involves "mimetic, and hence, rhetorical, self-reform," a departure from the Neoplatonists,
who stressed the ascent to an interior light at the expense of the historical
dimension of change in people's lives.[35] Augustine's story of Victorinus's conversion and the presence of Alypius in the garden suggest, in addition, that
conversion requires an audience; it must be publicly witnessed.[36] Mimetic self-
reform that is witnessed by an audience characterizes not only the conversions
of Victorinus and Augustine but the *Confessions* itself as a religious-rhetorical
text witnessed by its readers. The text leads readers to ask what connection
they can find between the role of Neoplatonism in Augustine's conversion and
the need for self-reform. How does self-reform relate, in turn, to the change in
self, and, finally, what role does deliberation play in conversion?

Neoplatonism provides an essential prerequisite for Augustine's change in
that it cures his literalism by leading him from an awareness of things known
by his mind to the role of his own mind in knowing them to a standard of truth
superior to his mind. This dialectical journey engages Augustine in thinking
through many general questions about the nature of God, questions (about the
materiality or immateriality of God, for example) that must be resolved before
he can understand God as transcendent. At the same time, but less frequently
noted by scholars, Neoplatonism is crucial to his conversion because of the
way it confronts him with the difference between truth and his opinion about
it (as in the case of his opinion that God is a material substance). Here we see
vividly the difference between a purely dialectical or contemplative ideal and a
rhetorical and religious conception of the apprehension of truth. Unlike dialectical truth, rhetorical and religious truth are relative to the *ethos* of the soul
of the knower, as here, when Augustine, having returned to himself, enters

"*mea intima*" and discovers the incommutable light: "He who knows truth or what truth is knows what that light is, and whoever knows the light, knows eternity. *Caritas* knows it. O eternal truth and true *caritas* and dear eternity. . . . When I first saw you, you received me, that I might see that there was something which I might see and that I was not the one to see it" (*Qui novit veritatem, novit eam, et qui novit eam, novit aeternitatem. Caritas novit eam. O aeterna veritas et vera caritas et cara aeternitas! . . . Et cum te primum cognovi, tu assumsisti me, ut viderem esse, quod viderem, et nondum me esse, qui viderem*, VII.x.11–15).[37]

Apprehension of the light as superior to the mind coincides with awareness of the incapacity of the self to see the light and the need for *caritas* to bring together the person (whose *ethos* prevents full vision) and the truth. Augustine discerns only enough of the truth to bring home what his *ethos* is not; that is, God repels him, making his sight rebound back on itself, so that he quakes with love and horror. Here we have an incomplete rhetorical transaction whose deformity bears witness to the religious power of an effect the witness cannot sustain. The *mysterium tremens* — being drawn toward God (logos) in love and repelled from him in terror implies a rhetorical orientation in its religious *pathos*, but it requires a substantial change in the human *ethos*, a change that can be accomplished only through *caritas*. *Caritas*, then, becomes the "fundamental discovery" of the *Confessions*, as for the *DDC*.[38] In this discovery Augustine transforms Aristotle's notion of *ethos*, the character created in a speech and through which a speaker connects with a hearer, into a more fundamental concept that connects the loving intent of God with the capacity to learn in the human being, allowing "one human heart to speak to another heart."[39] Thus, although it is true that when Augustine understands dialectically that the logos, God, is immaterial, he loses all doubt that "Truth is not" (VII.x.26), nevertheless, his conversion is not complete until all dimensions of his being are transformed.[40]

Through his reading of the Neoplatonists, Augustine discovers himself to be in the region of dissimilitude, far from God. Although he hears the voice that clamors, "I am that I am," hearing it as things are heard in the heart, and although the shadows of doubt fall away, the glimpse of truth is momentary and "through a glass darkly" (VIII.i). Fuller discovery of wisdom and happiness depends on his ability to gain sufficient strength to be moved to change his life; and he cannot find this until he embraces Christ, the mediator.

The importance of the incarnation of the Word for Augustine's rhetoric is well known.[41] Only when the divine unchanging Word reveals itself in the Word of the incarnation can human beings discover a road to truth and happiness. Only when this Word transforms a person's *ethos* — in Augustine's case the Neoplatonic *ethos* of pride—to the Christlike *ethos* of humility can that person change sufficiently to pursue and become more able to discern divine truth. This transformation of *ethos* comes about through freely given grace. If in *DDC* "*caritas*. . . formulated as the principle of 'love of God and love of neighbor,' becomes the means by which new wisdom is born,"[42] by leading to new readings of the Scripture, then in the *Confessions, caritas,* in cooperation with the reading of Scripture, leads to new interpretations of Scripture and of life.

Although it may be tempting to interpret the conversions in the *Confessions* as transformations of *ethos* alone by *caritas* (and, hence, as not involving the dimension of logos or even of *inventio*), the new lives and new understandings are born in a highly rhetorical activity of reading and meditating.[43] Reading takes place in the context of a person's struggles with deliberative issues. Both Ponticianus's friend, whose reading, meditation, and change are interspersed with agonies of deliberative uncertainty, and the narrator Augustine, whose account of his own reading is preceded by his analysis of a disease of the will, find themselves initially unable to choose a new life. Although in one sense they already grasp intellectually their new life as a search for wisdom and happiness, in another they do not understand this until their lives have changed sufficiently to embrace it.

The possibility for change appears only faintly earlier, in book VIII, chapter v, section 36ff., where Augustine represents himself as unable to overcome the old will of custom that holds him back, struggle as he might against it. Again in book VIII, chapters viii and ix, he relates his frustrations as his mind commands him to change but he is unable to obey. This rhetoric, in which the mind commands itself, fails to cure the disease that infects his volition, so that his many wills seek and deliberate over many goods without being able to resolve upon any. Deliberative conflict emerges into discovery only through the combination of reading, listening, meditating, and being moved rhetorically.

The activity of reading enacts a number of the effects that rhetoric was classically thought to produce. Ponticianus's friend changes after he begins to read and "wonders and is inflamed and in reading meditates about laying hold of a life" like Saint Anthony's (*et mirari et accendi, et inter legendum meditari arripere talem vitam,* VIII.vi.56–57). In Cicero's *De oratore,* Antonius expresses the idea that no substance can take fire without a spark, and no mind can absorb the force of oratory without being kindled or inflamed (*incendi,* II.189). In *DDC,* Augustine, writing of divinely inspired wisdom and eloquence, comments that the value of some passages in Scripture lies not so much in the way a good listener can be instructed by the text as in the way he warms to it (*accendit*) if it is ardently pronounced (IV.vii.21). The grand or moving style is especially commended for its power to inflame, to seize (*rapere*) and to convert the mind to action. In the *Confessions*, however, Ponticianus's friend attends not to the style of the conversion narrative but to the life of Anthony it narrates (the pattern of his life being the logos of that discourse), one that inflames him even in the act of reading to deliberate about leading such a life himself.[44] Seized by a holy love, this friend of Ponticianus becomes ashamed and angry with himself as he questions his former purposes, asking why he and his friend serve the state. The contrast between his own life and the life he reads about now leads to new emotions and new ideas of what constitutes happiness. He questions the wisdom of their serving the state when there is no higher role for them to aspire to than the one they fulfill as the emperor's friends; and he reflects upon the dangers and possible failures that attend the search for government employment, whereas "if I wish to become the friend of God, lo I am even now made it." Once he has deliberated, the friend of Ponticianus reads again and is "changed within" (*mutabatur intus*, VIII.vi.67). For as he read, the "flow of his heart pondered or turned round to" God and he "groaned," resolving on a new course and he said, "Just now I broke away [*abrupi*] from those hopes of ours" (VIII.vi.70–71).

Similarly, Augustine in the garden (VIII.xii), having been torn apart by the endless conflict between his will and his desires and frustrated by his inability to exercise continence, finally abandons the conflict, grieves for his incapacity to choose, and calls upon God for help, hearing the words "take up and read" sung repeatedly. He immediately begins to consider whether he has ever heard children sing in this way. Deciding he has not, he interprets the words as meaning that he should open the Bible and be bound by the first passage he reads. His interpretation is informed by his having heard that Anthony once believed that he had been commanded in the same way. In other words, Augustine's receptivity and interpretation of command and Scripture are influenced by the story of Anthony. Once he reads the passage "not in rioting and drunkenness, not in chambering and wantonness . . . but put ye on the Lord Jesus Christ," confidence infuses his heart and the shadows of doubt flee.[45] In book IX, chapter i, lines 7ff. Augustine implies that when he wept and despaired earlier in the garden, calling for divine aid, God's gracious love healed his divided self, allowing him to let go of his willing and nilling. His free will then emerged, and he read the passage from the Bible as having specific authority for him.[46] Because Alypius's failings are different, Alypius recognizes a different command as appropriate to him. Hearing and reading, then, are part of a deliberative activity in which Augustine determines what is authoritative for him, and they occur in a larger deliberative context which includes the stories of how Victorinus, Ponticianus, and his friends, as well as Augustine himself, examined alternative ways of life.

Rhetoric operates in books VI–VIII not so much through the structure and effects of particular formal speeches as through the interaction between readers and texts or verbal expressions. Rhetorical *ethos* is supplanted by *caritas* as a principle of communicability that links a speaker or author and a reader.[47] So when he remembers Alypius's transformation on hearing his bitter joke, Augustine comments that he meant no reproach but that God made use of his words: "From my heart and tongue you worked blazing coals with which you kindled his languishing mind . . . and cured it" (VI.vii.40–42).[48] Alypius then impelled himself "forth out of the deep pit" in which he had been caught, inspired to invention by the conflict between Augustine's words and his own life. This point of conflict operates in the same way as obscure passages in Augustine's biblical hermeneutics as described in *DDC* and perhaps even like *inventio* as a means of identifying the *constitutiones* (points of disagreement in a legal plea) in Cicero's rhetoric: all three locate the place of discovery in the contradiction between verbal formulations (*De inventione*) or between verbal formulations and belief (*DDC*) or between verbal formulations and life (*Confessions*).[49] In Augustine's two texts, the conflict opens the way to *caritas,* which turns the heart of the interpreter to new truths and to a new order of the emotions. It operates, not as a principle of closure, as is too often assumed by critics of Augustine's sign system, but, more commonly, as a principle of openness when readers discover new possibilities for their lives and for their understandings.[50]

Once Augustine discovers *caritas* as the love that casts out his conflicted willing and nilling (IX.i), he describes himself and his friends as permanently inflamed with *caritas* ("you shot through our heart with your charity and we carried your word transfixed in our bowels," IX.ii.14–15), with a flame never to be extinguished but only ignited more fiercely by the "cunning tongues" of those who attempted to contradict them. Torpor is gone, energy released, and Augustine's search is renewed: "My heart said to you, I have sought your face; your face Lord, will I seek" (IX.iii.41–2).

In sum, then, truth in the *Confessions* is something whose source the young Augustine discovers and for whose fuller reaches the narrator still searches. Even as late as book X, Augustine struggles with the difficulties of truth, representing it as a speaker from whom persons seek counsel and addressing truth with the comment that "you answer [those who seek counsel] clearly, but all do not hear you clearly" (*liquide tu respondes, sed non liquide omnes audiunt,* X.xxvi.4–7). Because the understanding of truth's counsel depends upon the character of the knower as well as the clarity of truth's response, human beings may fail in their search for wisdom. Within the compass of the *Confessions*, Augustine does not lose his sense of the shadows that darken the human mind. "There is still indeed a little light in men; let them walk, let them walk, that the darkness not overtake them" (X.xxiii.6–7).[51] Though the intellectual heaven of heavens may "know all at once, not from parts, not in an enigma, not through a glass darkly, but in the whole, manifest and face to face" (*nosse simul, non ex parte, non in aenigmate, non per speculum, sed ex toto, in manifestatione, facie ad facie,* XII.xiii), the human being's knowledge of God is more momentary, more elusive, and more mediated. Augustine's insistence on the brief and often mediated character of the human knowledge of God emphasizes the need for rhetorical tropes through which to apprehend him.

This mediated character of the human knowledge of God also affects the rhetorical character of the *Confessions* itself. The text is written in the rhetorical form of prayer, as a search for God in which the confessor is guided by the belief that he who seeks will find and, finding, praise (*quaerentes enim inveniunt eum et invenientes laudabunt eum,* I.i.13–14).[52] "Augustine introduces himself precisely as the seeker . . . and he concludes as the discoverer of the end of prudence as 'the Good lacking no good.' "[53] Augustine's word for finding or discovering is the same as the rhetorical term for to invent (*invenire*), the first division of Ciceronian rhetoric.[54] His epideixis (one of the three rhetorical divisions of speech) constructs an unusual rhetorical situation in which the speaker must search for the audience he wishes to praise. Augustine further represents himself as uncertain about whether to invoke God or to praise him, to know him or to call upon him. "But who can invoke you, who does not know you?" (I.ii.8–9), he asks, resolving the undecidability through faith but continuing his search for God as he continues to praise.

This rhetorical search for the knowledge of God, then, involves a relationship between human person and divine person that is mediated by prayer; knowledge emerges in the context of this relationship between persons, one in which human *ethos* and human limitation play a role. At the same time, Augustine affirms the religious character of his discovery of God by locating the agency of the inquiry in God. If we think, provisionally, of religion as originating in basic existential questions about the meaning of human life "as related to, indeed as both participating in and distanced from, what is sensed as the whole of reality," then prayer instantiates both a rhetorical and a religious relation.[55] In the *Confessions,* the stimulus for search and praise comes from God himself, for Augustine writes, "Man wants to praise you. You kindle [*excitas*] him, that he may delight [*delectet*] to praise you." The words "kindle" and "delight" produce further rhetorical echoes, calling to mind the Ciceronian emphasis on the powers to delight (*delectare*) the inattentive and to inspire (*excitare*) the lukewarm.[56] God, on whom men call, mysteriously rouses their hearts to praise, while Augustine himself arranges his many narrations before God not so that God can come to know him but rather, as he puts it, to "kindle my desires toward you and the desires of those who read this that we might all say: 'Great is the Lord and worthy of praise'" (*sed affectum excito in te et eorum, qui haec legunt, ut dicamus omnes: Magnus dominus et laudabilis valde*, XI.i.4–5). Because these narrations have an emotional as well as an intellectual purpose, they need to be viewed in light of a new rhetoric that has been reinvented and enlarged to include the "full range of classical rhetoric — *logos* and *ethos* and *pathos*."[57]

Augustine's rhetoric can best be understood through the work of contemporary rhetoricians who emphasize the powers of invention, including that of emotional appeal, rather than focusing on eloquence and style.[58] Cultural and intellectual historians are also showing how for earlier writers "emotion is . . . bound up with argument; the orator moves by giving reasons."[59] I have argued that this close tie between discovery and emotion is manifested from the beginning of Augustine's account of childhood language acquisition, where his theory of signs emphasizes the cognitive and emotional effect of language. Later in the text we find that although rhetoric can be manipulated to exert force upon others and thus denying them their freedom of will, it also can enable inquiry and Augustine's search for wisdom and a happy life.

Rhetoric and religion illuminate each other in additional fruitful ways. Augustine's criticism of corrupt forms of rhetoric — corrupt because they create an addictive relation between people and language — dramatizes how interconnected religious idolatry, linguistic fixity, and literalism may be. The Manicheans, as Augustine viewed them, reduced the search and discovery of wisdom to the word "Truth," and they reduced an infinite God to a material substance. Augustine does not reject the literal interpretation of parts of the Bible, but in *DDC* he insists on a thoughtful reading of the Word in light of the precepts "love God and love neighbor." A rhetorical understanding of the need for tropes at times complements and illuminates Augustine's insistence on spiritual reading and on God as distanced from human understanding. The *Confessions* also tests and ultimately includes deliberative activity that examines grounds of belief as part of a well-founded, well–thought through religious commitment, while he eschews skepticism as inadequate by itself. Finally, insofar as conversion implies a change of life and not just a shift in ideas, it involves human beings in deliberative activities. In these they compare the text with their own lives and are changed by the rhetorical arguments and emotions that emerge in this activity. These arguments are in accordance with a divine will that is fully expressed neither in the text alone nor in the reader but rather in the sparks thrown out from their interaction. The text has no absolute, accessible, intended author or meaning apart from the activity of reading and deliberating through which it lives.

Notes

I am grateful to Walter Jost for his thoughtful comments and careful editing of this essay.

1. James J. Murphy, "Saint Augustine and the Debate About a Christian Rhetoric," *Quarterly Journal of Speech* 46 (December 1960): 409. Augustine describes sophistical discourse in *De doctrina Christiana* [hereafter *DDC*], in *Patrilogiae Cursus Completus,* ed. J.-P. Migne, vol. 34 (Paris, 1887), III.xxx.48. Unless otherwise indicated, all references are to this edition and are given parenthetically in text. Translations are from Saint Augustine, *On Christian Doctrine,* trans. D. W. Robertson, Jr. (Indianapolis: Bobbs-Merrill, 1958).

2. See Debora K. Shuger, "The Philosophical Foundations of Sacred Rhetoric," Chap. 3 of this volume.

3. The words in quotation are from Richard McKeon, "Rhetoric in the Middle Ages," in *Critics and Criticism,* ed. R. S. Crane (Chicago: University of Chicago Press, 1952), 264. On the relation between philosophy and rhetoric in Augustine, see Mary C. Preus, *Eloquence and Ignorance in Augustine's* On the Nature and Origin of the Soul. American Academy of Religion 51 (Atlanta: Scholars, 1985), 2–33; and Marjorie O'Rourke Boyle, "Augustine in the Garden of Zeus: Lust, Love, and Language," *Harvard Theological Review* 83 (1990): 118ff. Boyle, however, emphasizes the importance of prudence in the *Confessions* in "The Prudential Augustine: The Virtuous Structure and Sense of His *Confessions,*" *Recherches Augustiniennes* 22 (1987): 129–50. Marcia L. Colish emphasizes the importance of language to Augustine's discovery of God in "Augustine: The Expression of the Word," in *The Mirror of Language: A Study in the Medieval Theory of Knowledge* (Lincoln: University of Nebraska Press, 1968, rev. ed. 1983), 16ff. On the importance of rhetoric for Augustine's thought, see Peter Brown, *Augustine of Hippo: A Biography* (Berkeley: University of California Press, 1967), and Henri Irénée Marrou, *Saint Augustin et la fin de la culture antique,* 4th ed. (Paris, 1958). Pages 196 and following of the latter are especially helpful with regard to the relation between rhetoric and philosophy.

4. See Ernest L. Fortin, "Augustine and the Problem of Christian Rhetoric," *Augustinian Studies* 5 (1974): 92ff.

5. *DDC* II.xxviii.57.

6. Fortin, "Augustine and the Problem of Christian Rhetoric," 93.

7. See ibid., 87ff.

8. Wayne C. Booth, "Rhetoric and Religion: Are They Essentially Wedded?" in *Radical Pluralism and Truth: David Tracy and the Hermeneutics of Religion,* ed. Werner G. Jeanrond and Jennifer L. Rike (New York: Crossroad, 1991), 62. For two notable exceptions that have informed the present study, see David Tracy, "Charity, Obscurity, Clarity: Augustine's Search for Rhetoric and Hermeneutics," in *Rhetoric and Hermeneutics in*

Our Time: A Reader, ed. Walter Jost and Michael J. Hyde (New Haven: Yale University Press, 1997), and Boyle, "Prudential Augustine."

9. Boyle, "Prudential Augustine," 233. See Cicero, *De officiis* 1.43.153. Boyle argues that Augustine uses Cicero's "topics concerning the attributes of persons" to invent his epideictic exhortation toward good and away from evil (132). See the following for the influence of Cicero on Augustine: Maurice Testard, *Saint Augustin et Cicero.* 2 vols. (Paris: Etudes Augustiniennes, 1958); J. B. Eskridge, *The Influence of Cicero upon Augustine in the Development of His Oratorical Theory for the Training of the Ecclesiastical Orator* (Menasha, Wis.: Collegiate/George Banta, 1912); C. S. Baldwin, "St. Augustine and the Rhetoric of Cicero," *Proceedings of the Classical Association* 22 (1925): 24–46.

10. See Aristotle, *Rhetoric* I.ii.1356aff; and Cicero, *De oratore* II.xl.175, and the surrounding argument.

11. See Aristotle, *Rhetoric* I.ii.1356aff; and Cicero, *De oratore* II.xl.175. The quotation is from Wayne C. Booth, "Rhetoric and Religion," 63.

12. Saint Augustine, *Confessionum.* In *Corpus Christianorum, Series Latina,* vol. 27 (Turnholti: Typographia Brepois editores pontificii, 1954–   ), I.vi. Unless otherwise indicated, all references are to this edition and are given parenthetically in text.

13. Boyle, for example, argues that Augustine makes a distinction between the "learning of speech for the communication of will" and "maturation to speech as the communication of intellect" ("Augustine in the Garden of Zeus," 120).

14. Brian Stock comments on the similarity between Augustine's account of language acquisition and his descriptions of interactions between writers and readers of texts in *Augustine the Reader: Meditation, Self-Knowledge, and the Ethics of Interpretation* (Cambridge: Harvard University Press, 1996), 25.

15. Tzvetan Todorov analyzes the communicative and designative aspects of the sign in *Theories of the Symbol,* trans. Catherine Porter (Ithaca: Cornell University Press, 1982), 36ff.

16. Augustine, *On Christian Doctrine,* 35. See Todorov, *Theories of the Symbol,* 41.

17. Brian Stock, *Augustine the Reader,* 9. See John R. Searle, *Intentionality: An Essay in the Philosophy of Mind* (Cambridge: Harvard University Press, 1983).

18. See Aristotle, *Rhetoric,* I.v.1360b, and Cicero, *De inventione* I.i.

19. For Cicero and Augustine on prudence, see Boyle, "Prudential Augustine," 133ff.

20. Eugene Vance, "Augustine's *Confessions* and the Grammar of Selfhood," *Genre* 6 (March 1973): 19.

21. Quintilian, *Institutio oratoria* VI.ii.3.

22. Augustine refers to how he came to love sorrows that were represented in fictions, that they "should touch or scratch me on the surface" (III.ii).

23. See Cicero, *De oratore* II.xlvi.192; and Quintilian, *Institutio oratoria* V.ii.26.

24. See Colish, *Mirror of Language,* 22.

25. See Aubrey Gwynn, *Roman Education from Cicero to Quintilian* (Oxford: Oxford University Press, 1926), 118. For the fragments themselves, see Harald Hagendahl, *Augustine and the Latin Classics,* Studia Graeca et Latina Gothoburgensia 20 (Göteborg: Elanders Boktryckeri Aktieholag, 1967), 1:81–94. Many of the fragments emphasize the search for a happy life.

26. Gwynn, *Roman Education,* 118–19.

27. See Saint Augustine, *De doctrina Christiana: Liber quartus,* ed. and trans. Thérèse Sullivan (Washington, D.C.: Catholic University of America Press, 1930), 144–45, para. 42.

28. Augustine, *On Christian Doctrine,* IV.xxv.161 (emphasis added).

29. The Manicheans, for example, had rejected the supposedly Christian literal view of man as a physical image of God, ridiculing the notion that God could be confined to the shape of a body (*Confessions,* VI.iii). When "image" is taken more spiritually to indicate the interior faculties of human beings, men can more properly be seen as images of God.

30. See Tracy, "Charity, Obscurity, Clarity," 254ff., on *DDC.*

31. David Tracy, *The Analogical Imagination: Christian Theology and the Culture of Pluralism* (New York: Crossroads, 1981), 20, 73.

32. Witnesses become an indispensable focus of the next books of his confession: witnesses to the power of words to convert, witnesses of changed lives — changed both for good, in the cases of Victorinus and Ponticianus, and, temporarily, for evil, when Alypius is seized by the spectacle of the games. Lady Continence, herself an allegorical figure, exhorts Augustine to change by surrounding herself with exempla.

33. See Olmsted, "Philosophical Inquiry and Religious Transformation," *Journal of Religion* 69, 1 (January 1989): 14–35.

34. Stock, *Augustine the Reader,* 71n1. Stock suggests that "the clue to his meaning is the adjective *admonitus,* a technical term that he [Augustine] frequently employs when referring to a divinely inspired 'external event that triggers an internal effect' " (72). Stock also refers in this regard to *De magistro* (n. 20), where the trigger is a sign, and to the conversion through the *Hortensius,* where error is pointed out and God's "advice" (*admonitio*) is manifested (3.4.21n23), observations that strengthen our sense of a rhetorical dimension in the dialectic shift to contemplation.

35. See Stock, *Augustine the Reader,* 105.

36. Ibid., 104.

37. As Marcia Colish puts it, "A person's moral state affects his ability to know the truth" (*Mirror of Language,* 23). See also page 48.

38. See Tracy, "Charity, Obscurity, Clarity," 265ff.

39. James J. Murphy, "The Metarhetorics of Plato, Augustine and McLuhan: A Pointing Essay," *Philosophy and Rhetoric* 4 (1971): 208. "Heart" here includes intelligence and should not be understood as distinguished from it.

40. See Olmsted, "Philosophical Inquiry."

41. See esp. Colish, *Mirror of Language,* 25ff. and 44ff.

42. See Tracy, "Charity, Obscurity, Clarity," 265.

43. Stock offers a detailed analysis of Augustine's representations of reading and meditation, especially in his introduction to *Augustine the Reader.* See also Ralph Flores, *The Rhetoric of Doubtful Authority* (Ithaca: Cornell University Press, 1984), chap. 2, pp. 44–65.

44. Stock analyzes this passage in detail in *Augustine the Reader,* 97ff., and offers detailed comments on various uses of *rapere.*

45. *St. Augustine's Confessions,* trans. by William Watts (Cambridge: Harvard University Press, 1976).

46. Stock offers an insightful reading of this part of the *Confessions* in *Augustine the Reader,* 107ff. Sarah Spence argues that Augustine's practice differs from Cicero's in that "he hesitates before accepting [the words he hears], and he interprets what he reads . . . [both are] essential characteristics of Christian persuasion" (*Rhetoric of Reason and Desire: Vergil, Augustine, and the Troubadours* [Ithaca: Cornell University Press, 1988], 79).

47. James J. Murphy makes an analogous point about the relation between the "didactic intent of a catechizer — the speaker — and the learning capacity of what he calls the 'hearer.'. . . Only Christian love (*caritas*) can supply this interconnection. This is in some ways a more sophisticated concept than that of Aristotle's *ethos,* because it posits the innate humanity of both speaker and audience member" ("Metarhetorics of Plato, Augustine, and McLuhan," 208).

48. Stock comments in the case of Alypius that "the meaning that was intended by God for Augustine cannot be traced to what they say, nor can the understanding that God intended for Alypius" (*Augustine the Reader,* 82).

49. Spence compares *DDC* and Cicero's *De inventione* with respect to how interpretation locates obscurities (*Rhetoric of Reason and Desire,* 100).

50. Consider, for example, that at IX.i Augustine writes that after casting out his willing and nilling, God "evoked" or "called forth" his free will; Augustine could then choose the author of the whole rather than being overattached to a part of the whole.

51. Peter Brown contrasts Augustine's sense of the darkness and mysteriousness of his inner self with Plotinus's more "reassuring" image of the "size and dynamism of the inner world" (*Augustine of Hippo,* 178ff.).

52. Spence describes Augustine's changes as from orator to *orans* (*Rhetoric of Reason and Desire,* 79). She and Preus envision him as moving from oratory to preaching. See Preus, *Eloquence and Ignorance,* 32–33.

53. Boyle "Prudential Augustine," 135.

54. See also Spence on *DDC* and Ciceronian rhetoric, *Rhetoric of Reason and Desire,* 94–95.

55. Tracy, *Analogical Imagination,* 20, 73.

56. In *DDC,* Augustine adapts the Ciceronian functions of rhetoric to teach, delight, and persuade (*docere, delectare, flectere*) to Christian purposes (*De doctrina Christiana,* ed. and trans. Sullivan IV.12–14, 27–31). Cicero uses forms of "*excitare*" at *De oratore* I.i.202.

57. Terry Eagleton, *Literary Theory: An Introduction* (Minneapolis: University of Minnesota Press, 1983), 205–6. Cf. David Tracy, "Charity, Obscurity, Clarity," 2.

58. Among these are Wayne C. Booth, *The Rhetoric of Fiction* (Chicago: University of Chicago Press, 1961, rpt., 1983); Booth, *Modern Dogma and the Rhetoric of Assent* (Chicago: University of Chicago Press, 1774); and Chap. 2 of this volume; Kenneth Burke, *A Rhetoric of Motives* (Berkeley: University of California Press, 1969); Marjorie O'Rourke Boyle, *Rhetoric and Reform: Erasmus' Civil Dispute with Luther* (Cambridge: Harvard University Press, 1983); and McKeon "Rhetoric in the Middle Ages."

59. Shuger, "Philosophical Foundations."

5

Rhetorical Theology: Charity Seeking Charity

MARJORIE O'ROURKE BOYLE

The religious piety of the humanists secured its perfect complement in rhetorical propriety. Such piety had established a tradition, from the Delphic wisdom of the ancients to the filial fear of the medievals, of the knowledge of self as creature, distinct from and lesser than God.[1] It shunned the irreverent curiosity that sought knowledge beyond the human measure and cultivated a reverent curiosity that promoted such mortal knowledge as might illuminate the divine revelation. It was a studied ignorance. Knowledge was not the end of humanist theology but a means to it. Those disciplines, notably grammar, that could interpret Scripture and tradition were assiduously applied. Implicit in this scholarship of editing and translating, of annotating and paraphrasing, was the belief that in reading or hearing the word of God, not only by sensory impression but also by volitional assent, the soul was conformed to that very Word in whom it had been uttered into being (John 1:1–3).[2] For this conformity the integrity of the text was essential. The humanists were thus zealous for erudition, but an erudition in the service of persuasion.

In persuasion humanist theology was governed by the rhetorical canon of decorum, which dictated attention to the subject and audience of the discourse.[3] Since theology was speech about God by and to mortals, a creaturely measure was to be observed. In expounding this propriety the humanists appealed to the piety of the very Son made man. Erasmus speculated that Christ spoke rhetorically to reveal and to conceal. He accommodated the divine truth to a universal understanding in tropes that were simple, not sophisticated, and available to all, whether illiterate shepherds or literate scribes.[4] As he was neatly paraphrased by Calvin, God stammers to human infancy as a mother to her babe.[5] This rhetorical method also sequestered the divine truth, since it could only be comprehended by the volitional assent of faith. It thus judged persons, separating the faithful from the faithless listeners, the shepherds from the scribes.[6] Erasmus not only regarded Christ as speaker but also revered Christ as Speech. The revelation that had been dispensed to the Jews through law and to the Greeks through philosophy was manifest to Christians as discourse.[7] This Logos was not the discrete utterance of the Vulgate rendition of *verbum* but the copious oratory of his own New Testament translation of *sermo*.[8] In imitating this paradigm the theologian was himself to be a rhetor, for the human complement to the divine generation was speech. Since man was created in the image of the Son as the eternally begotten discourse of the Father, it was speech, not reason, that distinguished him from beast. The Christian theologian was therefore to be a rhetorician not a logician. This vocation distinguished the humanists from the scholastics (whom Erasmus allied with the animals) in a methodological shift from inquiry to eloquence, from the dialectical question to the rhetorical period.[9]

In this exposition of the rhetoric of Christ and Christ as Rhetoric, another truth was inchoate, one whose exploration discloses the theological distinction between humanism and scholasticism. Christ spoke rhetorically because rhetoric is the language of the Holy Spirit, which he possessed in his mission. He breathed this Spirit upon persons in exhorting, consoling, instructing, admonishing, convicting, exciting their wills toward assent. "The words that I have spoken to you are spirit and life" (John 6:63). It is the same inspiration of the Spirit in Scripture, as extending the spiration of the Spirit in the Trinity, that quickens its letter to life: "For the word of God is living and active, sharper than any two-edged sword, piercing to the division of soul and spirit, of joints and marrow, and discerning the thought and intentions of the heart" (Heb. 4:12). It was from this divine inspiration that humanists like Petrarch, Erasmus, and Calvin received the Pentecostal spark that was their own genius. As Erasmus formulated the rhetorical program: "The special goal of theologians is to expound Scripture wisely; to render its doctrine according to faith, not frivolous questions; to discourse about piety gravely and efficaciously; to wring out tears, to inflame spirits to heavenly things."[10]

Rhetoric was not only pious but also pastoral, not merely appropriate toward God but persuasive toward people. This distinguished it from the dialectic that the scholastics adopted as their method: rhetoric had an efficacy not only to convince but also to convert. Dialectic seeks an act of the intellect, judgment, and secures its religious end in contemplation. Rhetoric seeks an act of the will, assent, and secures its religious end in conversion.[11] It was such conversion that Erasmus defined as the end of theology. The theologian had one focus only: to speak metamorphically, transfiguring man into God. "This is your first and only goal; perform this vow, this one thing," he instructed, "that you be changed, that you be seized, that you weep at and be transformed into those teachings which you learn." The program was the transformation of speech into act, of oratory into flesh, just as Speech had become incarnate.[12]

A particular efficacy of rhetoric toward this transformation defines it as the language of the Spirit that Christ spoke. Rhetoric is unitive. So is the Spirit. It is the Spirit who as the mutual love of the Father and the Son is the bond of the Trinity, and as their missionary love toward humans is the bond of Creation. To speak rhetorically, then, is to speak spiritually. The humanists appreciated the unitive power of rhetoric in three spheres: the bond of society, the integration of self, and communion with God. Rhetoric as the bond of society was indebted to the classical tradition that lauded speech as the cultural act. It distinguished humans from beasts and enabled them to found cities, establish laws, invent arts, and live the good life socially. It was communication for commonweal.[13] This social empathy was paralleled by a personal sympathy, indebted to the classical tradition that commended speech as the psychological act. By the education and therapy of speech a person could civilize himself, establishing law among his own unruly members, fashioning a personality, and living the good life individually. This was communication for integrity.[14] As a humanist exemplar Erasmus united these social and individual goals of discourse in his methodological masterwork *Diatriba,* by which he sought through deliberative rhetoric to bind the fracture of Europe and the fault of Luther.[15] Yet there was also speech as a theological act. Rhetoric had a power to foster, although not effect — *effect* being the verb of grace alone — a communion with God that secured the religious and theological ends of speech. Its religious end was that conversion to God by moral acts to which the will was persuaded. Its theological end was that union with God by mystical passions to which the will was enraptured. The ultimate conversion toward which rhetorical theology tended was that charitable union, and it is such transformation of the self in God that distinguishes its purpose from that of dialectical theology.

Dialectic seeks an act of the intellect, judgment, and secures its religious end in contemplation. Contemplation involves understanding, the comprehension of God, and wisdom, the right judgment of that apprehension. These are virtues of the speculative intellect and, superiorly, charismatic gifts.[16] The scholastic definition of theology was the formulation of Anselm: "faith seeking understanding."[17] Faith is a theological virtue and it resides in the intellect.[18] In scholasticism it seeks a virtue of the speculative intellect, understanding, and also understanding as a charismatic gift. Its speculative and charismatic crown is wisdom, by which it rightly judges what it understands. In the scholastic definition of theology, then, a theological virtue seeks a charismatic gift. In the humanist definition of theology, however, a theological virtue seeks a theological virtue, its proper perfection. Rhetoric seeks an act of the will, assent, and secures its religious end in conversion. Conversion involves charity alone. Charity is a theological virtue and it resides in the will. It is the consummate virtue and as such may only seek its own increase.[19] Here is the definitional shift from scholasticism to humanism in theology: from faith seeking understanding to charity seeking charity. It is paralleled by a psychological shift from the intellectual to the volitional, from the speculative to the experiential. The humanist reform of theology was indeed, as it eagerly acknowledged its imitation of the ancient method, a renaissance of the patristic tradition. It was, however, also what it disdained to acknowledge, a continuity with the medieval tradition of those mystical theologians from Bernard to Bonaventure and beyond who identified human excellence with the will rather than the intellect and who, not fortuitously, wrote rhetorically rather than dialectically about God.

The aspiration of scholastic theology may thus be convicted out of its own mouth by this simple consideration of the treatise on the habits in the *Summa theologiae* of Thomas Aquinas, whom the best of the humanists, Erasmus, considered the best of the moderns.[20] It clearly established the excellence of charity with its unitive end to faith with its contemplative end. Had Aquinas comprehended his own argument, its logic would have compelled him to rhetoric. Although he did not abandon his project, he was constrained upon its completion to judge it rhetorically with one of those tropes he so disdained, a mere metaphor: chaff.[21] This heap of knowledge was not in the judgment of the humanists any kindling for the fire of charity. It was damp chaff that emitted smoke — obfuscation — and quenched the flame. Lorenzo Valla assigned Aquinas to play the cymbals in the heavenly choir[22] because, as Paul declaimed, "If I speak in the tongues of men and of angels, but have not love, I am a noisy gong or a clanging cymbal" (1 Cor. 13:1). The humanists aspired to more than mortal or angelic voice: the breath of the Spirit: tongues of fire. As Erasmus encouraged theologians, God babbles to our infancy and we babble back; yet just as he stoops to human incompetence so should we mount to divine sublimity.[23]

This sublimity toward which the humanists ascended was the consummation of charity in mystical union. In this supernatural mission the Spirit perfects in the soul through the will by grace an experiential infusion of himself, as Charity, the spiritual union that participates by adoption in the essential unity that exists by nature between the Father and the Son.[24] This is utterly distinct from and utterly transcendent of the scholastic goal of contemplation, which completes the different and lesser theological virtue of faith. In contemplation there is only the quasi-union of the knower in the known, not the real union of the lover in the beloved. The union of charitable mysticism is, moreover, not knowing but unknowing. In the disavowal of John of the Cross "*Nescivi*. Then I knew naught."[25] This is so because, as Aquinas understood, the object of charity cannot be knowledge, because its object is the thing known, which is God himself.[26] There is an unknowing also in contemplative mysticism, but of a different nature. In contemplative mysticism the unknowing represents the failure of the speculative intellect, even as aided by the gift of understanding, to apprehend fully its object. In charitable mysticism the intellect is not even operative, or operated. The difference is as between clouded vision and no vision, the purblind and the blind. ("Love is blind.") The befogged vision of contemplation — its unknowing — will yield in glory to the manifest sight, "face to face" (1 Cor. 13:12). The nonvision of charity — its unknowing — will increase in glory to its own perfection in an eternal union: not the externality of facial regard but the internality of the self in God.

Theologically this justifies the claims of the humanists to superiority over the scholastics and explains the endurance of their method into the modern era, while scholasticism declined and ended as a historical episode. Although it is true that those scholastics who were religious-minded sought contemplation for charity, understanding in order to love, that end was merely on the horizon of theology, not integral to its definition. That charitable vision was obscured in the frigid and frivolous investigations lampooned by the humanists, as in the question whether God could have become incarnate in a beetle's asshole.[27] The scholastic method toward charity was, moreover, itself awry. The union of charitable mysticism does presuppose the perfection of the charismatic gifts, among them the contemplative graces of understanding and wisdom, the last of the charismatic gifts to be perfected on the threshold of the "mystical marriage," as the experience of John of the Cross attests; however, it is not wisdom but fear, filial fear. It is the solitary attachment of the will to God in poverty of spirit that ushers the kingdom of God by grace within, the Beloved into his chamber.[28] The humanists in their observance of fear through rhetorical propriety were thus more proximate to charitable union than were the scholastics in their cultivation of wisdom through dialectical certitude. Thus they gleefully declined the sage's crown for the fool's cap (and foolscap). One had to be, as Erasmus knew, a fool to play the rhetorician at theology. As Jacopone de Benedetti da Todi had rhymed:

> He who enters in this school
> Learns a new and wondrous rule:
> "Who hath never been a fool,
> Wisdom's scholar cannot be."[29]

Erasmus was confident that in his folly he imitated the Fool who had blessed such simplicity: "I thank you, heavenly Father, that you have hidden these mysteries from the wise and revealed them to the fools."[30]

It may seem that the fear of the humanists was not proximate to the charity of the mystics, since the rhetoric of mysticism appears to violate the canon of decorum. The rhetoric of charitable mysticism does not ruin decorum, however, but extends it. As charity increases, the understanding and judgment of what is fitting to speak about God becomes extravagant. Bernard of Clairvaux explained that because the reason for loving God is God himself, the way to love him is beyond measure.[31] Thus the way to speak of him in love is beyond measure. This exaggeration of language is evident in the mystical predilection for hyperbole and exclamation and for the imagery of eroticism and intoxication, as in the commentaries on the Song of Songs. To the religious mind such language seems indecent. Its rhetorical resorts offend the lesser love of filial piety, which regards the honor of God. This is spousal love speaking, however, and fittingly so, for it expresses an intimacy that exceeds the creaturely measure, which is filial fear. "Perfect love casts out fear" (1 John 4:18). The abandonment of self in God thus secures its perfect complement in an abandon of rhetoric. This union is ineffable, yet when flung back from spiritual to sensible reality the stunned tongue does loosen and speak, and not in a dialectical syllogism but in a rhetorical sentence. This rhetoric marks the failure of language to represent, not only because divine omniscience transcends human science but also because the experience itself is not cognitive: unknowing.[32] This rhetoric marks, however, the success of language to evoke, its consummate perfection, which is to speak charitably about Charity.

The rejection of rhetoric as the proper theological method betrays a servile fear, the fear of punishment, of damnation, that error and sin provoke. Theologians in the grip of this mercenary fear preferred the mathematical equation to the mystical union as a model for discourse. As Augustine confessed of his refusal, before conversion, to assent, he desired to be as certain of the divine mysteries as he was of the fact that three plus seven equals ten.[33] It was with such demand for apodictic evidence, absolute certitude (because if one does not know, he cannot believe, and if one disbelieves, one cannot be saved), that

Martin Luther grasped the kataleptic expression of justification by faith and clenched Zeno's fist around a dogma of absolute necessity.[34] He composed his masterwork, *De servo arbitrio*, in the forensic genre to condemn rhetoric itself as a theological method.[35] It was not fortuitous that Luther opted for ordinary language and literal sense as normative in theology.[36] He elected this rational method in rejection of the counsel of his confessor to take refuge in the wounds of Christ,[37] the mystical resolution to the anxiety about salvation that servile fear engendered.[38] There were two common cures in the sixteenth century for servile fear. They were classical therapies well established in medical theory with counterparts in the philosophical solutions to the epistemological problem of the criterion: Stoic clarity and Skeptic suspension.[39] In the question of free will, for example, Luther asserted Stoically for personal knowledge, while Erasmus deliberated Skeptically for consensual verisimilitude.[40] In the question of religious experience, for another example, Ignatius of Loyola formulated rules for the discernment and judgment of spirits, while John of the Cross advised oblivion and abandonment of them.[41]

Dialectic and rhetoric, certitude and plenitude, coercion and persuasion, the grip of logic and the lapse of love — these were the fundamental options that confronted John Calvin at the historical fork between the *via moderna* and the *via antiqua* in theology. Rhetoric is indeed, as many theologians feared, risky and messy. One might be burnt; one might be caught. The creative act could entail fault. Yet did not the original Creator risk the mess of the Original Sin, then redeem it in divine charity? It was this spiritual generosity that found its methodological complement in the "open hand" of rhetoric.[42] By humanist conviction, God could not be bound by the knots of logic yet he might be lured into the nets of love:

> Your head is held high like Carmel
> and its plaits are as dark as purple;
> a king is held captive in your tresses (Song of Songs 7:6).

So it was that the mystic theologian John of the Cross found Christ entangled in his hair:

> By that hair alone
> Which thou regardest fluttering on my neck
> Beholding it upon my neck, thou wert captivated.[43]

So it was that the poetic theologian Petrarch found himself entangled in Laura's hair: "Nor can I shake loose that lovely knot by which the sun is surpassed, not to say amber or gold: I mean the blond locks and the curling snare that so softly bind tight my soul, which I arm with humility and nothing else."[44] This was the classical symbol of ecstatic seizure, the tossing back of long hair in the wind, as when possessed Cassandra "flings her golden locks when there blows from the God the compelling wind of second sight."[45] The strand was one history. The perennial problem with enthusiasm was, Which spirit speaks? good or evil? To be virtuous rhetoric must attain its proper end, the good — theologically, the Good who is the Spirit. In the crisis of the sixteenth century over conflicting claims to that Spirit, Erasmus formulated the perfect rule. The presence of the Spirit is discerned by the Spirit alone — charity — and until that charity be manifest, the prudence of Gamaliel is to be practiced. If disunity rather than unity results from discourse, then the "rhetoric" is bedeviled sophistry.[46]

To imagine Calvin in his tidy cap as a theologian with his hair let down confronts the stereotype. Perhaps it is only odd to prop up his sagging tomes between the exclamation of two French mystics:

Charity! give me charity![47]

and

FIRE.[48]

Yet "he aspired — to use his own language — to be hot, not cool."[49] It was not only the classical tradition of rhetorical eloquence but also the Christian tradition of charitable mysticism that explains the origin and destiny of the theological method and scriptural hermeneutics of humanism. Although Calvin may have fallen short of eloquence and shy of mysticism, in his choice of the *via antiqua* rather than the *via moderna* he was on the right road, like the author of the psalms he cherished, a pilgrim with the song of the ascents.

Notes

1. For the classical background see Jean Defrades, *Les thèmes de la propagande delphique* (Paris: C. Klincksieck, 1954), 277–80, 284, 286; and for its Christian version, Pierre Courcelle, *Connais-toi, toi-même de Socrate à Saint Bernard,* 3 vols. (Paris: Etudes augustiniennes, 1974–75). For the degree of love, see Bernard of Clairvaux, *De diligendo Deo,* 8–10; and for servile and filial fear, Thomas Aquinas, *Summa theologiae* [henceforth *ST*], II-II, q. 7, art. 1; q. 19.

2. This parallels the mystical doctrine of the restoration of the image of God in the soul as propounded by the Cistercian masters Bernard of Clairvaux and William of St. Thierry and as originating in Neoplatonist philosophy.

3. See my *Erasmus on Language and Method in Theology* (Toronto: University of Toronto Press, 1977), 48–51; and my *Rhetoric and Reform: Erasmus' Civil Dispute with Luther* (Cambridge: Harvard University Press, 1983), 39–40.

4. Boyle, *Erasmus on Language and Method in Theology,* 117–27.

5. Ibid., pp. 44–45; cf. William J. Bouwsma, "Calvinism as *Theologia Rhetorica,*" Protocol of the Fifty-Fourth Colloquy, 28 September 1986 (Berkeley: Center for Hermeneutical Studies in Hellenistic and Modern Culture, 1987), 11.

6. Boyle, *Rhetoric and Reform*, 37.

7. Boyle, *Christening Pagan Mysteries: Erasmus in Pursuit of Wisdom* (Toronto: University of Toronto Press, 1981), 15–23.

8. Boyle, *Erasmus on Language and Method in Theology*, 3–31; Boyle, "Sermo: Reopening the Conversation on Translating at Jn 1,1," *Vigiliae christianae* 31 (1977): 161–68, with Calvin at page 161.

9. Boyle, *Erasmus on Language and Method in Theology*.

10. Ibid., 73.

11. Boyle, "Fools and Schools: Scholastic Dialectic, Humanist Rhetoric; from Anselm to Erasmus," *Medievalia et humanistica*, n.s. 13 (1985): 183.

12. Boyle, *Erasmus on Language and Method in Theology*, 73.

13. Ibid., 53–55.

14. Ibid., 39–48.

15. Boyle, *Rhetoric and Reform*, 14–17, 99–131.

16. Thomas Aquinas, *ST*, I, q. 68, art. 4; II-II, q. 8, q. 45.

17. Anselm of Canterbury, *Proslogion* 1.

18. Thomas Aquinas, *ST*, II-II, q. 4, art. 2.

19. Ibid., I, q. 66, art. 6, q. 67, art. 6; II-II, q. 23, art. 6, q. 24, art. 4.

20. Boyle, *Erasmus on Language and Method in Theology*, 206n43; J.-P. Massaut, "Erasme et Saint Thomas," in *Colloquia erasmiana turonensia: Stage internationale d'études humanistes, 12e Tours, 1969*, ed. Jean-Claude Margolin, 2 vols. (Paris: J. Vrin, 1972), 2:581–611.

21. See Boyle, "Chaff: Thomas Aquinas's Repudiation of His *Opera omnia*," *New Literary History* 28 (1997): 383–99. Special medieval issue.

22. Salvatore I. Camporeale, "Lorenzo Valla tra Medioevo e Rinascimento: Encomion s. Thomae — 1457," *Memorie domenicane* 7 (1976).

23. Boyle, *Erasmus on Language and Method in Theology*, 44–45.

24. This definition is indebted for its basic insight to William of St. Thierry, who writes that the Spirit effects in the soul by grace the same union that exists by nature between the Father and the Son (*Epistola ad fratres de Monte Dei* 263). This is repeated by John of the Cross, who better distinguishes between union and unity in *Cantico espiritual* 39.3–5. As their formulation does not distinguish between mystical union and any other infusion of charity, further clarifications have seemed necessary. The definition includes both degrees: the lesser union, which is conferred in the body repeatedly as a ravishment and penetration of exquisite delicacy; and the consummate union, which is conferred in ecstasy once only as an effacement and transformation of tremendous dynamism.

25. John of the Cross, *Cantico espiritual* 26.13–17, trans. E. Allison Peers, *Spiritual Canticle*, 3rd rev. ed. (Garden City, N.Y.: Doubleday, 1961), 396.

26. Thomas Aquinas, *ST*, I, q. 67, art. 6 ad 2.

27. Boyle, *Erasmus on Language and Method in Theology*, 54–56; Boyle, "Fools and Schools," 173.

28. John of the Cross, *Cantico espiritual* 26.3–4; cf. Thomas Aquinas, *ST*, II-II, q. 19, art. 9, 12.

29. Jacopone da Todi, *Laude* 87.15–18, trans. Evelyn Underhill in *Jacopone da Todi* (London: Dent, 1919), 283.

30. In his gloss of Matt. 11:25 in the *Moira* (1511 and 1514 eds.), Erasmus altered the Vulgate rendition of *parvuli* to *stulti*. Similarly in his first edition of the New Testament (1516) he rendered *nepioi* by *stulti* (*LB* VI, 62E, 274E). For the controversy over this philology with Diego Lopez Zuñiga, an editor of the Complutensian Polyglot Bible, see *Apologia respondens ad ea quae in Novo Testamento taxaverat Jacobus Lopis Stunica*, ad. loc. See also his *Paraphrasis in evangelium Matthei*, 11:25.

31. Bernard of Clairvaux, *De diligendo Deo* 1; cf. *ST*, II-II, q. 27, art. 6. [See also Chapter 13 in this volume: Stephen Webb, "Does Excess Have an Ethics? Theological Reflections on the Hyperbolic Imagination" — eds.]

32. [See Chapter 10 in this volume: Thomas A. Carlson, "Apophatic Analogy: On The Language of Mystical Unknowing and Being-Toward-Death" — eds.]

33. Augustine, *Confessionum libri tredecim* 6.4.6.

34. Boyle, "Stoic Luther: Paradoxical Sin and Necessity," *Archiv für Reformationsgeschichte* 73 (1982): 69–93; Boyle, *Rhetoric and Reform*, 47–57.

35. Boyle, *Rhetoric and Reform*, 58–98.

36. Boyle, "The Chimera and the Spirit: Luther's Grammar of the Will," in *The Martin Luther Quincentennial*, ed. Gerhard Dünnhaupt (Detroit: Wayne State University Press, 1985), 17–31.

37. For the relationship, see David Steinmetz, *Luther and Staupitz: An Essay in the Intellectual Origins of the Protestant Reformation* (Durham, N.C.: Duke University Press, 1980).

38. For an example of this mystical commonplace, see Bonaventure, *De perfectione vitae ad sorores* 6.2.

39. For the classical background, see the literature cited in my *Rhetoric and Reform*, 178n22, and also the discussion on pages 117–26.

40. Boyle, *Rhetoric and Reform*, 5–98.

41. Ignatius of Loyola, *Exercita spiritualia* 1, 314–36; for his alliance with scholasticism against humanism in 410–11, see my "Angels Black and White: Loyola's Spiritual Discernment in Historical Perspective," *Theological Studies* 44 (1983): 253–54; John of the Cross, *El subido del Monte Carmelo* 2–3.

42. For this classical metaphor, see Cicero, *Orator* 32.113; also Boyle, *Rhetoric and Reform*, 81–82.

43. John of the Cross, *Cantico espiritual* 31, trans. Peers, 432.

44. Petrarch, *Rime sparse* 197.7–11, trans. Robert M. Durling, *Petrarch's Lyric Poems: The "Rime Sparse" and Other Lyrics* (Cambridge: Harvard University Press, 1976), p. 343. Although this conceit is interpreted censoriously in literary criticism, for a theological appreciation of it and of Petrarch's aesthetics, consider my *Petrarch's Genius: Pentimento and Prophecy* (Berkeley: University of California Press, 1991).

45. See E. R. Dodds, *The Greeks and the Irrational* (Berkeley: University of California Press, 1951), 273, citing Euripides, *Iphigenia aulidensis* 758.

46. Boyle, *Rhetoric and Reform*, 132–61.

47. William of St. Thierry, *Meditativae orationes* 13.

48. Blaise Pascal, *Memorial*.

49. Bouwsma, "Calvinism as *Theologia Rhetorica*," 12.

6

Rhetoric, Conscience, and the Claim of Religion

WALTER JOST

One can only argue convincingly about goods which already in some way impinge on people, which they already at some level respond to but may be refusing to acknowledge.

— *Charles Taylor,* Sources of the Self

The Erasmian rhetorician who is foolish enough to write about religion, specifically about the individual and belief, speaks (as Kierkegaard said of himself) without authority.[1] But he or she is not necessarily speaking without warrant of any kind. As David Tracy has noted, "Any human being can interpret the religious classics because any human being can ask the fundamental questions that are part of the very attempt to become human at all, those questions that the religious classics address."[2] By "fundamental" and "religious" Tracy is referring to certain types of "limit-questions,"[3] which bear on the constitution of human life. Religious limit-questions disclose both the boundaries to this life — contingency, suffering, ignorance, death — as well as the boundaries of it: its possible "grounds" in reason, moral responsibility, duty, fear, love, creation, trust, joy. In some traditions the latter are included in the term "God" and are what skeptics of these traditions deem self-projections or illusions of one sort or another. Inquiry into the nature and limits of human life involves, among other things, reflections on *how* we come to interpret the limits and contours of that life, how we understand and interpret in order to locate meaning and truth, religious or otherwise.

In considering these matters I take my inspiration and point of departure from three ostensibly disparate sources: Stanley Cavell's "grammatical" (philosophical) investigations of human being-in-the-world — specifically his studies of an Emersonian "moral perfectionism" outside the pale (Cavell might say the pall) of religious faith;[4] Michael Novak's recently reissued *Belief and Unbelief,* which is subtitled "a philosophy of self-knowledge" and which, in good rhetorical fashion, aims at joining mind and heart in the inquiry into the possibility of religious belief;[5] and John Henry Newman's lifelong philosophic effort to articulate what he called a "grammar" and what elsewhere I have called a "rhetoric" of assent, particularly of religious assent or belief.[6] Together these thinkers offer resources for confronting the question of our human limits and for asking what we take our limits to be.

Certainly all three authors can be said to bridge the fast-disappearing gap between "grammar" (philosophy) and rhetoric. I am thinking here of rhetoric as a first-order discursive activity for effecting or changing belief or action (*rhetorica utens*).[7] So understood rhetoric includes, at one end of the spectrum, persuasion in explicitly indeterminate matters like practical ethics and politics, as it did in classical accounts of oratory, and at the other end, what modern rhetorical philosophers and theorists like Kenneth Burke or Ernesto Grassi call "identification" by means of symbolic action in *any* discursive field — including philosophy (or theology) in its most basic task of finding first principles (*arche*) or "grounds."[8] Like "persuasion" but allowing now for unintended effects and consequences, "identification" for Burke involves our actively identifying the nature (or "properties") of an indeterminacy — a situation, action, person, event — from an evaluative perspective; organizing our own moral and religious growth in terms of such identifications — that is, identifying ourselves with those identifications; recognizing that such identifications create disagreement and social discord between ourselves and others; and attempting, in our efforts to identify a person, situation, event, or problem, to get others to identify their interests — hence their identities — with our own (even if we, or they, do so without conscious intent).[9] All identification is thus more or less rhetorical because all identification is more or less situated, perspectival, and interested; once more, rhetorical identification ranges from familiar, quotidien problems to life's limit-situations.

Second-order "rhetorics" (*rhetorica docens*), accordingly, reflect on the nature of such discursive identifications in symbolic action and function in part as "how-to" manuals, providing cognitive re-sources (topoi) for effecting or achieving the desired identifications in matters that are susceptible of competing interpretations. Thought of in this way, Cavell, Novak, and Newman are all rhetorical philosophers as well as rhetorical theorists — a more useful term is "rhetorologists"[10] — who offer second-order rhetorics to illuminate first-order rhetorical activities, including their own: rhetorics of assent or belief (Newman), of intelligent subjectivity or understanding (Novak), and of the publicly accessible criteria and acknowledgments ("mutual attunements") underlying all speaking, reasoning, and knowing (Cavell). For the rhetorician, then, two connected questions arise: How does each philosopher understand distinctly rhetorical identifications to occur? and How, more specifically, does each philosopher portray the foundational limits of human beings as rhetorical creatures?

These different thinkers can initially be brought together by virtue of their similar orientations to thinking as continuous with practical living, their shared post-Enlightenment awareness of plural ultimate goods and the myriad forms self-autonomy can take, and particularly their similarly expansive uses of the word "conscience" to embody these concerns. A sentence from Stanley Cavell's early work on Thoreau begins to suggest some of the points I am after: "*Walden,* in its emphasis upon listening and answering, outlines an epistemology of *conscience.*"[11] In describing Thoreau's identification of American culture as self-destructively philistine and conformist, avoiding and even in flight from its own ideals, and in doing so in terms of a persuasive "conscience" calling us back "home," Cavell is probably thinking of Martin Heidegger's early phenomenological investigations of conscience in *Being and Time.*[12] For Heidegger the ontological structure of human being is care (*Sorge*), meaning both our responsibility to our factical "thrownness" in the world and our debt to our ownmost possibilities. And again for Heidegger, by virtue of conscience we human beings hear a (silent) summons not only calling us back from our lostness in the "they" (*das Man*) but charging us with responsibility for our past acts; and we can respond by answering the charge of "Guilty!" with renewed resolution to interpret and realize those indeterminate possibilities for being (ahead of us) that are especially our own.

But how do we effect those identifications? For Cavell, Thoreau's twofold project of living at Walden and writing *Walden* furthers Heidegger's investigation by enacting the drama of call-and-response in pragmatic, rhetorical terms only hinted at in Heidegger. In his text Thoreau performs his own conscience in a way that is pitched to show his neighbors how to renew their senses of themselves and their polity, their identifications and identities (hence, like the other texts I shall deal with here, *Walden* is both a *rhetorica utens* and a *rhetorica docens*). These include not only distinctly American ideals but more generally what it is to be a human being at all — that is, what Cavell calls the "criteria" and "acknowledgments" identifying the human condition and our "identification with" them. Cavell himself, similarly, seeks to reinvigorate his own culture's sense of its (our) moral, political, and philosophical possibilities, in part by retrieving the repressed philosophical legacy of such writers as Thoreau and Emerson. In effect both Thoreau and Cavell provide us with an art of discovering, and recovering, modes of agency through which we become more deeply human.

Michael Novak's *Belief and Unbelief* also derives in important ways from an Emersonian line of American pragmatism (cf. p. 73), and delineates a practical epistemology (a second-order rhetoric) of conscience, or of what the author more fully identifies as "intelligent subjectivity." "Fidelity to conscience" (6, 11, 12, and 181, passim) is fidelity to our own intelligent subjectivity and to our "drive to understand," that is, our desire to seek what is real about ourselves and our world amid ongoing contingency, indeterminacy, and change. At a pivotal moment in the text, within a passage that cites John Henry Newman's interest in Aristotelian *phronesis* extended "from ethics to other speculative concerns," Novak approvingly mentions a "wider view of pragmatism" than is popularly conceived, one pursued, for example, by the philosopher Morton White, who ties abstract speculation to practical reasoning: "Professor White, following Nelson Goodman, argues that a 'counterpart of conscience' is required to explain the [practical] decisions of philosophers and scientists. The inquiring mind feels the bite of the normative, of a quasi-conscience."[13] "Quasi," presumably because the concept of conscience gets extended beyond the orbit of practical conduct to include philosophic (or religious) concerns, just as it does in Thoreau, thereby making the two equally practical concerns; and "conscience," presumably because the enterprise of knowing, both a "knowledge-with" others and a "with-knowledge" (*conscientia*) of a shared world, entails claims of responsibility for past and future acts. Like Cavell, Novak investigates what is involved in discovering how we might come to decide on (how we might recognize or "acknowledge") what it means to be human and what the parameters of our existence might be.

Finally, it is no accident that Novak mentions Newman, inasmuch as another of the powerful sources of Novak's thinking was the philosopher Bernard Lonergan. Lonergan is known to have read Newman's *An Essay in Aid of a Grammar of Assent* (1870) six times, and his own epistemological insights show a marked Newmanian stamp.[14] We might say that Novak's book, first published in 1964, tries to do in our own time something of what Newman's *Grammar of Assent* (if not quite his *Apologia Pro Vita Sua* [1864])[15] sought to do a hundred years earlier, namely, reclaim religious belief, in part by stabilizing it in conscience, as a legitimate possibility for human life. For Newman, as for Bishop Butler before him, "conscience" refers to a natural, twofold capacity of the human mind that calls us to account for our deeds (our moral responsibility and debt) and to recognize our sinfulness and need to change (our moral and religious possibilities). Like Cavell and Novak, Newman addresses those limit-questions bearing on the nature and scope of human life: Who am I? Whence? Wherefore? Like them, he conceives of the self as the historically dynamic locus (topos) of conflict over what Novak calls belief and unbelief and what Cavell calls skepticism and its variants and alternatives, at the limits of the human world.

As a way of sharpening the point of this argument, then, I want to ask: How do what I am calling the rhetorical approaches and arguments of each of these authors work? That is, how does each author understand discursive arrival at fundamental or limit beliefs, and to what substantive fundamental beliefs about human beings and their world (about "conscience" variously described) does each philosopher seek to persuade us? We can begin with Newman, for he provides the most accessible account of the putative "claim" of reason and religion as rhetorical claims. My purpose here is not to lobby for or against any particular conception of religious belief but to suggest that arrival at religious belief involves the same sort of rhetorical methods and arguments as arrival at nonreligious belief and suggests the speciousness of the widespread academic dismissal of such religious faith as otiose (if not odious).

Newman's "Informal Inference" and the Centrality of "Antecedent Considerations"

In earlier work I established Newman's method of thinking, across the many subject matters he treated, as rhetorical both because he exhibits an elaborate first-order rhetorical practice in works like the *Apologia* and *The Idea of a University* (1853) and because he engages in second-order rhetorical philosophizing about coming to warrantable beliefs in indeterminate matters.[16] There I stressed the rhetorical nature of his theory of reasoning, but here I want to explore what reasoning for Newman rests on, which is perforce something other than further reasoning. More specifically, although I seek to recall Newman's notion of human reason in terms of a deliberative rhetoric that he considered more satisfactory than other approaches to reason and faith in his own time, I do so chiefly to show that Newman's rhetorical reason is stabilized and given minimal content and direction in "conscience," and that conscience functions as a rhetorical commonplace (topos) that indicates or "shows-forth" the human world under particular aspects, moral and religious, in ways that link Newman with Novak and Cavell.

This latter function — the showing-forth of a world under certain aspects or, said otherwise, the showing-forth of human existence "as" a field of persuasive inquiry, argument, judgment and action — is itself rhetorical in several ways: conscience is indeterminate to the extent that what it attends to can be variously interpreted; it uses an emotional and imaginative (metaphorical) language which is historically relative and changing; and (like any topos) it opens up a space for deliberation and competing arguments and actions. For Newman, in short, conscience cannot be rhetorically argued for, much less demonstrated, but it also cannot be dispensed with. To distinguish it from the deliberative inferential rhetoric which it supports and informs, I call its functioning *epideictic*, expanding the use of that term from classical rhetoric — the praise or blame of that which is already understood and valued — to include no less than the praise (and even thanks) for a world disclosed under certain aspects, a world that makes a practical "claim" on us.

Indeed "practice" for Newman was the ground and test for all theory and philosophy, much as it is in the pragmatism of, for example, William James (who admired Newman) or in the various neopragmatisms of our own time (when, unfortunately, Newman goes all but unnoticed).[17] In the empirical sciences it is comparatively otherwise, but in concrete, existential cases human beings differ too much, according to Newman, for us to be satisfied with abstract systems and grand theory. "Life is for action," he states in his essay "The Tamworth Reading Room" (1841): "If we insist on proofs for everything, we shall never come to action";[18] "Logic makes but a sorry rhetoric with the multitude." It does so because "deductions have no power of persuasion" (*DA*, 294, 293). As Newman expresses it in the *Apologia*, "To reconcile theory and fact is almost an instinct of the mind" (233). In the same vein Newman asks in the *Grammar of Assent*: "What is the meaning of the distrust, which is ordinarily felt, of speculators and theorists but this, that they are dead to the necessity of personal prudence and judgment to qualify and complete their logic? Science, working by itself, reaches truth in the abstract, and probability in the concrete; but what we aim at is truth in the concrete" (181).

In many ways these excerpts capture the essence of Newman's philosophical attitude and orientation. From his earliest writings in the Oxford sermons to the *Essay on the Development of Christian Doctrine* (1845) and the *Apologia*, to the late *Grammar of Assent* — religious classics all — Newman sought to resist and overcome two contrary approaches to religious belief: that faith in God and religious truths were objectively provable — or refutable — by "enlightened" (which is to say, secular) reason; or that they were a matter of romantic feelings, private intuitions, or will.[19] For his part Newman sought to avoid both approaches as severely reductive (if not destructive) of religious faith and of its dogmatic truths, for him much the same thing.

Newman set out to do this by discriminating two intertwined accounts of reasoning: the Enlightenment account, which he called "explicit reason" and later "formal inference," dealt with empirical fact, scientific generalization, and logical deduction; and what he called an "implicit" reason, later "natural" and "informal inference" — what I am calling rhetorical reasoning — which, properly employed, provides human beings with a justification for many of their beliefs, including belief in God.[20] Far from being distinct modes of reasoning, the formal is better understood as rooted in the informal and abstracted from it to consider those matters that are more amenable (given one's purposes) to exact treatment.

A good deal turns, therefore, on what Newman means by informal inference, what it includes and what it is grounded in. Central here is that such reasoning, while it can involve facts and logic, nevertheless also admits that all facts and logic depend more or less on what Newman variously names "prepossessions," "antecedent considerations," and "antecedent probabilities." Like Kant and the Romantics but in a far more rhetorical and dialogical fashion, knowledge of the world is mediated by the historically situated social self (*GA*, 252), whose values, experiences, and the like mediate the individual's views of our world, what he or she calls the real. Newmanian antecedent considerations are equivalent to what earlier thinkers like Edmund Burke and later hermeneutic thinkers like Hans-Georg Gadamer (following Heidegger) called "just" or "legitimate" "prejudices." They are similar to what the preeminently pragmatic Kenneth Burke, in part following John Dewey, later called our value-laden "interests" and "orientations,"[21] meaning those experiences, beliefs, opinions, judgments, actions that are not reducible to empirical fact, to logical or statistical calculation, or to epistemological or ontological determinacies. They are instead rhetorical resources for argument and interpretation just because they do not timelessly dictate what will be considered real but rather provide reusable argumentative materials and forms.

Like these other thinkers, then, Newman is referring to those more or less tacit practices, habits, cultural values, personal and social commitments, and so on that comprise our hermeneutical and rhetorical horizon of understanding: what Ludwig Wittgenstein calls *Lebensformen,* and Cavell our "mutual attunements." Although from within an individual's perspective not all antecedent considerations are equally susceptible of rhetorical selection and manipulation — on the contrary, some are more stable and fixed than others, while some are quite fixed indeed, providing in Wittgenstein's image the banks within which the individual's life flows — nevertheless, even from that perspective what an antecedent commitment entails may be ambiguous and culturally fluid, while to others they may be wholly contestable and negotiable.

In either case Newman's point is that we rely "always already" on such tacitly held considerations to interpret concrete, existential, problematic — which is to say, indeterminate — situations. Or more accurately, we either interpret those aspects of the world that present us with difficulties and challenges or we rely on previous and now fixed interpretations as settled judgments. By and large, problems do not come to us ready-made and sorted; we rely on antecedent considerations to organize, assess, and understand ourselves, other people, and complex situations and events. Indeed, in one of his letters Newman makes clear that this insight above all his others is central to his thought: "If I have brought out one truth in any thing I have written, I consider it to be the importance of antecedent probability in conviction. It is how you convert factory girls as well as philosophers."[22]

This informal mode of reasoning, then, whose materials are necessarily conditioned and colored by concrete antecedents, is recognizably rhetorical, for it constitutes a deliberative self-persuasion or identification regarding what are taken to be facts and (nonstatistical) probabilities — in short, what is real. Moreover, the most basic antecedent considerations, those which we recognize as enabling us to select facts and estimate probabilities, are equally rhetorical resources rather than Kantian categories or Platonic forms, for they provide culturally and historically relative rather than transcendental "first" principles for thought. In effect, the most basic antecedent considerations comprise rhetorical topoi that open up spaces for deliberation — open up even a world in which to deliberate — without dictating what will be found there.[23]

Informal inference, in short, is a mode of deliberative rhetoric that Newman describes as the "cumulation of probabilities, independent of each other, arising out of the nature and the circumstances of the particular case which is under review; probabilities too fine to avail separately, too subtle and circuitous to be convertible into syllogisms, too numerous and various for such conversion, even were they convertible" (*GA*, 187). As an example Newman cites the way a judge instructs a jury on what it means to exclude a "reasonable doubt" (211), in which what is reasonable is a matter of the established facts being interpreted by "converging probabilities" individually assessed by each juror and submitted to one another for discussion, dispute, and judgment. What is probable to one may not be to another simply because each may fit the facts into different framing narratives, lend them varying values and meanings, and assess them in light of differing experiences and expectations (212). So also for literary historians who debate the authorship of a text (212–13) and for those who offer syllogisms to prove that " 'God is a Being, which must of necessity be endued with perfect knowledge.' . . . To feel the true force of an argument like this, we must not confine ourselves to abstractions, and merely compare notion with notion, but we must contemplate the God of our conscience as a Living Being" (*GA*, 203–4). So theology itself is a rhetorical enterprise that weighs competing probable arguments within the established antecedent truths of the relevant fiduciary community.

Newman calls the perfection of informal inference grounded in antecedent considerations the "illative sense" and less frequently the architectonic faculty of "judgment." We have noticed that Novak observes how Newman extends Aristotle's notion of *phronesis* to encompass all reasoning in practical matters, including speculative questions treated in a concrete or "real" way.[24] This means, first of all, that ostensibly value-free scientific modes of argument are unequal to the interpretive mode of reasoning, the accumulation of myriad subtle probabilities, by which men and women come to faith. Thus Newman's cardinalatial motto is *cor ad cor loquitur* (heart speaks to heart), and he borrows the words of Saint Ambrose as the epigraph for the *Grammar of Assent:* "Non in dialectica complacuit Deo salvum facere populum suum," which we might elaborate as claiming that it is not by dialectic but rather by a noncoercive persuasion (or identification) operative within given topoi — in other words, by rhetoric — that God deigns to save his people.[25]

Second, Newman's extension of *phronesis* or prudence to all reasoning in the concrete means that any decision or judgment made by Newman himself about the ultimate limits of human life is stabilized in his own primary ante-cedent considerations, chief of which (reconfiguring the British tradition of natural theology and eighteenth-century moral philosophy) he identifies as "conscience."[26] One of Newman's most perceptive commentators notes that it is conscience that "underlies Newman's entire thought. All his greater works are ramifications and extensions of what he holds to be the significance of conscience in the life of man. In each of us what is human has its source in conscience."[27] Newman's rhetorical view of man, in short, locates a delib-erative persuasive reasoning grounded in the most important and pervasive antecedent consideration or topos of all: human conscience. How then, rhe-torically, do we make sense of that ground and its role in persuasive arguments for belief in God? And how, if at all, does Newman render appeals to con-science persuasive?

Conscience as the Rhetorical Place of Places

Although his language hearkens back to Shaftesbury and Butler in the eighteenth century, Newman's appeal to conscience is designed to appeal to an even more skeptical nineteenth century willing to concede even less by way of "common" places. Hence its possible use for our yet more skeptical twen-tieth century. Newman's claims for conscience are cast in terms of personal

experience, but experience proves to be a highly socialized and mediated activity susceptible of degrees of rhetorical *inventio*. Newman held that conscience affords individuals both a moral sense, or felt awareness, of right and
wrong and an awareness of absolute duty enjoined by a something—that is,
a Someone—superior and external to ourselves. These two aspects of conscience may be analytically distinguished but together they constitute a unity
of apprehension and function as rhetorical topoi ("moral sense" [a kind of
knowledge]/"duty" [a mode of action]) that, like all topics, open up lines of
argument for construing the world in their light. In this way conscience, the
light that allows us to see ourselves and the world in a certain way, affects all
our attempts at knowing ourselves and the world, providing a nonlogical basis
for reasoning. The question is, What sort of basis?

   In its religious aspect conscience constitutes, as Newman wrote in the Oxford sermons, "an essential principle and sanction of religion in the mind. Our
experiences of our conscience imply a relation between the soul and a something superior to it," a "supreme authority" (*OUS*, 18). Again, in spite of
the language here, Newman is not offering essentialist claims for a discrete
"faculty" of the mind filled with a determinate content, as though all con-
sciences situated all of us in the world in just the same way. Nor does his word
"imply" mean either "immediately" or "logically entails": the inference Newman makes from conscience to God is natural or "informal," hence comprised
of noncoercive probabilities and persuasives (that is, *pisteis*—a term familiar
to the Oxonian Newman), which in any individual case could take years to sift
and settle. Although he holds that conscience properly used informs all human
beings of a God who rewards and punishes (*GA*, 251), the particular doctrines
and rites of natural religion—that is, how this God is understood—vary with
time and place. Newman, in other words, is aware that conscience itself is
conditioned by family, society, and culture, although he is not further "concerned here with abstract [theoretical] questions" (*GA*, 252). In other words,
like Novak and Cavell (and Wittgenstein), Newman eschews *theory* about
how conscience is mediated in favor of *description* of what he takes to be part
of the natural practices of human beings.

   Equally, perhaps most, important, Newman's descriptive appeal to conscience is not exclusively either an empirical or a determinate proposition.
Experience cannot itself prove or even "justify" the doctrine of conscience
because any advertence to experience already presupposes a conscientious
inquirer, one for whom appeals to experience must (always already) be measured against his or her own conscience. Instead, conscience is itself the "*rule*
by which we test, interpret, and correct what is presented to us for belief" (*GA*,
231, emphasis added). It is a stable but dynamic standard or criterion against

which to measure what is real and unreal. We use our conscience in conjunction with our mind and will to negotiate the world that stands open before us, and the measure used is not proved or disproved, though it may be improved, or overthrown, in light of the various contradictions and conundrums it is required to negotiate.

Second, the concept of conscience possesses no single, determinate content composed of just such-and-such elements. Rather it is identified not by content but by "signs" — awareness of the moral, the call to duty, awareness of being judged, the desire to know more about the Judge and the hope and expectation of finding out.[28] As such conscience is a rhetorical topos to which one finds oneself (already) committed and which one explores prudentially, the most common of commonplaces shared by all but able to be elaborated in different, changing ways.

As an example Newman cites the "factory-girl" argument in Mrs. Gaskell's *North and South,* in which a poor working girl expresses her belief in an afterlife, implicitly basing this belief on the intimations of conscience, including her expectations of deliverance from God. About these arguments Newman says: "Here is an argument for the immortality of the soul. As to its force . . . will it make a figure in a logical disputation . . . ? Can any scientific measure compel the intellects of Dives and Lazarus to take the same estimate of it? Is there any test of the validity of it better than the *ipse dixit* of private judgment, that is, the judgment of those who have a right to judge, and next, the agreement of many private judgments in one and the same view of it?" (*GA*, 202–3). The reasoning, then, is just that informal inference which I have called deliberative rhetoric; however, what makes that reasoning possible are the moral and religious contents "opened up" or "shown forth" by the topoi (moral sense/duty) that make up human conscience.

Newman's talk of conscience as a "rule" with respect to which one's sense of reality is tested is what Wittgenstein would call a "grammatical" remark because it identifies criteria of what "counts" as a human being in a human world; and it is equally what I call a rhetorical remark because it topically opens up the space of moral and religious deliberation without dictating the results. More needs to be said about the grammatical-rhetorical nature of such talk, but to develop the inquiry I first want to turn to Novak, chiefly because Newman's own rhetoric on behalf of conscience no longer speaks directly to us, or so it seems to me. Not because his conceptual description is faulty or wrong — though it might be — but because it is inadequate to contemporary conditions and knowledge. Further quotations of Newman on conscience would, I think, necessarily unloose a crowd of plausible objections such as the following.

First, his doctrine (as one might expect) is male-biased, for Newman speaks almost exclusively of conscience as rule-governed, responsibility-centered, judgment- and justice-oriented, and placed under the yoke of an angry taskmaster (*GA*, 252). There is little talk here, except in passing, of intimacy, nurturing, care for community, and receptiveness.[29] Second, the doctrine is culturally biased as well: in spite of his awareness of other cultures, Newman has no way of providing for the lives of (to give but one example) the Japanese, for whom the alleged experience of an external Judge internally lodged is simply counterintuitive. Third, Newman's account is attenuated even as a description, unable to accommodate more than a century of psychoanalytic and sociological advances.[30] Finally, even if we wish to argue (as I would) that such objections are surmountable, Newman's account of conscience remains rhetorically inaccessible to most contemporary readers. In just the way that a Romantic appeal to experience of the land or of wilderness ("Nature") as supernatural simply fails to reach the hearts of most urbanites, so Newman's appeal to conscience as inner awareness of duty, not to mention of our "degraded, servile condition" (*GA*, 253) and our sinfulness, is registered, if at all, in disappearing ink. In short, the doctrine needs to be rethought — rhetorically reinvented — as, I believe, both Novak and Cavell recognize in different ways.

Novak's Criterial Appeal to Human Understanding

Charles Taylor has pointed out the widespread failure in the nineteenth century to recognize that the debate between belief and unbelief (religion and science) was a struggle between competing normative visions and not between a normative outlook (religion) and a value-neutral outlook (science).[31] Even many of those who wished to maintain for religion some room of its own, such as Matthew Arnold and F. D. Maurice, attempted to bring its contents into "scientific" line by reducing supernatural miracles and dogmas to ethical-moral (actional) demands, while scientistic philosophers like John Stuart Mill, Karl Marx, Thomas Huxley, and Herbert Spencer were content to override religion on putatively objective, empirical grounds. Newman never made this error, having always held that science as much as ethics and religion stands on antecedent first principles that are unprovable in any scientific way; but not until our own time have the normativity and rhetoric of science been acknowledged, allowing Newman's concern with practice and persuasion to emerge with full voice.

This philosophic, scientific, and social interest in practical action, utility, and the individual helps explain Newman's emphasis on conscience in terms of a practical command and duty. In our own time practical action (and power) are even more resonant terms, whether we meet them in the form of Nietzschean will-to-power, Sartrean decisionism, Foucauldian critique of power, Derridean deconstruction of authority claims, Marxist or New Historicist literary criticism, or the liberal neopragmatisms of Richard Rorty, Stanley Fish, and indeed Stanley Cavell. It is from within just such a concatenation of voices, in fact, and from within the circle of the individual and action in the world that Novak calls for a "civil conversation" (*Belief and Unbelief,* 15) to sort out and perhaps even begin to adjudicate these competing claims and normative positions. But on what common grounds? We might say that the debate over belief and unbelief of the nineteenth century, rendered unproductive by the dearth of agreed-upon grounds and standards of adjudication, is now made far more difficult by the greater, postmodernist plurality of voices and perspectives. Thus Novak can hardly take up the concept of conscience as Newman did, for he risks begging too many questions. By the same token, Novak does not look to escape his own antecedent considerations but rather only to reflect on and test them against the best competing arguments and fullest antecedent considerations. He needs, in effect, to reinvent the concept of conscience and thereby to shift the grounds of the conversation from allegedly commonly held feelings and experiences to . . . what?

Novak's answer is to transfer the contemporary conversation from the powers and limits of human beings to the nature and limits of human understanding. Whatever else is involved, all argument (all noncoercive philosophic rhetoric) about our place in the world, and the sort of world in which we find ourselves placed, presupposes "criteria" (73) of what it is to be a human being: "Inquiry about God begins with reflection upon the experiences proper to a human person, as a person" (75). Such criteria for Novak in turn depend upon criteria of what it is to know in the first place: it is to ask how we conceive of our own human understanding of ourselves and our world: "For what we mean by 'understanding' determines what we mean by 'man,' and what we mean by 'man' guides what we mean by 'God'" (81). Whereas in Newman conscience as the moral and religious experiences (including our feelings as cognitive indicators of the real)[32] of sin and judgment functioned as the rule by which we know reality, in Novak conscience as "intelligent subjectivity," recognized in self-reflection on one's own understanding, performs this criterial function: "The decision to believe springs from a decision about what in human experience is to be taken as the *criterion* of the real" (135, emphasis added), and this latter decision arises only from "the depths of intelligence" (123).

Let me try to be clear: what Novak calls a "decision" is the willingness in self-reflection to acknowledge that we are already using some standard for measuring the real, or to acknowledge that the standard we are using needs to be replaced with one that we see (recognize, acknowledge) is epistemically both prior and "better." For Novak that standard is human "understanding," which, though conceptually relatively open-ended, nevertheless involves increasingly better ways of *ordering* human experience of the world (78).

Moreover, in keeping with Newman's understanding of the horizonal nature of antecedent considerations, for Novak the decision to acknowledge human understanding as the unending pursuit of order, as the standard, is circular: "Every argument about deciding on the criteria by which to conduct one's inquiries and one's actions is of necessity circular: it begins from and returns to one's idea of one's self. To justify a theory about what knowing is, one must have a theory about the knower, i.e., the self."[33] Circularity, however, does not preclude change — it need not be vicious — for in self-reflection one can consider criticisms and alternatives and accept them; it means rather that one never starts from a tabula rasa and that if one's standard of measure itself changes, that change too will be a function (in part) of drawing on other antecedent considerations.

Like Newman, then, and like most other contemporary thinkers who reject Kant's distinction between *noumenon* and phenomenon, Novak argues that all descriptions of the world are mediated by the individual knower in community with others: one possesses no privileged access to any "world-as-such." Unlike Newman, however, Novak is able to accommodate a far greater plurality of voices (philosophical perspectives) on human beings and the world just because his shift from a putative common human "experience" to the formal necessity of some conception of human "understanding" is initially without content: conscience as intelligent subjectivity requires far less in the way of agreement than did Newman's claims about conscience as an awareness of morality and a superior Judge, and it requires nothing more than what even (for example) philosophical deconstructors like Heidegger or Jacques Derrida accept, namely a ground that may be (in classical philosophical perspectives) groundless (an *Ab-grund*). In rhetorical terms, conscience as intelligent subjectivity is thus more topically "open" a place than conscience as moral-religious awareness, and this is as it should be if Novak is to engage his intended audience. What, then, does intelligent subjectivity involve, and how does it function as the grammatical rule (criterion, standard) for deciding for or against religious belief?

For Novak, conscience as intelligent subjectivity consists in four activities, the first three of which constitute "understanding" — awareness, insight, and reflective judgment — and the last of which is the extension of these in the human ongoing drive to understand (8), that is, to establish a meaningful order that can survive criticism. Only our own understanding in the attempt to become aware of whatever we call real (including ourselves and our own understanding), to reflect on the real, to make judgments about the real, and to correct these judgments by understanding our errors and enlarging or changing our understanding, is, for Novak, the measure or rule of reality. What, then, are we to understand as the real?

Novak's answer to this question — that the real is not our empirical contact with the world (139ff.) but rather what we intelligibly (and interpretively, hence rhetorically)[34] make of that contact, in a word, the "intelligible"[35] — receives little elaboration in *Belief and Unbelief*, so we shall need presently to look to the work of Cavell as one plausible way to clarify the matter. About this deficiency of Novak's treatment of intelligibility, however, two things can be noted here. First, the deficiency is intentional, for it leaves the real as the intelligible a (relatively) open question subject to ongoing inquiry — a move which is fitting in the context of an argument designed to maximize contemporary voices, and the individual's drive to understand, in civil conversation. This position is open enough to accept, for example, the deconstructive insight into the fallacy of the metaphysics of presence, since the (Heideggerian) notion of a "groundless ground" taken up by Derrida and others is not, in Novak's view, incompatible with the human drive to understand the order of the world. Said otherwise, it is incompatible only if we accept the deconstructors' own antecedent consideration. That is, the chief conclusion of most radical deconstructivists — namely, that anything like Novak's "order," if it really is to be such, must be total, and that, since such totality has been shown historically to be unlikely, we get along better by admitting a general "disorder" or "arbitrariness" (of language, conventions, and the like) — this conclusion itself rests on the antecedent consideration, "either total order (as in a transcendental signified) or arbitrariness." But wherefore this choice? When we measure that conclusion against Novak's own account of "understanding" as the standard of the real, the former position can be said to be lacking precisely what the pursuit of understanding celebrates, namely, new and better answers to the quest for self-understanding of the order of the world. To be sure, this is not a logical argument that "defeats" deconstruction but is rather a rhetorical claim that the deconstructive horizon unduly, even dogmatically, limits the human scope for inquiry and action to its own claim on behalf of the arbitrary.

The second thing to note is that Novak is more open because whatever else the "intelligible" involves, it is not to be confused with classical or early modern (Enlightenment) rationalization (totalization, "metanarrative") of our experience; that is, the intelligible subsumes the deconstructive insight that all presences are invaded by absences without merely running into the sands of "undecidability." Newman understood this and Novak embraces it: "The drive to understand does not generate anticipations of rational order, necessity, cosmic harmony, or classical design. On the contrary, after a little experience, the drive to understand leads one to expect variety, many contingencies, an order that is often and at best statistical. . . . It leads one to expect surds and much that is unintelligible to men. One need not be a cosmic optimist, nor a rationalist, to believe in God" (134–35).

The importance of this latter insight, that the human drive to understand the real as the intelligible also involves acknowledging what is *"not* limited by what we can conceive or bracket in a rational system" (143, emphasis added), what escapes all logical and scientific knowledge (and to that extent unintelligible), will be considered below. Here I am interested in what Novak himself makes of our human drive to understand.

Having suggested the real as the object of the understanding, and the intelligible as the meaning of the real, Novak wants further to suggest that the most plausible candidate for the intelligible is a source without which "the intelligibility of the real is a mere accident and hence [wholly] unintelligible." Lest the intelligible become equivalent to the unintelligible (the predetermined or the arbitrary), in other words, Novak suggests an alternative, and "God" is the name he offers for this *arche* and telos of the human drive to understand.

Novak's claim, of course, is not that humans actually arrive in their understanding at this source or end; nor does it entail any traditional religious content (for example, a personal and loving divinity). On the contrary, the drive to understand remains unfulfilled, and its character may be said to be less a substantive content than an open place (topos) within which human life only seeks its fulfillment, pursuing endless formulations of a reality that is never fully formulated: "The drive to understand is like a source of light rather than like a basic cluster of undeniable self-evident premises or 'pinned-down' statements"—this, of course, is a most Newmanian sentiment. The drive to understand achieves, in short, a philosophical rather than a strictly a religious version of God: "The God of philosophy remains hidden, and does not reveal himself" (102).

In this appeal to the ongoing drive to understand as something other than ultimately arbitrary or predetermined, hence absurd—as other than wholly unintelligible—however, Novak proposes that the ongoing drive of human understanding is itself evidence for what it suggests, namely, a source and end of intelligibility such that, whatever it is in and by itself is best made sense of (made intelligible and significant) by appealing to our own intelligent consciousness. "God," again, is that telos and source: not strictly a "person" or "thing" or "cause," not an "intelligence" *simpliciter,* but rather the source of all intelligibility which humans best make sense of in an analogical (and hyperbolic) God-talk based on our own intelligent subjectivity.[36]

When all is said and done, then, it is not difficult to discern that Novak's argument, only the outline of which is visible here and in his book,[37] is but a more accessible version of the ontological proof for the existence of God.[38] It is, in fact, a distinctly rhetoricized version—even a Newmanian persuasion by way of informal ("real") inference, as Novak himself notes (xix)—about which we may say the following.

First, as a persuasive appeal the argument is not logically compelling, for it hangs loose at both ends: the move from the real as the intelligible to a (so to speak) "ultimate intelligible" that completes it is the same as the previous commitment to take one's human understanding (so defined) as criterial. This is not necessarily tautological, for understanding can change and self-correct; but it is grammatical and rhetorical. In other words, unless one takes the human drive to understand "as" evidence for an ultimate intelligibility ("God" so indicated), the argument unravels. Acknowledgment of criteria, in other words, involves the well-known hermeneutical circle noted by Newman (*GA,* 224: "My ideas are all assumptions, and I am ever moving in a circle") and Novak: "The outcome of any philosophical inquiry is determined by its starting place [rhetorical topos]. . . . The key focus for fruitful philosophical inquiry . . . concerns the question of 'horizon' " (*Belief and Unbelief,* 57).

Second, the argument is nonlogical and grammatical-rhetorical in another way. Because Novak, like Newman, understands the interpretive perspectivism involved in all understanding, he understands that all understanding is finite, partial, historically situated, "horizonal"—hence that any given interpretation of human beings and the world will necessarily be inadequate, involve surds, fail to be consistent, break down, and lack completeness. Newman knew this too, but by emphasizing it Novak puts to rout the usual accusations against believers as metanarrators obsessed with totalizing control and rational system. There is nothing in such philosophy (or theology consistent with it) that mandates embracing the metaphysics of presence.[39]

Finally, Novak's version of conscience and the ontological proof is a form of argument that implies a phenomenological-existential content without, however, insisting on what the experiential content is or must be. In this way it is continuous with Newman's turn to conscience while philosophically it broadens its appeal. On the other hand, we have now lost the personal aspect of Newman's notion of conscience—the implication of our actions and characters—and this loss may need to be made good before I finish. But we have gained a new or renewed common ground for discussion, namely, human understanding of the real. In order to advance our understanding of understanding and its "validation" in the philosophical or religious concept of "God" as rule and standard (criterion), I wish finally to turn to Stanley Cavell (and implicitly to Ludwig Wittgenstein), specifically to the notion of "criteria" (of our concepts) and their basis in "acknowledgments" (criteria in the sense of evaluative standard, as found above in Novak and Newman).

Recalling Criteria

I have said that "conscience" functions as a horizonal "place" of knowing and acting constituted by antecedent considerations that are themselves ultimately criterial, meaning that they provide a foundational (but not metaphysical) rule or standard by which to help measure the nature and scope of human beings and their world. From this basis may be inferred the concept and reality of "God" as source and telos of human understanding (Novak) or as personal other who judges and redeems us (Newman). We have suggested that whereas conscience-as-standard can be identified by its various substantive experiences (Newman) or formal activities (Novak), it cannot itself be "proved" to be the "correct" standard by which to measure humankind and the world, for it is simply the rule by which all limit-questions regarding true and false, correct and incorrect, meaningful and meaningless, rational and nonrational, probable and improbable are themselves established and answered. Conscience does not (even rhetorically) "prove" itself — antecedent considerations cannot rest on yet further antecedents, human understanding cannot require some prior human understanding without infinite regress — for conscience constitutes the original hermeneutic circle of humankind as a grammatical-rhetorical topos, that is, a place that we already hold (so it is claimed) in common. Conscience is an *epideictic* process not a deliberative product; it opens up and makes manifest the world "as" human.

On the other hand, I have also suggested that rhetoric and religion alike have undergone near-total loss or distortion in many intellectual quarters: held in contempt as either mere "enthusiasm" against, or in excess of, evidence or as crude wish-fulfillment and displacement of evidence, the not-so-artful dodge of the nihilist's Absurd. These attitudes are more concentrated versions of the larger threat of philosophical skepticism, in which knowledge of the world outside us and of other minds is permanently placed in question as epistemically disappointing just because it is objectively uncertain — beyond evidence, hence no "knowledge" at all.[40] According to Stanley Cavell such skepticism functions "as a place, perhaps the central secular intellectual place," of our culture,[41] a place packed with what Richard Bernstein has called "Cartesian anxiety," effectively separating human beings from the possibilities of conscience, however defined.

Is belief, then — either religious or philosophical faith — merely a matter of Humean custom or Nietzschean cowardice, as it seems to the skeptical mind? And if conscience is a matter merely of what we rhetorically say it is, then how do "we" choose among alternative world pictures held by the divergent groups with whom we might identify? How do we realize that this content of conscience, whether as "understanding" or as "moral and religious experience," furnishes the rule for what it is to be human — and divine? It is ultimately with the threat of skepticism in mind, and with historical moves either to acquiesce in or to attempt to overcome skepticism, that Cavell reads works of such Romantics as Wordsworth and Coleridge, or Thoreau's *Walden* (and even Wittgenstein's *Philosophical Investigations*), as an "epistemology of conscience," seeking electrically to recharge with renewed interest "lives of quiet desperation" and the muffled world in which they have stalled — recharge them with what "claims" our attention. What is the source of this claiming power?

Since it is not possible, even briefly, to sketch Cavell's overall philosophic project of rethinking the place of skepticism and thereby of philosophy, I wish to focus on the center of his concerns, his response to "other-minds skepticism," and specifically his recalling the role that conceptual "criteria" play in our knowing, including the limits of criteria and knowledge and their basis in so-called acknowledgments. I propose that his analysis recalls and extends my inquiry, while itself being recalled (called back and corrected) by it.

Because it is our knowledge of the ordinary world and of other beings as possessed of an inner life or mind that the skeptic calls into question, Cavell's magnum opus, *The Claim of Reason,* begins with the notion of the "criteria" resident in ordinary (natural) language and with related notions of the common and familiar as central both to Wittgenstein's philosophy and to his own way of going on with it. For Cavell criteria are "the means by which we learn what our concepts are and hence 'what kind of object anything is' ([*Philosophical Investigations*] 373)" (*CR*, 16); by the same token, confusion over criteria results when we lose hold of our concepts and thus of ourselves and our world. Criteria are (in J. L. Austin's language) "what we say when" we speak about, for example, "pain" or "understanding" or "knowledge" or "conscience," that by which we identify both concepts and their referents in terms of certain objects or behaviors or persons in certain circumstances. "Criteria . . . are the things by which we tell whether or not something is the case, which give us occasion to say that something is so, which justify us in what we say."[42] The appeal to what we "can" and "cannot," "do" and "do not" say in order to mean what we mean, and even to what we "must" mean, as Cavell puts it, when we say what we say, redirects us away from inner consciousness (intention) as the mediator of meaning and toward the outer scene, the myriad shifting "circumstances" of the natural language games we already know and share with others that contextualize both what we know about the world and what is still to be discovered.

As Hannah Pitkin puts the matter, Cavell's position is a "linguistic Kantianism" in which language and world are mutually constitutive;[43] it is therefore also "rhetorical" in Newman and Novak's sense of being relative to some community of speakers in specific situations, times, and places. In this way criteria, which make up a large part of what can be done with language, with what Wittgenstein calls the "grammar" of our words, also align speakers with one another in "mutual attunements" that are as much moral and political as epistemological. Using Novak's language, Cavell calls the criteria of ordinary language nothing less than the "conditions of intelligibility" of our understanding of and living in the world.[44]

Cavell's Kantianism is pragmatic and linguistic, then. For Cavell, Kant's project to overcome Humean skepticism — the position that we have no knowledge except of our own "ideas" (sense impressions and their combinations) — is both too little and too much. Kant's noumenon-phenomenon distinction, first of all, restricts knowledge to the latter by way of establishing the transcendental conditions of mind and reason that make objective, scientific knowing of phenomena possible and thereby loses what can be called our "interest" in the world — its vitality and our felt engagement with it as both objective and ours. But Kant's position is also too much, for it purports to overcome skepticism and thus loses what insight there is in skepticism, namely, its recognition of the limits of human being-in-the-world, our finitude and the logical uncertainty of all our knowing. By contrast, Cavell reads Romantic writers like Wordsworth as similarly preoccupied with the ravages of skepticism but calling us back to our practical interest in the "world" (things in themselves practically considered) as a function not of knowledge but of acceptance. Cavell's own project is thus to explore our linguistic possibilities as a nonanimistic version of the Romantic sense of the vitality of the world.[45]

We can put the skeptical threat this way: if judgments of reality, issued by us speakers of a natural (or "ordinary") language, depend on the criteria we use, and if criteria in turn are a matter of "agreements" and "attunements," how can we "know" the real at all?[46] We may say that we know, for example, that someone is in pain by virtue of the behaviors he or she exhibits. When the circumstances are right we say that these are pain-behaviors, hence criteria for recognizing pain itself. But the skeptic points out that the behaviors could be simulated, hence no criteria at all, and that we are always left with something missing — knowledge of what "must" remain hidden because it is "inner": the pain itself. The skeptical argument that applies to pain can apply to all criteria for knowledge of other minds: behavior can be simulated and thus, in principle, criteria will always fail as proof.

With this argument Cavell, notably, agrees: criteria allow us to predicate identity, not existence, to "identify" what we call something and thus to "identify with" it and with others (by means of what Cavell names "empathic projection" [*CR,* 421ff.]), and not to "prove" that some particular instance of something is the genuine article. We may take behaviors as pain-behaviors and hence, in the appropriate context, as criteria for pain; but we have no criteria telling us when to take something "as" pain-behavior, that is, telling us when to see another creature as possessed of an inner life. Criteria of inner life come to an end and presuppose a willingness on our part first to recognize another creature "as" capable of feeling, thinking, and so on, to identify with it and "see into its life." This willingness to recognize or acknowledge the human is what Novak called our "decision" about what to take "as" human and what Newman meant by using himself as a standard of the human: "My only business is to ascertain what I am, in order to put it to use. It is enough for the proof of the value and authority of any function which I possess, to be able to pronounce that it is human" (*GA,* 224).

If something can be said to be left out of the skeptical account of pain and the inner life, for Cavell it is the claim that another's pain, that another as human, makes on us. And this is a matter initially not of knowledge but of what we acknowledge, in the sense that it provides us with a measure or standard of interpretation: "[Acknowledgment] is not a description of a given response, but a category in terms of which a given response is *evaluated*" (emphasis added).[47] In this way Cavell's concept of acknowledgment functions as does Newman and Novak's concept of conscience — that is, as a grammatical standard by which another person, indeed a world, can be measured.

Although I cannot develop the point here, Cavell's account of acknowledgment is continuous with Wittgenstein's analysis of our stance toward the world as such and not only toward other minds; both positions turn on the notion of what I have called an *epideictic* rhetorical disclosure that underlies all argument and invites us to identification in the first place. Wittgenstein writes: "Where two principles really do meet which cannot be reconciled with one another, then each man declares the other a fool and a heretic. . . . I would 'combat' the other man, — but wouldn't I give him reasons? Certainly, but how far do they go? At the end of reasons comes *persuasion*." Or again: "I can imagine a man who had grown up in quite special circumstances and been taught that the earth came into being 50 years ago, and therefore believed this. We might instruct him: the earth has long . . . etc. — We should be trying to give him our picture of the world. This would happen through a kind of *persuasion* (ellipses in original)."[48] In *The Senses of* Walden, Cavell writes: "It is not quite right to say we *believe* the world exists (though certainly we should not conclude that we do *not* believe this, that we *fail* to believe its existence), and wrong even to say we *know* it exists (while it is equally wrong to say we *fail* to know this)." Rather our "relation to the world's existence is somehow closer than the ideas of believing and knowing are made to convey" (145). In both cases the world, and other minds, are not a function of knowing but of accepting, of acknowledging that which is epideictically both familiar to us (because prior) and a matter of interest or worth.

In this way the skeptic is not refuted but rather put in his or her place, subsumed by a larger "place" of publicly available criteria and acknowledgments, what we have been tracing out as the parameters of *con-scientia*. The skeptic's desire to "prove" the existence of others or the world, therefore, and her or his disappointment at the general failure to do so, is now exposed as a "flight from" or "avoidance of" the human condition, taking our "limits" as "limitations" and, out of disappointment over not getting something "better" (complete knowledge, proof, certainty, control), dismissing even what stands before us, what calls to us to take responsibility both for what we have and for what we have done or might do. What is acknowledged is itself not a matter of rhetorical deliberation because it is a matter of rhetorical *epideixis:* a showing-forth whose reality is not a conclusion but an attraction to matters that are the standard of worth. In all such rhetoric (Newman's, Novak's, Cavell's, Wittgenstein's) *ethos* subsumes logos; as Newman puts it, "We judge for ourselves, by our own lights, and on our own principles; and our criterion for truth is not so much the manipulation of propositions, as the intellectual and moral character of the person maintaining them, and the ultimate silent effect of his arguments or conclusions upon our minds" (*GA,* 196).

Recounting or recalling criteria of ordinary language, then — both in the senses of remembering them when they are forgotten and calling them back for correction and change when they are foiled or fail — criteria that are stabilized in our acknowledgments, makes up the activity of *con-scientia*. Another of Cavell's terms for the same set of concerns is "moral perfectionism," the "epistemology" of which is enacted (for example) in the works of Thoreau and Emerson, of Wittgenstein, and presumably of Cavell himself. "Moral (and political) perfectionism," because our criteria and acknowledgments are as much a function of values and interests as they are of perception and thought. And "moral perfectionism," because criteria are themselves perceptually relative and circumstantially or contextually applied; hence all claims to identify the real, and identify with it (*con-scientia*), are at best rhetorically partial, incomplete, and in transition from the less adequate to the more adequate, the imperfect to the improved.[49] Further, recalling criteria is an activity that requires us to stand outside ourselves—as Cavell puts it, to "neighbor ourselves"—in recognition of our always partial grasp of what we call the real, acknowledging others and the form of life and world we share, staking our all on them and it, while refusing to pretend to completeness or, skeptically, to despair about our limits. The chief way we neighbor ourselves is by locating or devising an Exemplar, a figure who provides ongoing perspectives (not merely static rules) by which we locate our moral, political, and epistemological quest for our better selves. As a stranger to us, the Exemplar enables us to become aware of our own incompleteness, to gauge the degree of lostness of our criteria, and to seek to redeem ourselves and the world.

Criteria, then, and the acknowledgments on which they stand, cannot be reduced to instruments of institutional conservativism, religious or political, simply because they are defeasible; acknowledgements are not mere opinions or beliefs but rather what it is claimed are natural human ways of acting and judging, deeper and more stable than arguable opinions and contestable claims to "knowledge" (*CR,* 111); and they require ongoing vigilance and self-transformation, allowing us to identify the world and identify with it but requiring us also to change those identifications when we encounter aporias, contradictions, and the like. Such attention to criteria—and to the claims made on us by virtue of our own acknowledgments—revivify our interest in the world and ourselves. For these, and for their maintenance and change, we are responsible because they remain a function of rhetorical disclosure rather than logical proof, which is to say what we (perforce) already use; and we listen to the call or claim of others and the world—our "ownmost possibilities"—on us.

Acknowledging Our Limits: Toward a Rhetoric of Theology and a Theology of Rhetoric

I have argued that Newman's appeal to the interpretation of experience to explain how we establish our limits and what those limits are avoided the scientism of his time, chiefly by bringing the resources of rhetoric to the analysis of assent; that Novak shifted the locus of interest from a personal call from God to a reflection on human understanding and its ability to recognize (acknowledge) the intelligible as a limit-idea that stabilizes human understanding without arresting it; and that Stanley Cavell's analysis of criteria and their basis in acknowledgments (invitations or attractions as well as claims) offers a way of extending Novak's account of the intelligible as well as Newman's account of antecedent considerations. Cavell does this by specifying the limits of knowledge in light of the need for responsible decision about what we take to be the standard of the real and how we locate that standard in what we do, in our form of life. His grounding of theoretical knowledge in what is practically lived and acknowledged is continuous with Newman's rhetorical (and pragmatic) account of conscience as something to which we might respond, for which we are responsible, and with Novak's similar account of the need for personal decision in what we take to be the real. All three, therefore, understand the question of fundamental commitments to involve will and choice in what we take to be our standard of measurement, construing these as our "acknowledgment of" only what we understand to make the world publicly ("objectively") intelligible. In Charles Taylor's terms, "One can only argue convincingly about goods which already in some way impinge on people, which they already at some level respond to but may be refusing to acknowledge."[50]

Both Novak and Cavell, moreover, present formal rather than experiential analyses which are, I believe, more hospitable than Newman's to the contemporary conflict of interpretations over religion, enabling a more civil discussion, unclouded by false dichotomies like the ones between science and religion or rationality and religion. Their formal analyses avoid such problems by overtly rhetoricizing all understanding while maintaining its objective integrity by appeals to public criteria and acknowledgments ("grammar") within a form of life. This is a crucial move, for it sidesteps the limited relativism of radical rhetoricians like Paul de Man or Stanley Fish, who divorce rhetoric from grammar, decision from evaluation, attraction from epistemic gain, and stabilize what would otherwise be a relativism in the will of interpretive communities.

On the other hand, Cavell's philosophic project is obviously not the only way to go on with Newman and Novak, nor is he wholly consistent with them. But he is useful, first because his interest in other-minds skepticism helps to bring back into the discussion what Novak lets drop in fact if not in principle, namely, the claim on us of the "other" as a person whom we avoid, or flee from, fearing not only what may be required of us in response (attention to the other, an offer of help) but, more important, what may be offered to us (the acknowledgment of us as responsible beings: a fearful prospect indeed!). Yet in our fear we take flight at the risk of so positioning ourselves as to be, as it were, blind both to persons and to our shared world. To refuse to acknowledge or to be acknowledged by another is thus the beginning of refusing to know at all. On Cavell's analysis we are faced with a personal claim on ourselves, on our way of living and not just our way of conceiving of the abstract intelligibility of things, a claim that requires ongoing self-transformation in the light of the self-partiality we inevitably discover. This is a claim also of community, extending and enriching what in Novak (and Newman) often seems to be the figure of the self alone with itself and its God. Cavell thus returns us to Newman's sense of the centrality of the claim of another person and not merely the claim of an idea of intelligibility, however personally appropriated. It is, in the end, a sense of the claim of reason as fundamentally a claim of love and will, of what Thomas Carlson, Wendy Olmsted and Marjorie O'Rourke Boyle variously identify as the *agape* or *caritas* central to rhetorical thinkers like Pseudo-Dionysius, Augustine, and Erasmus.[51]

Cavell is further useful because, as Stephen Mulhall has noted, his moral perfectionism is "intimately bound up with recognizably religious preoccupations."[52] Like another American grammaticus-rhetoricus, Kenneth Burke, Cavell can be said to travel a path parallel to Christianity yet ultimately opposed to it because it cannot meet the challenge of modernity.[53] What, in brief, is that challenge?

On Cavell's analysis, the modernist move away from Cartesian certainty has historically and philosophically involved the overthrow not only of epistemological but political and religious constraints on the autonomy of the human will as human measure and thus on human freedom of self-invention. Where the skeptic construed the limits of human knowing as "limitations" that destroyed the possibility of knowledge, the modern(ist) philosopher, moralist, artist, and political thinker accepts these limits as the human condition and begins to explore newly released possibilities for autonomous self-definition (hence the breakdown of traditional and the search for new criteria in all aspects of modern life).[54] In a distinctly Nietzschean vein, Cavell sees the Christian as self-positioned much like the skeptic, construing our bodily condition as a set of limitations that make human wisdom folly and that deflect us upward, toward religious faith in the divine. In keeping with this turn, the Christian, according to Cavell, construes the possibilities of human action in terms of passive suffering, in that way relinquishing responsibility and choice by avoiding acknowledgment of personal agency.[55] Either way — skeptical or Christian — our lot in life is reduced to a resigned avoidance of the modernist move to self-invention.

On the other hand, I propose that Cavell himself is open to the charge that it is he, not the Christian believer, who has failed to interpret our being-in-the-world adequately: that it is he who is engaged in his own disguised version of skepticism. By interpreting Christianity's call to accept suffering as a demand for passivity, hence as a limitation denying us something "better" — namely, a complete, liberal-modernist autonomy — Cavell himself skeptically sidesteps the possibility of the rhetorical claim of a divine other calling us to acknowledge our responsibility both to other persons and to himself through other persons. Inasmuch as it is Cavell himself who teaches the central importance that avoidance of or flight from the human condition plays in the skeptical retreat from knowledge — the flip side of the call to greater responsibility and love — Cavell's own avoidance can be understood if not endorsed: we need only recall both the offense (the surd, the ab-surd, the *Ab-grund*) that Christianity offers our understanding and the burden of responsibility which (on this understanding) God's acknowledgment of us involves. Indeed, without such a greater claim on or calling to us (the Christian would say, "without grace"), can a strictly secular interpretation of our being in the world even provoke, much less sustain, the claim of love as Cavell politically construes it? By dogmatically dismissing the possibility of religion on the spurious ground that it is a "limitation," Cavell may be elevating his own personal acknowledgments to the status of sole legitimizing principles. Yet on his own analysis the claim of the world religions to acknowledge and be acknowledged by human beings provides the same sort of grounds as Cavell's own project.

The avoidance of love, as Cavell calls it in his famous essay on *King Lear*,[56] derives from fear of recognition by the other. The question ultimately returns us to the place Newman occupied: Who is the other? Although Nietzsche, for example, has been accused of pursuing what Victoria Kahn on Machiavelli calls satanic self-aggrandizement of "perfect, self-originating agency,"[57] we have learned too much from Cavell to make the same accusation of him. But we have also learned from Cavell that the rhetorical claim of religion involves our desire to flee from this claim as much as to love the other; that the call to acknowledge is likely to be heard by us as a threat, a warning signal to STAY AWAY if we know what's good for us. The catch here is that at this level the claim of religion is not a matter of "knowing" (what's good for us) as the word is commonly used. Of course, it is also not, as Cavell notes, a matter of not-knowing, of know-nothingism. At this level of living, rather, we use words like "acknowledge," "accept," and "have faith in" and recall Coleridge's injunction about Christianity to "TRY IT!" On this understanding it may be that God is not dead, after all. On the contrary: if we cannot hear his call it may be because he speaks so insistently in so many languages and in so many voices — through the discordant voices of the world's "others," those whom we, Melvillian Bartlebys, prefer to decline to acknowledge as neighboring ourselves.

In the manuscript material left after Wittgenstein's death, some of which is collected in the volume entitled *Culture and Value* (1977), one passage in particular draws together many of the points I have been pursuing here. Wittgenstein writes: "It strikes me that a religious belief could only be something like a passionate commitment to a system of reference. Hence, although it's belief, it's really a way of living, or a way of assessing life. It's passionately seizing hold of this interpretation. Instruction in a religious faith, therefore, would have to take the form of a portrayal, a description, of that system of reference, while at the same time being an appeal to conscience."[58]

To speak of religious belief as a way of assessing life is to speak of it as a criterial standard, a set of lived acknowledgments that Wittgenstein finds continuous with conscience (understood, presumably, as motivated conduct), that Newman and Novak variously equate with conscience more broadly defined,[59] and that Cavell passes over as an avoidance of conscience understood as the liberal quest for human autonomy and self-definition. For all three, any fundamental belief as a form of life can be said to have a rhetorical claim on us, calling us from something other than our momentary needs and desires, subsuming them into a greater reality that defines our own. But only for Newman and Novak is a distinctly religious way of life an appropriate means of discovery and description. The rhetorical thinkers presented in this essay must answer this: What, or Who, is the other that is said to call? Or more generally, what are our limits?

Notes

My thanks to Wendy Olmsted and Michael Hyde for their comments on an earlier draft of this essay.

1. See Chapter 5: Marjorie O'Rourke Boyle, "Rhetorical Theology."

2. David Tracy, *Plurality and Ambiguity: Hermeneutics, Religion, Hope* (San Francisco: Harper and Row, 1987), 86; see also 88. Cf. Chapter 8: Paul Ricoeur, "Naming God."

3. David Tracy, *Blessed Rage for Order: The New Pluralism in Theology* (New York: Seabury, 1978), 92–109 and passim.

4. Pertinent works include Stanley Cavell, *The Senses of* Walden (Chicago: University of Chicago Press, 1972); Cavell, *This New Yet Unapproachable America* (Albuquerque: Living Batch Press, 1989); Cavell, *Conditions Handsome and Unhandsome: The Constitution of Emersonian Perfectionism* (Chicago: University of Chicago Press, 1990); Cavell, *In Quest of the Ordinary: Lines of Skepticism and Romanticism* (Chicago: University of Chicago Press, 1988); and Cavell, *The Claim of Reason* [hereafter cited in notes and text as *CR*] (Oxford: Clarendon, 1979), 16.

5. Michael Novak, *Belief and Unbelief: A Philosophy of Self-Knowledge*, 3d ed. (New Brunswick, N.J.: Transaction, 1994), 5.

6. See particularly John Henry Newman, *Newman's University Sermons: Fifteen Sermons Preached before the University of Oxford, 1826–1843* [hereafter cited in notes

and text as *OUS*] (London: S.P.C.K., 1970), 207, and Newman, *An Essay in Aid of a Grammar of Assent* [hereafter cited in notes and text as *GA*], ed. I. T. Ker (Oxford: Clarendon, 1985). On Newman as a rhetorical philosopher, see my *Rhetorical Thought in John Henry Newman* (Columbia: University of South Carolina Press, 1989), also notes 11 and 15.

7. The stress on warrantable belief is Wayne Booth's, derived chiefly from John Dewey. See Wayne Booth, *Modern Dogma and the Rhetoric of Assent* (Chicago: University of Chicago Press, 1974). In his translation of Aristotle's *Rhetoric*, George Kennedy defines rhetoric more expansively: "*Rhetoric*, in the most general sense, is the energy inherent in emotion and thought, transmitted through a system of signs, including language, to others to influence their decisions or actions" (*Aristotle On Rhetoric: A Theory of Civic Discourse*, trans. George Kennedy [New York: Oxford University Press, 1991], p. 7).

8. For Burke's rhetorical philosophy see especially *A Grammar of Motives* (Berkeley: University of California Press, 1969), and *A Rhetoric of Motives* (Berkeley: University of California Press, 1950). For Grassi's approach see, for example, "Rhetoric and Philosophy," *Philosophy and Rhetoric* 9 (Fall 1976): 200–216, "Why Rhetoric Is Philosophy," *Philosophy and Rhetoric* 20 (1987): 68–78, "Can Rhetoric provide a New Basis for Philosophizing? The Humanist Tradition," parts 1 and 2, *Philosophy and Rhetoric* 11 (Winter 1978 and Spring 1979): 1–18 and 75–97, and "Critical Philosophy or Topical Philosophy: Meditations on the *De nostri temporis studiorum ratione*," in Giorgio Tagliacozzo and Hayden V. White, eds., *Giambattista Vico: An International Symposium* (Baltimore: Johns Hopkins University Press, 1969), 39–50.

9. Burke, *A Rhetoric of Motives*, 24; cf. page 27: "The principle of Rhetorical identification may be summed up thus: The fact that an activity is capable of reduction to intrinsic, autonomous principles does not argue that it is free from identification with other orders of motivation extrinsic from it. Such orders are extrinsic to it, as considered from the standpoint of the specialized activity alone. But they are not extrinsic to the field of moral action as such, considered from the standpoint of human activity in general." See also Burke: "Sensation / Memory / Imitation / Story," the appendix to Chapter 2.

In sum my argument is that by identifying with God through conscience as moral sense and duty, as intelligent subjectivity, or as the acknowledgment of and by other people, we move beyond ourselves to identify with an extrinsic and larger order of motivation that changes us. That identification is at once rhetorical and religious because we need to think epideictically and deliberatively to discover more about the moral-religious order with which we identify.

10. The term is Wayne Booth's in *The Vocation of a Teacher: Rhetorical Occasions, 1967–1988* (Chicago: University of Chicago Press, 1988).

11. Cavell, *Senses of Walden*, 88, emphasis added.

12. See Martin Heidegger, *Being and Time*, trans. John Macquarrie and Edward Robinson (New York: Harper and Row, 1962); hereafter cited in notes and text as *BT*. For an account of Heidegger's project as rhetorical as well as hermeneutic, see Michael Heim, "Philosophy as Ultimate Rhetoric," *Southern Journal of Philosophy* 19 (Summer 1981): 181–95, and Walter Jost, "Philosophic Rhetoric: Newman and Heidegger," in Gerard Magill, ed., *Discourse and Context: Interdisciplinary Studies in John Henry Newman* (Carbondale: Southern Illinois University Press, 1993). On Heidegger, rhetoric, and con-

science, see Michael J. Hyde, "The Call of Conscience: Heidegger and the Question of Rhetoric," *Philosophy and Rhetoric* 27 (1994): 374–96, and Walter Jost and Michael J. Hyde, "Introduction: Rhetoric and Hermeneutics: Places Along the Way," in Walter Jost and Michael J. Hyde, eds., *Rhetoric and Hermeneutics in Our Time* (New Haven: Yale University Press, 1997), 1–42.

13. *Belief and Unbelief,* 72. Cf. *GA,* 228; also Michael Polanyi, "Authority and Conscience," in Polanyi, *Science, Faith and Society* (Chicago: University of Chicago Press, 1964).

14. See Bernard Lonergan, *Insight* (New York: Harper and Row, 1958); cf. Lonergan, *Understanding and Being: The Halifax Lectures on Insight,* in Elizabeth A. Morelli and Mark D. Morelli, eds., *Collected Works of Bernard Lonergan,* vol. 5.

15. John Henry Newman, *Apologia Pro Vita Sua* [hereafter cited in notes and text as *Apo*], ed. Martin P. Svaglic (Oxford: Clarendon, 1967), 233.

16. See my "Philosophic Rhetoric," 54–80, "On Concealment and Deception in Rhetoric: Newman and Kierkegaard," *Rhetoric Society Quarterly* (Winter–Spring, 1995): 51–74, and "What Newman Knew: A Walk on the Postmodernist Side," *Renascence* (Spring 1998).

17. For exceptions see Albert R. Jonsen and Stephen Toulmin, *The Abuse of Casuistry: A History of Moral Reasoning* (Berkeley: University of California Press, 1988), 162, 174, and Stephen Toulmin, "The Recovery of Practical Philosophy" in Toulmin, *Cosmopolis: The Hidden Agenda of Modernity* (Chicago: University of Chicago Press, 1990), 186ff.

18. John Henry Newman, "The Tamworth Reading Room," in Newman, *Discussions and Arguments* [hereafter cited in notes and text as *DA*] (London: Longmans, Green, 1891), 295.

19. John Locke's *The Reasonableness of Christianity* (1695) and William Paley's *A View of the Evidences of Christianity* (1794) a hundred years later (which features the argument from design in nature to the existence of God) fairly represent those who would defend some form of Christianity on putatively scientific grounds. Numerous works by others — notably David Hume's "Essay on Miracles," and works by Herbert Spencer, Thomas Huxley, and Auguste Comte, all written in the wake of Charles Lyell's *Principles of Geology* (1830–1833) and Darwin's *Origin of Species* (1859) — were thought to discredit faith as mere emotional "enthusiasm." On the other side of the divide, the anti-intellectual evangelicals within and outside of the Anglican Church embraced just such heartfelt enthusiasm, usually signaled in a conversion experience, as the mark of God's election. For accounts, see Walter E. Houghton, *The Victorian Frame of Mind, 1830–1870* (New Haven: Yale University Press, 1957). Newman notes his own conversion experience in the *Apologia*.

20. We should not misunderstand Newman on these two points. First, the distinction between formal and informal inference is not sharp; the two modes are on a continuum (or said otherwise, Newman recognizes what is now called, for example, the rhetoric of science). Second, Newman is aware that faith is a matter of grace from God, and no amount of human intellection can compel it. But Newman approaches faith from the human side and suggests that, depending on what we say is involved in human "reason," a faithful belief in and human relation to God (however incomprehensible God be in himself) can be eminently "reasonable" (*OUS,* 207).

21. See Edmund Burke, *Reflections on the Revolution in France* (Indianapolis: Bobbs-Merrill, 1955), and Hans-Georg Gadamer, *Truth and Method,* 2d rev. ed., trans. Joel Weinsheimer and Donald G. Marshall (New York: Continuum, 1993), 568. For connections between rhetorical reasoning and hermeneutics, see Robert Hollinger, "Practical Reason and Hermeneutics," *Philosophy and Rhetoric* 18 (1985): 113–22, and the introduction and the essays by Charles Altieri, Steven Mailloux, and Wendy Olmsted in Jost and Hyde, *Rhetoric and Hermeneutics in Our Time.* For Kenneth Burke see the appendix by Burke to Chapter 2 in this volume, and also John Dewey's notion of "interaction" between antecedent experience and external nature in *Experience and Nature,* 2d ed. (New York: Dover, 1929).

22. John Henry Newman, *The Letters and Diaries of John Henry Newman,* ed. Charles Stephen Dessain and Vincent Ferrer Blehl, 31 vols. (London: Thomas Nelson and Sons, 1961–), 15:381.

23. Perhaps the most discerning theorist dealing with this foundational function of topics is Ernesto Grassi; see note 8, above.

24. Newman distinguishes "real" from "notional" apprehensions and assents in the way he distinguishes informal from formal inference: in both cases, the real-informal refers to the intersubjective interpretations and judgments of people. For these points see *GA,* 54–68; see also Lonergan, *Understanding and Being,* lecture 5, "Judgment," pp. 109–32.

25. Newman is explicit on this point: "Words, which denote things, have innumerable implications; but in [formal] inferential exercises it is the very triumph . . . to have stripped them of all these connatural senses, to have drained them of that depth and breadth of association which constitute their poetry, their rhetoric, and their historical life, to have starved each term down . . . so that it may stand for just one unreal aspect of the concrete thing" (*GA,* 174).

26. Perhaps some readers recall Newman's quip, "Certainly, if I am obliged to bring religion into after-dinner toasts (which indeed does not seem quite the thing), I shall drink, — to the Pope, if you please, — still, to Conscience first, and to the Pope afterwards" (John Henry Newman, *A Letter to His Grace the Duke of Norfolk* [hereafter cited in notes and text as *Letter*] [Notre Dame, Ind.: University of Notre Dame Press, 1962], 136).

27. J.-H. Walgrave, *Newman the Theologian* (New York: Sheed and Ward, 1960), 342: "His teaching on the subject of conscience gives his whole thought its unity, cohesion and special character."

28. For Wittgenstein such a concept is called a "perspicuous representation." He writes: "The only way for us to guard our assertions against distortion — or avoid vacuity in our assertions [—] is to have a clear view in our assertions of what the ideal *is,* namely an object of comparison — a yardstick, as it were — instead of making a prejudice of it to which everything *has* to conform" (*Culture and Value,* trans. Peter Winch [Chicago: University of Chicago Press, 1980], 26e).

29. For an alternate view that acknowledges these aspects, see Carol Gilligan, *In a Different Voice: Psychological Theory and Women's Development* (Cambridge: Harvard University Press, 1982).

30. See Guyton B. Hammond, *Conscience and Its Recovery: From the Frankfurt School to Feminism* (Charlottesville: University of Virginia Press, 1993).

31. Charles Taylor, *Sources of the Self: The Making of the Modern Identity* (Cambridge: Harvard University Press, 1989), 402ff.; see also Leszek Kolakowski, *Modernity on Endless Trial* (Chicago: University of Chicago Press, 1990), 97ff.

32. See Chapter 8: Paul Ricoeur, "Naming God." For a lucid commentary on this essay, see James Fodor, *Christian Hermeneutics: Paul Ricoeur and the Refiguring of Theology* (Oxford: Clarendon, 1995), esp. chap. 6.

33. Novak, *Belief and Unbelief,* 64. Novak talks of "breaking" the circularity in moments of self-criticism, but I think he means to speak of succeeding, or failing, in attempts to *enlarge* the circle to accommodate divergent views or to reformulate views in accordance with the new information. Cf. *GA,* 235; also 208.

34. Novak, *Belief and Unbelief,* 122: "Everything depends on how I interpret the human experience at stake."

35. Cf. Novak, *Belief and Unbelief,* 139: "If I hold my hand in front of my face in perfect certainty that, in truth, my hand is in front of my face, one element in my certainty is my own first awareness; another is my sense of being awake and in at least normal spirits and self-possession. So it is not the case that what is known as real about my hand's being in front of my face is constituted by my seeing its brute, raw presence out there; what is known as real about it is constituted by judgment authenticating my qualifications for seeing it there at the present moment. . . . The real is not known by simply touching, seeing, or hearing, but by understanding and verifying: the real is not the tangible but the intelligible." The question then becomes how and where does "verifying" what we have located as the intelligible end.

36. On the hyperbolic imagination, see Chapter 13: Stephen Webb, "Does Excess Have an Ethics? Theological Reflections on the Hyperbolic Imagination."

37. Novak writes: "Attention to the drive to understand, its requirements and its implications, is the *first step* towards deciding the issue at its root. But the argument is not verbal. One must live for a certain little while in the alternative way of life if one wants to understand it well. Both ways of life [belief and nonbelief] can be lived, and nobly. The problem is to decide for oneself which way is most in accord with what it is to be a man, which, that is, is most in accord with the drive to understand" (*Belief and Unbelief,* 133, emphasis added).

38. For similar rhetorical versions, see Chapter 2: Booth, "Burke's Religious Rhetoric," and Booth, "Rhetoric and Religion: Are They Essentially Wedded?" in Werner G. Jeanrond and Jennifer L. Rike, eds., *Radical Pluralism and Truth: David Tracy and the Hermeneutics of Religion* (New York: Crossroad, 1991).

39. For an elaboration of the argument that religious belief and biblical theology need not entail an illusory "metaphysics of presence," see Brian D. Ingraffia, *Postmodern Theory and Biblical Theology* (Cambridge: Cambridge University Press, 1995); see also Chapter 17: James Fodor and Stanley Hauerwas, "Performing Faith: The Peaceable Rhetoric of God's Church," and Chapter 10: Thomas A. Carlson, "Apophatic Analogy: On the Language of Mystical Unknowing and Being-Toward-Death."

40. For a lucid history of British skepticism, see M. Jamie Ferreira, *Scepticism and Reasonable Doubt: The British Naturalist Tradition in Wilkins, Hume, Reid and Newman* (Oxford: Clarendon, 1986).

41. Stanley Cavell, "In Quest of the Ordinary: Texts of Recovery," in Morris Eaves and

Michael Fischer, eds., *Romanticism and Contemporary Criticism* (Ithaca: Cornell University Press, 1986), 184.

42. Hanna Fenichel Pitkin, *Wittgenstein and Justice* (Berkeley: University of California Press, 1972), 126. The reader is encouraged to consult Stephen Mulhall's excellent *Stanley Cavell: Philosophy's Recounting of the Ordinary* (Oxford: Clarendon, 1994), to which the present account is indebted.

43. Pitkin, *Wittgenstein and Justice*, 120. Cavell writes: "But now imagine that you are in your armchair reading a book of reminiscences and you come across the word 'umiak.' You reach for your dictionary and look it up. Now what did you do? Find out what 'umiak' means, or find out what an umiak is? But how could we have discovered something about the world by hunting in the dictionary? If this seems surprising, perhaps it is because we forget that we learn language and learn the world *together*, that they become elaborated and distorted together, and in the same places. We may also be forgetting how elaborate a process the learning is. We tend to take what a native speaker does when he looks up a noun in a dictionary as the characteristic process of learning a language. . . . But it is merely the end point in the process of learning the word" ("Must We Mean What We Say?" in Stanley Cavell, *Must We Mean What We Say?* [Cambridge: Cambridge University Press, 1969], 19).

44. Cavell, "In Quest of the Ordinary," 184.

45. For more on this question see Michael Fischer, "Accepting the Romantics as Philosophers," *Philosophy and Literature* 12 (October 1988): 179–89.

46. This is a familiar contemporary rhetorical position that theorists like Edward Said, Steven Mailloux, Stanley Fish, and Richard Rorty solve in different ways: by imposition of will (power), by whim (arbitrary choices of interpretive communities), or by Humean "custom" (moral and political habit).

47. Stanley Cavell, "The Avoidance of Love: A Reading of *King Lear,*" and Cavell, "Knowing and Acknowledging," in *Must We Mean What We Say?* 324 and 263, respectively. See also Chapter 11: Victoria Kahn, "Machiavellian Rhetoric in *Paradise Lost*": "Such defense takes the form of arguing not that force and fraud are simply evil, or that appearances are merely deceptive, but rather that the possibility of deception means that appearances must be interpreted, and that the activity of interpretation is itself an occasion of free will. Or to put it another way, "virtue" must be denaturalized so that it no longer appears as an object of perception but rather as an activity of interpretation."

48. Ludwig Wittgenstein, *On Certainty,* ed. G. E. M. Anscombe and G. H. von Wright, trans. Denis Paul and G. E. M. Anscombe (New York: Harper and Row, 1969), 611, 612, 262. Cf. page 378: "Knowledge is in the end based on acknowledgement."

49. Cf. *Conditions Handsome and Unhandsome,* 31.

50. Charles Taylor, *Sources of the Self* (Cambridge: Harvard University Press, 1989), 505.

51. See Chapters 10, 4, and 5 in this volume.

52. Mulhall, *Stanley Cavell,* 285.

53. For more on Burke, see Chapter 2.

54. In *Modernist Quartet* (Cambridge: Cambridge University Press, 1994), 26, Frank Lentricchia notes that Emerson — a major source of Cavell's meditations on Thoreau and conscience — proclaimed "private conscience" the "aboriginal reality" of the "present man."

55. Cf. Mulhall, *Stanley Cavell*, 301ff.

56. Cavell, *Must We Mean What We Say?* chap. 12.

57. See Chapter 11: Kahn, "Machiavellian Rhetoric." For a critique of Cavell see Charles Altieri, *Subjective Agency* (Oxford: Blackwell, 1994), 188–220.

58. Wittgenstein, *Culture and Value*, 64e.

59. Cf. Chapter 11: Kahn, "Machiavellian Rhetoric": "As Milton intimates in the homophones of Raphael's later warning, 'Know to know no more' (4.775), knowledge is predicated on negation, on the knowledge of limits. Furthermore, this limit is of ethical as well as epistemological importance, for absolute knowledge would itself be coercive and thus preclude virtue." Cf. also Basil Mitchell, "Newman as a Philosopher," quoted in David Goslee, *Romanticism and the Anglican Newman* (Athens: Ohio University Press, 1995), 146: "Newman anticipates Wittgenstein: there is no appeal from our actual practices, whether in thinking or acting, to any ideal, would-be neutral, standard of rationality."

PART **II**

Speaking of God

Here our contributors inquire into the rhetorical means that enable "believing in order to understand, and understanding in order to believe," exploring the ways the divine is named and considering the problems and limits of this naming. Manfred Hoffmann shows how the classical rhetorical offices of invention and disposition informed Erasmus's rhetorical interpretation of Scripture and his theologizing. The first, invention, involves facility with general and special loci (topoi), "drawn from the divine wisdom in Scripture (and also from nature)" and including such commonplaces as "faith, fasting, bearing evil, helping the sick, tolerating ungodly magistrates, avoiding offense to the weak, studying Holy Scripture, piety toward parents and children, Christian charity," and the like; later these were elaborately systematized by Erasmus under such heads as faith, hope, and charity, which in turn were organized within an elaborate scheme of broader topics. Thus "invention" stresses (as Olmsted also indicates in the rhetoric of Augustine) not sheer originality of thought so much as the ability to draw from commonly shared ideas and beliefs: "In the process of invention, the rhetorician first draws out from memory those ideas (res) that are suitable for the subject in question. Then words (verba) are chosen in such a way that they not only conform with those ideas and appropriately express the subject matter at hand but also carry an intellectual, aesthetic, and affective appeal through docere, delectare, and movere."

For Erasmus the rhetorical theologian next aligns and organizes his ideas as an integral whole, always with Christ as the *scopus* (head) and destination of scriptural interpretation or of commentary—that is, as a principle of both order and (temporal, historical) motion: "Both *ordo* and *gradatio* characterized his thought. . . . [Erasmus's] understanding of Christ's teaching as *orbis* and of his life as *fabula* is the most important case in point." "Disposition" in theology is thus not merely a pragmatic, much less an ornamental, activity but rather an essentially intellectual and ethical means of showing the organic nature of religious faith and life.

Implicit in the notion of drawing on loci or topoi to engender new insights is the notion of hermeneutical circles within which we all stand and which we neither can nor ought to try to avoid. Paul Ricoeur assumes the contingency of the hermeneutical (and rhetorical) circle of "believing in order to understand and understanding in order to believe": "Naming God only comes about within the milieu of a presupposition, incapable of being rendered transparent to itself," namely, the presupposition that "naming God is what has already taken place in the texts preferred by my [own] listening's presupposition." Hence the need for a "listening" (to Scripture, for instance), which is at the same time a recognition (or an "acknowledgment") of our limits. As Ricoeur puts it, "*Listening excludes founding oneself.*" How this naming (of what we hear when we listen) comes about within the referential and poetic dimensions of language, in particular the "polyphony" of Scripture, is the burden of Ricoeur's chapter, but its origin and end are, like the earlier chapter by Jost and the following chapters by Tracy and Carlson, concerned with limits and "letting go" of a will to mastery.

David Tracy transposes Ricoeur's discussion of different rhetorical registers of biblical speech into a dialectic of prophetic and mystical rhetoric, which in turn is illuminated by juxtaposition with the psychoanalysis of Freud and Lacan. These juxtapositions allow the suspension of "the question of the referent, if any, of all this religious God-talk and simply [allows us to] analyze the necessary emergence of 'god-terms' in all rhetorics." Tracy's mention of "god-terms" recalls Wayne Booth's discussion of Kenneth Burke's rhetoric of religion, which is now extended (as Burke meant it to be) to *all* rhetoric. With his concept of the unconscious, Freud listens to the "other" *within,* prophetically sharing with us what this other says. With his deconstruction of the unconscious other, Lacan forces us to acknowledge the limits of prophecy in light of the infinite signification of the unconscious. If Freud declares that where id was, there ego shall be, Lacan counters, where the consciousness of ego was, there the infinite subversive play of the unnameable shall be. Adjusted back into the matter of the powers and limits of theological rhetoric, Tracy notes:

"The question Does Lacan interpret Freud correctly? . . . bears remarkable resemblance to the question Does the apophatic mystic interpret the prophetic texts correctly?" and suggests that only an ongoing dialectic of self-and-other with mystical unknowing can do justice to the other that theologians would speak of.

This same dialectic is taken up and extended by Thomas A. Carlson, who questions whether contemporary interest in negative theological rhetoric (of the sort pointed to by Tracy in his use of Lacan) may mistake "for an ever desired but unknowable God a desiring human subject who remains opaque to itself," cautioning that a purely linguistic negativity can easily be confused with the "negative logic of Being-toward-God" in classical apophatic and mystical rhetorics. Carlson articulates in the thought of Pseudo-Dionysius three (not two) modes of theological language that are connected by "two different movements of negation." Whereas the first movement "unsays" all affirmation that corresponds "to the procession or advance (*prohodos*) of the divine 'out' of itself into the immanence of the cosmos," the second mode of negation passes beyond both assertion and denial: "This third, hyper-negative mode of theological language points beyond both procession and reversion, and it thus pertains to the superineffable goal of a reunion in which the created soul would have abandoned all thought." Carlson reveals an analogy between this "negative logic of Being-toward-God" and the "negative logic of Being-toward-death in contemporary . . . discourse on human finitude," challenging views of the "human subject's finitude, its situation in language, and its desire" that are current among theologians, literary theorists, historians and philosophers.

7

Erasmus: Rhetorical Theologian

MANFRED HOFFMANN

Invention

For Erasmus the source of theology is Scripture (and also good literature), and the subject matter of theology is the commonplaces (loci) drawn from the divine wisdom in Scripture (and also from nature). What is more, Christ is the center of Scripture and therefore the central hermeneutical principle of interpretation (even of good literature). But the way Erasmus interpreted Scripture and arranged theology was informed by rhetoric. The present task is, therefore, to explore in detail how interpretation, theology, and rhetoric are intertwined. To begin, it might perhaps help to suggest that Erasmus's formal principle of interpretation was theological (or better, Christological), while his material principle was rhetorical.

In applying the rules of grammar and rhetoric to the interpretation of Scripture, Erasmus gave grammar the first place: "Grammar claims primacy of place."[1] But this discipline ranges beyond establishing the lexical connotation of single words, their grammatical connections, and their location within the syntax of clauses and sentences. Determining in a passage the meaning of words and phrases as well as seeing the text within its context is propaedeutic to grammar, for "grammar is the art of speaking correctly (emendate)."[2] As such it is the foundation of all other disciplines: "The first task of education should be to teach children to speak clearly and accurately."[3] Grammar includes training in the classical languages and reading the best authors, that is, those whose good literature is especially conducive to moral utility.[4] Speaking correctly already involves discovering the broader and deeper dimensions of a text. So the line separating grammar and rhetoric is blurred; grammar serves rhetoric and interpretation in a preliminary way.

Even so, to make out the significance of a text as part of a larger linguistic context, the interpreter must apply, over and above the rules of grammar, the norms of rhetoric.[5] Only then is it possible to integrate the text into the order of nature and culture as reflected by language itself. Still, a theological understanding is not reached until the text is viewed as an integral part of the whole, namely, within the sweep of God's progressive revelation culminating in Christ's presence in Scripture. Scriptural interpretation provides the topoi which allow theologians to see God's speech in an order, a divine disposition reflecting the economy or dispensation of salvation.

Rules of grammar, principles of rhetoric, and theological topoi drawn from the story of Christ are instrumental for understanding Scripture on three increasingly significant levels.[6] These incremental stages of interpretation correspond to the historical, tropological, and allegorical methods of exegesis. In the same way that tropology and allegory make the transition from the letter to the spirit possible, rhetoric and theology enable the move from the particulars of grammatical knowledge to an understanding of an ordered whole that includes, respectively, the perspectives of nature and culture, and of salvation. Rhetorical theology thus helps not only to convey knowledge, morality, and a sense of the overall end in the process of human development in general but, what is much more, to inspire faith, love, and hope as the fundamentals of Christian existence.[7] Where theology is concerned, interpretation receives its hermeneutical principles from the teachings and life of Christ. Where rhetoric is concerned, the interpreter selects those of its norms that are useful to theology and accommodates them to sacred literature.[8] They are drawn particularly from the five functions of oratory: *inventio, dispositio, elocutio, memoria,* and *pronuntiatio* (finding, arranging, and expressing subject matter for discourse, plus memorizing and delivering speech).

When Erasmus mentions these five offices in his *Ecclesiastes,* he at once allegorizes them in reference to a living body. Since invention supplies the subject matter of speech, it compares with the bones of the body, which must be firm or else everything collapses. Next, disposition joins the parts of discourse fitly together and therefore is similar to the nerves. Because disposition orders speech to render it harmonious, it also makes the hearers teachable and facilitates the memory of the speaker. For one learns more easily and remembers better if what is said is properly ordered rather than scattered and confused. Elocution supplies the appropriate words and figures of speech. It thus resembles the flesh and skin of the living body, the comely clothing for bones and nerves. Memory is like the spirit, the life of the body, without which everything falls apart. Pronunciation is similar to the act and motion of the mind whereby the animal nature of the body is transformed into the spirit. This movement is as it were the life of life.[9]

This view suggests that oratory proceeds by means of a process with a beginning, middle, and end. Invention and disposition make up the beginning, elocution the middle, memory and pronunciation the end. This is the way authors compose speech. Interpreters, however, approaching a finished text, start in the middle, with identifying the signs of words and understanding the figures of speech. Then they move backward, through analyzing the disposition of the text, to the beginning, to the invention of subject matter. Last but not least, they advance toward the end, where they internalize the subject matter of the text by committing it to memory in order finally to deliver it, as expository discourse, into life. This delivery is reciprocal, both active and passive. Precisely as readers appropriate the subject matter for delivery, so the subject matter by virtue of its authority transforms them into what it says. In other words, by acquiring the text for delivery readers are being delivered by it; delivery and deliverance belong together.

We turn now to the question of how rhetorical invention functions in Erasmus's biblical exegesis and theology. We shall take first a look at the link between interpretation and invention in Erasmus's hermeneutic. In the next section we shall try to find out what interpretation and disposition have to do with one another. . . .

What interpreting a text has in common with both inventing and arranging it is that it is nothing less than the inversion of the process whereby the author conceives of, and orders, the subject matter under discussion. Author and interpreter are involved in the same hermeneutical process but they move in reverse directions.

The author begins by gathering thought (*res*) pertaining to the subject in question and suited to argumentation (*inventio*).[10] After that the author marshals these ideas by dividing and amplifying them, arranging them in such a way that the parts conveniently fit the order of the whole (*dispositio, ordo*).[11] That is to say, invention is to disposition what thought is to structure. The interpreter, on the other hand, traces the text in a secondary move from its ideas and structure to its origin in the author's mind. Therefore, the author's original move is more authoritative, whereas the interpreter's secondary move is more imitative. The interpreter is not at liberty to understand the text other than originally intended by the author. It is in this way that the dynamic of freedom and authority expresses itself regarding thought and structure: the freedom of interpretation is limited by the principle of imitation in terms of the interpreter's relation to the authority of the text.

Just as the author conceives of the subject matter, recognizes its internal structure, and arranges it coherently, so the interpreter analyzes the end product, discovers its structure, and follows it back to its beginning in thought. By analyzing the original disposition of the text, the interpreter becomes increasingly aware of the author's invention of thought so as eventually to participate in the original conceptualization of reality. More important, arriving at the origin of thought, the interpreter is so drawn into the author's world of ideas as to share in the same view of reality. Accordingly, while the author originally moves from the invention to the disposition of thought, the interpreter subsequently understands the particular text by moving toward, and finally becoming one with, the view of the whole. This movement of the mind toward the whole takes place by virtue of both memory, the internalization of the text, and delivery, the transformation of the body into spirit.

What the rhetoricians in the classical tradition meant by invention differs from our understanding of the term, namely, thinking out and producing something new. The modern mind is not at all squeamish about claiming originality for itself.[12] In the rhetorical tradition, however, invention seems to have been more a matter of imitating the best examples than of producing something novel. Even though some room was left for human individuality, particularly in the enthusiasm of poetic inspiration,[13] imitation of authority had not yet given way to the modern celebration of human autonomy and creativity. Rather, human individuality was understood more in terms of a commonly shared human nature.[14]

Erasmus insisted that imitation conform with one's own nature rather than being "enslaved to one set of rules, from the guidelines of which it dare not depart." "I welcome imitation . . . but imitation which assists nature and does not violate it, which turns its gifts in the right direction and does not destroy them. I approve imitation — but imitation of a model that is in accord with, or at least not contrary to, your own native genius."[15] Just as in general one should imitate models that reflect one's own nature, the biblical interpreter is not free to invent but must imitate Christ in order to have a nature that can really interpret the biblical text. This was a given which called for the reader's imitation of the Divine Word, Christ, not only by words but also by deeds. Erasmus raised the rhetorical concept of natural imitation to the higher power of the spiritual *imitatio Christi*.[16]

The importance of imitation is clear also from the part it plays as one of the four faculties that enable human beings to speak: *natura, ars, imitatio sive exemplum,* and *usus sive exercitatio.*[17] In fact, Erasmus deals with how these four capacities enable speech even before he turns to the rhetorical offices. But the four faculties are not all equally significant. The ability to speak derives above all from a natural tendency to imitate. "Already infants show a natural disposition for a certain teachableness by being able to imitate." Study and practice are only ancillary to nature, for "the usual obstacles of nature can be overcome by study and practice," inasmuch as they lend strength to the body and render both the mind keen and the memory reliable.[18]

There is for Erasmus an order of precedence governing the relation between nature, art, and use — and that precedence is indicated by the function of imitation. Nature and art belong together in such a way that, according to Quintilian, nature constitutes the origin of art, that is, the beginning of the knowledge and skills of speaking. Art thus arises from the observation of nature. "Nature provides the material for knowledge. Nature forms, knowledge is formed. Art is nothing without material; material without art possesses value; but the highest art is better than the best material."[19] Art must not be "art for art's sake." For artful speech makes the hearer wary of artificial traps and therefore reluctant to agree with sound insight: "Indeed, a speech that gives the impression of artifice is received coldly, viewed with suspicion, and feared as deceptive. For who would not be on his guard against someone setting out by the use of false glitter to get a hold over our minds?"[20] Rather, "it is the highest art to conceal art."[21]

Therefore, imitation must assist nature rather than violating it, improving its gifts rather than destroying them, being in accord with, rather than opposed to, one's own natural disposition.[22] And what is true of the imitation of nature by art in general applies also to memory and delivery. Knowledge, care, practice, and order must be added to a felicitous nature so as to prevent an artificial memory. Further, as for delivery, nature forms, and knowledge and use perfect, the human being: "it is best to follow nature" by imitating what is decent and avoiding what is indecent.[23]

In that sense, then, art imitates nature. This primary function of imitation governs its secondary function of acquiring and using the skills of art through study and practice. The use of art by imitating the best models serves, after all, nature in the first place and then art. Imitation links not only nature with art but also art with its use. In like manner, interpretation imitates the invention and disposition of the author's art, whereas the invention and disposition of the author's art imitates nature, its origin and goal.

While some people are endowed with such a happy natural disposition, says Erasmus, that they can clearly judge without the knowledge of dialectic and eloquently speak without the rules of rhetoric, our feeble nature is aided by rules and practice. Using art in imitation of nature thus makes the natural ability more certain and mature. Art by its use becomes a second nature. "The precepts of art do not help much unless through frequent use they go over into the habit as if into nature. Just as the experienced musician plays properly without thinking of measures and harmonies, so the preacher spontaneously knows what the present argument requires, even though he does not think of rhetorical precepts at all. In order to speak well it is expedient to take art lightly, even though from its use comes the ability of speaking."[24] Since this is so, it is the highest art to conceal art, to speak and write naturally, which is impossible unless art has been translated into nature, has become a second nature through imitation and use.

The rhetorical tradition taught that invention is imitative because it is predicated on *lectio, repetitio,* and *memoria* — a process that establishes images in certain places of the mind. "We must not neglect memory, the storehouse of our reading. Although I do not deny that memory is aided by 'places' and 'images,' nevertheless the best memory is based on three things above all: understanding, system, and care. For memory largely consists in having thoroughly understood something. Then system (*ordo*) sees to it that we can recall by an act of recovery even what we have once forgotten."[25] To aid memory and to organize what has been read, the student "should have at the ready some commonplace book of systems and topics, so that wherever something noteworthy occurs he may write it down in the appropriate column."[26]

In the process of invention, the rhetorician first draws out from memory those ideas (*res*) that are suitable for the subject in question. Then words (*verba*) are chosen in such a way that they not only conform with these ideas and appropriately express the subject matter at hand but also carry an intellectual, aesthetic, and affective appeal through *docere, delectare,* and *movere.* Therefore, reading and memorizing good authors (memorizing and repetition impress the ideas more firmly upon the mind) are the necessary prerequisites for invention, disposition, and elocution. There is no question that also for Erasmus this whole process of the mental formation of the orator (and conversely also the process of interpretation) was marked more by the ethos of imitation than by that of creative originality.

Once fixed upon the mind, ideas and their verbal images are available in the *copia verborum ac rerum,* the abundant storehouse of memorized knowledge.[27] But the mind does not stock this information at random. Inasmuch as the abundance of ideas and words already is shaped by an overall perspective of reality, that is, the system (*ordo*), the choice of ideas for a question to be considered and the selection of proper stylistic means to express it are largely dependent on a given, fairly solid but not rigid, linguistic structure. Accordingly, the rhetorical theorists understood memory to be a region with different places (topoi, loci) for different concepts. These proper places in which ideas and their corresponding words are embedded point to the significance of words and ideas within the overall order and consequently to their relevance for speech. The topography of words and ideas in the mind provides a system of coordinates expressing a worldview.[28]

Disposition

In the process of disposition (arranging, ordering),[29] the loci or topoi that were invented are arranged so as to function as constituent parts of speech. Ideas must be so aligned that they are integral to the order of the whole.[30] In this way, a natural order of discourse emerges that reflects as nearly as possible the order of nature. Now it was a generally held notion that nature manifests itself in two ways, namely, in the form of rest and motion, being and becoming.[31] The rhetoricians accordingly organized discourse as either reflecting a natural state or a movement, or as a combination of both. Further, the *ordo naturalis* could be changed into an *ordo artificialis* by means of *figurae* (schemata). Along with the *copia rerum ac verborum* for natural speech, then, the orator had to collect the *copia figurarum* to be able to render natural discourse artificial.[32]

While the principle of rest implied circularity, the principle of motion gave speech a linear direction. Without extension in time and space, the circle served as a symbol for the truth in a permanent, ontological system consistent in itself. The linearity of motion, on the other hand, expressed a process in time and space with a beginning, middle, and end (*initium, medium, finis*).[33] There is no doubt that these two principles decisively informed Erasmus's thinking as a whole. Both *ordo* and *gradatio* characterized his thought.[34] As we shall see, his understanding of Christ's teaching as *orbis* and of his life as *fabula* is the most important case in point.[35] Moreover, while he could simply place the literary form of rest side by side with that of motion, he preferred to combine natural circularity with historical movement in terms of an organic progress toward perfection (or, negatively, in terms of degeneration).

For instance, his view of the three cycles of the history of salvation (preceding Christ, concentrated in Christ, and following Christ) presents the gospel as both the fixed norm of Christ's teaching and the dynamic cause for a progressive development in the mission, tradition, and life of the church. However, this organic development turns out to be either positive or negative, depending on whether it gradually realizes the ideal norm or constitutes an increasing defection from it. Therefore, upon the period of preparation and revelation of the gospel followed a period of growth and decay.[36] Erasmus thus brought to bear on history two different but complementary perspectives, an optimistic and a pessimistic one (which are based on his dualistic notion of contrast and his trichotomic notion of transition, respectively). His theory of decay criticized historical conditions on the basis of the evangelical norm, while his theory of development respected the historical process as an organic development toward the goal, which is, however, already anticipated in the beginning by the evangelical norm.[37]

Dispositio included ordering the whole discourse by dividing it into its components (*divisio*). Now, Aristotle had distinguished in the human constitution three dispositions, one of excess and one of lack, with moderation in the middle keeping the balance between too much and too little. The rhetorical tradition adopted this advice for the disposition of discourse as much as for the disposition of the speaker.[38] Accordingly, the unity of the whole must not be sacrificed to the diversity of its parts, nor must the parts lose their particularity for the sake of the integrity of the whole. The part stands for the whole as much as the whole stands for the part.[39] It was inconceivable to classical thinkers that the order of speech should not follow the order of nature, which maintains its equilibrium by reducing the extremes of excess and want to a measure of proper proportion as far as the whole and its parts is concerned.

Erasmus made this rhetorical principle of *moderatio* a main criterion not only of his hermeneutic but also of his ethics (*temperantia*) and of his own life style. *Ego sum moderatior*: "My misdeeds amount to this: I am all for moderation, and the reason why I have a bad name with both sides is that I exhort both parties to adopt a more peaceable policy. Freedom I have no objection to, if it is seasoned with charity."[40] "My hesitancy and moderation have no other aim than to make myself useful to both parties."[41]

That Erasmus opted for the middle can be shown, where the *genera causarum* in the area of invention are concerned, by his preference for the *genus suasorium* over against the *genus iudiciale*.[42] Also, with regard to the *genera dicendi* in the area of elocution, he was partial to the *genus moderatum* between the *genus humile* and the *genus sublime*. Instead of setting one side against the other by either accusing and defending (judicial discourse) or praising and blaming (epideictic discourse), the deliberative discourse prudently weighs arguments on both sides of an issue in order to arrive at a probable solution. Similarly, the middle style serves to reconcile (*conciliare*) and to delight (*delectare*) by appealing to the milder *ethos*, in comparison with the simple style of proving (*probare*), on the one hand, and with the exalted style of moving (*movere*) and changing (*flectere*) by appealing to passion (*pathos*), on the other. So moderation, deliberation, and reconciliation belonged for Erasmus together.

Moderation is for Erasmus impossible unless one stands in the middle, seeks a balanced view, and lives a modest, temperate life. Only by avoiding too much and too little does the rhetorician acquire that sense of proportion (*modus*) which shows things, persons, and circumstances in their proper, convenient place within an overall order (*commoditas*). Not until Christians think, speak, and live from the center, Christ, can they accommodate to others (*similia similibus*), being all things to all people (*omnia omnibus*) by coming to terms and by the meeting of minds. A moderate approach persuades others to balance things out in their own minds so as to come to their senses and become levelheaded in their own behavior. Beyond the life of the individual, moderation should also govern the life in church and state, with regard to both doctrines and laws. It was this way of thinking that not only shaped Erasmus's method of interpretation (his emphasis on allegory reconciling letter and spirit) but also influenced his theological understanding (his view of Christ as mediator and reconciler).

As to *divisio,* both a dichotomous and a trichotomous pattern was at the rhetorician's disposal. The division into two parts was largely used to express opposition, even as the two opposites were taken as being ultimately held together by a basic unity. Or the whole could be structured in three parts, beginning (*exordium, caput, initium*), middle (*medium, progressus, profectus*), and end (*finis, consummatio, perfectio*).[43] The tripartite division could be changed into a duality in case the extremes of beginning and end were taken together and contrasted to the middle.[44] No matter how the whole was divided into its parts, however, the rhetorician was advised to observe moderation in the disposition of thought by avoiding too much or too little of ordering and dividing.

Erasmus's thinking . . . was determined by a basic dualistic structure. Even so, he was never content with stark opposition. Irreconcilable differences did not have the last word. Rather, harmony was the goal. However severe the split of reality, he made every effort to find a middle link that would throw a bridge across the gap.[45] The discovery of a connection between opposites established some kind of similarity and made the possibility of rapprochement appear on the horizon. With a third element inserted between two previously exclusive sides, the static structure of opposition yielded to a dynamic pattern of development, whereby the middle now functioned as progress between start and finish.[46] This rhetorical division of thought as a means of ordering discourse in accordance with the order of nature provides a crucial key to understanding Erasmus's way of making sense of reality.

While normal discourse was divided into three parts, drama followed a twofold rhetorical division, the thickening of the plot and the change in fortune as denouement (*catastrophe*). But the thickening of the plot could be subdivided into a preparation (*protasis*) and an intensification of the dramatic development (*epitasis*), which then rendered drama tripartite (*protasis, epitasis, catastrophe*). Erasmus saw in the tripartite division of drama an important rhetorical device to understand both the development of events in the Gospel accounts and the order of the history of salvation in general. In fact, for him the divine economy of salvation as articulated in the Apostles' Creed ran along the lines of a dramatic development from preparation to conflict to solution.[47]

To conclude our analysis of Erasmus's use of rhetorical disposition for his theological purposes, the last item to be dealt with is *amplificatio*. Amplification is that part of the disposition of thought which, in order to effect *utilitas*, enlarges and intensifies by means of art what is naturally given in speech.[48] Whether through *incrementum, comparatio, ratiocinatio*, or *congeries*, amplification was a favored means to extend a limited question concerning individual people and concrete situations (*quaestio finita*) into a general question or universally applicable thesis (*quaestio infinita*). Accordingly, the rhetorician used abstract commonplaces (*loci communes*), drawn from the topography of the mind, to seek probable answers, with the intention of eliciting a common sense, thereby moving the hearer/reader to agreement. However, the freedom of amplification had to be kept from becoming license by the demands of concision.[49] Therefore, the rule of moderation applied also here in terms of a balance between too much and too little expansion. The ideal for Erasmus was "artful artlessness, and copious brevity."[50]

The interplay of amplification and concision affected Erasmus's rhetorical style, his way of thinking, and his theology. Amplification became a paradigm for spiritual freedom. Erasmus's concept of expansion in terms of freedom prevailed especially in his understanding of the spirit: "The flesh makes narrow, the spirit enlarges. Where there is the spirit, there is charity; where there is charity, there fear is cast out; where there is no fear, there is freedom; where there is freedom, there is nothing that constricts."[51] "Sparse and confined are the banquets of the Jews who follow the flesh of the law, while the spirit spreads out far and wide and accepts all kinds of men. All love liberty, all need clemency."[52]

Just as rhetorical amplification raises speech from nature to art, so increasing and heightening occurs, theologically speaking, when one transcends the natural toward the spiritual, when one moves from narrow confines toward the spirit. Allegory widens the horizon from the restriction of the letter to the amplitude of the spirit.[53] The gospel spreads and becomes universal: "Unlike all else, the truth of the gospel seized, permeated and conquered within a few years every region the whole world over, attracting Greeks and barbarians, learned and unlearned, common folk and kings."[54] Charity enlarges by giving freely and abundantly (*largiri*); and above all, the gifts of largesse of the spirit set the human being free from the anxiety of the mind.[55] And what is true of the individual applies also to the church: "Thus was the kingdom of the gospel born and thus it grew and thus spread widely and was thus established, though for various reasons we see it now contracted into a narrow space and almost done away with, if you consider how large the whole world is. Fallen, we must rebuild it; contracted, we must spread it wide; unsteady, we must uphold it, using the same resources by which it was first born, increased, and grew strong."[56]

Again, the movement of spiritual freedom must not lead to libertinist excesses, but is to be balanced by what one can call theological concision; not the narrowness of the letter, the law, and the flesh, where freedom is constrained, but the concentration on Christ, where freedom is qualified by imitation. Rhetorical amplification, then, is checked by the notion of concision. Freedom is limited by authority. Even as art transcends nature through amplification, art nevertheless must imitate nature. Likewise, the freedom of the spirit is kept in balance by the concentration on Christ's teaching and by the requirement of imitating him.

As we return to interpretation in the light of what has been said about rhetorical invention and disposition, it is obvious that the interpreter must learn first to identify the parts in order to integrate them into the whole. However, the whole is more than the sum of its parts. The "one" excels the "many" because many parts pull apart while the "one" binds them together. This is why, on the one hand, rhetorical disposition has to be traced back to invention. But the grammatical, literal exegesis, on the other hand, needs to be enlarged by the tropological and allegorical method. The reduction to invention and the progression toward allegory go hand in hand. Concentrating on what the author said and enlarging the text to its spiritual meaning belong together the same way as concision and amplification, as authority and freedom do. But it is for Erasmus precisely the concentration on Christ as the Divine Word and on God as the author of divine speech that provides the freedom of spiritual interpretation and life.

The axiom that the whole is larger than the sum total of its parts implies also that the whole must be received as given and therefore as lying ultimately beyond the reach of the interpreter[57] — a fact that Erasmus acknowledges by his open-ended anagogical method and his admission of a sense of mystery. Despite our limited insight into the divine mystery, however, the whole is in fact revealed to the extent that God has spoken in the beginning and the end, by the original Word in nature and the final Word in Christ. And this whole is more important than the parts because it shows the larger significance of a text within the context of God's order of the world and of salvation.[58] Indeed, what the part is finally all about becomes clear only when it is viewed as a part of the whole rather than apart from the whole.

In other words, details are relevant in proportion to the way they fit in place in the overall picture. Beyond the general setting of nature and culture, it is the specific context of salvation as concentrated in the scopus Christ that elucidates the real locus each part holds within the whole. The importance of a variety of times, places, things, persons, and circumstances depends on their respective proximity to the center of reality, Christ. The proximity of a text to Christ qualifies it as having a corresponding measure of spiritual and moral value. The authority of a word rests on the extent to which it reflects Christ's teaching and life. The topoi in the mind of the interpreter which reflect the natural order must therefore be amplified by, and at the same time concentrated in, those theological loci that spring from the teaching and life of Christ. As the order of reality receives its ultimate focus in the scopus Christ, so the general topoi in the mind of the interpreter are now freed to be determined by the specific topoi of Christ's teaching.

The Harmony of Christ

The true meaning of the biblical text arises from its reference to Christ, the scopus at the center of the *orbis Christi,* the circle of his teaching and life. In his *Ratio verae theologiae,* Erasmus said: "The meaning which we draw forth from the obscure words must correspond to the circle of Christian doctrine, to its life, and finally to natural equity."[59] A more fully developed form of his statement reads: "As the whole circle of doctrine is in harmony with itself, so it is in agreement with his life, even with the judgment of nature itself. . . . The books of Plato or Seneca may contain teachings not dissimilar to Christ's. And Socrates' life may show certain similarities with that of Christ. Still, nowhere but in Christ do you find that circle and harmony in which all things are congruent in themselves. However inspired the words and pious the deeds of the prophets, no matter how renowned the holiness of Moses and others, such a circle is found in no human being."[60]

Accordingly, Christ's teachings are as consistent in themselves as they are consonant with his life. Doctrine and ethics belong together, allegory and tropology. This supreme unity of truth and harmony of life is what makes the *philosophia Christi* unique in comparison with all other philosophical schools. In addition to harmony and consonance with life, the truth of Christ's speech is clear from its simplicity and artlessness.[61] Only Christ's doctrine therefore is worthy of the symbol of the circle, the symbol of perfection. Like the circle, Christ's gospel is congruent with itself from start to finish (because it returns to its origin whence it came), is equidistant from its center at all times, and numberless, that is, fundamentally indivisible. As the concept *consensus* seems to express more the harmonious unity and inner consistency of the truth, so the concept *concentus* seems to bespeak more the euphony of the truth and the harmony of the virtuous life.[62] The truth is not only true to itself but also pleasant and therefore evokes both trust in agreement and love in concord. As doctrine and ethics belong together, we can say, so also doctrine, ethics, and aesthetics, that is, *docere, movere,* and *delectare.*[63]

Furthermore, the teachings of Christ are in agreement with the equity of nature, meaning that the consensus of truth in his doctrine and life reflects the equilibrium by which natural equity so balances justice with love that unity and harmony, concord and peace, arise instead of division and discord, violence and war. The symmetry by which nature balances justice and love to achieve harmony is thus a preliminary revelation of the truth in Christ. Likewise, the interpretation of the truth will reach consensus and concord only if it follows the principle of moderation.

Next to the symbol of the circle, Erasmus uses also the term *fabula.* He thus complements the rhetorical notion of rest, namely, of Christ's teaching in terms of fixed, permanent, and standing topoi, with that of dramatic development, narrating Christ's life story and beyond that recounting the history of salvation. Rather than signifying a myth or fiction, the *orbis totius Christi fabulae* tells the story of Christ, beginning before his birth and continuing after his death.[64]

Old Testament allegories and prophecies foreshadow him; angels, shepherds, and sages witness to him; and John the Baptist points to the lamb, the symbol of innocence. Then follow the events of Christ's earthly life: he increases in age and makes progress with God and humans; he speaks in the temple, a secluded place, and performs his first miracle in private at the wedding of Cana. This means that he makes his public appearance only after having been properly initiated by his baptism by John, his confirmation by his Father, and his temptation by the devil. Now that he is ready to begin his preaching office in public, he steps out of the arcanum.

After his death, Christ shows himself to his disciples and teaches them by his ascension to know the place to which they must strive. Finally, the divine Spirit renders them such as the master wished them to be. Begun with the prophets, the circle of Christ's story closes with the apostles. "But in all of this Christ was as it were his own prophet. Just as he did nothing that was not foreshadowed by the types of the law and announced by the oracles of the prophets, so nothing of note took place which he had not foretold his apostles."[65]

From this circle of Christ's story, the theologian can extract the main points (topoi) of Christian doctrine. "Examine his birth, education, preaching, or death, you find nothing but the perfect example of poverty, humility, indeed innocence." Another summation reads: "Innocence, gentleness, poverty, and aversion to ambition and arrogance." Boiled down to their shortest form, then, Christ's teaching and life reveal the three characteristic traits of innocence (and purity), simplicity (and gentleness), and humility (or lack of ambition and arrogance).[66]

Even before Erasmus recounted the story of Christ, he anticipated these three cardinal points in his summary of Christian doctrine on the basis of the New Testament sources: "Christ, the heavenly teacher, has established on earth a new people that totally depends on heaven. Because it distrusts all worldly protection, it is rich, wise, noble, powerful, and happy in quite another way. It strives for happiness by contempt of all earthly things. . . . It knows neither hate nor envy because its simple eye beholds no violent desires. . . . It is not titillated by vainglory since it applies everything to the glory of the one Christ. Nor is it ambitious . . . but rather of such innocence of character that even the heathens approve of its conduct. It is born again to purity and simplicity. . . . It considers concord the highest value. . . . This is the *scopus* put forth by Christ. . . . This is the new doctrine of our author, which no school of philosophers has ever handed down."[67]

While Erasmus's account of the *fabula* attributes these modes of conduct to Christ, the description of Christ's people applies them to ecclesiology.[68] Whether in their Christological or Christian significance, however, these qualities have obviously to do with a spiritual attitude issuing in a specific moral behavior. As the circle of Christ's teaching and life is characterized by consensus and harmony through innocence, simplicity, and humility, so Christian teaching and living imitate Christ and for this reason are conducive to concord and peace in both community and world. Now this orientation of Erasmus's thinking has frequently led to the conclusion that his philosophy of Christ is nothing but spiritual and/or moral. But it is precisely the connection of the *orbis totius Christi fabulae* with the equity of nature that points to an ontological ground for this Christian way of life. What is more, the theological ground for this Christian ethic is indicated by its connection with Christ, the divine mediator and reconciler, indeed the redeemer and author of salvation.[69]

It would be erroneous for us to assume that the essence of Christ's (and Christian) teaching and life consists only in moral instruction. As if to dispel this notion, Erasmus connected, in his further elaborations, these ethical qualities with the theological topoi of faith and love: "Christ impressed especially and continuously two things on his disciples, faith and love. Faith shows that we should place our confidence in God rather than in ourselves. Love urges us to deserve well from all."[70] Even though hope receives in the *Ratio* short shrift[71] and faith figures in this passage less than love, Erasmus makes it clear in other contexts that he concentrates the theological significance of Christ's teaching in the virtues of faith, love, and hope.[72] Nevertheless, in the *Ratio*, where he is primarily concerned with enjoining a theology of consensus in contrast to the scholastic dissensions, he emphasizes love as that source which engenders unity, peace, and concord in the face of division, violence, and discord: "Peace is our religion."[73]

Christian ethics, then, learns, in a preliminary way, a lesson from nature and therefore rests on an ontological foundation. But it is ultimately informed by a theological identity. While already the knowledge of natural equity gives Christians a general sense of unity, balance, and moderation, it is faith that marks their relation to God, love that characterizes their attitude toward God and their fellow human beings, and hope that orients them to the final goal, the happiness of the eternal communion with God. It is quite in line with Erasmus's thinking to conclude that Christ's harmony signifies a doctrine of faith, love, and hope in conjunction with a life of innocence, simplicity, and humility.

Theological Loci

Identifying in Christ's story both the essentials of his teaching and the characteristics of his attitude does not complete the task of interpretation. It is extraordinarily useful, says Erasmus, to prepare or adopt a list of theological loci into which everything one reads should be appropriately placed. Such commonplaces are, among others, faith, fasting, bearing evil, helping the sick, tolerating ungodly magistrates, avoiding offense to the weak, studying Holy Scripture, piety toward parents and children, Christian charity, honoring ancestors, envy, disparagement, and sexual purity. After the topics have been arranged in the order of the affinity or opposition of words and things (as in his *Copia*), whatever is found to be noteworthy in the books of the Bible should be incorporated according to concordance or dissonance. If appropriate, one could also glean from the ancient interpreters of the Bible, and even from the books of the heathens, what might be of future use.[74] Erasmus thus advised the theologian to systematize theological subject matter (drawn above

all from Scripture, but also from patristic interpretation, and even from classical authors) according to the principles of rhetorical invention.

This string of topoi in the *Ratio* gives at first sight the impression of having
been thrown together at random. On closer inspection we do find, among
various practical concerns, faith and love mentioned, if only in passing. Even
so, this juxtaposition of topoi fails to give us a clue as to what Erasmus might
conceive of as a systematic order of theological commonplaces. We have to
look elsewhere.

Fortunately, some eighteen years later he penned an outline in which faith,
love, and hope figure prominently. Our search for an order of theological loci
arranged by Erasmus himself leads us to the *Elenchus* and *Sylva* of the fourth
book of his *Ecclesiastes*.[75] Here, in what comes closest to a systematic blue-
print of his thinking, he lays out a dualistic framework, with God, Christ, and
the Spirit on one side, and the devil on the other.[76] Then follow God's hierarchies and the kingdom of Satan, God's and Satan's laws, virtues and vices in
general and in particular, and finally the extreme boundary line of virtue and
vice, and the end of Christian life. In all, then, two dominions are contrasted
with each other, each different in origin, association, laws, modes of behavior,
and ends, ranked in the order of rhetorical disposition (*initium, progressus,
consummatio*).[77]

The way Erasmus associated the three theological key concepts with this
schema indicates that faith has primarily but not exclusively to do with the
beginning (the triune God and God's rule, people, and law), that love functions foremost but not alone in the middle (virtues), and that hope orients the
Christian especially though not totally to the end (death, and the future glory
and happiness). This movement between *exitus* and *reditus* is to be organic,
that is, cumulative, and coalescent, meaning that in each stage, as one of the
three theological concepts assumes a major role, the two others are not elimi-
nated. Still, quite in line with his characteristic emphasis on *profectus* as the
transition between beginning and perfection, Erasmus greatly expands the
middle section on virtues and vices.[78]

Faith, love, and hope indicate three stages in the overall scheme. But they
function also in the middle part, where they are translated into the category of
Christian virtues and correlated, as species to genera, with the natural virtues.
Here the theological virtues of faith, love, and hope are seen as specific expressions of their corresponding counterparts, the philosophical virtues of prudence, justice, and fortitude. The fourth philosophical virtue, temperance, is
by no means left out but receives a prominent place in the middle of the
middle. Erasmus manages to fit it into his schema by assigning it the function

of a subspecies of justice-charity, thereby giving it a place in the center of the center.[79] This shows how singularly important the concept of temperance is in Erasmus's system. Balancing justice with love, temperance is the moral equivalent of the rhetorical principle of moderation which itself is predicated on the equity of nature.[80]

This triad in the center of the macrocosmic schema is again structured along the lines of the order of origin, progress, and end. Accordingly, charity-justice-temperance between faith-prudence and hope-fortitude obtains a middle place, marking it as that region where the progress happens between origin and end, faith and fulfillment, God and eternal bliss. Moreover, it is important to observe that it is temperance (or moderation, for that matter) that functions as the specific balance between justice and charity, ensuring that there is neither too much nor too little of either one or the other. This is why, in comparison with the other loci, the *chorus temperentiae et intemperentiae* commands much more space in the systematic outline of Erasmus's theology.[81]

From what has been shown so far, this much is clear: the circle of Christ's story (as ascertained by the historical method) offers insights into his way of life from which the interpreter abstracts (by means of tropology) the modes of his, and Christian, behavior (innocence, simplicity, and humility). But what is more, Christ's teachings are identified (by way of allegory) and concentrated in the theological concepts of faith, love, and hope. These are then interpreted as theological virtues and aligned with the philosophical virtues. Last but not least, the theologian is instructed to arrange these and other loci in a theological system of coordinates, into which all pertinent topoi are to be incorporated according to their concordance or dissonance, their similarity or dissimilarity.

This sequence of steps indicates that ethics precedes and succeeds theology. Nonetheless, Erasmus seems to insist that ethics does not give its quality to theology but rather receives its quality from theology. Just as allegory is the ultimate criterion of tropology, so theology governs ethics. Faith, love, and hope are first theological topoi before they become theological virtues, revealing then their affinity with the philosophical virtues. While servants proceed before the queen as harbingers and follow her as her train, they do not have priority and authority. Therefore, appearance notwithstanding, where the relation of teaching and life is concerned, it is on the whole clear that Erasmus intended for doctrine to come before life, for teaching to be prior to acting, for thought to go before deed. Just as epistemology constitutes the basis of morality, so theology is the foundation of ethics. Although Christian ethics is generally foreshadowed by the *aequitas naturae,* the natural virtues are to the theological virtues as genera to species, meaning that it is the special revelation in

Christ that discloses what natural reality is all about. Specificity is more valuable than generality.

Another point about the relation between teaching and life needs to be made. In the *Ratio* and in his *Paraphrases,* Erasmus narrates Christ's story in terms of growth toward maturity, with the pivotal point coming at the opportune moment when after a preparatory period Christ is ready to step out of the arcanum to preach his gospel in the open.[82] Two important motifs govern Erasmus's telling the story of Christ's circle: the gradualism of an organic development and the dualism of hiddenness and openness. . . . What concerns us at this point is the relation of the dynamic of Christ's life to the stability of his teaching.

Just as the first period of salvation history, Old Testament prophecy, is the time of preparation for Christ's coming, so in the beginning of his life, Christ is made ready for his preaching office. Then comes the central period of his public work up to his death. With his resurrection begins the third and final period that ends with the apostles' teaching and the outpouring of the Spirit. The first period is linked with the middle one, like the middle period to the last one, by prophetic prediction and fulfillment. It is prophecy that provides the mediation between the three periods. In the middle period, however, Christ's life is marked by the stages of a beginning, progress, and an end, the same tripartite development as the larger framework of the three periods of salvation history, with a preparation leading up to the middle part and its after-effects concluding it.

It is interesting to compare this arrangement in the *Ratio* of the three periods of beginning, middle, and end, including a tripartite middle part, with Erasmus's systematic layout of theological topoi in his *Ecclesiastes*. While the *Ratio* concerns more the dynamic of salvation history and Christ's life, the *Ecclesiastes* has to do more with the firm doctrines and the perennial teachings of Christ. Nevertheless, in the *Ratio,* Christ's teaching is concentrated in permanent, indivisible topoi, symbolized by the circle, whereas in the *Ecclesiastes* the systematic layout of theological topoi is couched in the tripartite arrangement of beginning, progress, and end.

Two patterns emerge that appear to characterize Erasmus's thinking as a whole: the *via* motive with a tripartite movement of beginning, middle, and end, and the topoi motif indicating the stability and coherence of the truth in a dualistic context. While the first pattern reflects the development of Christ's life, of salvation history, and of the Christian's improvement, the second pertains to both the perennial teachings of Christ and the firm doctrines of the church. The first seems to be oriented in the rhetorical notion of development in the *ordo artificialis*, the second seems to rest on the rhetorical notion of the *ordo naturalis*. In the disposition of speech, however, the rhetorician makes sure that there is an effective distribution of both.

This double perspective has much to say about the permanence of Christ's teachings over against the development and reformability of ecclesiastical practices that are to apply Christ's teachings to the various conditions in the history of his people.[83] While there are definite elements of doctrine that remain unchangeable (*akineta*),[84] others can become irrelevant, though not superfluous, as history progresses toward its consummation. And the same is true for the individual Christian's spiritual progress on the way of salvation. In other words, the teachings of Christ represent fixed points of Christian existence and the institution of the church. And yet they become the markers of the way in the development of Christian life and in the progress of the church toward perfection.[85]

This relation of the *via* motive and loci motif gives us clues to the peculiarity of Erasmus's own theology. He uses, on the one hand, a system of loci within which topics are arranged according to similarity and dissimilarity, with Christ representing the universal fixed point, the head and goal (scopus). This systematic layout of topics around a Christocentric focus is, on the other hand, animated by the notion of progress between beginning and end, whether in dramatic development in the telling of a story, the development of an argument in rhetorical discourse, the movement toward an allegorical understanding of a text, or moral improvement in life. In general, then, it is the coordination of form and dynamic, doctrine and narration, circle and progression, of the firm and movable, of motif and motive, of topos and *gradatio*, principles and application, teaching and life, that brings the characteristic manner of Erasmus's thinking to light.[86] This double perspective of his rhetorical theology (the cause, obviously, for his having been so often charged with ambivalence and ambiguity) can be ultimately traced to the relation between the freedom of organic growth and the authority of constant truth.

Abbreviations

Aristot.	Aristotle
Nic. Eth.	*Ethica Nicomachea*
Phys.	*Physica*
Rhet.	*Rhetorica*
ASD	*Opera omnia Desiderii Erasmi Roterodami.* Amsterdam: North Holland, 1969.
Aug.	Aurelius Augustinus
De doctr.	*De doctrina christiana*

CWE   *Collected Works of Erasmus.* Toronto: University of Toronto Press, 1974–.
Cic.   Cicero
  De or.   *De Oratore*
  Inv.   *De inuentione*
  Off.   *De officiis*
  Or.   *Orator*
Ep.   *Opus epistolarum Desiderii Erasmis Roterodami.* Ed. P. S. Allen, H. M. Allen, and H. W. Garrod. Oxford: Clarendon, 1906–58.
ERSY   *Erasmus of Rotterdam Society Yearbook.* Oxen Hill, Md.: The Society, 1981.
H   *Desiderius Erasmus Roterodamus: Ausgewaelte Werke.* Ed. Hajo Holborn und Annemarie Holborn. Munich: Beck, 1933. Rpt. 1964.
Her.   *Rhetorica ad Herennium*
HWP   Rudolf Eisler. *Historisches Woerterbuch der Philosophie.* Basil: Schwabe, 1971–.
LB   *Desiderii Erasmi Roterodami opera omnia.* Ed. Jean Leclerk. Leiden: Batavorum, 1703–6. Rpt. 1961–62.
Plat.   Plato
  Phaedr. *Phaedrus*
Quint. Inst. Quintilianus *Institutio oratoria*
RAC   *Reallexikon fuer Antike und Christentum.*

Notes

1. *De ratione studii* CWE 24 667. *Primum illud constat grammaticen esse disciplinarum omnium fundamentum, ex cuius neglectu quanta bonorum autorum ac disciplinarum vel interitus vel corruptela sit profecta* (*Ecclesiastes* ASD V-4 252:138–40).

2. *Ecclesiastes* ASD V-4 252:148. *Grammaticam dico . . . rationes emendate proprieque loquendi, quae res non contingit nisi ex multiiuge veterum lectione, qui sermonis elegantia praecelluerunt . . . Ad ea requiritur vocabulorum cognitio, quibus singulae res declarantur, tum eorum compositio; quorum vtrunque pendet non ab arbitrio disputantium, sed a consuetudine veterum, qui castigate loquuti sunt* (*Ecclesiastes* ASD V-4 252:141–55). Cf. Quint. Inst. 1,2,14; 4,1f.; 2–29; 5,1; 2–72; 6,1–45; 2,1,1–6.

3. *De pueris instituendis* CWE 26 319; *De ratione studii* CWE 24 669. Cf. ASD I-3 585–90; I-4 25:379; V-4 252:138–40.

4. *De ratione studii* CWE 24 667.

5. *De conscribendis epistolis* CWE 25 194–95. Cf. H 180:20f.; 187:1ff.; 10ff.; 190:15; ASD V-4 268:484ff.

6. See the sequence of grammar, rhetoric, and theological topoi in both the *Ratio* (roughly H 178:19ff.; 259:28ff.; 291:13ff.) and the *Ecclesiastes* (ASD V-4 252:138ff.; 268:484ff.; LB V 1071Cff.).

7. Cf. the structure and progression of the *Elenchus* (LB V 1071C–1083E).

8. *Ex rhetorum praeceptis aliqua delibemus, quae videntur ad Ecclesiastae munus accommoda* (*Ecclesiastes* ASD V-4 268:484–85). Cf. Aug. De doctr. 4,2,3–3,4.

9. *Ecclesiastes* ASD V-4 279:705–280:719.

10. Cf. for instance Plat. Phaedr. 236a; Her. 1,3,4; Cic. Inv. 1,7,9; De or. 1,31,142; Or. 13,44–15,49; Quint. Inst. 3,3,1–15.

11. Aristot. Rhet. 3,1,1; 3,13–19; Her. 3,4,7–5,9; 3,9,16–10,18; Cic. Inv. 1,14,19; De or. 1,31,143; 2,76,307–81,332; Quint. Inst. 7,pr 1–4; 7,1,1–63.

12. On the difference between the rhetorical concept of invention and the modern understanding of discovery and creativity see A. Hügli and U. Theissmann, art "Invention, Erfindung, Entdeckung" HWP 4, 544–52.

13. *Veteres poesim non arti, sed numinis afflatui tribuerunt* (*Ecclesiastes* ASD V-4 260:308).

14. On imitation cf. for instance Aristot. Rhet. 1,11,23; Her. 1,2,3; 4,2,2; Cic. De or. 2,22,90; Quint. Inst. 2,2,8; 5,25–26; 8,pr 16; 10,1,3; 24–131; 2,1; 10,5,19.

15. *Ciceronianus* CWE 28 441. "The true imitation tries not so much to say identical things as similar things, sometimes not even similar things but equivalent things" (*Ciceronianus* CWE 28 446). "Imitation is a matter of effort, likeness the result" (*Letters* 1334 / CWE 9 256:344).

16. For the influence of the *Devotio moderna* see for instance R. L. DeMolen *The Spirituality of Erasmus of Rotterdam* (Nieuwkoop: De Graaf, 1987) 35–67; R. J. Schoeck *Erasmus Grandescens: The Growth of a Humanist's Mind and Spirituality* (Nieuwkoop: De Graaf, 1988) 31–40. The relation between the rhetorical concept of imitation and the theological concept of *imitatio Christi* has not yet been explored.

17. Her. 1,2,3; 3,16,28; Cic. De or. 1,25,113; 32,145; 2,22,90; Quint. Inst. 1,pr 26; 2,17,1–19,3; 3,2,1–4; 5,1; 5,10,121; 6,4,12; 9,4,3–4; 120; 11,2,9. Erasmus defines nature, method, and practice in *De pueris instituendis* CWE 26 311–12: "By nature I mean man's innate capacity and inclination for the good. By method I understand learning, which consists of advice and instruction. Finally, by practice I mean the exercise of a disposition which has been implanted by nature and moulded by method. Nature is realized only through method, and practice, unless it is guided by the principles of method, is open to numerous errors and pitfalls. . . . Three strands must be intertwined to make a complete cord: nature must be developed by method and method must find its completion in practice."

18. *Ecclesiastes* ASD V-4 260:303–39. Cf. *De pueris instituendis* CWE 26 319; 320; 336.

19. Quint. Inst. 3,2,3; 2,19,3.

20. *Ciceronianus* CWE 28 368. *Ecclesiastes* ASD V-4 248:32–35.

21. *Ecclesiastes* ASD V-4 66:656; 248:32; IV-1A 153:210; *Letters* 531 / CWE 4 230:243–44; 1304 / CWE 9 146:46; *Ciceronianus* CWE 28 368. *Oportet igitur Ecclesiasten sibi notum esse, nec artem modo, verum etiam naturam suam in consilium adhibere* (*Ecclesiastes* LB V 967A). Cf. Aristot. Rhet. 3,2,4; Cic. De or. 2,41,177; Quint. Inst. 4,1,5–6.

22. *Ciceronianus* ASD I-2 704:16–18; 647:37ff.; *Ecclesiastes* V-4 236:950–51.

23. *Ecclesiastes* LB V 955C; 956B–D; 958C; cf. Her. 3,16,28f.; 22,35.

24. *Ecclesiastes* ASD V-4 250:80ff.; 106ff. Cf. Quint. Inst. 1,2,8.

25. *De ratione studii* CWE 24 671:5–10. Cf. Her. 3,16,28–24,40; Quint. Inst. 10,1,19.

26. *De ratione studii* CWE 24 672:24–27. *Ratio* H 291:13–35.

27. *De copia* ASD I-6. Cf. Quint. Inst. 10,1,5.

28. Quint. Inst. 11,2,13; 20; 23; 28; 36–38; 44. Cf. H. Lausberg *Elemente der lite-*

rarischen Rhetorik: Eine Enführung für Studierende der Romanischen Philologie (Munich: M. Hueber, 1963) 24.

29. *Ecclesiastes* ASD V-4 280:725; LB V 951E–955E. *Ratio* H 291:25. Cf. Aristot. Rhet. 3,13–19; Her. 3,4,7–5,9; 9,16–10,18; Cic. De or. 2,74,307–85,349; Or. 15,50; Quint. Inst. 7,1,1ff.

30. Cicero defines *ordo* as *compositio rerum aptis et accommodatis locis* (Off. 1,40,142); cf. Quint. Inst. 7,pr 3.

31. Aristot. Phys. 2,1,13ff. See F. P. Hager, art "Natur" *HWP* 6, 421–41.

32. H. Lausberg *Handbuch der literarischen Rhetorik: Eine Grundlegung der Literatur wissenschaft* (Munich: M. Hueber, 1960) 245–47; *Elemente* 27–28.

33. Lausberg *Handbuch* 242; *Elemente* 31–32.

34. On *gradatio* cf., for instance, ASD V-4 414:154–64; 346:486–88; 351:649f.; 352:667; LB V 970C; 1001F; 1002F; ASD V-3 289:90–91; LB VII 620B.

35. See below, "The Harmony of Christ."

36. *Ratio* H 199:13–201:34.

37. Cf. my book *Erkenntnis und Verwirklichung der wahren Theologie nach Erasmus von Rotterdam* (Tübingen: Mohr, 1972) 69–70; 189n146. See C. Augustijn "Erasmus und seine Theologie," in *Colloque érasmien* 55–56; 61–65. Erasmus cultivated both a Catholic sense for the traditional development of doctrine and a Protestant critique of tradition on the basis of the once-and-for-all evangelical norm. He would neither support the radical reformers who attempted to restitute the church to its primitive state, nor would he join the Catholic theologians who tended to use the gospel to justify the status quo of ecclesiastical tradition and practice. True to his moderate stance, he kept a balance between the theory of development and the theory of decay. His aim was the restoration of original goodness together with a process toward perfection. His advice was to nurture simple, steadfast faith as well as variable, accommodating prudence.

38. Aristot. Nic. Eth. 1108b, 11–13; Aug. De doctr. 3,21,31; 4,18,35; 25,55.

39. *Aristotelicum est primum rei summam et quasi capita proponere, dein per eadem vestigia recurrendo ad singulas partes quae sunt exactioris scientiae adiungere, exemplo artificum, qui prima manu deformant rude statuae simulachrum, mox ad singula membra redeunt iterum atque iterum, donec summam imponant manum* (*Ecclesiastes* ASD V-4 434:668–435:672). Cf. ASD V-4 388:550–53; 401:870–424:433; 448:964–72; LB V 1059F. On *synecdoche* see H. Lausberg *Elemente* 69–71.

40. *Letters* 1341A / CWE 9 340:1148–51. Cf. *Ecclesiastes* LB V 1080E.

41. *Letters* 1523 / CWE 10 448:202–449:204.

42. *Ecclesiastes* ASD V-4 270:502–10; 272:536–37; 310:562ff.; et al.

43. *Ecclesiastes* ASD V-4 412:135–414:164.

44. Cf. H. Lausberg *Handbuch* 241–42; *Elemente* 29.

45. *Paraphrase on Mark* CWE 49 21.

46. For references to Erasmus's use of the *initium-progressus-perfectio* division, see LB VII 190 A–B; 257A; ASD V-1 208:68ff.; 214:238; 231:774ff.; V-3 212:564f.; 236:914; IX-1 446:109f.; 452:259; LB V 953B; 1084C; L 324; LB X 1523F.

47. *Habes huius salutiferae fabulae protasim, epitasim et catastrophen, habes actus omnes ac scenas coelestis illius choragi ineffabili dispensatione digestas* (*Explanatio symboli* ASD V-1 218:358–60; *Purgatio* IX-1 451:252–452:269). *Homo bene conditus veluti*

protasis est, crux epitasis, resurrectio catastrophe (*Purgatio* ASD IX-1 452:290–91). *Adages* CWE 31 177:1–178:21 (*Catastrophe fabulae*).

48. On amplification in general see, for instance, Aristot. Rhet. 1,9,38; 2,18,4; 19,26; 26,1; Her. 3,3,6; Cic. De or. 3,26,104; Quint. Inst. 2,5,9; 8,3,40; 4,1–19; 9,1,27. Erasmus treated *amplificatio* primarily in the context of elocution, especially in connection with *adfectus* (*Ecclesiastes* LB V 968F–976D): The amplification of words produces *modus* the amplification of things makes for *adfectus* (cf. *De copia* ASD I-6 73:992–1002; 197:1ff.).

49. H. Lausberg *Handbuch* 145–46; 220–27; *Elemente* 35–39. *De copia* ASD I-6 30:85–32:112.

50. *Letters* 1304 / CWE 9 146:46.

51. *Psalmi* ASD V-2 240:512–14. *Amplissima est diuina sapientia, quae non est animalis sed spiritualis, eoque cor requirit amplum et capax* (*Psalmi* ASD V-2 240:539–40).

52. *Paraphrase on Mark* CWE 49 39.

53. *Scripturae tropis significari spiritualem amplitudinem, ac damnari angustiam. Illud habent peculiare res spirituales, quod ex contrariis gignantur contraria, quodque eadem res gignat contraria. . . . Sic Christi Spiritus ac diuina charitas eundem hominem, et laxat et contrahit, mollit ac durat, erigit ac deiicit, laxat ad benefaciendum omnibus, contrahit a cautionem, ne quem offendat, mollit ad vindictam, durat ad patientiam, erigit ad contemptum eorum qui obsistunt euangelio, deiicit a obsequendum omnibus amore Christi* (*Psalmi* ASD V-2 241:557–242:570).

54. *Letters* 1381 / CWE 10 69:283–85.

55. Cf., for instance, *Psalmi* ASD V-2 232:268–237:424; 266:352f.; *Ecclesiastes* V-4 448:964–72.

56. *Paraphrase on Mark* CWE 49 12. Cf. *Ecclesiastes* ASD V-4 182:961ff.; 146:304; LB V 953C.

57. Cf. Aug. De doctr.: *Ipsa tamen veritas connexionum non instituta, sed animadversa est ab hominibus et notata, ut eam possint vel discere vel docere: nam est in rerum ratione perpetua et divinitus instituta* (2,32,50); *Item scientia definiendi, dividendi, atque partiendi, quanquam etiam rebus falsis plerumque adhibeatur, ipsa tamen falsa non est, neque ab hominibus instituta, sed in rerum ratione comperta* (2,35,53).

58. *Nullo salutis periculo aberratur a germano sensu scripturae, modo quod accipitur congruat cum pietate et veritate; nec est leuis utilitas studii nostri, si quod interpretamur non faciat ad praesentem locum, modo faciat ad bonam vitam, et cum aliis scripturae locis consentiat* (*Psalmi* ASD V-2 246:724–27).

59. *Ratio* H 286:1–4.

60. *Ratio* H 210:4–211:4.

61. *Simplex est, iuxta tragici sententiam, veritatis oratio; nihil autem Christo neque simplicius neque verius* (*Ratio* H 280:4–5). "The language of the gospel is simple and artless" (*Letters* 1381 / CWE 10 73:389–90). Cf. *Adages* CWE 31 308:1–25; *Ratio* H 304:26–27.

62. *Hanc harmoniam, hunc omnium virtutum concentum in nullo sanctorum reperieris praeter quam in uno Christo Iesu* (LB VI *5r). "Sweet and tuneful indeed is the concerted sound when love, chastity, sobriety, modesty, and the other virtues sing together in harmonious variety. . . . And this music will be the more pleasing to God if

performed by a numerous choir in harmony of hearts and voices" (*Letters* 1304 / CWE 9 158:462–76).

63. *Ratio* H 209:3; 210:33, 211:28–30; 222:36–223:1. Although *consensus* and *concentus* are used interchangeably (cf. Cic. De or. 3,6,21, referring to Plato), for Erasmus, *consensus* has perhaps more to do with the convincing *vehementia* of the Divine Word and *concentus* more with its attractive *suavitas* or *jucunditas*.

64. *Ratio* H 209:1–211:10.

65. *Ratio* H 210:22–26.

66. *Enchiridion* H 59:25–26; 63:11–13; 75:20; 91:8; *Ratio* H 203:23–24; 31–32; 210:2–4; 220:11ff.; 264:21–22; 280:5. "But men who are like this child in humility, simplicity, and innocence are held in the highest regard by me. For it is fair that those should be dearest to me who are most like me" (*Paraphrase on Mark* CWE 49 117). These qualities occur again and again in Erasmus's theological writings as character traits of both Christ and the Christians, especially their leaders. By contrast, the catalogue of vices Erasmus repeatedly draws on seems to be derived from Stoic ethics which singles out as the foremost vices *luxuria, avaritia, ambitio,* and *superstitio.* Cf. R. Staats, art "Hauptsünden" *RAC* 13, 738.

67. *Ratio* H 193:24–195:1.

68. The allegorical interpretation combines Christology and ecclesiology. Cf. F. Krüger *Humanistische Evangelienauslegung: Desiderius Erasmus von Rotterdam als Ausleger der Evangelien in Seinen Paraphrasen* (Tübingen: Mohr, 1986) 109–17; my article "Church and Ministry" *ERSY* 6 (1986) 15.

69. *Est irrefutabilis auctoritas, quae sic summa est in Christo, ut pene sit sola* (*Ecclesiastes* LB V 1008B; cf. *Purgatio* ASD IX-1 472:832–41). Christ is not only the *unicus auctor et recte sentiendi et beate vivendi* (*Enchiridion* H 110:18) but also *unicus humanae salutis auctor* (*Paraclesis* H 141:2). Christ is the redeemer (*Purgatio* ASD IX-1 473:850) and "No one can find salvation unless he believes that Jesus is the author of all salvation. For the source of evangelical salvation is a divinely inspired belief in Christ, the Son of God" (*Paraphrase on Mark* CWE 49 105).

70. *Ratio* H 237:17–19. *In his enim duobus sita est summa felicitatis humanae, ut per oculum ac lumen fidei citra errorem videat homo quid sit expetendum, quid fugiendum, per caritatem exsequatur quod dictavit fides. Fides gignit caritatem, caritas vicissim alit fidem bonis operibus* (*Ecclesiastes* LB V 1080B). "This is the first principle of the evangelical doctrine: to believe what you hear and to have faith in what is promised" (*Paraphrase on Mark* CWE 49 79). Cf. LB VII 649–50.

71. Dionysius the Areopagite too considered hope the lowest of the heroic virtues (*Hierarchies* 40).

72. For instance, *Ecclesiastes* ASD V-4 84:89–85:92; 247:21; LB V 1078E–1080E; *Paraphrasis in epistolam ad Corinthios priorem* VII 901E–F. Cf. Aug. De doctr.: *Quidquid in sermone divino neque ad morum honestam, neque ad fidei veritatem proprie referri potest, figuratum esse cognoscas. Morum honestas ad diligendum Deum et proximum, fidei veritas ad cognoscendum Deum et proximum pertinet. Spes autem sua cuique est in conscientia propria, quemadmodum se sentit ad dilectionem Dei et proximi, cognotionemque proficere* (3,10,14; cf. 15; 16).

73. *Ratio* H 245:34–35. "Through my Spirit I shall act in them, as you have asserted

your truth in me; hence they too, like the limbs of one body, holding fast to one head and quickened by one Spirit, will cling fast to each other in mutual unanimity. . . . Conflict of opinion deprives teaching of its trustworthiness" (*Paraphrase on John* CWE 46 197). *Summa nostrae religionis pax est et vnanimitas* (Ep. 1334:217). *Mea pax, quam vobis do, vos conciliat Deo. . . . Pax, quam vobis relinquo, mutua concordia conglutinans vos inter vos, reddet sodalitium vestrum invictum adversus omnia, quae potest mundus, aut Satanas hujus mundi princeps* (*Paraphrasis in Ioannem* LB VII 612E).

74. *Ratio* H 291:13–31. "But principles of this kind, which like ballast in a ship do not allow the mind to be tossed to and fro by the waves of fortune and events, cannot be drawn from any better or more reliable or more effective source than the study of the gospel" (*Letters* 1333 / CWE 9 237:195–99). Cf. *De ratione studii* CWE 24 672:24–26.

75. *Ecclesiastes* LB V 1071C–1087F.

76. In a way Erasmus's system resembles that of the rules of Tychonius (*Ecclesiastes* LB V 1059A–1061C), except that Tychonius contrasts Christ and his body, the church, in the beginning (rule 1) to the devil and his body at the end (rule 7), whereas Erasmus contraposes God and the devil from the start. At this point, as elsewhere, the influence of Dionysius the Areopagite on Erasmus should be examined.

77. The letter "To the Pious Reader" following Erasmus's *Paraphrase on John* summarizes similarly the Gospel both in terms of a center (faith, love, and hope) and of two spheres: heavenly-earthly; spiritual-physical; the triune God–the tyrant Satan; the children of God in heavenly fellowship vs. Satan's confederates; resources and consolations on each side; and rewards for each in the afterlife (*Paraphrasis in Ioannem* LB VII 649–50; cf. CWE 46 226–27).

78. *Ecclesiastes* LB V 1085D–1087E.

79. *Ecclesiastes* LB V 1080D–E.

80. *Aequitas . . . est legum moderatio* (*Ecclesiastes* ASD V-4 313:621). Cf. Cic. De or. 1,56,240.

81. *Ecclesiastes* LB V 1087A–D.

82. *Ratio* H 209:32–210:2.

83. At *Ecclesiastica Hierarchia, quoniam Divinis regitur legibus, & Christi immutabilibus institutis, semper eodem statu sit oportet, licet in ritibus nonnullis ac caeremoniis sit nonnulla varietas* (*Ecclesiastes* LB V 1071F).

84. *Adages* CWE 32 43–44; *Psalmi* ASD V-3 304:619; *Paraphrasis in Mattheum* LB VII 145B–146E; *Hyperaspistes* L 256; 506. "Another thing . . . which would reconcile many nations to the Roman church . . . would be a readiness not to define everything over a wide field . . . but only such things as are clearly laid down in Holy Writ or without which the system of our salvation cannot stand. For this a few truths are enough, and the multitude are more easily persuaded of their truth if they are few" (*Letters* 1039 / CWE 7 126:235–41).

85. See above, note 37.

86. In my book (*Erkenntnis* 52–53), I had interpreted Erasmus's combination of *ratio* and *methodus* from this systematic perspective and identified *ratio* with a deductive method and *methodus* with an inductive method of inquiry (see M. O'Rourke Boyle's critique in *Language: Erasmus on Language and Method in Theology* [Toronto: University of Toronto Press, 1977] 64–65). But Erasmus simply substituted the Greek word

methodus for the Latin *via* used by the rhetoricians in the formula *ratio et via* (see, for instance, Her. 1,2,3; Cic. Inv. 1,4,5; De or. 1,15,113; Quint. Inst. 5,1,3). Martin Bucer annotates: "Called by the Greeks *methodus;* which word Theodorus translates as *viam rationemque docendi.* Quintilian divides grammar into two parts: method and history. By method he means what Cicero calls *viam, artem et rationem.* . . . Again, elsewhere he translates *methodus* as *breve dicendi compendium,* as if there were a short cut by which we could travel to knowledge" (*Martini Buceri Opera omnia* 3,128; quoted in T. H. L. Parker *Calvin's New Testament Commentaries* [London: S.C.M. Press, 1971], 31).

8

Naming God

PAUL RICOEUR
Translated by David Pellauer

Few authors have the gift or the talent to write "What I Believe." Yet more than one listener to Christian preaching may stand ready to describe the ways they understand what they have heard. I am one of these listeners.

Presupposition

To confess that one is a listener is from the very beginning to break with the project that is dear to many, and even perhaps all, philosophers: to begin discourse without any presuppositions. (We could speak simply of the "project of beginning," for to think without presuppositions and to begin to think are one.) Yet it is in terms of one certain presupposition that I stand in the position of a listener to Christian preaching: I assume that this speaking is meaningful, that it is worthy of consideration, and that examining it may accompany and guide the transfer from the text to life, where it will verify itself fully.

Can I account for this presupposition? Alas, I stumble already. I do not know how to sort out what is here "unravelable" situation, uncriticized custom, deliberate preference, or profound unchosen choice. I can only confess that my desire to hear more is all these things, and that it defies all these distinctions.

But if what I presuppose precedes everything I can choose to think about, how do I avoid the famous circle of believing in order to understand and understanding in order to believe? I do not seek to avoid it. I boldly stay within this circle, in the hope that, through the transfer from text to life, what I have risked will be returned a hundredfold as an increase in comprehension, valor, and joy.

Shall I tolerate the fact that thinking, which aims at what is universal and necessary, is linked in a contingent way to individual events and particular texts that report them? Yes, I shall assume this contingency, so scandalous for thinking, as one aspect of the presupposition attached to listening. For I hope that, once I enter into the movement of comprehending faith, I shall discover the very reason for that contingency, if it is true that the increase in comprehension that I expect is indissolubly linked to testimonies to the truth, which are contingent in every instance, and rendered through certain acts, lives, and beings.

Text

Naming God only comes about within the milieu of a presupposition, incapable of being rendered transparent to itself, suspected of being a vicious circle, and tormented by contingency. This is the presupposition: Naming God is what has already taken place in the texts preferred by my listening's presupposition.

1. Do I therefore place texts above life? Does not religious experience come first? My presupposition does not say that nothing can be taken as religious "experience" — be it a feeling of "absolute dependence," a response to a will that precedes me, an "ultimate concern" at the horizon of all my decisions, or "an unconditional confidence" that hopes in spite of . . . everything. These are some of the synonyms of what has been called faith, those at least that are most familiar and closest to me. So understood, faith is certainly not an act that can be reduced to any act of speaking or any piece of writing. This act represents the limit of any hermeneutic because it is the origin of all interpretation.

But the presupposition of listening to Christian preaching is not that everything is language; it is rather that it is always within a language that religious experience is articulated, that one hears it in a cognitive, practical, or emotional sense. More precisely, what is presupposed is that faith, inasmuch as it is lived experience, is *instructed* — in the sense of being formed, clarified, and educated — within the network of texts that in each instance preaching brings back to living speech. This presupposition of the *textuality* of faith distinguishes *biblical* faith ("bible" meaning book) from all others. In one sense, therefore, texts do precede life. I can name God in my faith because the texts preached to me have already named him.

Yet if I do not put texts above life, do I not nevertheless give writing a privilege that really belongs to speaking? Do we not call these texts the Word of God? And is not preaching a speech event? If there is an abstraction and a hypostasis of the text that I will fight against below, the contrary abstraction, that of a dialogue or an encounter between an I and a thou, calls for similar reservations. An apologetic that is based just on dialogue tends to make us completely lose sight of what is unique to instruction through texts. Examining some specific texts below will reveal how the purely dialogical interpretation of the relation between God and humanity is too narrow and exclusive. I limit myself here to calling the dialogical scheme into question on the simple level of the communication of discourse; that is, on the plane of a text's being addressed to and received within a community of interpretation.

Someone may readily say, recalling Plato's critique of writing in his *Phaedrus,* that when living speech is given over to "external marks" such as letters and written signs, communication is irremediably cut off. Something is lost that belongs to the voice, the facial expression, and the common situation of interlocutors in a face-to-face setting. This is not false. It is even so true that the reconversion of writing into speech aims at re-creating a relation not identical to, but analogical to, the dialogical relation of communication. Yet it does so precisely beyond the "scriptuary" step of communication and with its own characters that depend on preaching's posttextual position. What the unilateral apologetic for dialogue misunderstands is the extraordinary promotion that happens to discourse in passing from speech to writing. By breaking away from the bodily presence of a reader, the text also breaks away from its author — that is, from the intention the text is supposed to express, from the psychology of the person behind the work, from the understanding that person has of himself or herself and of his or her situation, from his or her relation as author to an initial public, the original target of the text, and all at the same time. This triple independence of the text with regard to its author, its context, and its initial audience explains why texts are open to innumerable "recontextualizations" through listening and reading that are a reply to the "decontextualization" already contained in the very act of writing or, more exactly, of publication.

2. If I make believers scribes, will it be long before I make them literary critics? Taken in the closure of their own textuality, my texts will then close in upon themselves. They will be open to other texts that they cite or that they transform, but the interplay of intertextuality will only come to be more separated and closed off from the side I have called life. What I call the hermeneutical approach (or simply the theory of interpretation) is exactly the refusal of this "literary" hypostasis of the text, simply substituted for that of dialogical speaking. I would like to develop two arguments against this hypostasis.

A text is first a link in a communicative chain. To begin, one of life's experiences is brought to language. It becomes discourse. Then this discourse is differentiated into speech and writing, with the privileges and advantages of which I have spoken. Writing, in its turn, is restored to living speech by means of the various acts of discourse that reactualize the text. Reading and preaching are such actualizations of writing into speech. A text, in this regard, is like a musical score that requires execution. (Some critics, reacting against the excessive emphasis on the text itself, even go so far as to say that it is "the reader in the text" who completes its meaning, for example, by filling in its lacunas or resolving its ambiguities, that is, by straightening out its narrative or argumentative order.)

Cut away from speaking-becoming-writing and writing-becoming-speaking, the text is no more than an artifact of critical method. This artifact may, in turn, be put in a series with other artifacts, as we place a book alongside other books in a library. Intertextuality in the proper sense of the word is such a library. And other less classificatory, more genetic operations may be applied to this constructed series. The old *Quellenforschung* already practiced this game of referring one text to another in a genetic filiation. The quoting of the code in the theory of intertextuality that today replaces the borrowing of a message basically belongs to this same family of procedures: abstract a text from the communicative chain, put it near or together with another equally abstract text, then make a whole out of these texts in genetic or structural series. The illusion is the same, that of believing that one has understood a text better when one knows another text from which it arises through borrowing or quotation.

Yet it does not suffice to replace a text in the communicative chain in order to overthrow the hypostasis of the text itself. Its most central hypothesis must be attacked, namely that writing brings about a fundamental mutation in discourse concerning the relation between "sense" and "reference." This mutation would abolish the question of reference solely to the benefit of the sense. By reference is meant discourse's character of relating itself to an extralinguistic reality—what above I called the lived experience that is brought to language—before any bifurcation within discourse into speech and writing. By sense is meant, within the perspective of abolished reference, a network of relations purely internal to the text, whether it be a question of a hierarchical relation by which units of a lower rank are integrated into units of a higher rank, a relation between the surface message and the underlying codes, a combination of various codes within the same text, or the quotation of some codes external to the text considered within the relation of intertextuality mentioned above.

The hermeneutical thesis, diametrically opposed to the structuralist thesis — not to structural method and inquiry — is that the difference between speech and writing in no way abolishes the fundamental function of discourse (which encompasses these two variations: oral and written). Discourse consists of the fact that someone says something to someone *about something*. "About something" is the inalienable referential function of discourse. Writing does not abolish it but rather transforms it. In oral discourse, face-to-face interlocutors can, in the final analysis, refer what they are talking about to the surrounding world common to them. Only writing can, by addressing itself to anyone who knows how to read, refer to a world that is not there between the interlocutors, a world that is the world of the text and yet is not in the text. Following Gadamer, I call this "the 'thing' or issue of the text." This issue of the text is the object of hermeneutics. It is neither behind the text as the presumed author nor in the text as its structure but unfolded in front of it.

This same consideration applies to biblical texts. God, who is named by the texts held open, by my desire to listen, is, in a way still to be spoken of, the ultimate referent of these texts. God is in some manner implied by the "issue" of these texts, by the world — the biblical world! — that these texts unfold.

By so orienting the hermeneutical axis of my meditation toward the issue of the text, I recognize the vanity of an inquiry oriented toward the text's author that would seek to identify God as the voice behind the narrative or prophetic voice. I am well aware that a long tradition identified revelation with inspiration, in the sense of an insufflation of meaning that made God a sort of overarching author of the texts wherein faith instructs itself. But if the word "revelation" means something, its meaning is to be sought on the side of the issue the texts tell about, as an aspect of the biblical world.

Poetic

How do I respond to the following objection? This defense of the referential dimension of a text only holds for discourse of a descriptive character: ordinary discourse about the things of life, scientific discourse about the world's physical entities, historical discourse about events that really happened, sociological discourse about actual instances of existing societies. The referential theory discourse stops at the threshold of poetic discourse. There, language celebrates itself. Or if it does seem to refer to something, it does so to the extent that it expresses emotions that are wholly subjective and that add nothing to the description of the world. Thus naming God is, at best, a poetic activity, without any bearing on description; that is, without any bearing on true knowledge of the world.

I do assume provisionally the assimilation of biblical texts to poetic texts. I will speak below about the manner in which the Bible is a poem, albeit unique and, in this sense, eccentric. I do assume this assimilation because I object to the theory that reduces the referential function to descriptive discourse in order to allow only an emotional function to poetic discourse. (I note in passing that the structuralist reduction of literary texts to their immanent sense depends largely on a theory wherein poetic discourse has already been stripped of its referential function because of the subterfuge of the opposition between descriptive and nondescriptive discourse. What is held to be essential, in effect, is that "literature" occurs in the nondescriptive zones of discourse, whether it takes the form of fictive narration, lyric, or an essay. It is a matter, therefore, of directly refuting this theory of poetic discourse, independent of its link to literary structuralism; for example, in the form it assumes in Anglo-Saxon logical positivism.)

If some have held the poetic function of discourse to exclude its referential function, this was because, at first, the poem (again understood in a wide sense that includes narrative fiction, lyricism, and the essay) suspends a first-order referential function, whether it is a question of direct reference to familiar objects of perception or of indirect reference to physical entities that science reconstructs as underlying the former objects. In this sense, it is true that poetry is a suspension of the descriptive function. It does not add to our knowledge of objects. But this suspension is the wholly negative condition for the liberation of a more originary referential function, which may be called second-order only because discourse that has a descriptive function has usurped the first rank in daily life, assisted, in this respect, by science. Poetic discourse is also about the world, but not about the manipulable objects of our everyday environment. It refers to our many ways of belonging to the world before we oppose ourselves to things understood as "objects" that stand before a "subject." If we have become blind to these modalities of *rootedness* and *belonging-to* [*appartenance*] that precede the relation of a subject to objects, it is because we have, in an uncritical way, ratified a certain concept of truth, defined by adequation to real objects and submitted to a criterion of empirical verification and falsification. Poetic discourse precisely calls into question these uncritical concepts of adequation and verification. In so doing, it calls into question the reduction of the referential function to descriptive discourse and opens the field of a nondescriptive reference to the world.

It is this nondescriptive reference to the world that is awkwardly covered over by the traits of the emotional function of poetic language. As though emotions were simply "subjective"! What we here are calling emotions, in the wake of poetic language, are precisely modalities of our relation to the world that are not exhausted in the description of objects. Basic emotions such as fear, anger, joy, and sadness express ways of belonging to things as much as ways in which we behave in relation to them; all the more reason why feelings, temperaments, moods, and *Stimmungen,* expressed, shaped, and instructed by poetic language, should throw us into the midst of things.

I will not hesitate to say, given the rapid pace of this refutation of positivism in poetics, that it seems to me that this referential function of poetic discourse conceals a dimension of revelation in a nonreligious, nontheistic, nonbiblical sense of the word, yet a sense capable of furnishing a first approximation of what revelation in the biblical sense might signify.

To reveal is to uncover what until then remained hidden. Now, the objects of our manipulation dissimulate the world of our originary rootedness. Yet in spite of the closed-off character of our ordinary experience, and across the ruins of the intraworldly objects of everyday reality and science, the modalities of our belonging to the world trace out their way. Revelation, in this sense, designates the emergence of another concept of truth than truth as adequation, regulated by the criteria of verification and falsification: a concept of truth as manifestation, in the sense of letting be what shows itself. What shows itself is each time the proposing of a world, a world wherein I can project my ownmost possibilities.

Hence, naming God, before being an act of which I am capable, is what the texts of my predilection do when they escape from their authors, their redactional setting, and their first audience, when they deploy their world, when they poetically manifest and thereby reveal a world we might inhabit.

Biblical Polyphony

It is the naming of God by the biblical texts that specifies the religious at the interior of the poetic.

1. A preliminary remark: the very word "God" primordially belongs to a level of discourse I speak of as *originary* in relation to utterances of a speculative, theological, or philosophical type, such as: "God exists," "God is immutable and omnipotent," "God is the first cause," and so on. I put theological utterances on the same speculative side as philosophical utterances inasmuch as theology's discourse is not constituted without recourse to concepts borrowed from some speculative philosophy, be it Platonic, Aristotelian, Cartesian, Kantian, Hegelian, or whatever. For the philosopher, to listen to Christian preaching is first of all to let go [*se depouiller*] of every form of ontotheological knowledge. Even — and especially when — the word "God" is involved. In this regard, the amalgamation of Being and God is the most subtle seduction.

Modern philosophy accomplishes this letting go of knowledge about God in a certain fashion with its own resources. I am thinking principally of Kant and his general conception of philosophy as knowing our limits. There the index of this letting go is the idea of a "transcendental illusion" that Reason necessarily produces whenever it undertakes to forge a knowledge of God by way of "objects." The paralogisms and antinomies thus become for critical reason the ascetic instruments by which it is led back to itself within those boundaries where its knowledge is valid.

But this letting go of the knowledge of God through the resources of critical philosophy has no apologetic value, even in its negative form. For if a first hubris is knocked down, that of metaphysical knowledge, a second one replaces it, that of a knowledge that is no longer metaphysical but transcendental. This knowledge makes the "I think" the principle of everything that is valid. This knowledge does not stand on the side of objects to be known but on the side of the conditions of possibility of knowing, therefore on the side of the subject. The idea of a subject that posits itself thus becomes the unfounded foundation or, better, the foundation that founds itself, in relation to which every rule of validity is derived. In this way, the subject becomes the supreme "presupposition."

Listening to Christian preaching also stands in the order of presuppositions, but in a sense where presupposition is no longer self-founding, the beginning of the self from and by the self, but rather the assumption of an antecedent meaning that has always preceded me. *Listening excludes founding oneself.* The movement toward listening requires, therefore, a second letting go, the abandoning of a more subtle and more tenacious pretension than that of ontotheological knowledge. It requires giving up [*dessaisissement*] the human self in its will to mastery, sufficiency, and autonomy. The Gospel saying "Whoever would save his life will lose it," applies to this giving up.

This double renouncing of the absolute "object" and the absolute "subject" is the price that must be paid to enter into a radically nonspeculative and prephilosophical mode of language. It is the task of a philosophical hermeneutic to guide us from the double absolute of ontotheological speculation and transcendental reflection toward the more originary modalities of language by means of which the members of the community of faith have interpreted their experience to themselves and to others. It is here where God has been named.

2. A second remark. The naming of God, in the originary expressions of faith, is not simple but multiple. It is not a single tone but polyphonic. The originary expressions of faith are complex forms of discourse as diverse as narratives, prophecies, laws, proverbs, prayers, hymns, liturgical formulas, and wisdom writings. As a whole, these forms of discourse name God. But they do so in various ways.

Indeed, it is worth noting that each of the forms of discourse just mentioned encompasses a particular style of confession of faith where God is named in an original fashion. This is why we miss what is unique about biblical faith if we take categories such as narrative, oracle, commandment, and so on as rhetorical devices that are alien to the content they transmit. What is admirable, on the contrary, is that structure and kerygma accommodate each other in each form of narration. It is within this mutual accommodation of the form and the confession of faith that the naming of God diversifies itself.

The whole of contemporary exegesis has made us attentive to the primacy of the *narrative* structure in the biblical writings. The theology of the Old Testament is first established as a "theology of traditions" around several kernel events: the call of Abraham, the Exodus, the anointing of David, and so forth. The naming of God is thus first of all a narrative naming. The theology of traditions names God in accord with a historical drama that recounts itself as a narrative of liberation. God is the God of Abraham, Isaac, and Jacob. He is, therefore, the Actant of the great gesture of deliverance. And his meaning as Actant is bound up with the founding events in which the community of interpretation recognizes itself enrooted, set up, and established. It is these events that name God.

In this regard, the naming of God in the resurrection narratives of the New Testament is in accord with the naming of God in the deliverance narratives of the Old Testament: God called Christ from the dead. Here, too, God is designated by the transcendence of the founding events in relation to the ordinary course of history.

In this sense, we must say the naming of God is first of all a moment of the narrative confession. God is named in "the thing" recounted. This is counter to a certain emphasis among theologies of the Word that only note word events. To the extent that the narrative genre is primary, God's imprint is in history before being in speech. Speech comes second inasmuch as it confesses the trace of God in the event.

But my concern here is not to deal with the problems of narrative. It is rather to insist upon the variety of ways of naming God that the listener to the Word discovers in the texts of his or her predilection.

The well-known opposition between narration and prophecy first solicits the listener's attention. In narration, no one seems to be speaking. It is as though the events recounted themselves. God, then, is named in the third person within the horizon of the recounted event. In prophecy, the prophetic voice announces itself in the consciousness of being called and sent: "The word of the Lord came to me, saying 'Go and proclaim in the hearing of Jerusalem.'" God is now signified as the voice of an Other behind the prophetic voice. To put it another way, God is named in a double first person, as the word of another in my word. It is easy to understand how, through forgetting the narrative genre and the other genres where God is also named, a certain hypostasis of the prophetic genre could have led to identifying revelation and inspiration and to the entire "subjectivization" of the naming of God. God, named as the voice behind the voice, becomes the absolute subject of discourse. We then break off the essential dialectic between the narrative and the prophetic. We first break it at the level of grammatical persons, the prophetic "I" being always balanced by the narrative "He." But it is also broken at the level of the events themselves, for prophecy is not just its own voice but also what is intended by the event, as with narration. Without locking prophecy into the prediction of the future, prophecy does bear forward toward "the day of Jahweh," concerning which the prophet says it will not be a day of joy, but of terror. This collision between an imminent threat and the remembrance of the founding events introduces a fault into the very meaning of the recounted history. The tension between narration and prophecy thus is expressed in a dialectic of the event, and it gives rise to a paradoxical understanding of history as simultaneously founded in remembrance and menaced through prophecy. In this way, even in the prophetic genre, God is named in and through the event and not just as the voice behind the voice.

All the other genres of discourse in which biblical faith has found expression must be brought together, not just in an enumeration that would juxtapose them, but in a living dialectic that will display their interferences with one another. Thus the prescriptive discourse of the Torah, separated from narrative discourse and prophetic discourse, tends to shrink to the dimensions of an imperative that Kant held to be both heteronomous, owing to its origin as a commandment, and conditional, owing to its conjunction with promises and threats. God is then named as the author of the law. Taken in itself, this naming is not false. It is part of the meaning of this naming that I perceive myself as designated in the second person by God: "*You* shall love the Lord your God with all your heart, and with all your soul, and with all your might." I am this "you." But the meaning of this double naming of God as the law's author and of myself as face-to-face with him is illumined only in the dialectic between prescriptive discourse and the other forms of discourse.

First, the teaching of the Torah is organically linked to the founding events recounted in the great deed for which the Exodus constitutes the kernel. In this way, the promulgation of the law is organically linked to the narrative of deliverance. To this overlapping of the prescriptive and the recitative is added the concrete character of the time of apprenticeship that is attached to the idea of the Covenant, concerning which the modern notion of an imperative expresses only the most abstract trace.

The concrete character of the teaching is confirmed if we also bring together the commandment and the prophetic commission. This, too, designates the prophet as a summoned second person: "(You) go proclaim." The person sent was thus personalized as "you" by the prophetic voice. Then this "you" became the "I" of the double voice of the herald. A similar dialectic of persons is produced by what we could call the ethical voice: the "you" of the summons becomes the responsible "I."

The dialectic of the ethical and the prophetic that is the counterpart of the dialectic of the ethical and the narrative extends beyond the exchange between the prophetic and the ethical voices. It is inscribed in the movement of the commandment, which, in turn, is deployed into the minutia of the innumerable commandments or compressed into the single goal of sainthood and the single commandment of love. The new law, the new covenant, express, if we may put it this way, an ethic based on prophecy. God is then named as the one who says, "A new heart I will give you, and a new spirit I will put within you; and I will take out of your flesh the heart of stone and give you a heart of flesh."

The New Testament takes this interplay of exchanges to the extreme. The new commandment taken up from Deuteronomy leans on the evangelical narrative of the life of the Liberator, and it is through the remembering of the Resurrection and under the sign of the promises of a universal resurrection that the Kingdom of God allows itself to be understood.

Yet the naming of God in narrative, prophecy, and prescription must not be deprived of the enrichment brought by wisdom and hymns. Wisdom is not just contained in the wisdom writings. Overflowing the framework of the Covenant, its meditation bears on the human condition in general. It is directly addressed to the sense and nonsense of existence. It is a struggle for sense in spite of nonsense. Unjust suffering has a central place here to the extent that suffering itself poses its enigma at the juncture between the order of things and the ethical order. This is why wisdom does not so much speak of what ought to be done as of how to endure, how to suffer suffering. The naming of God here is less personalized than in prescription or in prophecy, whether the nothingness of God be brought face-to-face with the incomprehensibility of God in terms of his silence or his absence, or if wisdom itself be celebrated as a barely personalized transcendent entity. A wholly other voice than the prophetic voice or the ethical voice may be heard, which has some traits in common with the narrative "He." At its limit, wisdom discourse encounters a hidden God who takes the anonymous and inhuman course of things as his mask.

The relation to God is internalized in another way with the hymns of celebration, supplication, and thanksgiving. It is no longer just humanity who is a "you" for God, as in the prophetic commission or the ethical commandment. God becomes a "you" to the human you. This movement toward a double second person reaches its highest point in the psalms of recognition just as the movement toward the double first person culminates in the prophetic voice as the voice of an Other.

Thus God is named in diverse ways in narration that recounts his acts, prophecy that speaks in the divine name, prescription that designates God as the source of the imperative, wisdom that seeks God as the meaning of meaning, and the hymn that invokes God in the second person. Because of this, the word "God" cannot be understood as a philosophical concept, not even "Being" in the sense of medieval philosophy or in Heidegger's sense. The word "God" says more than the word "Being," because it presupposes the entire context of narratives, prophecies, laws, wisdom writings, psalms, and so on. The referent "God" is thus intended by the convergence of all these partial discourses. It expresses the circulation of meaning among all the forms of discourse wherein God is named.

Limit-Expressions

The referent "God" is not just the index of the mutual belonging together [*appartenance*] of the originary forms of the discourse of faith. It is also the index of their incompleteness. It is their common goal, which escapes each of them.

Indeed, that God is designated at the same time as the one who communicates through the multiple modalities of discourse just discussed and who also holds back is why the dialectic of the naming of God cannot be transformed into a form of knowledge. In this regard, the episode of the burning bush (Ex. 3:13–15) has a central significance. Tradition has rightly named this episode the revelation of the divine name. This name is precisely unnameable. To the extent that to know a god's name was to have power over him, the name confided to Moses is certainly that of the being whom humanity cannot really name; that is, hold at the mercy of our language. "Then Moses said to God, 'If I come to the people of Israel and say to them, "The God of your fathers has sent me to you," and they ask me, "What is his name?" what shall I say to them?' God said to Moses, 'I am who I am.' And he said, 'Say this to the people of Israel, "I am has sent me to you.""" Thus the appelative "Jahweh" — He is — is not a defining name but one that is a sign of the act of deliverance. Indeed, the text continues in these terms: "God also said to Moses, 'Say this to the people of Israel, "The Lord, the God of your fathers, the God of Abraham, the God of Isaac, and the God of Jacob, has sent me to you": this is my name for ever, and thus I am to be remembered throughout all generations.'" Far, therefore, from the declaration "I am who I am" authorizing a positive ontology capable of capping off the narrative and other namings, instead it protects the secret of the "in-itself" of God, and this secret, in turn, sends us back to the narrative naming through the names of Abraham, Isaac, and Jacob, and by degrees to the other namings.

This recession into infinity of the referent "God" is suggested by the particular structure of certain other forms of the discourse of faith that we have not yet spoken of, which especially belong to the New Testament and more particularly to Jesus' preaching about the Kingdom of God. There, God is named at the same time the kingdom is named. Yet the kingdom is only signified through parables, proverbs, and paradoxes for which no literal translation can exhaust their meaning. This indirect character of the naming of God is especially noteworthy in the parables. We find in them a narrative structure that recalls that of the theology of traditions, yet there are considerable differences. The narration is unfolded less in terms of large historical frescoes of an epical style than as compressed into brief little stories of everyday life whose narrative form recalls that of tragedy or comedy. What is more, just as drama conjoins a "plot" and a "theme" in its structure (*mythos* and *dianoia* in the vocabulary of Aristotle's *Poetics*), the parable has a "point," one signified by the plot itself, and which may easily be converted into a proverb (just as a proverb may become the "point" of a parable if the proverb is given a plot).

It is as plot and as point that the parabolic narrative undergoes a transference of meaning, a metaphorical displacement which, through the crisis and the denouement of the story recounted, obliquely intends the kingdom: "The Kingdom of God is like a . . . " In this way, the parable joins a metaphorical transfer to a narrative structure. But this is not the whole story nor even what is essential. For what carries the literal meaning toward the metaphorical meaning is a characteristic of the plot and the point that is related to a similar characteristic that can be better read from these other forms of discourse.

In the eschatological saying, it is the calculating of the times practiced by apocalypticists that is subverted. "The Kingdom of God is not coming with signs to be observed; nor will they say, 'Lo, here it is!' or 'There!' for behold the Kingdom of God is in the midst of you." The same transgression affects the ordinary use of the proverb, which is meant to provide guidance for living in ordinary circumstances. Paradoxes and hyperboles dissuade the hearer in some way from forming a coherent project of his life and from making his existence into a continuous whole. Paradox: "For whoever would save his life will lose it; and whoever loses his life for my sake and the gospel's will save it." Hyperbole: "But if any one strikes you on the right cheek, turn to him the other also; and if one would sue you and take your coat, let him have your cloak as well; and if any one forces you to go one mile, go with him two miles." In the same way that the proverb—submitted to the law of paradox and hyperbole—only reorients by first disorienting, the parable—submitted to what I call the law of extravagance—makes the extraordinary break forth in the ordinary. Indeed, there is no parable that does not introduce into the very structure of the plot an implausible characteristic, something insolent, disproportionate; that is, something scandalous. Thus it is the contrast between the realism of the story and the extravagance of the denouement that gives rise to the kind of drift by means of which the plot and its point are suddenly carried off toward the Wholly-Other.

If we now bring together what has been said about the unnameable name signified in the episode of the burning bush and this kind of transgressing of the usual forms of the parable, the proverb, and the eschatological saying through the concerted use of extravagance, hyperbole, and paradox, a new category appears that we may call the category of limit-expressions. This is not a supplementary form of discourse, even though the parable as such does constitute an autonomous modality of the expression of faith. It is rather a question of an indication or a modification that undoubtedly affects every form of discourse through a sort of passing over to the limit. If the case of the parable is exemplary, it is because it combines a narrative structure, a metaphorical process, and a limit-expression. In this way, it constitutes a short summary of the naming of God. Through its narrative structure, it recalls the original rootedness of the language of faith in narratives. Through its metaphorical process, it makes manifest the poetic character of the language of faith as a whole. And finally, in joining metaphor and limit-expression, it furnishes the matrix for theological language inasmuch as this language conjoins analogy and negation in the way of emminence: "God is like . . . , God is not . . . "

Poem of God or Poem of Christ?

Some will object that the preceding meditation is too "biblical," if one may put it this way, and not "Christian" enough. I have followed the spoor of the naming of God through the Bible without insisting on the specificity of the naming of God in the New Testament. In opening my run through the various modalities of discourse, I have considered the narration of the Exodus and that of the Resurrection as arising from the same narrative genre. In closing it, I have placed the Unnameable Name from the episode of the burning bush face-to-face with the limit-expressions from the New Testament. As one kind of justification, I might limit myself to asserting that my topic was "God," not

"Christ." But I do not want to elude the objection that holds that the poem of Christ has replaced the poem of God, following the formula of Christian atheism that God is dead in Jesus Christ, with the consequence that the referent "God" recedes to the rank of a simple cultural given that needs to be neutralized. I do not want to avoid this objection because it calls into question the very hypothesis of this meditation, namely that the New Testament continues to name God. I will not hesitate to say that I resist with all my strength the displacement of the accent from God to Jesus Christ, which would be the equivalent of substituting one naming for another.

I hold that what Jesus preaches is the Kingdom of God, which is inscribed in the naming of God by the prophets, the eschatologists, and the apocalyptics. What is the Cross without the cry, "*My God, My God,* why hast thou forsaken me?" inscribed into the naming of God by the psalmist? And what is the Resurrection if it is not an act of God homologous to that of the Exodus? Hence a christology without God seems to me as unthinkable as Israel without Jahweh. And I do not see how it could avoid becoming diluted into an individual or collective anthropology, one that would be entirely horizontal and stripped of its poetic power.

If one says that the God we ought to renounce knowing has made himself known in Jesus Christ, this proposal does not make any sense unless, in confessing the initiative of Jesus' words, we name at the same time Jesus' God. Jesus' humanity is not thinkable as different from his union with God. Jesus of Nazareth cannot be understood apart from God, apart from his God, who is also the God of Moses and the prophets.

Perhaps we can no longer write a christology beginning from above, that is, beginning from Trinitarian speculation, in relation to which the event of Jesus would be contingent. Yet neither can we write a christology beginning from below, that is, beginning from the historical figure of the man Jesus of Nazareth — unless at some point it intersects with the whole naming of God that encompasses Jesus' message and his message *about God*. This point of intersection is the place where Jesus is signified and understood by the confessing community as "the man whose existence is determined by the God he proclaimed" (Pannenberg). What sense would this expression have if we were not capable of understanding together — that is, under the form of the most extreme tension and conflict — God's determining the existence of Jesus *and* the naming of God by all the biblical texts? Perhaps, with Pannenberg, we need to enlarge this circle to include the whole of history, to the extent that we need to see it as the history of the question concerning God and the history of the failure of the quest for God.

Some may say that the relation between the christological ground and this mediation through the whole of history of the names of God is circular. Certainly it is circular. But this circle must itself be courageously assumed. Everything, in one sense, begins with the Cross and Resurrection. But the Cross does not allow itself to be spoken of or understood as the relinquishment of God except in relation to all the signs of God's weakness that belong to the whole naming of God. And the Resurrection may be understood only through the memory of God's liberating acts and in anticipation of the resurrection of every human being.

Hence, it is perhaps the task of christology to maintain, in the interior of the *same* meaning space, as the two antagonistic tendencies of the *same* naming, the celebration of total power, which seems to dominate the Old Testament, and the confession of total weakness, which seems to be declared by the New. It would then be necessary to discover that, on the one side, the total power of the biblical God, once stripped of Greek ideas of immutability and impassivity, already leans toward the total weakness signified by the contestation and failure of God. But it would also be necessary to understand symmetrically that the *kenosis,* signified by the Cross, ceases to be the simple idea that some today would like to draw toward the idea of the death of God, as soon as it is put in relation with the power expressed through Jesus' preaching of the kingdom and the Christian community's preaching of the Resurrection. In this way, the New Testament announces a power of weakness that needs to be dialectically articulated along with the weakness of power that the other namings of God suggest.

In no way do I deny the difficulty of this dialectical labor. It must avoid the constraint of the logic of identity as much as the license of the logic of difference, as well as any false appeasement of the dialectic. The doctrine of the Trinity did this labor for one epoch of thought. A similar labor ought to be undertaken today, one that would take up the whole space of the naming of God and its discordant concordance.

Poetics and Politics

I would like now to link my investigation of the multiple namings of God to my earlier proposal about the revelatory power of poetic language. Three remarks will demarcate the transfer from the text toward life.

1. First, a preliminary question. Shall I take up the idea that the naming of God depends on the poetic word? I will reply: in a certain sense and up to a certain point.

This sense is the one I tried to establish above, which I will summarize in three points. (a) Poetic language is language that breaks with everyday language and that is constituted in the crucible of semantic innovation. (b) Poetic language, far from celebrating language for itself, opens up a new world, which is the issue of the text, the world of the poem. (c) The world of the text is what incites the reader, or the listener, to understand himself or herself in the face of the text and to develop, in imagination and sympathy, the *self* capable of inhabiting this world by deploying his or her ownmost possibilities there. In *this* sense, religious language is a poetic language. Here, the word "poetic" does not designate a "literary genre" that could be added to narration, prophecy, and so on, but the overall functioning of all these genres as the seat of semantic innovation, as the proposition of a world, and as the instigation of a new understanding of oneself.

But religious language is not simply poetic. Or, if one prefers, it is so in a specific manner that makes the particular case a unique one, an eccentric one. What differentiates it is precisely the naming of God. All the literary genres we have referred to, from narration to parable, constitute "speaking about God." This specificity does not abolish any of the poem's characteristics. Rather it adds to the common traits of the poem the circulating of an overarching referent — God — that coordinates the texts at the same time that it escapes them. Touched by God's "name," the poetic word undergoes a mutation of meaning that needs to be circumscribed.

One might be tempted to attach this mutation of meaning exclusively to the role of the limit-expressions (the Unnameable Name, paradox, hyperbole, extravagance). These limit-expressions surely do have the immense virtue of making us aware of the specificity of religious language, but they do not entirely constitute it. They only work within the milieu of a fundamentally analogical or metaphorical language, itself engendered by the narrative, prescriptive, prophetic, and finally parabolic naming of God. These limit-expressions serve to qualify, modify, and rectify this analogical language.

This can be demonstrated in the following way. Narratives, prophecies, laws, and so on, are not established at the level of the concept but at that of the schema. As Kant says concerning the schema of a concept, these are the procedures and methods for providing images not for the concept, nor even for the Idea — as in the theory of aesthetic ideas in the *Critique of Judgment* — but for the Name. Or, to use another vocabulary more familiar to modern epistemology, these schemas are models; that is, rules for producing figures of the divine: models of the monarch, the judge, the father, the husband, the rabbi, the servant. These models are not just, or even principally, models for figures of the divine, but are models for figures of God's accompanying his people, human beings, all of humanity. These schemas or models remain very diversified and heterogenous, and are incapable by themselves of forming a system.

After all, the only systems are conceptual systems. Yet their propensity is toward anthropomorphic representation, toward becoming an idol. The functioning of the model, therefore, must be set within a dialectic of the Name and the Idol. The Name works on the schema or model by making it move, by making it dynamic, by inverting it into an opposed image. (Thus God assumes all the positions in the figures of the family: father, mother, spouse, brother, and finally Son of Man.) Just as, according to Kant, the Idea requires the surpassing of not only the image but also the concept, in the demand to "think more," the Name subverts every model, but only through them.

The role of limit-expressions must be understood within the framework of this dialectic of the Name and the Idol. They are the model's complement and corrective. They are, following a remarkable analysis of Ian Ramsey's, the model's qualifiers.

We may not therefore reduce the mutation of poetic language in religious language, under the pressure of the naming of God, to the single game of limit-expressions. It is the models and their qualifiers taken together that are the seat of this mutation. The result is that the poetics of the name of God — which is expressed principally in the models' labor — is not abolished but intensified through paradox, hyperbole, and all the primary expressions that give rise to the "negative way" at a higher degree of conceptuality (itself only conceivable in relation to the analogical way for which it is the complement and the corrective).

2. My second remark will take us a decisive step along the trajectory from poetics to politics. If I have so resisted the temptation to concentrate all my attention on the subversive character of limit-expressions in relation to the metaphorical character of models, it is in part because the combined interplay of models and their qualifiers continues in a wholly significant fashion in the *practice* that results in the transfer from texts to life.

This practice, it should not be necessary to emphasize, is not external to our understanding the texts of faith. On the one hand, these texts do not exhaust their meaning in some functioning purely internal to the text. They intend a world, which calls forth on our part a way of dwelling there. It is part of the essence of poetics to "remake" the world following the essential intention of the poem. In this sense, the *applicatio* spoken of by the older hermeneutics is indeed the terminal moment of understanding. I prefer to use another language here, but one that I maintain is rigorously synonymous: to understand oneself in front of the text. In its turn, understanding oneself in front of the text is not something that just happens in one's head or in language. It is what the Gospel calls "putting the Word to work." In this regard, to understand the world and to change it are fundamentally the same thing.

Now, in a hermeneutic that puts the accent exclusively on limit-expressions, the self-understanding that corresponds to the demand of the text also takes on an extreme character, the one that Kierkegaard, for example, pushed so far. The logical and practical force of the limit-expressions of Scripture will not be to recommend some type of conduct, whatever it may be, but rather to bring about within the heart of ordinary experience, be it ethical or political, a general suspension to the benefit of what we may symmetrically call life's *limit-experiences*. Of course, the consonance between those limit-experiences and the limit-expressions is not inevitably or uniquely translated into those experiences of catastrophe that Karl Jaspers calls limit-situations: fault, failure, death, struggle. Limit-experiences can also be culminating experiences of creation and joy. Yet they all have in common the surpassing of the ethical and the political at the expense of the positive, although always precarious and provisory, role of the analogical "models."

3. These "models" can nourish an ethical and political reflection inasmuch as they govern the anticipation of a liberated and revived humanity. On this point, I entirely follow André Dumas in his recent attempt (in his *Political Theology and the Life of the Church*) to ground the transition from what he calls metatextual existence to political engagement on the functioning of some typical models from the Old and New Testaments. I also agree with him that the most "telling" [*parlant*] of these models is that of the "fratriarchal" struggle on the horizon of possible reunions. Still, I do not think that in order to assure this transition we may *substitute* a political theology for a hermeneutical one. Just as hermeneutical theology pays heed to the theologies of God's transcendence, to the extent that it preserves the specificity of the naming of God at the heart of the biblical poem, it also attends to political theologies. And it does so in numerous ways. First, in its textual aspect, hermeneutics does not place the accent on the dialogical relation between the author and the reader, or even on the decision taken by the listener to the Word, but rather — and essentially — on the world of the text. It models self-understanding on this world of the text. If language does not exist for itself but in view of the world that it opens up and uncovers, then the interpretation of language is not distinct from the interpretation of the world.

Hence self-understanding in the face of the text will have the same amplitude as the world of the text. Far, therefore, from being closed in upon a person or a dialogue, this understanding will have the multidimensional character of biblical poetics. It will be cosmic, ethical, and political. I hold, therefore, that a hermeneutic that takes the world of the text as its central category does not run the risk of privileging the dialogical relation between the author and the reader or any personal decision in the face of the text. The amplitude of the world of the text requires an equal amplitude on the side of the *applicatio*, which will be as much political praxis as the labor of thought and language.

There is another reason for not substituting a political theology for a hermeneutical theology: If a hermeneutical theology opens in this way to political practice, as one of the dimensions of application that fulfills understanding, it does not in turn become absorbed therein, inasmuch as it is first of all precisely and fundamentally a poetics. If I have so sought to preserve the poetic qualification of the naming of God, it is to preserve the precious dialectic of poetics and politics. Certainly, human existence is political existence. Yet the texts within which Christian existence understands itself are not political to the extent that they are poetical. Thus the models for a partnership [*compagnonnage*] between God and his people and the rest of humanity constitute what I will call a poetics of politics, which, in order to receive a properly political qualification, needs to be articulated through analyses, knowledge, interests, organizations, and so on. To use a Weberian language, I will say that these models only reach the political by nourishing an ethics of conviction that is always irreducible to one of responsibility, which, let it not be forgotten, is also the ethic of the limited use of violence.

9

Prophetic Rhetoric and Mystical Rhetoric

DAVID TRACY

Introduction: Impasse and Exodus

Perhaps we have finally reached the end of the more familiar discussions of Freud and religion. Surely we do not need another round of theologians showing the "ultimate concern" in the works of Freud. Nor do we really need psychoanalysts announcing, once again, that religions are finally, indeed totally, illusion. Orthodox religionists have long since noted the many obvious religious analogues in Freud's work: the founding of the orthodox church, the purges of the heretical "Gnostic" Jung and the "Anabaptist" Adler, the debates over the translations of the sacred texts and their proper modes of interpretation. Orthodox Freudian psychoanalysts have amply demonstrated the psychological realities embedded in many religious phenomena: the obsessional nature of some religious rituals, the overdetermined character of all religious symbols, and even, at times, the original patricide in totemic and monotheistic religions alike. In each case, the list could easily be extended. But should it? Or might it not prove more fruitful to reflect on the clashing rhetorical strategies in this clash of claims? Each rhetorical strategy has now proved its usefulness and its limits. These limits are now clear to everyone except those religionists who cannot help finding religion anywhere a serious concern (that is, literally everywhere) and those psychoanalysts incapable of noticing anything in religion except neurosis. For both these latter analyses, everything is finally the same thing. The only rhetorical strategy approved is a myth of the eternal return of more of the same.

Behind these two exhausted rhetorical moves lie two exhausted rhetorics: on the one side, a rhetoric of "pure science" that is neither pure nor notably scientific; on the other side, a rhetoric of "pure religion" that makes all religions so pure, so loving, so nice that no recognizable historical expression of religion fits the portrait. Even the entry of philosophy can often increase the problem rather than, as promised, resolve it. For any philosophy which effectively denies the reality of the unconscious in favor of its usual claims for consciousness and pure reason can hardly help. Sometimes the philosophies straightforwardly deny that the unconscious means anything other than the preconscious (Jean-Paul Sartre and Simone de Beauvoir). At other times, more fruitful strategies are forged as when philosophers admit the challenge of psychoanalysis and then see what philosophical analysis might have to say in return (Paul Ricoeur and Stanley Cavell).[1] This second kind of move does lead to a new mutual challenge of psychoanalysis and philosophy: at least when Ricoeur's Hegel (rather than Kant) or Cavell's Wittgenstein (rather than Bertrand Russell) helps the post-Freudian philosopher speak back in the presence of, rather than by means of the denial of, the unconscious.

Theologians have an even more difficult task than the philosophers. They, too, are tempted to deny any connection between those two notoriously overdetermined phenomena: the unconscious and religion. They, too, may prefer to rush back to safer rhetorical ground — the endless Western debate on "theism" and "atheism." In arguments for or against the existence of God, after all, there is no unconscious and there often may as well be no historical religion either. On this question of God, all is determined, nothing is overdetermined. Here a consciousness free of any unconscious can have one last fling — proving or disproving "God." Has "God" become the one clear and distinct idea left? Alternatively, "God" may become, for many, the favorite candidate for the "transcendental signified" — briefly mentioned before everyone rushes on to more interesting candidates like the "subject." The problem in all this is that God, religiously construed, is not primarily the problem of consciousness but the question of the unconscious. Mystics (and Jacques Lacan) know this. Most philosophers, theologians, and psychoanalysts do not. This is what makes Lacan's reading of Freud theologically interesting. At last the question of God is not who can produce the best philosophical argument on the implications of consciousness. Nor is the question who (Peter Gay or Hans Küng) can give the best explanation for the fact that Freud's atheism was chronologically prepsychoanalytical.[2]

The first question is not even what is the referent of all this God-talk — or, for that matter, all this talk of the unconscious. Rather the Lacanian reading of Freud suggests a more interesting question: What is the rhetorical character of Lacan's reading of Freud if construed as similar to the clash of two familiar religious rhetorics, the prophetic and the mystical? This new question, to be sure, has its own problems. It can seem to assume that we are all clear on the conflicting psychoanalytic rhetorics of Freud and Lacan, which, despite some fine studies, we are not.[3] The question can also seem to assume that we are all clear on the rhetoric of religion, which, again despite some good studies, we are not.[4] Despite these difficulties, the new question does have one advantage: it allows all rhetorical analysts to suspend the question of the referent, if any, of all this religious God-talk and simply analyze the necessary emergence of "god-terms" in all rhetorics, whether explicitly religious ones like those of the classic prophets and mystics or classically secular ones like Freud's and Lacan's.

To clarify the question itself, the following steps seem appropriate: first, analyze the "rhetoric of religion" and the emergence of "god-terms" in all rhetorics via Kenneth Burke (the best rhetorical analysis of religion available to date);[5] second, complicate Burke's general rhetoric of religion by introducing the more specific and contrasting rhetorics of the two classic religious types — the prophet and the mystic; third, see whether the classic conflict between prophetic and mystical rhetorics may illuminate the analogous clash between the rhetorics of Freud and Lacan. On this reading, the question, Does Lacan read Freud accurately? becomes uncannily similar to the familiar theological question, Can a mystic read correctly the prophetic texts she or he claims to be interpreting? In neither case is the answer self-evident. But by recalling the conflicting rhetorics of prophet and mystic, we may find a new way to suggest what is really at stake in the rhetoric of psychoanalysis itself: that is, the conflicting rhetorics of Freud and Lacan.

The Rhetoric of Religion: Kenneth Burke

Burke has been well described as an "analytical and moralizing therapist of the human mess."[6] Burke, as a good rhetorician, is principally interested in changing fundamental attitudes. We can, he urges, transform our temptations to scientism, romanticism, absolutism, monomania, and so on into a fundamental attitude which, while contemplating generic necessities, can allow us to "dance with tears in our eyes." One can name this Burkean "fundamental attitude," as Burke does, his own "neo-Stoic" resignation. One can also understand it (as I tend to do) as tragicomic: that is, the "representative anecdote" for Burke is closer to the *Oresteia:* three tragedies followed by a satyr play.

This, at least, is the rhetorical structure of *The Rhetoric of Religion*. And since that work rhetorically analyzes our most fundamental attitudes it can serve as a good clue to Burke's own ultimate vision as a tragicomic one. We can use Burke's rhetoric of persuasion on generic necessities in the same way we (most of us, I suspect) have learned to use other great "analytical and moralizing therapists of the human mess" (Aeschylus, Augustine, Calvin, Edwards, Freud, Marx, Nietzsche, and others). All these "masters of suspicion" do provide persuasive analyses of the unnerving presence of certain generic necessities in the human mess. More exactly, there are certain fundamental attitudes in human beings which are frightening (and deserve some good analysis and sometimes, as Freud knew, even moralizing).[7] There are good persuasive reasons why, in concrete cases (for example, Freud's Dora), such analyses do illuminate what the problem may be. For many of our "masters of suspicion" the analysis can quickly become a totalizing interpretation of the "human situation."

But exactly here Burke's own candidate for a generic necessity is illuminating: namely, the drive to perfection seemingly incumbent upon all language use of any terministic screen. This Burkean rhetorical tool does analytically illuminate the totalizing temptation in all positions, including the masters of suspicion and retrieval; the rhetoric of deliberation on a multiplicity of goods; the absolutisms endemic to religion; the scientism endemic to science; the imperialism endemic to rhetoric; and the monomania endemic to most insights — recall René Girard in *Violence and the Sacred* yielding to a kind of monomaniacal totalizing of a good insight.[8]

The heart of Burke's tragicomic vision claims that endemic to human beings (and best disclosed in their language) is a drive to perfection. This drive, when analyzed, discloses a remarkable ambiguity: our creativity is dependent on this drive (and it is the best thing about us). At the same time, we are "rotten with perfection." We turn every insight, every creative activity, into a total system. (Art, science, and religion become Romanticism, scientism, absolutism; technology becomes *Helhaven* on the moon.) What then, in this situation, can we do? We can analyze this entelechy (enter Burke's two rhetorical strategies, dramatism and logology).[9] We can accept our fate by accepting *this* generic necessity. We can cultivate a fundamental attitude that is tragicomic (Freud-Lacan?) and, by that cultivation, we can "purify war" by turning war into, not peace (impossible on this perspective), but conversation, perspective by incongruity, irony, or, as Burke prefers, "dancing with tears in our eyes."

If we are persuaded of the need for a rhetoric of persuasion on fundamental attitudes like Burke's, then our problem becomes a familiar one: How persuasive is Burke's account of this generic necessity (the drive to perfection) and how does it relate to alternative accounts of generic necessities (Augustine, Marx, Freud, Nietzsche, and others)? What is unfamiliar and significant about this new kind of Burkean rhetorical analysis of perfection, however, is that even if Burke's account of the drive to perfection is persuasive, he has also built into his choice what other accounts of the radical ambiguity of the "human mess" possess less clearly: that is, the very necessity and ambiguity of perfection as the key generic necessity leads one to be suspicious of the key itself. This aspect of Burke's rhetoric of persuasion is, I think, more subtle (and, therefore, more persuasive?) than many alternatives. His major competitor for this particular subtlety would seem to be Nietzsche — at least the "new Nietzsche," that honorary French thinker of *différance*. This is probably the reason Burke is sometimes made an honorary member of the "new rhetoric": if Nietzsche can become French, why not Kenneth Burke?

The *Rhetoric of Religion* becomes the ne plus ultra text of all Burke's rhetorics of persuasion on attitudes. Burke is interested in religions because he is interested in attitudes:

> The subject of religion falls under the head of *rhetoric* in the sense that rhetoric is the art of *persuasion,* and religious cosmogonies are designed, in the last analysis, as exceptionally thoroughgoing modes of persuasion. To persuade men toward certain acts, religions would form the kinds of attitude which prepare men for such acts. And in order to plead for such attitudes as persuasively as possible, the religious always ground their exhortations (to themselves and others) in statements of the widest and deepest possible scope, concerning the authorship of men's motives.[10]

The first two sentences of this crucial passage seem a clear illustration of Burke's enterprise: if rhetoric has to do with a persuasion to action by changing attitudes, then study that phenomenon which changes attitudes most "thoroughly." This is also the key to Burke's shift from considering "poetic" language as the privileged instance of "language as symbolic action" to "religious" language as the privileged instance of "language as such as motive." Religions are more "thoroughgoing" than poetic speech or dramas. They will not simply cancel out what we learned under the rubric "dramatism" but (by their greater abstractness, generality, and thoroughness) they will move the analysis of rhetorical persuasion to more general, more thorough, fundamental attitudes.

Hence we need a new form of analysis of this "ultimate" rhetoric of persuasion: namely, a new rhetorical enterprise named logology. But here some confusion enters: that is, logology will be a rhetorical discipline that will study words-about-words and since words-about-words discloses a drive to perfection in all words, then we must study *words*-about-God (god-terms). Is that why we need a rhetoric of religion? Well, not quite — for it seems that it is not so much religion we need to study but "theology." Why? It cannot simply be that theology is more verbal than religion, although that is true and Burke mentions it. For Burke's earlier dramatism already taught us (did it not?) not to have a simple contrast between words and actions.

Something else is at stake — and something, as Burke likes to say, "complicated." My guess is this: religions help Burke to reflect principally on a radicalized, generalized rhetoric of persuasion to attitudes; theologies help Burke to reflect principally on radicalized, generalized analysis of generic necessities (namely, the drive to perfection in all language).

Only logology can move our concerns past all "privileged cases" (whether drama, poetry, or religion) to a study of words as such (words-about-words). But we should still search for some "privileged case" that can at least initiate our analysis. Choose, then, "words-about-God," god-terms. An analysis of "words-about-God" reveals a generic necessity to all words, language, namely, the drive to perfection. God-language (for radical monotheists, at least) is perfection-language — recall Charles Hartshorne on the logic of perfection in God-language.[11] But the "early" Burke already argued that the peculiarity of human beings is that as "symbolic animals," human beings are language-beings. They learn by learning negatives (the prophetic negatives "thou shalt not") in order to create once they learn that they cannot stop going to the end of the line — the line of the widest possible generalization, the most perfect language for the truly creative act — to god-terms. (God *as* Pure Act; Genesis as Pure Act, as origin determining the whole cycle of terms: creation-covenant-guilt-redemption which seem narrative-temporal but are synchronic-systemic.)[12]

We are driven to perfect our creations, our language. We are driven, wherever we begin, to god-terms. The basic necessity for the symbolic animal is to speak, to learn negatives, to create and *not* to stop. Perfection is our telos — which seems to mean, paradoxically, that end *is* origin. Once we acknowledge that nontelos — telos via rhetorical analysis of privileged god-terms — we learn a generic necessity (our necessary drive to perfection) that becomes a vision of "transcendence" informing our move back to history ("the cave"?). Our freedom, as true freedom is determined (reenter Calvin, Spinoza, and Freud). Even "symbol" and "animality" (those two generic necessities of the "symbol-making animal") seem to meet as our creative, symbolic power of words drives us to a perfection-language which returns history to nature, freedom to necessity, and narratives like Augustine's *Confessions* and Genesis to an atemporal cycle of terms. End is origin.[13]

Prophetic Rhetoric and Mystical Rhetoric: Freud and Lacan

Burke's analysis shows, in rhetorical terms, the further meaning of Hegel's or Hartshorne's philosophical interpretations of God-language as perfection-language. A rhetorical analysis, moreover, has one advantage over more purely dialectical enterprises: it opens to an acknowledgment of the reality of the unconscious in the words we use and the god-terms we inevitably employ. The "rottenness of perfection" position of Burke suggests at best ambiguity and, at the limit, overdetermination in all our conscious god-terms.

However, Burke's properly general analysis of the rhetoric of religion as a drive to perfection-language needs further specificity. For religious languages arrive in two basic forms: the rhetoric of the prophet and the rhetoric of the mystic.[14] First, the prophet: the prophet hears a word that is not his or her own. It is Other. It disrupts consciousness, actions, deliberations. It demands expression through the prophet. The prophet is not his own person; something else speaks here. Only on behalf of that Other may the prophet presume to speak her or his warnings, interruptive proclamations, predictions, and promises. Driven by a perfection-language needing god-terms to disclose this Other who or which speaks through the prophet, she or he cannot but speak. The others ordinarily do not want to listen. If matters get bad enough (and they usually will, given the "human mess"), others may begin to listen: first to the puzzling words of the prophet; then to the disturbing words of the Other in those words; then to the word of that Other in themselves. Some listen, some come for help, some are healed. Their healing will rarely prove a full recovery but, like Peter Brown's Augustine or Freud's Dora, more like a continuous convalescence.[15] For consolation from all sorrow they must go elsewhere — to those who deny the Other. For the rhetoric of the prophet can only listen and help them hear the words of the Other in themselves.

Prophets have good reason to be discouraged about how few will listen. "Let him who has ears to hear, hear" is not a ringing assurance of success. Sometimes the prophets reflect their own fury at this Other who insists on speaking in them: witness the lamentations of Jeremiah and many of the letters of Freud. At other times this fury will disclose itself in the gaps, the fissures, the repressions of the prophet's own too-clear prose.[16] At still other times, the prophets (or their successors) will yield to more reflective moods. They will face the fact that people seem to demand, not a word of the Other, but a consolation that cannot be given. They will note that the prophetic word is also "rotten with perfection." Ecclesiastes, that oddest of biblical books, is, rhetorically, that kind of work; so is *Civilization and Its Discontents*.

Freud was not a conquistador. His rhetoric was that of a prophet. Through his words — as clear, definite, and, at the same time, self-interruptive as those of Amos — some Other spoke. Like all prophets, he would not let his prose indulge itself in what, for the prophet, must be viewed as the obscure and bizarre allegories of an apocalypticist nor the weird, uncanny obfuscations of the mystic. He needed words that allowed the unconscious to speak and words persuasive enough to entice others to listen to that Other. But only clear, everyday words rendered with classic humanist restraint could allow that Other to be heard in such manner that others might hear and be persuaded. Freud called his god-term Logos — not mystery, not Other, not law.[17] He called his discipline scientific. Science was for him, as for most in his period, the longed-for language of perfection after other languages (art, religion, myth) had failed. He often wanted to believe that his rhetoric was purely scientific. Happily, it was also something else:[18] a rhetoric of corrigibility, clarity, and a search for evidence that does resemble science; a prose whose subtlety and restraint does resemble Goethe's; yet both that scientific and that humanist prose were finally an interruptive one — constantly interrupted, even disrupted, by the voice of the Other. By trying to render that subversive reality of the unconscious into seemingly scientific and humanist prose, Freud's powerful prophetic rhetoric challenged the ordinary prose of science and humanism alike as surely as the classic prophets' rhetoric, however clear and definite, smashed against the iconic proses, the idols, of the people. The prose becomes more and more polyvalent as it turns upon others and itself through the strange stories it narrates so well and the even stranger fissures and lapses it harbors within its own definiteness.

Finally every word, including every word about words, becomes not merely ambiguous and polyvalent, as Burke sees, but overdetermined and disseminating — as Freud saw. The very material reality of these words of the Other invades all words — even the scientific words of Freud, the humanistic prose, the care and search for clarity and harmony. In that sense, Freud's persuasive prophetic rhetoric becomes, in his greatest texts, something like a kabbalistic palimpsest filled with words whose very materiality are the central clues to the revealing and concealing of the Other-in-words.[19]

Freud may have wished to produce a purely scientific body of work. In one sense, he did. But he also produced something more — a prophetic rhetoric of persuasion to the Other. He may have called his god Logos but he was no neo-Platonist. As a "godless Jew," he consciously ignored the prophets, the rabbis, and the kabbalists only to have their most typical rhetorical strategies emerge in his own German-Greek humanist prose. Even as a Greek, he was odd: he praised Logos as much as any Platonist in the first academy but often wandered out of Plato's academy to attend to the forbidden texts of Aeschylus and

Sophocles. Like so many Greeks of the classical age, he also seemed to long for some other wisdom, some other god-term than Logos. As Herodotus makes clear, for the classical Greek imagination, Egypt became the land where another wisdom — the wisdom of the Other? — may lie. Thus did the great Greek-Jew Freud often travel in his imagination to Egypt. Even Moses must become an Egyptian. Then his "murder" by the Jews and his puzzling Exodus from the homeland of Egypt might finally be intelligible.[20] Even Plato and Pythagoras — with their god Logos — must have learned from Egypt.

Freud's god-term was not "God" — and surely not the radically monotheistic God of Ahkenaton and Moses. It was also not really Logos, nor was it the radically monotheistic science of the philosophes and the nineteenth-century scientists. His god-term was not even the Unconscious. Indeed, the discovery of the unconscious teaches once again the most ancient of Jewish commands: the god-term should remain unnameable; it is not to be named. All we have are the words of the Other: material words to be deciphered and even then only partially understood by this nonbelieving prophet and this nonobservant kabbalist. What Freud sometimes wanted — from his god-term Logos — was a stabilizing rhetoric of the topics. What he received — from the Other in the unconscious — was a radically destabilizing prophetic rhetoric of the tropes. Lacan spotted this secret of the prophet with all the self-confidence of a mystic assuming that only he could understand what the prophet really meant. For mystics, unlike prophets, have no hesitation in allowing the destabilizing discourse of the Other the fullest sway.

Mystical religious discourse is startlingly different from prophetic discourse. Both are driven by an impulse toward perfection in their words about the Word. Both seem driven by an Other who speaks. For the prophet, the Other is Word acknowledged in a word of proclamation ("Thus says the Lord") that disrupts the prophet's own consciousness and disseminates the ego.[21] For the prophet, that Word, as One, demands a new center of unity beyond the ego. For the prophet is not her or his own person. The prophet, as responsible to the *fascinans et tremendum* of the Word, must become a new, responsible self — responsible to others, to history, to the cosmos, because made a responsible self by the Other-as-Word.[22] Only by losing the self can a new self be gained. The Word, the god-term named God, must remain Other or else the other in the new, responsible self cannot speak. The great Western monotheistic traditions (Judaism, Christianity, Islam) live by and through this prophetic rhetoric on the one God and the newly unified, responsible, othered self.

For many Eastern mystical traditions this prophetic discourse on God and the self is a symptom of the deeper problem, not an expression of the solution. For the most radical of these traditions, the Ch'an and Zen forms of Mahayana

Buddhism, the prophet clings to a double illusion: that there is an Other that is Other (and thereby to be worshiped and trusted as "God") and that there is a self at all. Only by letting go of this form of primary ignorance (*advaita*) can all clinging and ultimately all desire cease. There is no "God" and there is no "self." Since there is not even a real nirvana and a real samsara, we must also not cling to enlightenment itself. For nirvana and samsara are one — one (more exactly, "not two") in their emptiness — but not one in the union/encounter of the prophet and the covenanting God, not one in the radical identity of the Hindu Shankara's Brahman-beyond-God and Atman-beyond-the-self.

This most radical of Buddhist mystical rhetoric illustrates, by its very radicality, certain crucial features of all mystical traditions: even the usually marginalized strands of mysticism in the Western prophetic traditions, even that of Buddhism's greatest opponent — the Vedantic tradition of Hinduism — even that of the return of the Other in the "other-power" of Pure Land Buddhism. For all mystics want to say something more than the prophet is willing to say — and say it as what the prophet really meant or should have meant. Zen Buddhist rhetoric does have certain affinities with some Western rhetorics — but not, I believe, with either Freud or Lacan. Rather Zen Buddhist rhetoric is far more like Derrida's. Indeed Nagarjuna and Derrida,[23] with all their differences, are natural allies with their insistence on nonpresence, their attempts to undo dialectic dialectically, and their disclosures of the radical instability of all linguistic attempts to secure a determinate meaning. Even the "undeterminate" will not suffice: Derrida's *différance* is not a candidate for a new transcendental category; Nagarjuna's no-self is not a doctrine, for it neither exists nor does not exist; both discover the play of Nothingness behind the mere nihility of all tragic humanisms obsessed with a "self."

However, this kind of radical Zen and deconstructionist discourse does not really fit the kind of rhetoric in the destabilizing tropes of Lacan. For an analogy to Lacan, we must return to the Western monotheistic traditions and note a peculiar kind of apophatic mysticism emerging there. The rhetoric of the great Western love-mystics (Bernard of Clairvaux, Teresa of Avila, John of the Cross) may attract a Julia Kristeva with her post-Lacan and anti-Derrida semiotic rhetoric of a subject-in-process in transference love.[24] But all — literally all — that interests Lacan in Teresa of Avila is her *jouissance* and the excess and radical negations it discloses.[25] But that all is everything and the clue of the radically apophatic, but not Zen, rhetoric of Lacan.

Mystics in prophetic traditions (as all Western monotheisms are) always have problems. Unless they are very cautious in their marginalized place, some prophet (or more likely, some hierarch with prophetic pretensions) will accuse them of betrayal. Where is the God of the prophets in the Godhead-beyond-

God of Meister Eckhart? Where are the energetics of Freud's unconscious in the linguistic Unconscious of Lacan? Where is the radically monotheistic God and the responsible self in the apophatic Jewish, Christian, and Muslim mystics? Where is Freud's god Logos, and where is the ego in the uncontrollable prose and the unnerving tropes of Lacan? Have the Western apophatic mystics betrayed the prophets for neo-Platonism? Has Lacan betrayed Freud for Hegel and Heidegger?

At first, it may seem that monotheism is still honored by the mystics and a scientific Logos is honored by Lacan. For the mystic will try to reduce the world portrayed in the Bible to its most basic elements (God, world, soul) in order to observe their structural relationships. Mystics almost always have some basic grammar as their first move. Even Buddhists have the language of "dependent originations." Even Eckhart possesses a highly peculiar grammar of analogy.[26] Lacan will also pay his tribute to structural relationships (and, thereby, "science") as his first move. Indeed, he will insist that only Saussure's linguistics (unfortunately not available to Freud) can render scientific the discovery of the unconscious — an unconscious, of course, structured like a language. Every apophatic mystic in the monotheistic prophetic traditions will answer their critics in much the same way: unfortunately, the prophets who wrote our sacred texts did not have available to them a grammar of the structural relationships of God-world-soul; fortunately, this grammar is now available to interpret the text correctly.

If the grammatical-structuralist move is the only move that the mystic makes, then all may be well: as the love-mystics hoped, as religious metaphysicians like Aquinas insist, as the Jungians with their strangely morphological if not structuralist archetypes believe, as all structuralists, from Saussure to Lévi-Strauss, find sufficient.

But what if a second move is made? What if the apophatic element in mystical discourse takes a radical turn? Then, as in Pseudo-Dionysius, John Erigena, and Eckhart, the basic structural elements themselves (God-world-soul) dissolve into one another as self-negating, self-dissolving. When Eckhart paradoxically prays, "I pray to God to save me from God," he is not speaking classical prophetic rhetoric of humble submission to the will of God. He is rather apophatically moving. But where? Perhaps, after all, into a radical mystical rhetoric of the Other, the "Godhead beyond" the prophets' God? When Eckhart proclaims a vision of "Leben ohne Warum" as a model for the self which is no-self he is far, indeed, from the responsible self of the prophets as well as far from the agapic-erotic self of the Christian love-mystics. When Lacan informs us that "the unconscious is structured like a language" only then to insist that there is no unitary sign since the signifiers and not the signifieds rule (S/s), we are far, indeed, from the "sign" of Saussure and the god Logos of the scientific side of Freud. We are somewhere else. Perhaps in the discourse of the Other? Perhaps in the apophatic excess of *jouissance?* Surely not in the ego.

Like Eckhart with his strange appeals to the more orthodox analogical rhetoric for God-language of his fellow Dominican Thomas Aquinas, Lacan will also occasionally appeal to more orthodox views of the Other. Hence Lacan will appeal to the dialectical rhetoric of the Other in that strangest of orthodox Lutherans, Hegel, and the rhetorical poetics on "Language Speaks" in that oddest of post-Catholic Catholics, Heidegger.[27] In Lacan's rhetoric there speaks, it seems, not only the Unconscious but the Other of the two most significant Greek-Christians of modernity, the Protestant Hegel and the Catholic Heidegger. Both of them, after all, often read as gnomically as Eckhart (whom, not surprisingly, they both respected). Both of them also wanted an end to "theism" and "atheism" alike in favor of an Other who is finally allowed to speak. The orthodox psychoanalytic institutions may expel Lacan as firmly as the papal commission at Avignon condemned certain propositions of Eckhart. Yet both would continue to insist on their higher orthodoxy: for them, only the mystic understands what the prophet really meant for only the mystic knows both the basic structure of the whole and its radically destructuring actuality.

But even the mystic may eventually find it necessary to adopt a prophetic rhetoric and proclaim the word of the Other. Otherwise, the others in their secure institutions will trivialize and reify the words of the Other once again. If necessary, prophetic actions may follow: leave the official institution, open a new one, close it, and start again is an all too familiar prophetic activity. The careers of Eckhart and Lacan are often as uncannily parallel as their apophatic rhetorics. Neither was interested in either "theism" or "atheism." That quarrel they left to those who did not understand the Other at all. They wanted *jouissance* and the uncanny tropes familiar in the authentic speech of the Other.

The question Does Lacan interpret Freud correctly? therefore bears remarkable resemblance to the question Does the apophatic mystic interpret the prophetic texts correctly? Despite the decrees of Avignon, the case of Eckhart is still open; so is the case of Lacan. If the prophetic rhetoric needing interpretation is itself, often despite itself, also a speech of the Other, it also becomes mystical rhetoric. Then the chances are reasonably good that a mystical interpretation may take hold. And if the mystic, however reluctantly, is forced into a prophetic role, the chances are even better. But neither the theist nor the atheist, neither the scientistic scientist nor the romantic mythologist (Jung?), need enter this debate. The debate between the prophet and the mystic is elsewhere. It is beside itself. It is a rhetoric of the Other.

Notes

1. See Paul Ricoeur, *Freud and Philosophy: An Essay in Interpretation,* trans. David Savage (New Haven: Yale University Press, 1970); Stanley Cavell, "Psychoanalysis and Cinema: The Melodrama of the Unknown Woman," in Francoise Meltzer, ed., *The Trial(s) of Psychoanalysis* (Chicago: University of Chicago Press, 1988), 227–58.

2. Peter Gay, *A Godless Jew: Freud, Atheism, and the Making of Psychoanalysis* (New Haven: Yale University Press, 1987); Hans Kung, *Freud and the Problem of God,* trans. Edward Quinn (New Haven: Yale University Press, 1979).

3. Patrick J. Mahoney, *Freud as a Writer* (New York: International Universities Press, 1982); Samuel Weber, *The Legend of Freud* (Minneapolis: University of Minnesota Press, 1982).

4. Representative studies may be found in Robert Alter and Frank Kermode, eds., *The Literary Guide to the Bible* (Cambridge: Harvard University Press, 1987).

5. Kenneth Burke, *The Rhetoric of Religion* (Berkeley: University of California Press, 1970).

6. In an unpublished paper by David Smigelskis for the Seminar in Rhetoric in the Committee on Analysis of Ideas and Study of Methods at the University of Chicago, 1984.

7. On this aspect of Freud, see Philip Rieff, *Freud: The Mind of a Moralist* (Chicago: University of Chicago Press, 1979).

8. René Girard, *Violence and the Sacred,* trans. Patrick Gregory (Baltimore: Johns Hopkins University Press, 1977).

9. For two studies of Burke, see Frank Lentricchia, *Criticism and Social Change* (Chicago: University of Chicago Press, 1983); William H. Rueckert, *Kenneth Burke and the Drama of Human Relations* (Berkeley: University of California Press, 1982). For the present analysis, besides *The Rhetoric of Religion,* Burke's central texts are *The Philosophy of Literary Form* (New York: Vintage, 1941), *A Grammar of Motives* (Berkeley: University of California Press, 1969), and *A Rhetoric of Motives* (Berkeley: University of California Press, 1969).

10. Burke, *Rhetoric of Religion,* v.

11. Charles Hartshorne, *Man's Vision of God and the Logic of Theism* (Chicago: Willett, Clark, 1941).

12. See Burke's unusual analysis of Genesis in *Rhetoric of Religion.*

13. A Burkean conclusion remarkably similar to that of Mircea Eliade on cosmogonic myths. See Mircea Eliade, *The Myth of the Eternal Return* (Princeton: Princeton University Press, 1971), and Eliade, *The Sacred and the Profane: The Nature of Religion,* trans. William R. Trask (New York: Harper and Row, 1961).

14. The same contrast can be made by distinguishing "manifestation" and "proclamation": see Chapter 8: Paul Ricoeur, "Naming God," as well as his "Manifestation and Proclamation," *Journal of the Blaisdell Institute* 12 (Winter 1978), and my own refor-

mulation in *The Analogical Imagination: Christian Theology and the Culture of Pluralism* (New York: Crossroad, 1981).

15. Peter Brown, *Augustine of Hippo: A Biography* (Berkeley: University of California Press, 1970).

16. For a good example see Francoise Meltzer, "The Uncanny Rendered Canny: Freud's Blind Spot in Meeting Hoffmann's 'Sandman,'" in Sander L. Gilman, ed., *Introducing Psychoanalytic Theory* (New York: Columbia University Press, 1982), 218–39.

17. Sigmund Freud, *The Future of an Illusion* (New York: Vintage, 1975).

18. A reinterpretation of Wittgenstein's remarks on Freud leads to a similar conclusion, as argued in the doctoral dissertation "Psychoanalysis, Grammar, and the Limits of Critique," by Charles Elder (University of Chicago, 1991), and by Jacques Bouveresse in *Wittgenstein Reads Freud: The Myth of the Unconscious,* trans. Carol Cosman (Princeton: Princeton University Press, 1995).

19. This textual resemblance is not dependent on historical influence. The latter claim seems far more dubious: for the claim itself, see David Bakan, *Sigmund Freud and the Jewish Mystical Tradition* (Boston: Beacon, 1975). For rhetorical analyses of the classical "Jewish" ways of reading texts, see Susan A. Handelman, *The Slayers of Moses: The Emergence of Rabbinic Interpretation in Modern Literary Theory* (Albany: State University of New York Press, 1982), and Harold Bloom, *Kabbalah and Criticism* (New York: Seabury, 1975).

20. Sigmund Freud, *Moses and Monotheism* (New York: Vintage, 1967).

21. Cf. James Luther Mays and Paul J. Achtemeier, eds., *Interpreting the Prophets* (Philadelphia: Fortress, 1987) and Alter and Kermode, *Literary Guide to the Bible.*

22. See Richard H. Niebuhr, *Radical Monotheism and Western Culture* (New York: Harper and Row, 1970).

23. See Robert Magliola, *Derrida on the Mend* (West Lafayette, Ind.: Purdue University Press, 1984). This difference may also help interpret the differences of Lacan and Derrida: on the latter, see Barbara Johnson, "The Frame of Reference: Poe, Lacan, Derrida," in Johnson, *The Critical Difference: Essays in the Contemporary Rhetoric of Reading* (Baltimore: Johns Hopkins University Press, 1980).

24. Julia Kristeva, *Tales of Love,* trans. Leon S. Roudiez (New York: Columbia University Press, 1987).

25. Lacan and the *école freudienne,* "God and the Jouissance of the Woman," in Juliet Mitchell and Jacqueline Rose, eds., *Feminine Sexuality* (New York: Norton, 1982), 137–49.

26. On Eckhart, see *Meister Eckhart: The Essential Sermons, Commentaries, Treatises, and Defense,* ed. and trans. Edmund Colledge and Bernard McGinn (New York: Paulist Press, 1981). See also John Caputo, *Heidegger and Aquinas: An Essay on Overcoming Metaphysics* (New York: Fordham University Press, 1982).

27. On Lacan's relationships to Hegel and Heidegger, see the representative studies of William Richardson, Edward Casey, and Antoine Vergote in Joseph H. Smith and William Kerrigan, eds., *Interpreting Lacan* (New Haven: Yale University Press, 1983).

10

Apophatic Analogy: On the Language of Mystical Unknowing and Being-Toward-Death

THOMAS A. CARLSON

And the bold request which goes up the mountains of desire asks this: to enjoy the Beauty not in mirrors and reflections, but face to face. The divine voice granted what was requested in what was denied, showing in a few words an immeasurable depth of thought. The munificence of God assented to the fulfillment of [Moses'] desire, but did not promise any cessation or satiety of the desire. He would not have shown himself to his servant if the sight were such as to bring the desire of the beholder to an end, since the true sight of God consists in this, that the one who looks up to God never ceases in that desire. For he says: You cannot see my face, for man cannot see me and live.
— Gregory of Nyssa, Life of Moses, 2.232–33

For love is strong as death.
Song of Songs 8:6

The rhetorical modes of "negative" or "apophatic" theology — and of its twin, "mystical" theology — have since the 1970s attracted serious inquiry and extended discussion not only among theologians but also among literary theorists, historians, psychoanalytic theorists, and philosophers, who tend to share three interconnected concerns: the human subject's finitude, its situation in language, and its desire. Among post-Heideggerian thinkers in particular, the fascination with textual and discursive traditions deriving from the negative theology of Pseudo-Dionysius (flourished ca. 500) almost always involves a fascination as well with the radically finite, desiring subject of language — to the point that one might suspect contemporary interest in negative theology to constitute at bottom a concern with negative anthropology.[1] Indeed, in light of the insistent conjunction between reflection on negative theological rhetoric and reflection on the finitude of human existence, one might rightly ask whether these contemporary approaches to the apophatic traditions simply mistake for an ever desired but unknowable God a desiring human subject who remains opaque to itself. Do they constitute a misguided effort to baptize the abysses of a purely human, linguistic existence with the name of apophatic theology's mystically unknowable and thus unnameable God?[2] This question can be answered — or better, suspended — insofar as we gain access to a point at which the negative logic of Being-toward-God within classic apophatic and mystical rhetorics reveals a strikingly forceful analogy to the negative logic of Being-toward-death in contemporary (largely Heideggerian or post-Heideggerian) discourse on human finitude. The present essay aims to open such access.

The Apophatic Rhetoric of Mystical Unknowing: Dionysian Foundations

The traditions of apophatic theology in Western Christianity derive primarily from the Eastern writings of the Pseudo-Dionysius, who claimed to be — and was long accepted as — Dionysius the Areopagite, the Athenian convert of Saint Paul who appears in Acts 17:34. Including the treatises *Divine Names, Mystical Theology,* and the *Celestial* and *Ecclesiastical Hierarchies,*[3] the Dionysian writings were viewed in the Middle Ages as having an authority whose antiquity was surpassed only by that of the Bible itself. Accordingly, Dionysius's influence in the Middle Ages actually matches that of Augustine,[4] and although the Dionysian vision shapes medieval theology, spirituality, and aesthetics in manifold ways, one can see at the heart of this influence, and at the heart of contemporary interest in Dionysius, the distinctively Dionysian uses of language — above all in its "negative" forms and functions.[5] Here, then, we should briefly explicate the forms and functions of negativity in Dionysian rhetoric by situating them within the overall framework of the Dionysian system.

"Apo-phasis," an "un-saying" that denies or negates, constitutes the most noted rhetorical mode of the mystical traditions that derive from Pseudo-Dionysius, and its operation stems from the premise that God must ultimately

remain inconceivable and therefore ineffable. Following the logic of this premise, any thinking discourse concerning God must finally proceed negatively
and paradoxically by removing or undoing thought and language, precisely
through the linguistic practice of apophasis or unsaying, about the God who
would only thus be known rightly—that is, as unknown. The rhetoric of
apophasis, by attempting to transcend language through language, serves as
the indispensable vehicle for a spiritual practice that seeks a knowledge of the
unknowable. The language of apophasis in Dionysius, however, is never fixed
or final, for it always operates only in and through its tension with the *kataphatic* or affirmative modes of language that it seeks to undo.

   Furthermore, contrary to those who would imagine "negative" or apophatic theology as the mere reversal of "affirmative" or kataphatic theology
within a straightforward, binary system, Dionysius in fact deploys three distinct modes of theological language, which are informed and linked by two
different movements of negation.[6] The apophatic or unsaying mode of language, in other words, will itself need to be negated or unsaid. The Dionysian
uses of language thus involve an affirmative or kataphatic mode, a negative or
apophatic mode, and a doubly negative or "hyper-negative"[7] mode of the
apophatic which we can identify as the "mystical." These three modes of
language function as a whole to promote or embody a spiritual practice that
would lead the created soul toward a "mystical unknowing," or *agnosia*, of
the God who remains in principle and in experience inconceivable and ineffable. The logic that determines Dionysius's threefold language is therefore not
merely theoretical or speculative but practical, for the operations of Dionysian
language determine at the most concrete levels the spiritual and liturgical
activities of the individual and community who seek an ineffable God.[8]

   By means of this theological language, Dionysius articulates a cosmic order
and a movement of the created soul within that order which are both essentially ecstatic: the cosmos as a whole is structured and driven by the ecstatic
self-giving of divine love or eros (which Dionysius identifies with *agape*),[9] and
to that divine love the constitutive desire of created beings ecstatically answers. The "cause of the universe"—which Dionysius understands in terms of
"the Beautiful and the Good"—is "beguiled by goodness, by love, and by
yearning and is enticed away from his transcendent dwelling place and comes
to abide within all things" (DN 712B); correspondingly, those things themselves "must desire, must yearn for, must love, the Beautiful and the Good"
(DN 708A). In this world where "all being drives from, exists in, and is returned toward the Beautiful and the Good" (DN 705D), the causal Beauty (*to
kalon*) of the divine generously calls (*kaleo*) all beings to be, and "it is the very
longing for beauty which actually brings them into being" (DN 704A). All

movement in this Dionysian world, then, as articulated in the movement of Dionysian language itself, proves at bottom to be a movement of love, a dynamic of call and response between divine generosity and created desire — an erotic circle in which "both the desire and the object of that desire belong to the Beautiful and the Good" (DN 712B).

Within the threefold framework that Dionysius constructs to articulate such cosmic order and movement, the three modes of theological language correspond to three modes of the divine within its causal relation to the cosmos.[10] Dionysius articulates this threefold arrangement succinctly in his *Mystical Theology:*

> What has actually to be said about the cause of everything is this. Since it is the cause of all beings, we should posit and ascribe to it all the affirmations we make in regard to beings [*pasas tas ton onton tithenai kai kataphaskein theseis*], and, more appropriately, we should negate all these affirmations [*kai pasas autas kurioteron apophaskein*], since it surpasses all being. Now we should not conclude that the negations [*apophaseis*] are simply the opposite of the affirmations [*kataphasesin*], but rather that the cause of all is considerably prior to this, beyond privations, beyond both every denial and every assertion [*huper pasan kai aphairesin kai thesin*]. (MT 1000B)

As Dionysius here indicates, the first mode of theological language, the affirmative or kataphatic, makes positive statements about God that are based analogically on a knowledge of God through creation, for as creative Cause, God "has the names of everything that is" (DN 596C), "every attribute may be predicated of him" (DN 824B);[11] this mode of language therefore corresponds primarily to the procession or advance (*prohodos*) of the divine "out" of itself into the immanence of the cosmos, and in this sense affirmative or kataphatic language signals the creative, loving ecstasy of the divine.[12]

The second mode of language, the "apophatic" mode strictly speaking, negates or removes all affirmations made in the kataphatic mode in order thereby to signal the transcendence of the creator over all he creates, to signal that while "in" all things, the Cause of all "is also superior to them because he precedes them and is transcendently above them" (DN 824B19). The "unsaying" movement of apophatic language is aphairetic (from *aphaireo*, to take away, remove, deprive), and thus it functions most notably through the negative force of the alpha privative: removing any thought, discourse, or name that might be affirmed of the divine in the kataphatic mode, the negative prefix "a-" articulates the divine as mind "not thought on" (*nous a-noetos*), as unsaid word (*logos a-rhetos*), as utterly name-less (*an-onumos*). Through such negation or removal, through such deprivation, this second mode of language articulates and promotes a return movement (*epistrophe*) of the created soul beyond the totality of created beings, including itself, back toward the transcendence of the creative divinity; in this sense apophatic language corresponds to an erotic ecstasy of the creature.

Finally, the third, or "mystical" mode of language in Dionysius — who in fact originates the phrase "mystical theology" — passes beyond both affirmation and its simple negative reversal through the use of a doubly negative or doubly apophatic rhetoric of "hyper-" terms. Following a rigorous "neither/ nor" logic, Dionysius uses the preposition and prefix "hyper-" to indicate that the divine finally remains (in its *mone*) beyond (*huper*) both simple affirmation (*kai thesin*) and simple negation (*kai aphairesin*). According to this mystical mode of hyper-negative language,

> there is no speaking of [the cause of all], nor name nor knowledge of it [*oude logos autes estin oute onoma oute gnosis*]. It is neither darkness nor light, neither error nor truth [*oude skotos estin oute phos, oute plane oute aletheia*]. Of it there is neither assertion nor denial [*oude . . . thesis oute aphairesis*]. We make assertions and denials of what is next to it, but never of it, for it is both beyond every assertion [*huper pasan thesin*], being the perfect and unique cause of all things, and, by virtue of its preeminently simple and absolute nature, free of every limitation; it is also beyond every denial [*huper pasan aphairesin*]. (MT 1048B)

Whereas the absolute simplicity of the divine pertains both to "the assertion of all things" and to "the denial of all things" (*he panton thesis, he panton aphairesis*), theological language can finally rest in neither, since the divine ultimately remains beyond both — "beyond every assertion and denial [*to huper kai thesin kai aphairesin*]" (DN 641A). Passing in this way beyond assertion and denial, beyond both kataphatic thesis and the apophatic removal (*aphairesis*) of every thesis, this third, hyper-negative mode of theological language points beyond both procession and reversion, and it thus pertains to the superineffable goal of a reunion in which the created soul would have abandoned all thought (or nonthought) of beings, including itself, within the God beyond Being. It is precisely because that union itself can never be articulated directly in language — either affirmative or negative — that it requires the movement of a hyper-negative language which neither simply affirms nor simply negates, neither simply posits nor simply removes, but rather oscillates endlessly, excessively, between these two poles.[13]

The excessive oscillation in Dionysius between affirmative and negative modes of language embodies, or perhaps engenders, a desire for God that comes to no end, not even — or indeed especially — in the highest union with

God. For according to Dionysius, union with God intensifies desire rather than sating it; the closer the soul moves toward God, the greater its desire grows, to the point where the soul is entirely consumed and thereby undone. A central figure for such desire in Dionysius is the seraphic angel — the highest of those beings whose basic condition is desire for God (DN 716A), the divine messenger who in moving closer to divine union becomes ever more ecstatic and burns in the flame of its consuming love for God, the figure of language whose voice of praise therefore becomes most intense on the threshold of dissolution.

Within the history of Christian spirituality, this Dionysian understanding of desire and divinizing union (the *henosis* that Dionysius equates with *theosis*) stands clearly in line with the radical expectation or *epektasis* that character-izes the return to God in Gregory of Nyssa (d. 395), and it likewise stands in sharp contrast to the satiety which return to God brings for Origen (d. ca. 253).[14] According to the Dionysian scheme, all created beings exist by strain-ing dynamically, ecstatically, between the nothingness from which they are called by the incomprehensible love of God and that same unknowable God for whom they therefore endlessly yearn. As we have noted, the cosmic beauty (*to kalon*) through which this divine goodness manifests its hiddenness func-tions precisely in and as a language — that of the call (*kaleo*, to call, to sum-mon) which brings all beings to be (see DN 701D, 704A, 704B). Dionysius's basic modes of theological language embody this structure and movement of call and response, at the center of which remains the superineffable goodness to which created beings long to return. Among those modes, the two "nega-tive" modes especially function to lead the created soul back to God. But how precisely do the negative modes of language effect such a return?

Through the negation of thought and language pertaining to things and beings in the world, the negative modes of theological language are intended to carry the soul toward that God who is "beyond Being," the God who — recalling the Platonic and Neoplatonic "Good beyond Being" (*epekeina tes ousias*) — is not a being but rather a not-being, or literally a no-thing. God for Dionysius not a being or thing, and insofar as thought and its language pertain only to beings or things, they cannot open access to God except in their being negated or undone. But such negation must itself be negated if it is truly to be unknowing, for a negation that simply reverses affirmation, a determinate negation, still knows what it is doing. The goal or summit of such double negation, then, is the mystical "unknowing" in which the soul would be un-done or deprived of all thought and language as such — affirmative or negative. Such a radical undoing or deprivation would therefore imply the absence or impossibility of any "experience" that requires a thinking subject of language.

Thus, the logic of the "hyper-negative" rhetoric that marks the summit of Dionysian theology concerns not only the incomprehensibility and ineffability of God but also the dispossession of the self in its movement toward such a God. In his *Mystical Theology*, Dionysius explains: "By an undivided and absolute abandonment of yourself and everything, shedding all and freed from all, you will be uplifted to the ray of the divine shadow which is above every-thing that is" (MT 997B–1000A). The self abandons itself in and through the denial and transcendence of all beings, a denial and transcendence that are themselves denied and transcended; such a redoubled negation and abandon-ment — carried out through a self-negating negative language, or a radically "self-subverting utterance"[15] — alone make possible the impossible knowledge of an unknowable God. Dionysian language does not simply describe this abandonment and denial but indeed constitutes their very movement.

The impossible knowledge of God, which Dionysius articulates as the "un-knowing" (*agnosia*) toward which his theological language would carry or drive the soul, marks the mystical summit wherein union with God would undo the self as a subject of language. Literally hyperbolic, such language throws the subject of language beyond both its language and its subjectivity, into a "nowhere" or "nothing" of experience. Dionysius figures this utopic summit of unknowing by reference to Moses' encounter with God on Mount Sinai:[16]

> But then [Moses] breaks free . . . , away from what sees and is seen, and he plunges into the truly mysterious darkness of unknowing. Here, renouncing all that the mind may conceive, wrapped entirely in the intangible and the invisible, he belongs completely to him who is beyond everything. Here, being neither oneself nor someone else [*oute heautou oute heterou*], one is su-premely united by a completely unknowing inactivity of all knowledge, and one knows beyond the mind by knowing nothing [*to pantelos de agnosto tes pases gnoseos anenergesia kata to kreitton henoumenos kai to meden ginos-kein huper noun ginoskon*]. (MT 1001A)

Dionysius's mystical unknowing of the God who is nothing would mark the summit of the soul's spiritual path, but at that hyper-negative, agnostic sum-mit the soul is neither itself nor another — and therefore cannot be present or self-present in the consciousness or language of any experience. In this regard, the apophatic movement of Dionysian theology would concern not so much an experience of absence as an absence of experience.[17] Or, as Michael Sells puts it, "The nonintentional aspect of apophasis runs up against the modern concept of experience," for "if the nonintentionality claims of apophatic mys-tics are taken seriously, and if experience is, by definition, intentional, it necessarily follows that mystical union is not an experience."[18] The union of mystical unknowing lacks both the intentional self and the intended object that could render experience and its language possible. The desire for God in Dionysius is never sated, therefore, precisely because the subject of language can never be present or self-present in the experience of that which it desires.

For this reason also, the threefold movement of theological language in Dionysius, like the desire it embodies and sustains, remains radically open, for it aspires toward that which it cannot reach. Just as the subject of thought is not and cannot be present in the experience of mystical unknowing, so the doubly apophatic language that carries the soul toward such unknowing cannot articulate it as such. To know beyond mind by knowing nothing, therefore, is to name the unnameable according to a hyperbolic, hyper-negative rhetoric in which infinite polyonymy constitutes the reverse side of a radical anonymity—that is, an anonymity which the subject as such cannot speak, even through unspeaking. The escape from language never occurs within language, where the ever-desiring subject knows only an endless oscillation between naming and unnaming, a ceaseless and excessive proliferation of language which speaks an emptiness that keeps language ever open.

The Negative Logic of Death: Heideggerian Meanings

This hyperbolic openness of language in the Dionysian naming of the unnameable calls to mind in striking fashion contemporary understandings of language that would insist on the radical finitude of the mortal subject who is constituted by or through language. In its finite, transcending relation to death, that subject of language relates to the possibility of its own impossibility, a possibility that, like the naming of the unnameable, can never be actualized as such—and for that reason remains irreducibly open. An indispensable starting point for such understandings of the mortal subject is the Heideggerian analysis of death, whose traces can be discerned throughout contemporary approaches to the relation between language and death in finite existence. In looking briefly here at Heidegger's understanding of death, therefore, I shall be able to situate my reading of Dionysius's apophatic rhetoric of mystical unknowing in relation to a dominant contemporary understanding of human finitude and its significance.

In the well-known existential analysis that he carries out in his epoch-making *Being and Time* (1927),[19] Heidegger defines finite human existence, or *Dasein,* as "Being-in-the-world" (*In-der-Welt-sein*), and he defines the worldhood of that world—without which Dasein simply is not (and vice versa)—as a primordial totality of referential relations that constitute the "significance"

(*Bedeutsamkeit*) in terms of which Dasein exists understandingly.[20] Dasein is at bottom a being that deals understandingly in significance, and precisely this understanding involvement in significance confers Dasein's ontic-ontological distinctiveness — for through such involvement, and through it alone, Dasein's very Being is an issue for Dasein. According to the well-known formulation, Dasein is "a being for which, in its Being, that Being itself is an issue [*Das Dasein ist Seiendes, dem es in seinem Sein um dieses selbst geht*]" (SZ 236; H. 191), and it is in this sense that Heidegger defines Dasein's Being as "care" (*Sorge*); Dasein can care about its Being, its Being can be an issue for Dasein, only in the measure that Dasein deals in significance.

Within the existential analytic of Dasein, then, Heidegger will seek (in Division 1 of *Being and Time*) to delineate the three equiprimordial structures of the care that defines Dasein's fundamental Being (facticity, existence, falling), and in turn (in Division 2) he will ground those structures in the three correspondingly equiprimordial modes of temporality (the having-been, the futural, the present). Although I cannot explicate Heidegger's existential analytic fully here, I shall briefly highlight certain aspects of Dasein's facticity and existence in order to illuminate the sense in which, as "factical existence," Dasein is fundamentally a "thrown Being-towards-death" (*geworfene Sein zum Tode*).

As factical existence Dasein always already finds itself "thrown," or inescapably situated, in a world of significance where Dasein exists, or projects itself understandingly, according to its finite but fundamentally open possibility, its fundamental ability "to be." Always already situated in a context of significance that it does not ground, Dasein has likewise always already taken up its existence by projecting itself understandingly according to the necessarily limited but never fully exhausted possibility opened by that context. The structure of this factical existence or "thrown projection" must also be understood temporally: in its Being, Dasein is articulated ecstatically between a "past" that it cannot have been present to ground and a "future" that it will never be present to actualize. It exists essentially as always already "having-been" and as ever yet "to be." This never present but always operative past (which "is" only as "having-been") and this never present but ever operative future (which "is" only as yet "to be") signal precisely the "nullity" (*Nichtigkeit*) of which Dasein is the thrown-projecting basis. The ultimate horizon of such nullity is the futural horizon of death, against which Dasein projects every possibility of its existence. Indeed, Heidegger will define Dasein's fundamental Being, care, straightforwardly as "Being-towards-death" (SZ 378; H. 329). But how are we to understand that death and its relation to the significance of Dasein's existence?

In *Being and Time*'s analyses of death (especially §§ 46–53), Heidegger defines death as the radical possibility of the impossibility of my existence or Being-in-the-world: "Death is the possibility of the absolute impossibility of Dasein [*die Möglichkeit der schlechthinnigen Daseinsunmöglichkeit*]" (SZ 294; H. 250). This possibility of death can be seen as "radical" in at least two ways. First, it constitutes the ultimate horizon of all other possibilities and thus confers the singular wholeness of Dasein's potentiality-for-Being. Second, and most important for my concerns here, it remains irreducible: the possibility of death is a possibility that itself can never become actual for the being whose possibility it nevertheless is. Thus, as Heidegger will put it, the possibility of death is both my "ownmost" (*eigenst*) and my "uttermost" (*äusserst*) (SZ 294; H. 250). It gives to me what is singularly and wholly my own — namely, an ultimate possibility that I alone can face and that delimits the whole of my potentiality-for-Being. And it marks at the same time the absolute limit of my potentiality-for-Being the being that I am — namely, Being-in-the-world. What is the significance of this limit, or what is the tie between this limit and the possibility of significance as such?

Insofar as I am or exist toward death, my Being in its very significance remains open. This is because the significance of my Being is understood in terms of possibility, and at its most fundamental level that possibility is defined by its openness. To say that my existence is my essence in the Heideggerian framework is to say that I am defined, as Being-in-the-world, by my potentiality-for-Being, by my fundamental ability "to be" — which implies that at every moment I exist, I am constitutively yet "to be," or I am always still "not yet" what I am "to be." In other words, insofar as I exist, insofar as my Being is defined by potentiality, I am never yet all that I can be, I have never yet completed my Being, which thus remains irreducibly open. This openness is conferred by death precisely insofar as death marks the possibility of an impossibility, for the "realization" of the possibility of death would undo my constitutive ability to be; it would close this potentiality-for-Being that defines me.

The openness of my Being, then, is given by death insofar as my death as such eludes all possible experience. In this sense death itself might be seen as hyperbolic: it would throw me beyond myself so as to undo me. I exist toward death as toward a transition or going-over (*Übergang*) that I could not, as the being I am, ever actually experience, because death marks the collapse of the structure in terms of which all possible experience might be projected and articulated in its significance: "When Dasein reaches its wholeness in death, it simultaneously loses the Being of its 'there.' The transition [*Übergang*] to no-longer-Dasein [*Nichtmehr-Dasein*] lifts Dasein right out of the possibility of experiencing this transition and of understanding it as something experienced [*aus der Möglichkeit, diesen Übergang zu erfahren und als erfahrenen zu verstehen*]" (SZ, 281; H. 237). Constitutively "not yet" at its end, Dasein "will be" in death there where it cannot be: where the "there-ness" or "worldhood" of Dasein's world — that is, the significance structure of Dasein's potential Being — no longer holds. In this sense, Heidegger insists, Dasein cannot be at its end, for such an end closes all "Being-there" or Being-in-the-world, and thus all possible significance; rather, Dasein always exists potentially toward its end, which it cannot realize as such in any actual, significant experience.

The fact that death remains ever "not yet" for Dasein, that this "not yet" remains irreducible, indicates the radical character of the ontological possibility that defines Dasein, and that character is decisive for understanding Dasein's relation to death. As distinct from all the particular possibilities that Dasein might in fact actualize within the course of its existence, the ontological possibility of death, or "death as possibility," "gives Dasein nothing to be 'actualized,' nothing that Dasein, as actual, could itself be [*Der Tod als Möglichkeit gibt dem Dasein nichts zu 'Verwirklichendes' und nichts, was es als Wirkliches selbst sein könnte*]" (SZ 307; H. 262). Heidegger elaborates this radical form of possibility by distinguishing between "expecting" or "awaiting" (*erwarten, gewärtigen*) and "anticipating" (*vorlaufen*).

The radical possibility of Dasein's impossibility, a possibility not susceptible of any actualization or experience, must be distinguished from "something possible," which might be expected or awaited. "To expect something possible," Heidegger indicates, "is always to understand it and to 'have' it with regard to whether and when and how it will be actually present at hand" (SZ 306; H. 262). In such an expecting of "something possible," one reduces the possibility of the possible to actuality, "one leaps away from the possible and gets a foothold in the actual. It is for its actuality that what is expected is expected" (SZ 306; H. 262). By reducing the possible to the actual in this fashion, by thus "having" it "with regard to whether and when and how," Dasein would become intent on the possible, it would represent the possible to itself so as to render it manipulable or calculable — drawing it into the realm of "what is attainable, controllable, practicable, and the like" (SZ 305; H. 261). Death, by contrast, which remains irreducible to intention or representation, remains likewise incalculable.

Therefore, rather than expect death, which is not something that can become actual for me, I would relate to death through "anticipation" (*Vorlaufen*), which is characterized precisely by the fact that it does not reduce possibility to an actuality-in-reserve but rather maintains possibility as possibility — in all its incalculability. In the anticipation of death, Heidegger explains, "one does not tend towards concernfully making available something actual; but as one comes closer understandingly, the possibility of the possible just becomes 'greater' [*sondern im verstehenden Näherkommen wird die Möglichkeit des Möglichen nur 'größer'*]. The closest closeness which one may have in Being towards death as a possibility, is as far as possible from anything actual [*Die nächste Nähe des Seins zum Tode als Möglichkeit ist einem Wirklichen so fern als möglich*]" (SZ, 306–7; H. 262). The possibility of the possible just becomes "greater" through anticipation because the possibility at issue constantly proves incommensurable with the actual.

Withdrawing itself absolutely in the very measure that Dasein comes near to it, the possibility of death marks an incalculable limit that finally remains without measure, and it is precisely this hyperbolic incalculability, this excess of death over the actual, that renders death irreducible to representation: "The possibility [of death] reveals itself to be such that it knows no measure at all, no more or less, but signifies the possibility of the measureless impossibility of existence [*die Möglichkeit der maßlosen Unmöglichkeit der Existenz*]. In accordance with its essence, this possibility offers no support for becoming intent on something [*auf etwas gespannt zu sein*], 'picturing' to oneself the actuality which is possible [*das mögliche Wirkliche sich 'auszumalen'*], and so forgetting its possibility" (SZ 307; H. 262). As an incalculable "limit without measure," death signals an impossibility that remains — perhaps contrary to expectation — fundamentally generous, for it sets all possibility free as possibility. In doing so, at the same time, it eludes representation, or it exceeds the imagination, precisely because to represent or picture it would be to reduce it to an actuality that exhausts or forgets possibility as such. Just as the representation or image of God in Dionysius finally blocks a knowledge of God as unknowable, so any representation of death would seek to make it "actual" or "actually present" in such a way as to forget its excessive character as the radical possibility of an impossibility.

As the horizon of all possibility that itself remains impossible, as that which is anticipated but never realized, death marks the horizon of significance which "in itself" would mark the collapse of significance. So long as Dasein exists according to the possibility of its Being, the structure of that possibility — the worldhood that articulates the significance of such Being — remains irreducibly open.

This would mean that Dasein's essentially hermeneutic mode of Being remains radically open for Dasein precisely because Dasein exists finitely: as thrown-projection, Dasein is ever already under way — and never yet finished — with the "interpretation" or unfolding of its understanding involvement in the possible significance of its existence: "As understanding, Dasein projects its Being upon possibilities. This Being-towards-possibilities which understands is itself a potentiality-for-Being, and it is so because of the way these possibilities, as disclosed, exert their counter-thrust [*Rückschlag*] upon

Dasein. The projecting of the understanding has its own possibility — that of developing itself [*sich auszubilden*]. This development of the understanding we call 'interpretation' [*Auslegung*]" (SZ 188; H. 148).

Based on this approach to interpretation, Heidegger's definition of "meaning" is determined by — indeed, coincident with — the basic existential structure of Dasein:

> That which can be Articulated in a disclosure by which we understand, we call "meaning" [*Sinn*]. The concept of meaning embraces the formal existential framework of what necessarily belongs to that which an understanding interpretation Articulates. Meaning is the "upon-which" of a projection in terms of which something becomes intelligible as something; it gets its structure from a fore-having, a fore-sight, and a fore-conception. In so far as understanding and interpretation make up the existential state of Being of the "there," "meaning" must be conceived as the formal-existential framework of the disclosedness which belongs to understanding. Meaning is an *existentiale* of Dasein, not a property attaching to beings. (SZ 193; H. 151)

Because it is a function of Dasein's existential structure, meaning for Dasein is both ever already operative and never yet fully realized: it issues in the interplay between Dasein's "fore-structure" and its "projection." The "ever already" of Dasein's fore-structure and the irreducible "not yet" of its projection-according-to-possibility are precisely what render the meaning of Dasein's existence always circular and never closed: "The 'circle' in understanding belongs to the structure of meaning, and the latter phenomenon is rooted in the existential constitution of Dasein — that is, in the understanding which interprets" (SZ 195; H. 153). Insofar as meaning is rooted in the existential constitution of Dasein, it issues only in relation to the ultimate horizon of that existential constitution — the horizon of death, whose possibility, precisely, is ever already at issue for Dasein but never yet realized.

From this perspective, death in Heidegger might be seen as analogous to the God in Dionysius who marks the source and horizon of thought and language that can itself never actually be reached by a thinking subject of language. In the Heideggerian terms that I have summarized here, death would constitute the horizon of understanding and interpretation whose meaning no understanding or interpretation will ever exhaust.

Naming the Unnameable and the Possibility of Impossibility: Apophatic Analogy

More precisely, the operative analogy here is one of relation: the relation of the created soul to God in Dionysius proves analogous to the relation of finite existence to its death in Heidegger. Just as the Dionysian soul exists ecstatically between the nothingness from which it is called and the finally unnameable God for whom it endlessly yearns, so in Heidegger, Dasein exists, as a thrown-projection that understands and interprets, between a past that it cannot ground and a future that it anticipates but never actualizes. In both cases, the one who exists thoughtfully in language, or the one who exists understandingly through interpretation, always stands in relation to a term that ultimately eludes thought and language, a term that escapes understanding interpretation — a term that marks, in short, a certain figure of "the impossible." Precisely because both relations are relations to "the impossible," the analogy through which we would relate those relations must itself constitute an "apophatic analogy."

In the Dionysian framework, that around which thought and language circle in endless desire is the inconceivable and ineffable love or generosity of a God beyond Being. According to a logic that ties the possible to the impossible, the soul relates to God through a thought of the unthinkable and a naming of the unnameable: all thought and language that prove possible, all thought and language that the soul might actually live and experience (affirmatively or negatively), circle around that which remains impossible — to name, to comprehend, to be sated by a God who at every moment remains yet to be desired, yet to be thought, and yet to be named.

In Heidegger, the relation of finite existence to its death likewise ties the possible to the impossible. Death marks a possibility that itself remains at every moment possible, at every moment "not yet" actual, and in this sense it signals the impossible. Just as I cannot, as a thinking subject of language, actually be present to experience mystical union with the Dionysian God, so as Dasein I cannot meaningfully "be" there where my death would "occur," for such an "occurrence" would mark the collapse of the very significance structures that define me, the closure of the possibility whose understanding interpretation constitutes the meaning of my existence.

In both Dionysius and Heidegger, then, a temporality or movement of radical anticipation goes hand in hand with a fundamental openness of language or interpretation; such anticipation issues in relation to an irreducible "not yet" whose trace language and interpretation bear. For Dionysius that "not yet" holds open the movement of an endless desire within the created soul's relation to God; the return or reversion to God does not lead to satiety (as in Origen's *apokatastasis*) but remains ever a straining forward, an *epektasis* without end (as in Gregory of Nyssa). For Heidegger an irreducible "not yet" appears in Dasein's relation to a death that can never be realized; that "not yet" constitutes the ultimate term of a temporality and an understanding existence that remain radically open because finite. The insatiable desire of the created soul in Dionysius is embodied or enacted in a ceaseless play between the naming and unnaming of a God who is both all in all and nothing in anything—an unknowable and ineffable God toward whom the knowing subject of language can move only asymptotically. Likewise, the futural movement of mortal existence in Heidegger is embodied or enacted in a hermeneutic mode of Being, an understanding interpretation of meaning, that cannot reach closure precisely because its finite temporality never actually arrives at its own ultimate horizon.

In both Dionysius and Heidegger, radical anticipation concerns at bottom the relation between, on the one hand, a finite being's situation in language and, on the other, that which essentially eludes language even as language constantly points toward it. From a Heideggerian perspective, all language would relate to death insofar as the horizon of death holds open the existential structures of significance that ground the meaning of language, which thus necessarily speaks a gap between itself and the death toward which it would point; as long as the significance of language remains operative, as long as meaning is understandingly interpreted, Dasein exists and so has not "reached" the death of which it might nevertheless speak. There where Dasein would have "reached" death—strictly speaking, an impossibility—the significance of language would have collapsed absolutely. Language can therefore circle around death but never attain it. Similarly, from the Dionysian perspective, language pertaining to God would speak of God in the mode of an "as" that constitutes, as Jean-Luc Marion puts it, an "index of inadequation" between our language and the God to whom it would refer.[21] The movement of mystical unknowing would signal the irreducibility of such inadequation, and the hyper-negative language of such unknowing would succeed only by continually failing to articulate that "place" or "moment" where the soul knows God through unknowing.[22] The language of mystical unknowing thus circles around its God in a hyperbolic naming which speaks the radical anonymity that sustains the soul's insatiable desire.

This intimate interplay between radical anticipation and openness of language would justify our comparison between a naming of the unnameable in the rhetoric of mystical unknowing and the possibility of impossibility within the Heideggerian discourse on Being-toward-death. Such a comparison finds a forceful formulation in Jacques Derrida, who also points to the resemblance between the death in which Dasein can no longer be and the mystical moment in which the speaking being can no longer speak: "All the apophatic mysticisms can also be read as powerful discourses on death, on the (impossible) possibility of the proper death of the being-there that speaks, and that speaks of what carries it away, interrupts, denies, or annihilates its speaking as well as its own Dasein."[23] From this Derridean perspective, which my own analyses here confirm, the apophatic rhetoric of Dionysian mysticism proves analogous to the discourse required by the structure and movement of finite, mortal existence.

But how are we to take that analogy? Does the analogy imply that the God articulated (or not articulated) in a Dionysian apophaticism is "really" death — or, conversely, that death is really a God? Not at all, for the operative analogy is an apophatic one.

Denying the confusion or identification of God and death, our apophatic analogy derives its force from the undecidability that prohibits such an identification. Precisely because both the God of mystical unknowing and the death of Heideggerian Dasein remain "in themselves" inaccessible to the presence of any experience for a thinking subject of language, the two terms can be neither identified with nor distinguished from each other. In both cases the term "in itself" remains strictly unknowable and ineffable — and thus, from the perspective of a knowing subject in language, neither identical nor distinct. It is precisely this neither/nor of identity and distinction that makes analogy the most forceful means of approaching the rhetoric of mystical unknowing and the language of death in relation to each other.

Now, if we find through our readings in Dionysius and Heidegger that such an apophatic analogy proves compelling at some formal or structural level, an important question remains: Is the analogy in the end not rather contrived? While recognizing that Dionysius does not really define the mystical unknowing of God in terms of death, and that Heidegger does not actually analyze Being-toward-death in terms of a Being-toward-God,[24] we might nevertheless answer this question negatively insofar as the resonance between a theological rhetoric of the unnameable and an existential logic of death finds explicit elaboration in the textual history of apophatic discourse itself (and perhaps also insofar as that same history may have influenced Heidegger's analysis of finitude).

Theo-thanato-logy: Historical Confirmation and Contemporary Directions

As a signal toward the significance of "death" within the textual history of apophatic discourse, I point here to one major instance: the *Itinerarium mentis in Deum,* by the thirteenth-century Franciscan Saint Bonaventure. This masterpiece of Dionysian mysticism culminates literally in a "death" of the soul that Bonaventure articulates by means of a thoroughly Dionysian rhetoric.

Working toward the conclusion of his itinerary, Bonaventure cites a key passage from Dionysius's *Mystical Theology* on the mystical unknowing that demands abandonment of world and self: "For transcending yourself and all things, by the immeasurable and absolute ecstasy of a pure mind [*immensurabili et absoluto purae mentis excessu*], leaving behind all things, and freed from all things [*omnia deserens et ab omnibus absolutus*], you will ascend to the superessential ray of the divine darkness."[25] This transcending abandonment of self and world into the divine darkness, articulated in and through the hyper-negative language of the Dionysian "hyper-" terms, ultimately appears to Bonaventure as the Christic death that closes the *Itinerarium*. The fire of love enkindled through the passion of Christ appears as a consuming fire of death, and that death becomes the supreme movement through which Bonaventure thinks and expresses God's inconceivability and ineffability, the central term through which he signals the relation of the created soul to its incomprehensible God.

The soul that would see the unknowable God can do so only if it loves that death wherein the soul loses itself:

> But if you wish to know how these things come about, ask grace, not instruction, desire, not understanding, the groaning of prayer not diligent reading, the Spouse not the teacher, God not man, darkness not clarity, not light but the fire that totally inflames and carries us into God by ecstatic unctions and burning affections. This fire is God and his furnace is in Jerusalem [Isaiah 31:9]; and Christ enkindles it in the heat of his burning passion, which only he truly perceives who says: My soul chooses hanging and my bones death [Job 7:15]. Whoever loves this death can see God because it is true beyond doubt that man will not see me and live [Exodus 33:20].[26]

This passage brings together and reinforces in a most remarkable way the central themes I have attempted to trace concerning the tie between a language of the unknowable, unnameable God and a logic of death. In doing so it confirms historically and textually the analogy whose rhetorical and logical grounds I have been unfolding. Patterning his entire work in relation to the six wings of the seraph, who, as we saw with Dionysius, is the angel — and thus the figure of language — consumed by the flame of insatiable desire for God, Bonaventure recommends as the way into God not the teacher but the Spouse: the ever-sought and ever-desired Spouse from the Song of Songs, love for whom is "strong as death" (8:6). And it is precisely that death for Bonaventure which, articulated christologically, gives expression to Dionysius's mystical unknowing — which Dionysius himself figured through the story of Moses, who learns in Exodus 33:20 precisely what Bonaventure here reminds us: that "one shall not see [God] and live."[27]

This single example — part of a larger field whose exploration we are just now beginning[28] — should suffice to indicate that later traditions of apophatic, and especially Dionysian, mysticism have themselves made explicit what in Dionysius's own language remained largely implicit: namely, that the relation of mystical unknowing, which demands (or ensues from) a hyper-negative discourse through which the subject of language is undone, might actually be articulated most forcefully in terms of the soul's dissolution or "death."[29] At issue in such an articulation, no doubt, are the complex ties that so often and so intimately bind the language of negative theology to a language of negative anthropology, for, as Denys Turner has indicated, "If, in my deepest inwardness, I and God meet in a union beyond description and beyond experience, then an apophaticism of language about God and an apophaticism of language about the 'self' are obviously intimately connected."[30] On the basis of my discussion here, I would argue that this connection between two apophaticisms — one of God and one of self — might be approached not only within single thinkers from particular historical moments (here, Bonaventure) but also between figures who stand at some historical and conceptual distance (here, Dionysius and Heidegger). By juxtaposing Dionysius's negative language of God and Heidegger's negative discourse on the self, I have attempted to suggest a possible way of bringing together, on the one hand, inquiry into the historical traditions of mystical theology (and its anthropology) and, on the other, contemporary approaches to the mortal subject of language and desire. At issue in such an attempt would be the precise nature of the relation between a traditional apophaticism of God and a contemporary apophaticism of self. In order to think the two together without identifying or distinguishing them, I propose the language of apophatic analogy.

For if the subject of language cannot be present there where it most intimately approaches the God it desires, or if the subject of language cannot experience the death that delimits all experience, then the theological and thanatological movements of language must equally speak a desire for experience that is never satiated. Accordingly, a naming of the unnameable — theological or thanatological — would mark a possibility of the impossible. And if we attempt to articulate these two figures of the impossible by affirming that love of God may indeed be strong as death, then the theological and thanatological would remain inextricably bound, and a language of apophatic analogy might bring the experience of such death to life.

Notes

1. The impact of Heideggerian and post-Heideggerian thought on contemporary discussion of the apophatic and mystical traditions is remarkable in its scope. A list of works in which that impact is significant specifically for the discussion of Pseudo-Dionysius

would have to include the early and usually overlooked essay of Christos Yannaras, *De l'absence et de l'inconnaissance de Dieu d'après les écrits aréopagitiques et Martin Heidegger* (Paris: Editions du Cerf, 1971; appeared originally in Greek in 1967); the much-discussed works of Jean-Luc Marion, *L'Idole et la distance* (Paris: Grasset, 1977) and *God Without Being*, trans. Thomas A. Carlson (Chicago: University of Chicago Press, 1991; French original, 1982); the later and even more discussed essays of Jacques Derrida, "How to Avoid Speaking: Denials" and "Post-Scriptum: Aporias, Ways and Voices," trans. John P. Leavey, Jr., in H. Coward and T. Foshay, *Derrida and Negative Theology* (New York: State University of New York Press, 1992); and the deconstructive approach of literary theorist and poet Kevin Hart, *The Trespass of the Sign: Deconstruction Philosophy and Theology* (Cambridge: Cambridge University Press, 1989). The Dionysian thinker most often discussed in Heideggerian and post-Heideggerian contexts is, of course, the later, medieval mystic Meister Eckhart, and the best treatments of Eckhart in these contexts remain Reiner Schürmann's *Meister Eckhart: Mystic and Philosopher* (Bloomington: Indiana University Press, 1978; originally in French, 1972) and John Caputo's *The Mystical Element in Heidegger's Thought* (Athens: Ohio University Press, 1978). On the question of language and desire in late medieval and early modern mysticism, see especially Michel de Certeau's *Mystic Fable*, vol. 1: *The Sixteenth and Seventeenth Centuries* (Chicago: University of Chicago Press, 1992; French version, 1982).

2. As Jean-Luc Nancy asks in *Des lieux divins* (Mauvezin: Trans-Europ-Repress, 1987), 5.

3. Citing these works parenthetically as DN, MT, CH, and EH, respectively, I rely on the English edition of the complete Dionysian corpus in *Pseudo-Dionysius: The Complete Works*, trans. Colm Luibheid (New York: Paulist, 1987). Citations will be given according to the pagination of J.-P. Migne's Greek edition (*Patrologiae cursus completus. Series graeca*, vol. 3, Paris, 1857–1866), but I cite the Greek text from the new critical edition, *Corpus Dionysiacum*, vols. 1 and 2, ed. Beata Regina Suchla, Günter Heil, and Adolf Martin Ritter (Berlin: Walter de Gruyter, 1990, 1991). The best brief introduction to Dionysius in English can be found in Bernard McGinn's *Foundations of Mysticism*, volume 1 of *The Presence of God: A History of Western Christian Mysticism* (New York: Crossroad, 1991), 157–82.

4. As Hans Urs von Balthasar puts it, the influence of Dionysius's theology is "scarcely less than that of Augustine . . . and one can see virtually all medieval philosophy up to the Aristotelian renaissance and the whole of theology up to Thomas as derived from the fecundity of these two" (*Glory of the Lord*, vol. 2, trans. Andrew Louth, Francis McDonagh, and Brian McNeil [New York: Crossroad, 1984], 148).

5. In addition to offering the Middle Ages some of its most decisive formulations on the modes of theological language (kataphatic, apophatic, and mystical) and on the stages of spiritual practice (purification, illumination, perfection), Dionysius also gave to medieval culture an immensely influential conception of the cosmos in hierarchical terms, a systematic ordering of angels and their significance, and a theology of light that would prove foundational for Gothic aesthetics.

6. The best discussions of the irreducibly threefold character of the Dionysian system can be found in René Roques, "De l'implication des méthodes théologiques chez le pseudo-Denys," *Revue d'ascétique et de mystique* 119 (1954): 267–74; Hans Urs Von

Balthasar, "Denys," in *Glory of the Lord,* vol. 2; Jean-Luc Marion, "La Distance du Réquisit et le Discours de Louange: Denys," in *L'Idole et la distance* (Paris, Grasset, 1977); and Michel Corbin, "Négation et transcendance dans l'oeuvre de Denys," *Revue des sciences philosophiques et théologiques* 69 (1985): 41–76. See also the approach of Denys Turner in *The Darkness of God: Negativity in Christian Mysticism* (Cambridge: Cambridge University Press, 1995).

7. My thanks to Bernard McGinn for having suggested this term to indicate the second level of negation which passes beyond (hyper-) the mere reversal of kataphatic affirmation. With equally suggestive power, Michel Corbin describes this third mode of Dionysian language as a "redoubled negation" (op. cit.).

8. For extended discussions of the liturgical in Dionysius, see R. Roques, *L'Univers dionysien: Structure hiérarchique du monde selon le Pseudo-Denys* (Latour-Maubourg: Editions du Cerf), and Paul Rorem, *Biblical and Liturgical Symbols Within the Pseudo-Dionysian Synthesis* (Toronto: Pontifical Institute of Mediaeval Studies, 1984).

9. As Dionysius indicates in DN 709B: "So let us not fear this title of 'yearning' (erōtos onoma), nor be upset by what anyone has to say about these two names, for, in my opinion, the sacred writers regard 'yearning' and 'love' (agapēs) as having one and the same meaning."

10. The threefold character of the Dionysian system, of course, is indebted to the pagan Neoplatonism of Proclus (410–485). On that debt, see H.-D. Saffrey, "New Objective Links Between the Pseudo-Dionysius and Proclus," in Dominic O'Meara, ed., *Neoplatonism and Christian Thought* (Albany: State University of New York Press, 1982), and Stephen Gersh, *From Iamblichus to Eriugena* (Leiden: Brill, 1978).

11. The key biblical ground for this view is Romans 1:20, which indicates that "since the creation of the world, the invisible noumena of God have been perceived through the things that have been made." For Dionysius's citation of this passage, see DN 700C and Letter IX, 1108B.

12. On the crucial notion of divine ecstasy, see Bernard McGinn, "God as Eros: Metaphysical Foundations of Christian Mysticism," in *Historical Theology and the Unity of the Church: Essays in Honor of John Meyendorff* (Grand Rapids, Mich.: Eerdmans, 1995); and Kevin Corrigan, "Ecstasy and Ectasy in Some Early Pagan and Christian Mystical Writings," in William J. Carrol and John J. Furlong, *Greek and Medieval Studies in Honor of Leo Sweeney, S. J.* (New York: Peter Lang, 1994).

13. In this light one can easily see why the logic of Jacques Derrida's *différance* seemed so readily to call for comparison to the apophatic traditions. On Derrida's initial response, see "Différance," p. 6 in *Margins of Philosophy,* trans. Alan Bass (Chicago: University of Chicago Press, 1982). For his more recent and more nuanced approach, see especially "How to Avoid Speaking: Denials," and "Post-Scriptum: Aporias, Ways and Voices," op. cit.

14. On Gregory's important notion of infinite progress in desire, which grows out of God's fundamental incomprehensibility, see especially these remarkable passages from *The Life of Moses,* trans. by Abraham J. Malherbe and Everett Ferguson (New York: Paulist, 1978): "And the bold request which goes up the mountains of desire asks this: to enjoy the Beauty not in mirrors and reflections, but face to face. The divine voice granted what was requested in what was denied, showing in a few words an immeasurable depth of

thought. The munificence of God assented to the fulfillment of his desire, but did not promise any cessation or satiety of the desire. He would not have shown himself to his servant if the sight were such as to bring the desire of the beholder to an end, since the true sight of God consists in this, that the one who looks up to God never ceases in that desire. For he says: You cannot see my face, for man cannot see me and live" (2.232–33); "This truly is the vision of God: never to be satisfied in the desire to see him. But one must always, by looking at what he can see, rekindle his desire to see more. Thus, no limit would interrupt growth in the ascent to God, since no limit to the Good can be found nor is the increasing desire for the Good brought to an end because it is satisfied" (2.239). See also the numerous passages in Gregory's commentary on the Song of Songs (e.g., J.174/M.888; J.246–47/M.941; J.321/M.1000). The crucial difference between a thought of satiety and one of epektasis will have to do with whether one understands God to be limited or unlimited. As contrasted with Gregory, Origen holds that, in order to be knowable, God cannot be unlimited. On this, see *On First Principles*, book 2, chapter 9, § 1, trans. G. W. Butterworth (Gloucester, Mass.: Peter Smith, 1973): "For we must maintain that even the power of God is finite, and we must not, under pretext of praising him, lose sight of his limitations. For if the divine power were infinite, of necessity it could not even understand itself, since the infinite is by its nature incomprehensible."

15. Denys Turner develops this phrase in *Darkness of God*.

16. For a helpful discussion of the role played by this Exodus story in generating and shaping the language of Christian mystical discourse, see Turner's *Darkness of God*, chap. 1, "The Allegory and Exodus," especially pp. 16–18.

17. On this, see Turner's objection to "the contemporary preoccupation with mysticism as 'experience'" — in which he perceives a "theological positivism" that parallels "the philosophical positivisms of our own century": "For just as the philosophical positivists made a sharp division between the first-order experiential bedrock of 'sense experience' and the second-order theoretical reflection upon the language of experience, so there are those for whom there is, as it were, a 'mystical' equivalent to sense experience — equivalent in its 'immediacy' and subjectivity, equivalent in its foundational character, equivalent in its freedom from theoretical presupposition — in terms of which theological truth is capable of being verified or falsified" (*Darkness of God*, 262). For Turner's development of the distinction between negative experience and the negativity of experience, see especially pages 259–65.

18. Michael Sells, *Mystical Languages of Unsaying* (Chicago: University of Chicago Press, 1992), 214.

19. Citations from Heidegger's *Being and Time* will be given parenthetically as SZ for the English and H. for the German. The English translation (at times modified) is by John Macquarrie and Edward Robinson (Oxford: Basil Blackwell, 1962); the 16th German edition is *Sein und Zeit* (Tübingen: Max Niemeyer, 1986).

20. On worldhood and significance, see *Being and Time*, § 18.

21. See Marion, *Idole et la distance*, pp. 233 ff. In an approach that is in many ways similar to mine in this regard, Michael Sells's *Mystical Languages of Unsaying* provides a complex and insightful analysis of apophatic language's fundamental openness, which Sells shows to be a function of apophatic language's self-critical character: "Apophasis is a discourse in which any single proposition is acknowledged as falsifying, as reifying. It is

a discourse of double propositions, in which meaning is generated through the tension between the saying and the unsaying" (12). For a schematic account of the principles of apophatic language, see especially pages 207–9. Turner's notion of the "self-subverting" utterance offers a similar way of approach; see *Darkness of God,* esp. 21–25, 42–46, 252, 270.

22. In this regard, Sells is again interesting: the apophatic movement where language undoes itself functions as a "meaning event" that constitutes a "mimetic reenactment" of the mystical union (see *Mystical Languages of Unsaying,* esp. 6–10 and 213–17). The extreme paradox, of course, would be that language seeks to reenact mimetically the strictly singular or incomparable.

23. Derrida, "Post-Scriptum," 290–91.

24. Heidegger does come close, however, to indicating a connection like the one I am developing here when he notes that "it is no accident that the phenomena of anxiety and fear, which have never been distinguished in a thoroughgoing manner, have come within the purview of Christian theology ontically and even (though within narrow limits) ontologically. This has happened whenever the anthropological problem of man's Being towards God has won priority and when questions have been formulated under the guidance of phenomena like faith, sin, love, and repentance" (SZ 492; H. 190).

25. *Mystical Theology,* 997B–1000A, quoted in Bonaventure's *Itinerarium,* 7.5. As Henry Duméry notes on p. 104 of his translation of the *Itinerarium* (Paris: J. Vrin, 1960), Bonaventure here follows the translation of John Scotus Eriugena. For the English translation of Bonaventure, I use *The Soul's Journey into God,* in *Bonaventure,* trans. Ewert Cousins (New York: Paulist, 1978).

26. Bonaventure, *Soul's Journey into God,* 7.6.

27. Here in Bonaventure's *Itinerarium* we can see a clear and decisive instance of the attempt to articulate in Dionysian terms a connection between the ineffability of God and a death or dissolution of the self. Historically, then, my analogy is not at all contrived. But what about the specifically Heideggerian interpretation of death and its relation to Dionysian thought? Although I cannot develop it here, we might at least hypothesize a significant connection, if not through Bonaventure, a Dionysian mystic who may have influenced the early Heidegger, then perhaps more certainly through Meister Eckhart, a Dionysian mystic who undoubtedly did so. Indeed, Meister Eckhart's *"abgescheidenheit"* could well provide a concrete link between, on the one hand, the Dionysian approach to unknowing in terms of a removal or abandonment of beings and, on the other, the Heideggerian understanding of death as an *Abschied vom Seienden,* a discharge or departure of/from beings that literally constitutes a decease (from the Latin *decessus,* a departure, death).

On the influence of Bonaventure, Eckhart and other religious (especially mystical) figures in the early formation of Heidegger's thought, see the studies of Theodore Kisiel, *The Genesis of Heidegger's Being and Time* (Berkeley: University of California Press, 1993), and John van Buren, *The Young Heidegger: Rumor of the Hidden King* (Bloomington: Indiana University Press, 1994). See also the important earlier article of Thomas Sheehan, "Heidegger's 'Introduction to the Phenomenology of Religion,'" *The Personalist* (July 1979): 312–24.

On the Dionysian ground of Eckhart's *abgescheidenheit* or "detachment," see "On

Detachment": "All the powers of the soul are racing for the crown, but it will be given only to the soul's being—and Dionysius says: 'The race is nothing but a turning away [*ein abkeren*] from all created things and a uniting oneself with what is uncreated.' And as the soul attains this, it loses its name, and it draws God into itself, so that in itself it becomes nothing [*ze nihte wirt*], as the sun draws up the red dawn into itself so that it becomes nothing. Nothing else [*kein dinc dan*] will bring man to this except pure detachment [*abgescheidenheit*]," in *Meister Eckhart: The Essential Sermons, Commentaries, Treatises and Defense*, ed. Edmund Colledge and Bernard McGinn (New York: Paulist, 1981), 292 [German version, "Von Abgescheidenheit," in Meister Eckhart, *Die Deutschen und Lateinischen Werke*, ed. Josef Quint, volume 5 of *Die Deutschen Werke* (Stuttgart: Kohlhammer Verlag, 1963), 427–28]. Interpreted in terms of death to the world and self, Eckhart's thought of "detachment" would involve also the related interplay I have been tracing between apophatic dispossession of self and insatiable love or desire. On detachment and death, see, for example, Sermons 12, 29, and 39 in *Meister Eckhart: Teacher and Preacher*, ed. Bernard McGinn (New York: Paulist, 1986). On the movement of unending love, see Eckhart's citation of the pseudo-Bernardine *Epistle on Charity*: "The person who has longed to desire cannot be satiated by desire. Desire is the soul's hunger. The soul that truly loves God is not satiated by love. Because the God he loves is love, he loves love, and to love love is to make a circle so that there is no end to love," in *Meister Eckhart: Teacher and Preacher*, 180.

28. A field that would concern, beyond death itself, the entire problematic of negative anthropology, from its major formulation in the early medieval Dionysianism of Eriugena through the late medieval mysticism of Marguerite Porete and Eckhart to the early modern writings of Nicholas Cusanus or Angelus Silesius and perhaps also into the contemporary world.

29. For an excellent overview of death and its articulation in mysticism (especially German), see Alois Haas, "Mors Mystica: Thanatologie der Mystik, inbesondere der Deutschen Mystik," *Freiburger Zeitschrift für Philosophie und Theologie* 23, no. 3 (1976): 304–92.

30. Turner, *Darkness of God*, 6.

PART III

*The Rhetoric of Excess, Difference,
and the Sublime*

The contributors in our third section stress the ambiguities that attend any use of hyperbolic, sublime, or negative language and figures — language and figures that can both promote human self-aggrandizement and open us to divinely inspired insight.

According to Victoria Kahn's reading of Milton's *Paradise Lost,* what appears to be sublime could instead be a "satanic, parodic version of the Word." Linguistic mediation requires an interpretive act to distinguish the true from the false. Kahn argues that Milton's representation of Satan's refusal to interpret the divine prohibition against eating enacts the fixity of a mind that refuses to acknowledge limitations on its knowledge and that supplies its own meaning instead, without attending to the need for interpretation. Negation, as in the prohibition against eating of the Tree of Knowledge, "makes thought possible, at the same time that it makes the closure of absolute knowledge impossible, for us." But for Milton, "this impossibility is the condition of virtue." In different ways, several of our contributors argue for tropological and other readings that acknowledge a gap between the sign and what it might express and between the human understanding of the divine and divinity itself. In Part I, for example, Wendy Olmsted noted that in Scripture according to Saint Augustine's rhetoric, the looseness of the relations between signs and meanings permits multiple interpretations. For this reason, human beings may read Scripture in relation to their own lives and discover different ways to change, while also discovering new aspects of God's charity.

Susan Shapiro discusses the complex ways in which rhetoric, for Emmanuel Levinas, serves ideological totalities — idolatries of one sort or another: "The problem with rhetoric, for Levinas, is that it is both embedded in and expressive of ideology." What grounds Levinas's thinking is not an immanent ontology in league with rhetoric but a transcendent ethics that rises above philosophy and rhetoric, and even above Habermas's quasi-transcendental conditions for critiquing rhetoric and philosophy. Moreover, to the degree that rhetoric-as-eloquence slips the disciplining conditions of the public realm and serves private reflection, its threat to the truth increases. The question then becomes, for Shapiro, whether Levinas locates in the "saying" of "prophecy" an essentially rhetorical or a-rhetorical (or even anti-rhetorical) discourse: "It is a discourse beyond or otherwise than both rhetoric and philosophy that, however (. . . I argue both with and against Levinas), participates in and draws upon both."

Stephen Webb similarly confronts the danger that figure and rhetoric, more generally considered, might constitute only deception or exaggeration. Webb argues that excess and hyperbole easily become mere exaggeration or "hype," "a linguistic discharge" that grounds Levinas's thinking, "achieves nothing lasting or permanent," unless these figures can be made theologically meaningful by being linked to a context of action. Because in Webb's view, religious beliefs have too often been understood by modern secularists as crudely exaggerated illusions serving compensatory needs within a culture, the excess and hyperbole of Christianity are best understood in relation to the praxis of love and of gift giving, where " 'too much' of a good exaggeration can be 'just right.' "

Because hyperbole signals "profusion and exuberance," it also can release language from a merely instrumental function — but only if the hyperbolic "is" denies the metaphorical "as if" in a demand either "to find love everywhere God is" or to see in every "finite other . . . an infinite demand for justice and compassion." Only in the context of such demands can excess be both meaningful and ethical. Webb considers these issues in relation to the thought of Levinas, Jacques Derrida, and John Caputo, examining hyperbole as "another name for difference."

11

Machiavellian Rhetoric in Paradise Lost

VICTORIA KAHN

Such an one was that Macchiavile, *who perswaded men to governe in this world, partly by fraud, partly by force, and partly by fortune: and not by the divine providence, whereat hee jested immitating therein, not only* Julian *and those prophane heathens which said of the Israelites,* Where is now theyr God *(making mocke of theyr religion) but also (and that effectually) that cankered Serpent, which hearing that God had forbidden* Adam *and* Heva *the Tree of Knowledge of good and evill, scoffed at Gods word, and saide:* Tush, it is nothing so: yee shall not die, but ye shall be as Gods.

— *John Carpenter,* A Preparative to Contention

Better than any other single figure in Milton, Satan in *Paradise Lost* exemplifies the intersection of rhetoric, theology, the Machiavel, and the republican.[1] Perhaps the most famous nondramatic Machiavel of the Renaissance, Satan is a skillful orator and casuist, who uses rhetorical force and fraud to wheedle and coerce his fellow fallen angels. Not surprisingly, the topics of Machiavellism — the relation of *virtù* or virtue to success, means to ends, persuasion to coercion, force to consent — appear regularly in his speeches. What is surprising, or truly diabolical, however, is the way Satan attributes the stereotypically Machiavellian understanding of these topics to God. While in his use of force and fraud and his pretensions to absolute rule Satan resembles the Machiavellian Charles I, his republican rhetoric suggests that God is as coercive and manipulative as the Stuart monarch. In a kind of ironic comment on the mutual appropriation of each other's arguments by royalists and parliamentarians, Satan speaks the language of republicanism in order to cast God as the Machiavel.[2]

Milton's decision to have Satan the Machiavel occasionally speak as a republican has given rise to a number of interpretations. For some readers, Satan represents not only Charles I but also Milton's disillusionment with Oliver Cromwell, the hypocritical puritan. Satan may also reflect Milton's own doubts concerning the revolutionary cause or the adequacy of a secular language of politics.[3] For other readers, Satan's obvious misuse of republican language, along with his own tyrannical behavior, shows that the language of earthly politics is inapplicable to heaven and vice versa. Satan is wrong to expect heaven to be a republic; rather, heaven is the only legitimate absolute monarchy, and kings act hubristically when they style themselves as God.[4] Still other critics argue, conversely, that the human language of absolutism is inapplicable to divine rule, which proves on examination to be a meritocracy based on virtue rather than force.[5] Here it turns out that an analogy can be drawn between divine and human rule, precisely the one Satan refuses to recognize.

In this chapter I suggest a different approach to the issue of Satan's republican rhetoric. Rather than seeing the conjoining of the Machiavel and the republican as evidence of Milton's disillusionment with the revolutionary cause, I believe Satan is one of Milton's best arguments for its validity. Just as Machiavelli argues for building a republic on the assumption of human corruption and for a rhetorical politics that integrates the resources of force and fraud into the arsenal of persuasion, so Milton begins *Paradise Lost* with Satan in order to show that rhetorical and political indeterminacy, which his contemporaries stigmatized as Machiavellian, is also the condition of free will. As Mary Ann Radzinowicz has argued, "Satan's rebellion is political as well as spiritual, no mere subplot but part of a repeated pattern, a design in which failure itself enforces the doctrine of free choice."[6] Satan does not speak as a republican simply to illustrate that the language of republicanism — of virtue, debate, consensus, and dissent — can be appropriated for evil purposes but also to show that it must be capable of being so appropriated for virtue to be meaningful. Furthermore, Christian virtue here is not the simple opposite of Machiavellian *virtù* but rather structurally analogous to it in that both aim to articulate, without equating, intention and effect, virtu(e) and success. And just as the force and misrepresentation of the stereotypical Machiavel are part of the rhetorical politics of the mature Machiavellian, so too Milton aims to make the resources of the Machiavel part of his own politics, as well as of his

Machiavellian justification of the ways of God to men. What Satan stigma-
tizes, in the language of the Machiavel, as force and fraud, turns out to be the
condition of virtue and knowledge in the making. In the following pages I
analyze Milton's exploration of the indifferent resources of the Machiavel, by
looking briefly at Satan's rhetoric in books 1 and 2 of *Paradise Lost,* and then
in greater detail at his encounter with Sin and Death, and his rhetoric in
prelapsarian Eden.

Satan's Rhetoric in Books 1 and 2

Satan's rhetoric consistently asks us to rethink the relationship between
the stereotypical *virtù* — or force and fraud — of the Machiavel, republican
virtù, and Christian virtue. Although Satan the Machiavel initially seems the
opposite of the republican and the puritan saint, who share a concern with
virtuous — in the sense of ethically responsible as well as effective — political
action, it gradually emerges that force and fraud are not only an instrument
but also a condition of republican and Christian virtue. Here we begin to see
how the Machiavel and the republican are not simply mutually exclusive for
Milton — not only because the republican will on occasion use the Machiavellian tools of force and fraud but also because the Machiavel and republican are
two possibilities of the rhetorical politics that Milton and Machiavelli share to
different degrees.

In Satan's account, God is a Machiavel who fraudulently concealed his
power in order to trick the angels into rebelling; once they did, he revealed
himself as the de facto ruler by virtue of his greater power (1.91–124). Although Satan acknowledges God as the de facto "Conqueror (whom I now /
Of force believe Almighty)" (1.143–44) and hopes to use similar "force or
guile" to wage war against God in return, he also rejects — when it serves his
purposes — the argument for the legitimacy of de facto power: "That Glory
never shall his wrath or might / Extort from me" (1.110–11). In rationalizing
his defeat, Satan contrasts God's rule by coercion and fraud to his own leader-
ship and the "united force" of the devils, which are the result of "free choice,"
"merit," and "consent" (2.19–24, 388). Here Satan rehearses the republican
interpretation of the Machiavellian topics of force and consent, virtue and
success, opposing the de facto arguments for the Engagement as well as for
absolute, monarchical power. In this account, the force and fraud of the stereotypical Machiavel are antithetical to republican virtue, and this antithesis is
only confirmed when we recognize that it is not God but Satan who is the
hypocritical Machiavel, using republican rhetoric merely to advance his own
tyrannical ends.

Yet if Satan appears to suggest the incompatibility of Machiavellian *virtù* and republican virtue, a more complicated picture soon begins to emerge from his overdetermined rhetoric. Like Machiavelli, Milton plays with classical and Christian meanings of virtu(e), not in order to separate them completely but rather to explore the various possible relations between them. For example, when Satan refers to the fallen angels' "wearied virtue" (1.320), he implies that *virtù* is not equivalent to success; if it were, he would be God and the fallen angels his followers in heaven. Yet he also suggests that the fallen angels are physically weary (wearied *virtù*) because they are ethically weak (wearied virtue). He thus implies in spite of himself that ethical virtue is the basis of God's power, that, in God's case at least, virtue does guarantee success.

In a later passage, the narrator plays with the meanings of "virtue" in order to explore the relation between *creaturely* virtue and *virtù;* he describes the fallen angels who bend toward Satan,

> With awful reverence prone; and as a God
> Extol him equal to the highest in Heav'n:
> Nor fail'd they to express how much they prais'd,
> That for the general safety he despis'd
> His own for neither do the Spirits damn'd
> Lose all thir virtue; lest bad men should boast
> Thir specious deeds on earth, which glory excites,
> Or close ambition varnisht o'er with zeal. (2.478–85)

Here, too, the meaning of "virtue" is overdetermined, hovering between *virtù* and Christian virtue. At first glance, the meaning seems clear: the fallen angels praise Satan's heroic valor or *virtù,* not his Christian virtue. Yet, the next lines can be construed in at least two ways. The first is that, precisely because even the fallen angels demonstrate *virtù* in deeds excited by glory or ambition, no creature on earth is able to boast of similar deeds: all such claims to agency are diabolical and thus merely "specious"; the specious deeds of *virtù* are no sign of Christian virtue.[7] Here we already begin to see how *virtù* might not be simply the opposite of ethical virtue: for if human action is "specious" and Christian virtue takes the form of faith alone, then *virtù* comes to stand for the supposed achievement of deeds with ethical consequences.

This brings us to the second possible interpretation of the passage, according to which Milton wishes to preserve rather than deny the element of *virtù* in Christian virtue. For, as I have suggested elsewhere, Milton rejects the Lutheran argument against freedom of the will and the possibility of working toward salvation. In this light, the devils' actions are not specious; their responsibility for their deeds is precisely what allows them to be "damn'd."

(Perhaps here we might even understand the opposition between the fallen angels and "bad men" to suggest that whereas the devils preserve some "virtue," "bad men" are those who pretend to deeds that are not their own.) Accordingly, when the devils complain later in book 2 that their "free virtue" is enthralled "to Force or Chance" (2.551), we understand that they have freely chosen to enthrall themselves. Similarly, when Satan declares the inefficacy of divine force — "That Glory never shall his wrath or might / Extort from me" — he takes responsibility for his own actions and thus justifies God's behavior and his own damnation: God will not extort praise, not because he is incapable of exercising such power but because true praise — like virtue — cannot be coerced. "Spirits damn'd" are still possessed of "virtue," in the sense of the free will to alter their own condition. Thus, if there is no necessary connection between Christian virtue and *virtù,* neither are they simply opposed.

Abdiel's response to Satan in book 6 similarly complicates the relationship of virtue to *virtù:*

> O Heav'n! that such resemblance of the Highest
> Should yet remain, where faith and realty
> Remain not; wherefore should not strength and might
> There fail where Virtue fails, or weakest prove
> Where boldest; though to sight unconquerable?
> His puissance, trusting in th' Almighty's aid,
> I mean to try, whose Reason I have tri'd
> Unsound and false; nor is it aught but just,
> That he who in debate of Truth hath won,
> Should win in Arms, in both disputes alike
> Victor; though brutish that contest and foul
> When Reason hath to deal with force, yet so
> Most reason is that Reason overcome. (6.114–26)

Here Abdiel notes Satan's fraudulent likeness to God, as well as Satan's "puissance . . . to sight unconquerable," at the same time that he expresses the faith that virtue and success, virtue and *virtù,* will correspond. He thus calls attention to the existence of force and fraud, and the necessity of angelic force to combat Satan's troops, even as he asserts that God's power is on the side of the angels. Abdiel tries to negotiate, as Milton does in *Areopagitica,* between the exercise of virtue in the realm of appearances and of things indifferent, and the conviction that "Truth is strong . . . [and] needs no policies" (Hughes, 747). And as Milton does in *Areopagitica,* he suggests that the likeness of Truth and Error, of Satanic *virtù* and Christian virtue, as well as the lack of necessary correspondence between virtue and success, intention and effect, are inevitable aspects of action in the realm of appearances. Yet Abdiel also implies by his syntax that the indifference of *virtù* is divinely ordained: "His puissance, trusting in th' Almighty's aid / I mean to try" locates the origin of satanic as well as angelic power in God. He thus makes the realm of things indifferent a gift of God, in which virtue may be achieved only because it may also fail.

Milton similarly complicates the relationship between the stereotypically Machiavellian *virtù* of force and fraud and Christian virtue in Satan's description of God in his final address to the fallen angels in book 1. Here Satan unwittingly shows that what is stereotypically Machiavellian from one perspective is Christian from another:

> O Myriads of immortal Spirits, O Powers
> Matchless, but with th' almighty, and that strife
> Was not inglorious, though th' event was dire,
> As this place testifies, and this dire change
> Hateful to utter but what power of mind
> Foreseeing or presaging, from the Depth
> Of knowledge past or present, could have fear'd
> How such united force of Gods, how such
> As stood like these, could ever know repulse?
> For who can yet believe, though after loss,
> That all these puissant Legions, whose exile
> Hath emptied Heav'n, shall fail to re-ascend
> Self-rais'd, and repossess thir native seat? (1.622–34)

Here Satan rehearses his earlier description of God's fraudulent concealment of his superior power, but with a difference. Once again he claims that the cause of defeat was insufficient knowledge; but he also reveals that even absolute knowledge would have been insufficient in the circumstances: "What power of mind / Foreseeing or presaging, from the Depth / Of knowledge past or present" could have anticipated Satan's defeat? The following line — "For who can yet believe, though after loss" — reads, at first glance, as a gloss on those that precede it, as though to suggest that even the actual experience of the fall can't make the fall believable to Satan. Yet in shifting from knowledge to belief, Satan implicitly acknowledges that what is insufficient knowledge from one perspective is the occasion of faith from another; that what the Machiavel and his critics would call fraud — the intentional discrepancy between appearance and reality or, in the case of God, between free will and foreknowledge — is the condition of human action. As Satan admits, it is precisely because experience does not provide conclusive evidence, that he can believe in, and act on, his ability to "re-ascend."

As this brief discussion of Satan's rhetoric suggests, the *virtù* of the Machiavel is not simply opposed to republican or Christian virtue. Rather, *virtù* is a thing indifferent, whose force, fraud, and concern with effective human action are both instruments and conditions of Christian virtue. If we now turn to Satan's encounter with Sin and Death in book 2 of *Paradise Lost,* we can analyze more closely how Milton exploits the indifference of rhetorical figures to anatomize human agency and justify the ways of God to men. Here, too, the Machiavel and the republican prove to be related.

The Allegory of Sin and Death

Like *Comus,* Satan's encounter with Sin and Death allegorizes Milton's own fears regarding the stereotypical Machiavellism of rhetorical virtuosity, his fears that poetic power might be allied to the forces of rebellion rather than true revolution. At the same time, in its rhetorical form and its biblical allusions, the episode aims to justify Milton's poem by illustrating that the resources of the Machiavel can also be appropriated by the Machiavellian republican: "For neither do the Spirits damn'd / Lose all thir virtue" (2.482–83). The episode not only invites us to think about the Machiavellian topics of force and consent, means and ends, but also illustrates the inseparability of Milton's rhetoric of indifference from his defense of Christian liberty. The stereotypically Machiavellian indeterminacy of rhetorical figures here becomes a justification of free will. In dramatizing that the force and fraud of allegory, and the indeterminacy of rhetoric, are conditions of republican *virtù,* Milton turns the culture's fear of Machiavellian rhetoric on its head and makes the fallen Machiavel the best argument for a republic of saints. The rhetorical form of this episode needs to be taken seriously if we are to understand Milton's Machiavellism.[8] In the following pages I focus first on the allegory of Sin and Death and then on the critical reception of the episode as an example of Miltonic sublimity. As we will see, Milton's allegory criticizes allegory from within, at the same time that his sublime defense of agency dramatizes the Machiavellian underside of sublimity.

In considering how the allegory of Sin and Death helps us meditate on the Machiavellian dilemmas of action in the realm of indifference, it may be useful to recall both Angus Fletcher's remarks about the daemonic Machiavellism of allegorical agency and George Puttenham's about the Machiavellism of allegory. Together, their comments begin to suggest why Satan the Machiavel tends toward allegory, and why allegory should be a particularly powerful rhetorical device for meditating on the paradoxes of agency, both Machiavellian and Christian.

Fletcher uses the term *daemonic* in a morally neutral sense, to describe a world in which "supernatural energies and consuming appetites are the sole means to existence." And he draws an explicit parallel between the daemonic agent and the stereotypical Machiavel: "Like a Machiavellian prince, the allegorical hero can act free of the usual moral restraints, even when he is acting morally, since he is moral only in the interests of his power over other men."[9] Yet though free from moral restraints, the allegorical agent seems not only possessed *of* an intellectual or physical *virtus* (41) but also possessed *by* external force, driven by an "appetite of dominion" (52). He thus combines the appearance of "unrestrained will" with "a maximum of restraint" (68–69). Allegorical fixity is simply the other side of daemonic agency. Satan the Machiavel is such a daemonic hero: in assuming a radically contingent universe, one governed by *fortuna* and susceptible to the machinations of his own unrestrained will, he snakes himself into a "fixed mind" (*PL*, 1.97). He also gives rise to allegorical figures who reflect his own reified sense of agency. If, according to Fletcher, the allegorical hero often seems to operate in a world of daemonic powers, a world in which mental functions are compartmentalized and personified, it is not all that surprising that the daemonic hero appears, conversely, to generate allegorical figures from his own forehead.

In his *Arte of English Poesie,* Puttenham offers a slightly different account of the Machiavellism of allegory but one that is equally important for understanding Satan's encounter with Sin and Death. For Puttenham, allegory or "false semblant" is a figure that depends on force and fraud, the wresting of signification and the resulting "dissimulation": ∫And ye shall know that we may dissemble, I meane speake otherwise then we thinke, in earnest aswell as in sport, under covert and darke termes, and in learned and apparant speeches . . . and finally aswell when we lye as when we tell truth. To be short every speach wrested from his owne naturall signification to another not altogether so naturall is a kinde of dissimulation, because the wordes beare contrary countenaunce to th' intent."[10] Allegory thus raises the question of the relationship of force and signification. Puttenham implies that every trope that wrests signification disguises meaning under a false appearance, regardless of whether one is lying or telling the truth. He thus suggests that the forceful breach of allegory, which opens a space between words and intent, language and meaning, makes the attainment of truth contingent upon the possibility of falsehood. Without this split produced by dissimulation, neither truth nor falsehood would be possible. Allegory, for Puttenham, may be termed the "chief ringleader and captaine of all other figures, either in the Poeticall or oratorie science" (197), "as it is supposed no man can pleasantly utter or perswade without it" (196). Thus if Fletcher's allegory is a figure of force and compulsion, Puttenham suggests that allegory's forceful wresting of signification — or fraud — is a condition of meaning in general.[11]

Satan's encounter with Sin and Death dramatizes both aspects of allegory: the episode does not simply allegorize Satan's force and fraud and thereby equate force and fraud with allegory; it also stages a critique of such an equation by showing that the possibility of Machiavellian force and fraud is a condition of all signification and agency. Allegory comes to signify a false conflation of interpretation with perception, and — as in *Areopagitica* and *Comus* — the false delegation of ethical responsibility; at the same time, it also embodies a structure of linguistic difference that is the condition of meaningful human action. In its ambivalent rhetoric — at once parodic and sublime — the episode dramatizes the indeterminacy or indifference that is a condition of interpretation and free will.

We can begin to get at the indifference — the ambivalence and polysemousness — of this allegory by noting its high degree of self-reflexivity. This self-reflexivity is apparent first of all in the descriptions of Sin and Death. Traditionally, allegory was seen both as the representation of what is by nature obscure to human understanding and as itself an obscure form of representation. We can only know God or divine truths indirectly or allegorically but, in accommodating these truths to human understanding, allegory also presents them under a veil. Thus Demetrius in his *On Style* associates allegory with darkness and night, and Vossius writes that "by its obscurity [allegory] resembles the darkness of night, which easily terrifies the fearful."[12] The obscure representation of Sin and Death thus functions as a kind of allegorical parody of allegory. That is, in personifying the unknowable or unrecognizable, the descriptions should make Sin and Death clearer to us, but the descriptions themselves merely double the original obscurity of these terms. This is especially true of Death, "the other shape / If shape it might be called that shape had none" (2.666–67). Obscurity and darkness also attend Satan's conception of Sin: "dim [his] eyes, and dizzy swum / In darkness" (2.753–54).

Sin's narration of her birth is another self-reflexive, parodic moment of the allegory; her account alludes to one prominent allegory of the birth of Christ in the Renaissance at the same time that it anatomizes the production of allegorical figures as a process of projection and, to use Fletcher's vocabulary, compartmentalization of functions:

> Hast thou forgot me then, and do I seem
> Now in thine eye so foul, once deem'd so fair
> In Heav'n, when at th' Assembly, and in sight
> Of all the Seraphim with thee combin'd
> In bold conspiracy against Heav'n's King,
> All on a sudden miserable pain
> Surpris'd thee, dim thine eyes, and dizzy swum

> In darkness, while thy head flames thick and fast
> Threw forth, till on the left side op'ning wide,
> Likest to thee in shape and count'nance bright,
> Then shining heav'nly fair, a Goddess arm'd
> Out of thy head I sprung: amazement seiz'd
> All th' Host of Heav'n; back they recoiled afraid
> At first, and call'd me *Sin* and for a Sign
> Portentous held me; but familiar grown,
> I pleas'd, and with attractive graces won
> The most averse, thee chiefly, who full oft
> Thyself in me thy perfect image viewing
> Becam'st enamor'd, and such joy thou took'st
> With me in secret, that my womb conceiv'd
> A growing burden.(2.747–67)

On one level, Sin's description of her birth is a parody of God's generation of the Son, since the latter was traditionally allegorized as the birth of Athena in the Renaissance.[13] But Sin also describes the moment of her birth as the projection of Satan's thoughts of rebellion and conspiracy, force and fraud: Sin springs out of Satan's head as he and his fallen angels are joining together "in bold conspiracy against Heav'ns King" (2.750–51). As Kenneth Knoespel has informed us, the Hebrew word for sin, *pesha*, means rebellion. Thus the generation of Sin from Satan's conspiracy serves not only to dramatize etymology[14] but also conversely to gloss the independent or self-regarding activity of the imagination, with its concomitant claim to unmediated agency, as sinful rebellion.[15]

The passage just quoted provides a further allegorical comment on the relation of linguistic mediation to rebellion. As a number of critics have remarked, the birth not only dramatizes etymology but also gives rise to a "linguistic event" of its own: "amazement seiz'd / All th' Host of Heav'n; back they recoil'd afraid / At first, and call'd me *Sin*, and for a Sign / Portentous held me" (2.758–61).[16] Sin seems unfamiliar, and this unfamiliarity is tied to recognizing Sin as a sign of something else, a warning. It is familiarity or habit, here described as a narcissistic identification ("Thyself in me thy perfect image viewing / Becam'st enamor'd"; 2.764–65), which leads to a misrecognition of Sin's otherness, that is, to the deepest sin: "familiar grown, / I pleased, and with attractive graces won / The most averse" (2.761–63).[17] In these lines Milton allegorizes rebellion as the refusal to recognize the mediation of signs, as the narcissistic desire to conflate self and other. Thus what is an allegory of narcissism and identification on the one hand proves to be an allegory of the necessity of allegory — of linguistic mediation and difference — on the other.

This point can be clarified by turning to some of the analogues and subtexts of Sin's narrative. To begin with, Satan's response to Sin suggests the familiar Augustinian distinction between signs that are to be used and those that are to be enjoyed. For Augustine, "all things are to be used (*uti*), that is, treated as though they were signs, God only to be enjoyed (*frui*), as the ultimate signification. To enjoy that which should be used is reification, or idolatry."[18] Satan's enjoyment of Sin involves an idolatry of the sign rather than a recognition of the signified—a form of self-reflection that precludes genuine engagement with the text or the external world. When we take into account Sin's seduction of Satan, we could say that allegory panders to the reader and thus obstructs the kind of rational exercise of the will which is the precondition of right reading and of virtue. In not leaving room for the reader's own activity, this pandering might just as easily be described as a kind of violence or coercion, a violence that is later dramatized in Death's rape of Sin. From this perspective, the passage can be read not only as a critique of the allegorical reification of meaning but also as a defense of reading allegorically; such a defense of allegory is also a defense against it, for to read allegorically is to take the figure of Sin as a sign, a warning.

Satan's "enjoyment" or lust may parody the dangers of antinomianism as well. It is significant in this context that excessive allegorizing was associated with antinomian tendencies in the seventeenth century, and that antinomianism was often conflated with libertinism by its critics. As James Turner has written, "In mid-seventeenth-century polemic . . . radical 'enthusiasm' was associated with the abuse of Genesis and the attempt to recover an Adamite relation to the body. This was supposed to involve either naturalistic sexual freedom or ascetic hatred of the flesh, and sometimes both at once." At times such "paradisal antinomianism" took the form of engaging in sex or sin in order to cast it out (a kind of parody of the Miltonic "trial by what is contrary").[19] The incestuous coupling of Satan and Sin would thus figure in particular the antinomian abuse of—or refusal to be constrained by—the "letter" or sign (*PL*, 2.760), with its attendant dangers of libertinism. Satan's coupling with Sin would also figure the way in which the assumption of radical indeterminacy or immediacy turns into its opposite: the bondage of the will.

Here we can further clarify the dialectical implications of Milton's self-conscious allegory of allegory by examining his biblical source. The genealogy of Sin and Death from lust derives from the Epistle of James, whose canonical status was controversial in the Renaissance not least because of its Pelagian or, in seventeenth-century discourse, Arminian argument for justification by works and thus for free will.[20] The passage reads: "Let no man say when he is tempted, I am tempted of God for God cannot be tempted with evil, neither tempteth he any man: But every man is tempted, when he is drawn away of his own lust, and enticed. Then when lust hath conceived, it bringeth forth sin and sin, when it is finished, bringeth forth death" (1.13–15). In his preface to the epistle, Luther objected, "Flatly against St. Paul and all the rest of Scripture, [James] ascribes righteousness to works . . . . [and] does nothing more than drive to the law and its works; He calls the law a 'law of liberty,' though St. Paul calls it a law of slavery, of wrath, of death and of sin."[21] As John Tanner has argued, however, it is precisely the Pelagian emphasis on individual responsibility in the passage from James that serves to condemn Satan in our eyes:[22] the autogeneration of Sin from Satan's forehead figures the responsibility of the sinner for his fall (as Adam says of man in book 9 of *Paradise Lost*, "Within himself / The danger lies, yet lies within his power: / Against his will he can receive no harm" [9.347–49]); Satan's failure to recognize Sin is a failure to recognize his own responsibility. It is also a failure to recognize that what is the law of death and sin from one perspective is the law of liberty and works from another, and that if sin takes the form of a sign, it is signs, conversely, that allow for the recognition of sin.

Satan's error lies, paradoxically, in his refusal to read, to accept the necessity of interpretation and the possibility of error. He thus substitutes, both structurally and thematically, determinism for freedom, fate for faith and free will. Here, too, "fixed mind" and force or compulsion coincide.[23] Signs that should ideally point to something else simply point back to themselves. Precisely because Satan's narcissistic identification with the allegorical figure of Sin precludes genuine recognition of otherness, allegory in relation to Satan figures the danger of seduction by and idolatry of literature rather than, as it was traditionally presumed to do, providing armor against it. The episode could thus be said to perform its own immanent critique of the idea of an autonomous cultural realm of literature: the claim to unmediated imaginative activity is itself a form of violence, of reification and rebellion.

The preceding analysis has suggested the way the allegory of Sin and Death functions as a thing indifferent that may have positive as well as negative implications or uses in the poem. If the episode represents the stereotypical Machiavellism of allegory, it also criticizes such force and fraud as well. In so doing, it points to an alternative mode of reading the obscurity and failed referentiality we have noted in the representation of Sin and Death and in Sin's account of her encounter with Satan. Borrowing from the more appreciative critics of the poem, we can redescribe this indifference in terms of the rhetorical category of the sublime. My aim in doing so is to situate the previous analysis in relation to the critical reception of the episode from the seventeenth century onward, and to show how even the encomiastic category of the sublime refigures the Machiavellian indifference of allegory.

In "On Paradise Lost," prefaced to the 1674 edition of the poem, Andrew Marvell recorded how he feared Milton would "ruin . . . / The sacred Truths to fable and old Song," and "perplex . . . the things he would explain"; yet, in the end Marvell was "convinc'd," and commended Milton's "verse created like [his] Theme sublime" (Hughes, 209–10). Later readers followed suit, often singling out the perplexity of the Sin and Death episode as one of the chief examples of the Miltonic sublime. Commenting on the line, "Rocks, caves, lakes, dens, bogs, fens and shades of death" (*PL*, 2.621), Edmund Burke wrote: "This idea or affection caused by a word ['death'], which nothing but a word could annex to the others, raises a very great degree of the sublime; and it is raised yet higher by what follows, a '*universe of death*.' Here are again two ideas not presentable but by language; and an union of them great and amazing beyond conception. Whoever attentively considers this passage in Milton . . . will find that it does not in general produce its end by raising the images of things, but by exciting a passion similar to that which real objects excite by other instruments."[24] And Samuel Taylor Coleridge, commenting on the description of Death in *Paradise Lost,* argued in a similar vein: "The grandest efforts of poetry are where the imagination is called forth, not to produce a distinct form, but a strong working of the mind, still offering what is still repelled, and again creating what is again rejected; the result being what the poet wishes to impress, namely, the substitution of a sublime feeling of the unimaginable for a mere image."[25]

Burke's and Coleridge's comments nicely capture the ambivalence of the sublime. On the one hand, it seems as though the poet's deliberate failure of representation allows greater freedom to the reader's imagination; on the other hand, the reader's failure to imagine anything precisely serves to refer the reader to what is described by Coleridge as "a sublime feeling of the unimaginable" but that has been described by other theorists of the sublime as an identification with a higher power, one that transcends the faculties of perception and imagination. Luther's description of the law in his *Commentary on Galatians* provides one example of the religious experience of the sublime: "Wherefore this is the proper and absolute use of the law, by lightning, by tempest and by the sound of the trumpet (as in Mt. Sinai) to terrify, and by thundering to beat down and rend in pieces that beast which is called the opinion of righteousness."[26] The abasement of the sinner proves to be an uplifting experience insofar as it makes him aware of his own sinfulness and thus receptive to divine grace. From this perspective the sublime descriptions of Satan, Sin, and Death serve as a counterplot to their infernal activities, by inviting the reader to contemplate his own divine nature. Similarly, according to Marvell, Milton's sublime style effectively transforms his potentially satanic poetic activity into divinely inspired prophecy: "Just Heav'n thee like *Tiresias* to requite / Rewards with Prophecy thy loss of sight."

Milton may have intended the sublime allegory of Sin and Death to convey an explicitly republican message as well. As Annabel Patterson and others have recently reminded us, Longinus's discussion of the sublime — which was available to seventeenth-century readers in English translation, as well as in Latin and Greek — explicitly linked the sublime to political liberty and to democracy. Marvell, in particular, seems to have noted the republican dimension of the Miltonic sublime in his prefatory poem to *Paradise Lost*. As Patterson has observed, Marvell's image of Milton as "a latter-day Samson braced to bring down the pillars of his society upon the heads of its leaders" "reverberates with Milton's invocation in the *First Defence* of the 'heroic Samson,' who 'still made war single-handed on his masters, and . . . slew at one stroke not one but a host of his country's tyrants.' "27 In the preceding pages we have seen how the generation of Sin allegorizes the illegitimate rebellion of the individual sinner and of the self-regarding imagination; I would now like to suggest that Satan's confrontation with Death be read as a related critique of monarchical authority. For, like Machiavelli, Milton's aim here and elsewhere in *Paradise Lost* is not simply to stage the indifference of rhetorical figures but also to show how they may be appropriated by the religiously motivated republican.

Satan's challenge to Death is represented as a repetition and parody of his rebellion against God's throne. When Death first appears, it "seem'd his head / The likeness of a Kingly Crown had on" (2.672–73). And when Satan refuses to recognize Death's authority, Death surmises he is "that Traitor Angel . . . / Who first broke peace in Heav'n and Faith, till then / Unbrok'n, and in proud rebellious Arms / Drew after him the third part of Heav'n's Sons / Conjur'd against the Highest" (2.689–93). Both in his revolt against heaven and in his encounter with Death, Satan's assumption is that kingly power is merely de facto political power that may be challenged by equal and opposing power. This assumption is dramatized in the lines in which Satan and Death — like allegorical figures from *The Faerie Queene* — are indistinguishable in battle:

> Each at the Head
> Levell'd his deadly aim; thir fatal hands
> No second stroke intend, and such a frown
> Each cast at th' other, as when two black Clouds
> With Heav'n's Artillery fraught, came rattling on. (2.711–15)

Unlike Satan's challenge to God, Satan's contest with Death is merely a conflict of equal powers. As such, the passage looks forward to the War in Heaven and to Abdiel's remarks, discussed above, on the indifference of reason, arms, and military *virtù* (6.114–26). And as in Abdiel's speech, so here the narrator implies that this indifference is itself divinely ordained: both fight with "Heav'n's Artillery."[28]

The fact that Death is an allegorical projection of Satan's own desire for absolute rule may also suggest that Milton intends for us to see kingship as a deadly allegorical projection and alienation of the subject's true freedom. In *The Reason of Church Government* (1642), Milton had written that the authority of the civil magistrate seems originally "to have been placed, as all both civil and religious rites once were, only in each father of family" (Hughes, 678) but that in time magistracy was grounded in reason and persuasion. And in *The Tenure of Kings and Magistrates* (1649), Milton argued against Robert Filmer that "the law was set above the magistrate," and that eventually kings and magistrates "received allegiance from the people, that is to say, bond or covenant to obey them in execution of those laws which they, the people, had themselves made or assented to. And this ofttimes with express warning, that if the king or magistrate proved unfaithful to his trust, the people would be disengaged" (Hughes, 755). In a later passage already mentioned, Milton rebutted Filmer's and others' coupling of 1 Peter 2:13 with Romans 13:

> Therefore kingdom and magistracy, whether supreme or subordinate, is without difference called "a human ordinance" (1 Pet. ii, 13, &c.), which we are there taught is the will of God we should alike submit to, so far as for the punishment of evildoers and the encouragement of them that do well. "Submit," saith he, "as free men." But to any civil power unaccountable, unquestionable, and not to be resisted, no, not in wickedness and violent actions, how can we submit as free men? "There is no power but of God," saith Paul (Rom. xiii), as much as to say God put it into man's heart to find out that way at first for common peace and preservation, approving the exercise thereof; else it contradicts Peter, who calls the same authority an ordinance of man. It must also be understood of lawful and just power. (Hughes, 758–59)

In juxtaposing Satan's illegitimate "conspiracy against Heav'n's King" (2.751) with his initial refusal to recognize the kingly authority of his son, Milton calls attention to the indifference of dissent. What is illegitimate dissent from God becomes legitimate dissent from an allegorical figment of absolute authority. As in the passage just cited from *The Tenure of Kings and Magistrates,* where Milton asserts that the power to contract is the power also to disengage, so here the power to alienate agency is also the power to reassume it. The allegorical conflict of Satan and Death both dramatizes and ironizes the royal fiction of absolute, patriarchal authority. It thus indirectly provides a defense of republicanism.

Yet in the end, Milton's indifferent rhetoric touches the category of the sublime as well. Although from one perspective the sublime may be equated with true prophecy and republicanism, from another the sublimity of Sin and Death simply replays the problem posed by the Machiavellian indifference of the allegory in a higher key. For according to some modern critics, in the experience of the sublime, reason "stages" a failure of that form of representation that assumes an analogy between cognition and vision, understanding and the phenomenal world, in order to make room for the nonphenomenological activities of reading and writing — of prophecy in the seventeenth-century sense of exegesis.[29] The imagination fails to comprehend nature, but this failure allows reason to recognize its independence from nature. As Donald Pease has written, "Instead of locating the source of the sublime in its former locus, i.e., in external nature, the imagination redirects Reason to another locus, within Reason itself, where Reason can re-cognize astonishment as its own power to negate external nature."[30] In doing so, however, reason simply displaces to this ostensibly higher level, "within Reason itself," the question of its own authority. Like allegory, the literary category of the sublime raises questions concerning the relation of authority and interpretation, free will and determinism, which are central to Milton's theological and political concerns: if sublimity can be staged, how does one tell the difference between a satanic or Machiavellian self-aggrandizement and divinely inspired prophecy or poetry? How does one tell the difference between legitimate and illegitimate dissent?[31] In confronting the reader with the Machiavellian possibilities of its indifferent rhetoric, the episode looks forward to dilemmas faced by Adam and Eve in books 4, 8, and 9 of *Paradise Lost*.

Machiavellism in Eden

Satan's encounter with Sin and Death has usually been perceived as something of an anomaly in *Paradise Lost*. From the eighteenth century on the allegory was regularly praised as sublime while being criticized as inappropriate to the otherwise nonallegorical epic. Although admitting that "the descriptive part of this allegory is . . . very strong and full of sublime ideas," Joseph Addison complained, "I cannot think that persons of such a chimerical existence [Sin and Death] are proper actors in an epic poem." Samuel Johnson irritably echoed this complaint in his *Life of Milton*: "This unskilful allegory appears to me one of the greatest faults of the poem."[32] And although modern readers have preferred to see the "fault" of allegory as a deliberate rhetorical strategy, they have also isolated the episode by associating allegory exclusively with a fallen mode of language.[33] Rather than being a form of sublimely inspired language or divine accommodation, allegory in this case is a satanic, parodic version of the Word.

The preceding pages have begun to suggest, in contrast, that the structures of linguistic difference and indifference that we observed in the Sin and Death episode — the emphasis on the mediation of signs and the varied uses of rhetorical figures — are constitutive of prelapsarian experience as well.[34] The fact that the Sin and Death episode can be described both as an allegory and as a critique of allegory is thus part of the larger argument of the poem. Yet if linguistic mediation exists in Eden, the poet still wants to distinguish between true and false versions of it. Thus the distinction that Christianity has traditionally marked with the Fall, Milton places within Eden itself, though this does not mean that Adam and Eve are somehow fallen before their acts of disobedience. In particular, *Paradise Lost* shows that the structure of the prohibition not to eat of the Tree of Knowledge is the same as that of the law of postlapsarian experience (the prohibition is already a law), and that the differential structure articulated by the law is a condition of freedom as well as slavery. Whether the law is perceived as enabling or not is a function of reading, which in either case depends on the law in order to negate it.

This point may be clarified by returning to Luther's objections to the Epistle of James. The Lutheran view of the law as a law of slavery consequent upon the Fall would seem to underlie any strict differentiation between pre- and postlapsarian experience. Although Pelagius might suffice for a description of the original Fall, as fallen creatures we are incapable, according to Luther, of willing freely. Yet in *Paradise Lost,* Milton takes issue with this Lutheran position. That Sin is first a sign means conversely that signs (linguistic mediation) allow for the recognition of the possibility of sin. In glossing the genealogy of Sin and Death in the Epistle of James, Milton's allegory thus suggests that sin shares a linguistic structure not only with the postlapsarian law but with the prelapsarian prohibition, and that, in both cases, this linguistic structure is a condition of virtue. In the following pages I consider the command not to eat from the Tree of Knowledge as an example of linguistic mediation and the linguisic constitution of virtue in prelapsarian Eden; I then analyze Satan's Machiavellian rhetoric in book 9 in similar terms. Just as the divine prohibition exemplifies the linguistic mediation that is a condition of virtue, so Milton uses the disjunction between intention and language in Satan's rhetoric—his Machiavellian fraud—to explore the way in which the wresting of signification is a condition of all agency and meaning.

It is significant that we first see the Tree of Knowledge from Satan's vantage point, for the poet's description emphasizes that "virtue" is tied to right use:

> Thence up he [Satan] flew, and on the Tree of Life,
> The middle tree and highest there that grew,
> Sat like a Cormorant; yet not true Life
> Therby regain'd, but sat devising Death
> To them who liv'd; nor on the virtue thought
> Of that life-giving Plant, but only us'd
> For prospect, what well us'd had been the pledge
> Of immortality. (4.194–201)

The narrator uses "virtue" to mean the power of the Tree of Life—just as in book 9 Eve will refer to the virtue of the Tree of Knowledge and of other plants in the garden. But "virtue" also retains its ethical sense as the faculty that governs and is a consequence of right use. It is right use that converts the Tree of Life from a mere object to a "pledge" or sign of God's promise of immortality. The ethical indifference of the Tree—that it can be used well or badly, that it can be construed as a pledge or a mere plant—is thus a condition of virtue in both senses of the word. As in the Sin and Death episode, Satan's literal-minded perception is reflected in his "devising Death": in scriptural terms, the letter killeth but the spirit giveth life.

Like the Sin and Death episode, this passage on the Tree of Life prepares us for Adam's description of God's command against eating from the Tree of Knowledge. Adam describes the prohibition in a way that explicitly ties its linguistic structure to the possibility of virtue. Two aspects of his account are important to note: first, the prohibition signifies that the recognition of sin is a linguistic rather than a merely perceptual activity; second, as a sign, the prohibition is intended to establish the difference between coercion and persuasion. God "requires," Adam tells Eve,

> From us no other service than to keep
> This one, this easy charge, of all the Trees
> In Paradise that bear delicious fruit
> So various, not to taste that only Tree
> Of Knowledge, planted by the Tree of Life,
> So near grows Death to Life, whate'er Death is,
> Some dreadful thing no doubt; for well thou know'st
> God hath pronounc't it death to taste that Tree,

The only sign of our obedience left
Among so many signs of power and rule
Conferr'd upon us, and Dominion giv'n
Over all other Creatures that possess
Earth, Air, and Sea. Then let us not think hard
One easy prohibition, who enjoy
Free leave so large to all things else, and choice
Unlimited of manifold delights:
But let us ever praise him, and extol
His bounty, following our delightful task
To prune these growing Plants, and tend these Flow'rs,
Which were it toilsome, yet with thee were sweet. (4.420–39)

Here it is clear that although Adam does not understand the word "death," he does understand the prohibition as a test of obedience.[35] The partial obscurity of the prohibition is thus analogous to the obscurity of Sin and Death; in both cases it functions as a boundary or limit. The sign is thus, in a curious way, performative rather than cognitive. It refers Adam and Eve to the limits of cognition but recuperates this failure of cognition ("whate'er Death is / Some dreadful thing no doubt") in the recognition of the task of obedience to God's word: "For well thou know'st / God hath pronounc't it death to taste that Tree." As Milton intimates in the homophones of Raphael's later warning, "Know to know no more" (4.775), knowledge is predicated on negation, on the knowledge of limits. Furthermore, this limit is of ethical as well as epistemological importance, for absolute knowledge would itself be coercive and thus preclude virtue. At the same time, the prohibition itself is clearly a sublime obstacle, a limit that tempts one to "think hard"—that is, beyond the boundary it establishes; and to think of that activity as hard which formerly—that is, without thought—was easy and so without virtue. Negation makes thought possible, at the same time that it makes the closure of absolute knowledge impossible, for us. But this impossibility is the condition of virtue. Just as the Mosaic law is given to fallen man to allow for the recognition of sin (12.287–308), so the prohibition is given to Adam and Eve as a sign which, as it articulates difference, allows for genuine choice, reason, and obedience. And this articulation of difference is itself predicated on the doctrine of things indifferent. As Milton writes in *Christian Doctrine,* "It was necessary that something should be forbidden or commanded as a test of fidelity, and that an act in its own nature indifferent, in order that man's obedience might be thereby manifested. For since it was the disposition of man to do what was right, as a being naturally good and holy, it was not necessary that he should be bound by the obligation of a covenant to perform that to which he was of himself inclined; nor would he have given any proof of obedience by the performance of works to which he was led by a natural impulse, independently of the divine command" (Hughes, 993). In Milton's analysis, the Tree of Knowledge is itself a thing indifferent, and it is this indifference that makes possible the test of virtue constituted by the prohibition. Or, to put it another way, as in the passage on divine ordinance and human order in *The Tenure of Kings and Magistrates,* Milton diminishes the difference between God's command and human discretion in things indifferent by making the former a test of the latter.

If the prohibition establishes the fact of linguistic mediation in prelapsarian Eden, it is not surprising that Adam and Eve's prelapsarian experience in book 9 of *Paradise Lost* rehearses many of the issues we saw dramatized in Satan's encounter with Sin and Death. Satan's narcissistic refusal to recognize the mediation of signs is refigured in book 9 as Eve's narcissistic blindness to Satan's fraud. Yet if Milton allegorizes stereotypical Machiavellism in the Sin and Death episode as the unwarranted claim to self-origination and imaginative power, in book 9 of *Paradise Lost* Machiavellism appears as well in its more familiar form of rhetorical deception and hypocrisy. Even more than in books 1 and 2, Satan appears in book 9 as the archetypal hypocrite, using fraud and malice (9.55) to wage war against Adam and Eve. And, as in those earlier books, part of Satan's Machiavellism involves ascribing the stereotypically Machiavellian use of force and fraud to God himself, while claiming in his own case and that of the fruit that appearances are truthful. As with Satan's speeches to the fallen angels in books 1 and 2, here too Milton implies that what is rhetorical force and fraud from one perspective is the condition of virtue from another.

Satan is the original of William Bradshaw's Machiavel, who manipulates the realm of appearances so that "scant any thing is as it appears, or appears as it is."[36] In addition, in a particularly diabolical twist, Satan makes even those things that appear as they are seem different. Debating about the proper means to serve his ends, Satan

> Consider'd every Creature, which of all
> Most opportune might serve his Wiles, and found
> The Serpent subtlest Beast of all the Field.
> Him after long debate, irresolute
> Of thoughts revolv'd, his final sentence chose
> Fit Vessel, fittest Imp of fraud, in whom
> To enter, and his dark suggestions hide
> From sharpest sight: for in the wily Snake,
> Whatever sleights none would suspicious mark,

As from his wit and native subtlety
Proceeding, which in other Beasts observ'd
Doubt might beget of Diabolic power. (9.84–95)

Satan's deliberations lead him to the conclusion that suspicious behavior in a creature one expects to be suspicious will not be suspicious. This reasoning simultaneously parodies and illustrates Machiavelli's remark that "men in general judge more by the sense of sight than by the sense of touch, because everyone can see but only a few can test by feeling. Everyone sees what you seem to be, few know what you really are."[37] "Sharpest sight" will be its own undoing, because its suspicion takes the form of perceiving, that is, trusting the appearance of, "sleights" and "fraud."

Once he has assumed the form of the serpent, Satan's rhetoric consists of making distinctions between appearance and reality, intention and effect, means and ends, *virtù* and success, only in order then to argue for their correspondence on the basis of apparent evidence or sense certainty. In particular, according to Satan, physical sight guarantees intellectual insight. In fact, all of Satan's arguments in book 9 can be organized around the sense of sight in a way that makes his rhetoric an elaborate pun. Thus the serpent appeals throughout book 9 both to Eve's sight and to her desire to be seen. He calls attention to the shallowness or superficiality of mere sight as opposed to the depth of insight (9.544: "Beholders rude, and shallow to discern"). In this way, his rhetoric turns sight into desire and thus into a sense of absence (9.535–36: "gaze / Insatiate"). At the same time, he asks Eve not to think or be on guard: "Wonder not, sovran Mistress, if perhaps / Thou canst, who are sole Wonder, much less arm / Thy looks." Then, having established the difference between two kinds of looks, fairness, and perception (9.538, 605–6), the serpent argues for their identity by referring to himself as evidence:

Queen of this Universe, do not believe
Those rigid threats of Death; ye shall not Die:
How should ye? by the Fruit? it gives you life
To Knowledge. By the Threat'ner? look on mee,
Mee who have touch'd and tasted, yet both live,
And life more perfet have attain'd than Fate
Meant mee, by vent'ring higher than my Lot.
Shall that be shut to Man, which to the Beast
Is open? or will God incense his ire
For such a petty Trespass, and not praise
Rather your dauntless virtue, whom the pain
Of Death denounc't, whatever thing Death be,
Deterr'd not from achieving what might lead

To happier life, knowledge of Good and Evil;
Of good, how just? of evil, if what is evil
Be real, why not known, since easier shunn'd?
God therefore cannot hurt ye, and be just;
Not just, not God; not fear'd then, nor obey'd:
Your fear itself of Death removes the fear. (9.683–702)

What is interesting about this passage is the way Satan argues inconsistently both for the truth of sense evidence and for God's Machiavellian use of fraud. He appeals to the evidence of his own appearance— "Look on me"— to suggest both that God's "rigid threats of Death" are fraudulent and that the Machiavellian use of force would disable any claims to legitimacy: "God . . . cannot hurt ye, and be just." The same is true of the divine prohibition construed as a threat: Eve's "fear itself of Death removes the fear," because such fear is construed as evidence of coercion. Yet in describing God as a Machiavel, Satan admits the possibility of deception that undermines any strict claim for the correspondence between appearance and reality. In so doing, he betrays the Machiavellism of his pretension to unmediated experience.

Satan's rhetoric also makes clear that the appeal to sense evidence is tied to a particular interpretation of "virtue" as natural strength or innate power. As in books 1 and 2, Milton plays with the word "virtue" in a way that invites us to reflect on the relationship between the natural virtue of herbs, plants, and fruit in the Garden, and the ethical virtue of obedience, which is dependent upon the linguistic intervention of God's prohibition. Thus Satan describes the orbs of heaven, whose "known virtue appears / Productive in Herb, Plant, and nobler Birth / Of Creatures animate" (9.110–12); and, reflecting on why God created the Earth, he wonders if God's "virtue spent of old now fail'd / More angels to create" (9.145–46). In both cases "virtue" may be construed as productive power. In a similar vein, the fruit of the Tree of Knowledge is repeatedly described as possessed of, in Eve's words, a "virtue . . . / Wondrous indeed, if cause of such effects" (9.616, 649–50). Just before the fall, Eve praises the Tree's "Virtues" (9.745); in describing the Tree as both "Fair to the eye" and "of virtue to make wise" (9.778, 779), she once again suggests that the appeal to sense evidence and the construction of "virtue" as a natural power and unfailing cause of specific effects are two sides of the same coin.

Yet, as Milton argues in the passage quoted above from his *Christian Doctrine* and as Eve herself implies in the "separation colloquy" when she presents Milton's argument in *Areopagitica* ("What is Faith, Love, Virtue unassay'd"; 9.335), such natural or innate "virtue" is itself a thing indifferent, one that needs to be tested or tried before it can be called Christian virtue. The prohibition provides for just such a denaturalization of virtue through the mediation of signs. Even Satan suggests as much when he urges Eve to show an epic *virtù* or "dauntless virtue" by trespassing God's prohibition (9.694). He thus implies, in spite of himself, that the natural "virtue" of the Tree is nothing compared to the virtue Adam and Eve exercise by being obedient to—or disobeying—God's command.

The linguistic play with "virtue" helps us to understand Milton's Machiavellian defense against the force and fraud of the Machiavel. Such defense takes the form of arguing not that force and fraud are simply evil, or that appearances are merely deceptive, but rather that the possibility of deception means that appearances must be interpreted, and that the activity of interpretation is itself an occasion of free will. Or to put it another way, "virtue" must be denaturalized so that it no longer appears as an object of perception but rather as an activity of interpretation. Accordingly, all of book 9 is governed by an opposition between knowledge construed as cognition of an object (knowledge as possession) and knowledge construed as an activity of choice. The first kind of knowledge is associated with perception and with reasoning by analogy. The second kind is identified with obedience to God and faith, for which there can be no merely perceptual evidence. The impossibility of such evidence might seem to guarantee the harmlessness—the inefficacy— of deceptive appearances or, to use Puttenham's words for the trope of *evidentia,* "counterfait representation." Yet if appearances—and the realm of things indifferent—are reasoned away, learning and the right exercise of virtue are impossible.

Thus the problem that Eve faces when confronted with Satan disguised as "mere serpent in appearance" (9.413) is the same problem faced by the postlapsarian Redcrosse in book 1 of *The Faerie Queene:* the problem, that is, of Puttenham's "false semblant." In a garden that includes both the "fair appearing good" (9.350) that is the snake and the "fair appearing good" that is Adam, no single rule of interpretation (whether according to analogy or the inversion of simple irony) will suffice. Rather, it is precisely the absence of such an a priori rule that makes reading (construed not as the possession of knowledge but as the activity of choice) possible. Eve's error does not arise from the entirely rational assumption of the snake's good intentions (she has every right to expect the "subtle" snake to be as innocuous as the "mazy error" of the streams of paradise) but from her subjection of faith and of the divine prohibition to the serpent's view of human reason—from a reading for knowledge that refuses to accept the knowledge of human limitations. Accordingly, with the serpent's help, Eve reasons in contradictory fashion, both analogically and ironically. For once she assumes with the serpent that she can accede to divine knowledge by reasoning analogically from appearances, she leaves herself open to (the misconstruction of) a mere Outside. Milton's nonallegorical poetic is not at all designed to solve the ethical and epistemological problems dramatized by Spenserian allegory or by the allegory of Sin and Death; for what is allegory by one name is *enargeia* or *evidentia* by another.

Fittingly, Milton conveys his criticism of a phenomenological approach to reading not only thematically but also intertextually. If we return to the scene of seduction, we can see that although the pleasing appearance of the serpent dazzles Eve even before it speaks, Milton's allusive style seems to place the reader in a different position. For the comparison of the serpent to a ship (9.513) recalls Virgil's description of the Trojan Horse. We are reminded of the sliding — or falling (*lapsus*) — wheels that allow the horse to slip into the city (*inlabitur urbi*), and the approach of the Greek ships, whose departure from Tenedos (*Aeneid*, 2.254–67) recalls a similar departure of the snakes (*Aeneid*, 2.203, 225) who devoured Laocoön. The reader is thus tempted to think that the cognoscenti of Virgil are in a position of superior knowledge in comparison with Eve, and that their knowledge of Virgil provides them with proof of why Eve should not have fallen: that is, the snake is a Trojan Horse. But allusion here also functions as a trope of evidence and, in doing so, undermines the reader's supposed superiority: if we do not remember that Virgil, like Homer, is an "erring" narrator (*PL*, 1.747), we should note that the Virgilian passages to which Milton alludes do not tell a story of simple deception (according to which appearances are in ironic contradiction to what they really signify) but rather of a double misreading — for the Trojans believe Sinon's lies but they do not believe Laocoön's truth. We are thus gradually forced in book 9 to confront the fact that knowledge per se, knowledge of allusion, knowledge of the deceptiveness of appearances (and one is tempted to add aesthetic knowledge in particular — as the model of disinterested, independent inquiry) is not a guarantor of virtue.

Yet while Satan's rhetoric plays with the unreliability of appearances and so undermines the possibility of a phenomenological account of reading, it also makes clear that deceit and misrepresentation are not the invention of the devil: they are not created *ex nihilo*. If conventional signs are distinguished from natural signs insofar as the former involve the "will to signify" (as Saint Augustine argues in *On Christian Doctrine*), Satan does not introduce conventional signs into Eden.[38] He simply makes explicit what was already a potentiality of human language: the possibility of misrepresentation is a constitutive part of representation just as the possibility of choosing wrongly is a constitutive part of free will. In other words, all human language is arbitrary, which is to say, in the root sense of the word, willful. The question is, whose will is being served? Satan's sin, then, is not in using language arbitrarily but rather in turning that arbitrary language into an object: by making language seem to signify "naturally," in short, by arguing that knowledge can be acquired as, or in the form of, a natural object (the Tree of Knowledge), and so reifying it. Like Augustine, Milton makes clear that the first wrong choice is the choice to think of language and Christian knowledge as objects rather than as activities of choice.

That Milton aims to defeat Satan and his "rebellious rout" not by denying the conventionality of signs but by admitting it — and then by arguing that this conventionality is itself an assertion of free will (and thus a justification of God's ways) — is apparent in the treatment of Adam's fall. Since Adam falls neither by force nor by fraud, he undermines this stereotypical Machiavellian paradigm (itself associated with Satan's rhetoric throughout books 1 and 2): the Fall is not primarily a problem of external misrepresentation but of self-deception. Eve is righter than she knows when she says of her fall to Adam:

> who knows
> But might as ill have happ'n'd thou being by,
> Or to thyself perhaps: hadst thou been there,
> Or here th' attempt, thou couldst not have discern'd
> Fraud in the Serpent, speaking as he spake;
> No ground of enmity between us known,
> Why tree should mean me ill, or seek to harm. (9.1146–52)

Although Eve claims to be reading (eating) for knowledge, her remarks here betray her necessary ignorance (the necessary limits of knowledge), an ignorance Adam accepts only in order to *choose* to reject it. When he warns Eve "not to taste that only Tree / Of Knowledge, planted by the Tree of Life, / So near grows Death to Life, whate'er Death is, / Some dreadful thing no doubt; for well thou know'st" (4.423–26), the syntax of the lines dramatizes the inseparability of knowledge and ignorance. Yet in the end, "he scrupl'd not to eat / Against his better knowledge, not deceiv'd" (9.997–98). Milton's aim in both scenes of the Fall is to shift the definition of reading from reading for the acquisition of cognitive knowledge to reading as the activity of choice, a choice that if correctly made presupposes a different kind of knowledge as its foundation. Thus, whereas Satan argues (9.756) that "good unknown / Sure is not had" (knowledge as possession), Milton replies with Eve that "in such abundance [of the yet unknown] lies our choice" (9.619–20).

I have argued that the Sin and Death episode is an exemplary instance of Milton's ambivalent or, in theological terms, indifferent rhetoric. In Sin's narration of her encounter with Satan, we are offered an allegorical parody of allegory; and in Satan's encounter with Death, we are offered an allegory and critique of monarchical power. From one perspective (which we can identify with Sin's description of Satan's response), allegory implies a fallen mode of reading since it reifies signification and precludes any genuine encounter with otherness, any genuine exercise of deliberation and choice among possible meanings. From another perspective, the episode provides an allegorical critique of reading allegorically and so dramatizes the indifference of this rhetorical mode. From this second perspective, allegory exemplifies a structure of signification that characterizes pre- as well as postlapsarian experience. One burden of the episode is thus to show that signs, including prohibitions and laws, are not simply a consequence of the Fall but the precondition of any genuine ethical choice: language itself is a thing indifferent that can be used well or badly.

Milton thus uses what contemporaries stigmatized as the Machiavellian indeterminacy of language, its potential for force and fraud, as an argument for free will. In so doing, as we have seen, he provides us with a rhetorical theology and rhetorical politics, both more concerned to stage than to resolve the paradoxes of Christian doctrine.[39] Like the rhetoric of *The Prince*, Milton's rhetoric dramatizes the dilemmas of agency in a world in which our actions are partially governed by *fortuna*—or entirely foreseen by God. Furthermore, like Machiavelli's allegorical figure of Fortune as a woman, Milton's allegorical critique of allegory aims to dramatize—and to free virtue from—the threat of reification in the face of pure contingency (fortune) or pure determinism (the Calvinist God). In both cases, the critical or enabling aspect of such allegory might be described as a mode of reading or reasoning, in which the failure of immediate perception gives way to an elevating activity of interpretation, one that restores to the subject the conviction of free will.

In this light, Milton's remark in *Areopagitica*—"Reason is but choosing," a remark that describes the activity of Adam, Eve, and the reader of *Paradise Lost*—is the exemplary Miltonic narrative in little: it posits the passage between epistemology and ethics. Faced with the limits of human cognition, the reader exercises judgment in the realm of things indifferent and in so doing performs his or her divinely ordained ethical task. The problem, of course—and it is the problem of Reformation hermeneutics—is how does one tell the difference between the satanic self-aggrandizement of "perfect, self-originating agency"[40] and those decisions and actions that do not simply claim to be but are obedient to a higher power? Here we are reminded of the possibility that reason might act as a stage Machiavel, pretending a failure of knowledge in order narcissistically to "discover itself freshly in an attitude of awe."[41] Satan's narcissism in his encounter with Sin enacts this theatrical possibility. As Milton was well aware, if ethical discretion in things indifferent can be staged or parodied, this also raises questions concerning Milton's own rhetorical defense and education of the reader's ethical judgment. We know not only from the Sin and Death episode but also from the poet-narrator's self-descriptions, which frequently echo earlier descriptions of Satan, that Milton was himself sensitive to this dilemma. Milton stages the plot and counterplot of allegory in the Sin and Death episode not only to try to distinguish between legitimate and illegitimate dissent, reformation and rebellion, but also to meditate on the satanic and Machiavellian dimension of justifying the ways of God to men. Just as *fortuna* was for Machiavelli both the occasion of *virtù* and the threat to its realization, so for Milton the satanic Machiavel signifies the realm of indifference that is both a threat to, and the occasion of, virtue. Not least disturbing in the conflation of truth and the realm of things indifferent is the suggestion that the exercise of Christian virtue may be inseparable from a self-aggrandizing, stereotypically Machiavellian *virtù*. But for Milton this possibility is the risk one must take in order to reunite virtue and *virtù* in the proper exercise of Christian liberty.

In contrast to those many critics who have asserted that Milton was only interested in the Machiavelli of the *Discourses,* the preceding pages have shown that Milton was fully aware that the Machiavel and the republican theorist are two aspects of rhetorical politics, and that what contemporaries stigmatized as the indeterminacy or indifference of rhetoric in the figure of the Machiavel is also the condition of political virtue. Like the proponents of the oath of Engagement, Milton exacerbated this indeterminacy in the rhetoric of his prose and poetry, not in order to argue as they did for the necessity of allegiance to the arbitrary authority of de facto political power but rather to insist on the exercise of deliberation and action in the contingent world of political affairs. Like Machiavelli, Milton was aware that the indeterminacy of rhetoric could serve as a dialectical critique of the status quo, a means of unmooring custom and ideology and making room for a republic of virtuous citizens or saints. Like the critics of Machiavelli, Milton knew that the cost of such indifference was the Machiavel.

Notes

Unless otherwise identified, all citations from *Paradise Lost* are from John Milton, *Complete Poetry and Major Prose,* ed. Merritt Y. Hughes (Indianapolis: Bobbs-Merrill, 1957), cited parenthetically in text by book and line number; other citations to Hughes's edition are cited parenthetically to "Hughes."

1. In thinking about Milton's rhetoric in *Paradise Lost,* I have benefited in general from the work of Stanley Fish, especially "Things and Actions Indifferent: The Tempta-

tion of Plot in *Paradise Regained*," *Milton Studies* 17 (1983): 163–85, and "Driving from the letter: Truth and Indeterminacy in Milton's *Aeropagitica*," in *Re-membering Milton*, ed. Mary Nyquist and Margaret W. Ferguson (New York: Methuen, 1987), 234–54; and from Leslie Brisman, *Milton's Poetry of Choice and Its Romantic Heirs* (New Haven: Yale University Press, 1973); Patricia Parker, *Inescapable Romance: Studies in the Poetics of a Mode* (Princeton: Princeton University Press, 1979), 114–58; William Kerrigan, *The Sacred Complex: On the Psychogenesis of* Paradise Lost (Cambridge: Harvard University Press, 1983); Sanford Budick, *The Dividing Muse: Images of Sacred Disjunction in Milton's Poetry* (New Haven: Yale University Press, 1985); and Joan S. Bennett, *Reviving Liberty: Radical Christian Humanism in Milton's Great Poems* (Cambridge: Harvard University Press, 1989). Particular debts will be indicated in the notes below.

2. On Satan's use of republican language and his description of God as a tyrant or absolute monarch, see Stevie Davies, *Images of Kingship in* Paradise Lost (Columbia: University of Missouri Press, 1983); Christopher Hill, *Milton and the English Revolution* (Harmondsworth, Eng.: Penguin, 1979), 365–75; Bennett, *Reviving Liberty*, 33–58; Blair Worden, "Milton's Republicanism and the Tyranny of Heaven," in *Machiavelli and Republicanism*, ed. Gisela Bock, Quentin Skinner, and Maurizio Viroli (Cambridge: Cambridge University Press, 1990), 225–46. On Milton's self-consciousness about the use of the same vocabulary for opposing political purposes, see Worden, "Milton's Republicanism," 239, and especially Mary Ann Radzinowicz, "The Politics of *Paradise Lost*," in *Politics of Discourse*, ed. Kevin Sharpe and Steven N. Zwicker (Berkeley: University of California Press, 1987), 216.

3. See Worden, "Milton's Republicanism," 240, 243; Hill, *Milton and the English Revolution*, 365–75.

4. See Worden, "Milton's Republicanism," 243; Davies, *Images of Kingship*; and Northrop Frye, *The Return of Eden* (1965; Toronto: University of Toronto Press, 1975), 103–11.

5. See Radzinowicz, "Politics of *Paradise Lost*," 209–11; Bennett, *Reviving Liberty*, 24–26 and chaps. 2 and 3.

6. Radzinowicz, "Politics of *Paradise Lost*," 217.

7. In his note on this passage, Alastair Fowler suggests this reading. He glosses "lest . . . boast" as "so that men ought not to boast," and refers the reader to Eph. 2:8f: "by grace are ye saved . . . Not of works, lest any man should boast" (*Paradise Lost*, ed. Alastair Fowler [London: Longman, 1968]).

8. In considering the Sin and Death episode, I have benefited in particular from the following works: Philip J. Gallagher, " 'Real or Allegoric': The Ontology of Sin and Death in *Paradise Lost*," *ELR* 6 (1976): 317–35; Kenneth Knoespel, "The Limits of Allegory: Textual Expansion of Narcissus in *Paradise Lost*," *Milton Studies* 22 (1986): 79–99; Stephen M. Fallon, "Milton's Sin and Death: The Ontology of Allegory in *Paradise Lost*," *ELR* 17 (1987): 329–50; John S. Tanner, " 'Say First What Cause': Ricoeur and the Etiology of Evil in *Paradise Lost*," *PMLA* 103 (1988): 45–56; Ruth H. Lindeborg, "Imagination, Inspiration and the Problem of Human Agency in *Paradise Lost*," unpublished paper; Steven Knapp, *Personification and the Sublime: Milton to Coleridge* (Cambridge: Harvard University Press, 1985). I have also discussed this episode in "Allegory and the Sublime in *Paradise Lost*," in *Milton*, ed. Annabel Patterson (London: Longman, 1992), 185–201.

9. Angus Fletcher, *Allegory: The Theory of a Symbolic Mode* (Ithaca: Cornell University Press, 1964), 68.

10. George Puttenham, *The Arte of English Poesie* (Kent, Ohio: Kent State University Press, 1970), 197.

11. This discussion of Puttenham is indebted to an unpublished paper on book 1 of *The Faerie Queene* by Neil Saccamano.

12. Cited by Debora K. Shuger, *Sacred Rhetoric: The Christian Grand Style in the English Renaissance* (Princeton: Princeton University Press, 1988), 160. The quotation is from *Gerardi Joannis Vossi commentariorum rhetoricum, sive oratorium institutionum libri sex* (1606).

13. See the note to this passage in *Paradise Lost*, ed. Alastair Fowler.

14. On the Hebrew etymology of sin, see Kenneth Knoespel, "Limits of Allegory," 82. In *Milton's Spenser: The Politics of Reading* (Ithaca: Cornell University Press, 1983), Maureen Quilligan also discusses this passage in terms of etymological wordplay but does not note the Hebrew meaning of sin. For the association of sin and sign, Merritt Hughes refers us to Dante's "trapassar del segno" in *Paradiso*, 26.115–17 ("Beyond Disobedience," in *Approaches to "Paradise Lost,"* ed. C. A. Patrides [London: Edward Arnold, 1968], 188–89).

15. I was helped to see this point by the unpublished paper of Ruth H. Lindeborg. See also Maureen Quilligan's chapter, "The Sin of Originality," in *Milton's Spenser*.

16. On Sin's birth as a "linguistic event," see Knoespel, "Limits of Allegory," 82.

17. See Luther's remarks in his *Lectures on Genesis* (*Luther's Works*, ed. Jaroslav Pelikan [Saint Louis: Concordia, 1955], 1:166) on the sins which are so fully ingrained "that they not only cannot be fully removed but are not even recognized as sin."

18. John Freccero, *Dante: The Poetics of Conversion*, ed. Rachel Jacoff (Cambridge: Harvard University Press, 1986), 108.

19. James Grantham Turner, *One Flesh: Paradisal Marriage and Sexual Relations in the Age of Milton* (Oxford: Clarendon, 1987), 84, 87–88. Turner glances at the Sin and Death episode when he writes in a discussion of the allegorical interpretations of German mysticism and Neoplatonism: "Indeed, the grotesque figure of Sin [in *Paradise Lost*] . . . may parody the excesses of neo-Gnostic myth making."

20. On the identification of Pelagianism and Arminianism by seventeenth-century Calvinists, see, for example, A. S. P. Woodhouse, ed., *Puritanism and Liberty* (London: Dent, 1938), 54.

21. Martin Luther, "Introduction to the Epistle of Saint James and Saint Jude" (1545), in *Works of Martin Luther*, 55 vols., ed Jaroslav Pelikan and Helmut T. Lehmann (Philadelphia: Muhlenberg, 1932), 6:478.

22. Tanner, " 'Say First What Cause,' " 48.

23. In " 'Say First What Cause,' " Tanner makes a similar point, though he does not comment on the significance of the allegorical form of Sin and Death in this context: "Milton's myth thus exposes the irrationalism that lies at the core of ostensibly rational free-will explanations. It acknowledges that, at the deepest level, complete self-determination begins to look more like compulsion than free choice" (49).

24. Edmund Burke, quoted in *Milton 1732–1801: The Critical Heritage*, ed. John T. Shawcross (London: Routledge and Kegan Paul, 1972), 236.

25. Samuel Taylor Coleridge, quoted in Knapp, *Personification and the Sublime*, 8.

26. Martin Luther, *Commentary on Galatians,* in *Martin Luther: Selections from His Writings,* ed. John Dillenberger (Garden City, N.Y.: Anchor, 1961), 141. The passage recalls Botero's description of the sublime in his *Aggiunta* on reputation.

27. Annabel Patterson, "The Good Old Cause," in *Reading Between the Lines* (Madison: University of Wisconsin Press, 1993), 256. Patterson discusses seventeenth-century editions and translations of Longinus, and the political dimension of Longinus's discussion of the sublime, on pp. 258–66. The evidence for the direct influence of Longinus on Milton is circumstantial; Patterson notes that John Hall's translation was dedicated to Bulstrode Whitelock, "one of the most important, though moderate, members of the revolutionary council of state," and a friend and colleague of Milton's. On the republican dimension of Marvell's poem, see also Andrew Eric Shifflett, "Paradox and Politics in English Neostoic Literature," Ph.D. diss., Princeton University, 1993. Shifflett demonstrates that Marvell is echoing Ben Jonson's poem to Thomas May ("To My chosen friend, . . . Thomas May"), the translator of Lucan's republican epic the *Pharsalia.* Shifflett, following Christopher Hill, reads "That Majecty which through thy Work doth reign" as a joke shared by the republicans Marvell and Milton (161).

28. The political significance of this indifference may be clarified by noting that the battle between Satan and Death is an oedipal struggle. It was a commonplace of seventeenth-century political theory—most famously articulated by Robert Filmer's *Patriarcha*—not only that the king was a metaphorical father to his people but that his power had its origin in the actual power of the father over his family, a power that descended from father to son. In the conflict between Sin and Death, we have instead a father and son each claiming absolute authority, and neither recognizing the other. In making the oedipal conflict of Satan and Death into a conflict of de facto political powers, Milton mocks the patriarchal model of political authority.

29. See Thomas Weiskel, *The Romantic Sublime* (Baltimore: Johns Hopkins University Press, 1976), 40–41; Neil Hertz, "The Notion of Blockage in the Literature of the Sublime," in *Psychoanalysis and the Question of the Text,* ed. Geoffrey H. Hartman (Baltimore: Johns Hopkins University Press, 1978), 71–76; and Knapp, *Personification and the Sublime,* 74ff. On prophecy as exegesis, see John Milton, *Christian Doctrine,* in *The Complete Prose Works of John Milton,* 8 vols., ed. Don M. Wolfe et al. (New Haven: Yale University Press, 1973), 6:582 and 584 (book 1, chap. 30). I am grateful to Victoria Silver for calling my attention to this definition of prophecy in the seventeenth century.

30. Donald E. Pease, "Sublime Poetics," *boundary 2* 12/13 (1984): 264.

31. Cf. Jonathan Arac, "The Media of Sublimity: Johnson and Lamb on *King Lear,*" *Studies in Romanticism* 26 (1987): 209ff., on the sublime as allowing rebellion or reinforcing conformity; and Ronald Paulson, "Burke's Sublime and the Representation of Revolution," in *Culture and Politics: From Puritanism to the Enlightenment,* ed. Perez Zagorin (Berkeley: University of California Press, 1980), 241–69, esp. 248–52, on the political ambivalence of the sublime.

32. Joseph Addison, *Critical Essays from the Spectator,* ed. Donald F. Bond (New York: Oxford University Press, 1970), nos. 309 and 273, pp. 102, 68; Samuel Johnson, *Lives of the English Poets,* 2 vols. (London: Dent, 1961), 1:110. Steven Knapp discusses eighteenth-century objections to the Sin and Death episode in *Personification and the Sublime,* 51–65.

33. See Anne Perry, *Milton's Epic Voice: The Narrator in* Paradise Lost (Cambridge: Harvard University Press, 1963), 116–46. See also Quilligan, *Milton's Spenser*, 95: "Allegory is the genre of the fallen world, for in a prelapsarian world, at one with God, there is no 'other' for language to work back to since there has been no fatal division. No distance, no divorce, no distaste between God and man, who has not yet known the coherence of good and evil in the rind of one apple tasted."

34. For a related argument, see Budick, *Dividing Muse*, 48, 73, 79.

35. This is a traditional understanding of the prohibition. See Martin Luther, *Lectures on Genesis*, 154: "It was God's intention that this command should provide man with an opportunity for obedience and outward worship, and that this tree would be a sort of sign by which man would give evidence that he was obeying God." See also the gloss on this passage in the Geneva Bible, and *Paradise Lost*, 3.93–95.

36. William Bradshaw, *A Treatise of Things Indifferent* (London, 1605), marginal gloss on 25.

37. Niccolò Machiavelli, *The Prince*, ed. and trans. Robert M. Adams (New York: Norton, 1977), 51.

38. Saint Augustine, *On Christian Doctrine*, trans. D. W. Robertson, Jr. (Indianapolis: Bobbs-Merrill, 1958), 34.

39. I borrow the phrase "rhetorical theology" from Charles Trinkaus, *In Our Image and Likeness*, 2 vols. (London: Constable, 1970).

40. Knapp, *Personification and the Sublime*, 3.

41. Weiskel, *Romantic Sublime*, 41.

Rhetoric, Ideology, and Idolatry in the Writings of Emmanuel Levinas

SUSAN E. SHAPIRO

As the audience for Emmanuel Levinas's philosophical and Jewish thought has grown, his claim that ethics rather than ontology is first philosophy has become a more familiar—if resisted—view. This claim is central to Levinas's thought and indeed, as will be made clear, figures importantly in relation to problems of rhetoric, ideology, and idolatry within discourse. For without the priority of ethics, a critique of these functionings would, for Levinas, be impossible. In order to demonstrate the importance, relations among, and shifting character of the problems of rhetoric, ideology, and idolatry in Levinas's writings, I shall first briefly trace his claim that ethics is prior to ontology—that it is first philosophy—and then introduce within this context the basic problems to be addressed in this essay.

For Levinas, ethics is found in the response to and responsibility for the demand (or "command") emerging from the vulnerability, mortality, and nakedness of the "face" of the other person and not in the pure intention to do good emerging from the self. In this way, Levinas seeks to locate ethics in relation to the other person rather than within the self. The self exists, of course, before this command is received, but this self is not yet ethical. Furthermore, that the self must respond to the command emerging in relation to the other does not mean that ethics must inescapably be grounded in the self and ontology. The ethical revolution of the self that is responsible to the other person destabilizes the self. This very revolution, this turning over, is both constituted and enacted through the priority of ethics. Ethics, however, is ethically — and not, thereby, ontologically — prior, and it is only from the perspective of this ethical responsibility and turn that this priority can be recognized and enacted. Levinas argues that an ethics which is not first but which follows and is grafted onto ontology will necessarily fail to attend to the alterity of the other person. It will ultimately be reducible to its grounding in ontology and the self. Thus Levinas uses the terms "transcendence" and "height" for this priority to distinguish it as that which is not "grounded" in ontology. Ethics is found in the movement toward the other in difference and beyond the self-same. In transcending the same through "substitution" for and "proximity" to the other person, a critique of the same, a displacement of the self, and an assumption of responsibility for the other are simultaneously performed.

For Levinas ontology — grounded for him, by definition, in the same and the self — cannot generate a thoroughgoing critique of ideology but will always already produce yet further instances of ideology. "Totality" signifies for Levinas an ideology in which the self dominates the other; it is another name for empire. Levinas seeks to intervene from within this totality, to point beyond it to the alterity of the other person and to the self's obligation to her or him. Attending to the irreducible otherness of the other person ruptures the containment and the closure of the same in a totality. The opening of the self to the other is enacted through this attending to the command; it ruptures the complacency and ultimate self-containment of the self.

What is it, then, that makes possible or enacts this asymmetrical relation of responsibility to and for the other person? How does totality become ruptured? These are important and difficult questions for Levinas, for there is within discourse a double that haunts it, subverting the possibility of transcendence. One of the names of this shadow or double is "rhetoric." Its function is to maintain the ideology of totality by so infiltrating discourse that distinguishing between reality and its shadow is (nearly) impossible. The ability to critique ideology and to act ethically is at stake in being able to distinguish between discourse and its other within, that is, rhetoric. Thus, transcendence would be impossible without such an ideology critique of rhetoric. Further, for Levinas the problem of idolatry occurs when the distinction between discourse and rhetoric collapses. For rhetoric would always refer within — but never beyond — totality, making impossible the ethically orienting transcendence of what Levinas terms the "Holy" as opposed to the immanence of the "Sacred." Embracing the immanence of the Sacred, with its concomitant inability to critique ontology by transcending it ethically, is tantamount to idolatry. Thus, Levinas equates the inability to critique ideology and the institution of idolatry. The role of rhetoric in both ideology and idolatry is significant here. Further, the argument that ethics, and not ontology, is first philosophy is subject to this very problem of the rhetorical shadowing and return to totality. I shall thus pay close attention to the use of the term "rhetoric" in Levinas's thought and its relation to the ethical critique of ideology and idolatry.

Rhetoric: Levinas's Shifting Views

In his earliest and best-known treatment of rhetoric, Levinas figures its functioning somewhat negatively:

> Our pedagogical or psychagogical discourse is rhetoric, taking the position of him who approaches his neighbor with ruse. And this is why the art of the sophist is a theme with reference to which the true conversation concerning truth, or philosophical discourse, is defined. Rhetoric, absent from no discourse, and which philosophical discourse seeks to overcome, resists discourse (or leads to it: pedagogy, demagogy, psychagogy). It approaches the other not to face him, but obliquely — not, to be sure, as a thing, since rhetoric remains conversation, and across all its artifices goes unto the Other, solicits his yes. But the specific nature of rhetoric (of propaganda, flattery, diplomacy, etc.) consists in corrupting this freedom. It is for this that it is preeminently violence, that is, injustice — not violence exercised on an inertia (which would not be a violence), but on a freedom, which, precisely as freedom, should be incorruptible. . . . Justice consists in recognizing in the Other my master. . . . Justice is the recognition of his privilege qua Other and his mastery, is access to the Other outside of rhetoric, which is ruse, emprise, and exploitation. And in this sense justice coincides with the overcoming of rhetoric.[1]

Although I agree with some recent critics of Levinas that, in a restricted sense of the term, he can well (and perhaps may even best) be understood as advocating a kind of ethical rhetoric, in most of Levinas's thought and for most of his interpreters this claim would seem nonsensical if not pernicious.[2] And although I affirm a qualified rehabilitation of rhetoric in Levinas's thought, I do so only after a close look at how Levinas treats rhetoric in both his earlier and later writings. I do not wish to claim, even in principle, that Levinas has no problem with rhetoric, for he surely does. Furthermore, it is not clear to me that these pejorative understandings of rhetoric are finally overcome in Levinas's later writings, even though they do offer a more equivocal treatment of rhetoric.[3] I will both seek to understand and take seriously his negative claims about rhetoric, for only after and through attending to these critiques can we reevaluate the status and significance of rhetoric for an ethical discourse such as Levinas's in pursuit of justice.

Rhetoric in Levinas's Early Writings

Levinas's early writings elucidate the deceptiveness of rhetoric through comments on Plato's *Gorgias, Phaedrus,* and *Republic*.[4] In this view, rhetoric is considered an illusory and shadowy knack with speech that imitates, haunts, and would supplant being or truth. As such, it is the other of philosophy residing within it as its double. The task of philosophy might be understood as the critique of rhetoric and its separation from properly philosophical discourse. This splitting between rhetoric and philosophy is certainly a familiar gesture and citing Plato as the locus classicus for this opposition is also common. As Levinas notes in "Ideology and Idealism,"

> This is rhetoric in the platonic sense, which according to *Gorgias* flatters the listeners and which "is to the judicial art what cooking is to medicine" (465c); a rhetoric felt in all the fullness of its ideological essence, as "an image of a kind of political art" (463d). Such is rhetoric according to the *Phaedrus*, a force of linguistic illusion, independent of any flattery and of any interest: "not only in connection with judicial debates, nor in connection with all those of the popular assembly... but ... in connection with any use of speech ... one will in the same way make anything resemble anything else" (261d–e; ellipses in original). Such is the rhetoric that applies, not to speech that seeks to win a case or a position, but rhetoric that eats away the very substance of speech, precisely insofar as it "functions in the absence of all truth." Is this not already the possibility of signification that is reducible to a game of signs detached from meanings? From now on, we face an ideology more desolate than all ideology, one that no science could rehabilitate without running the risk of being bogged down in the very unproductive game that it sought to break up. This threatening ideology hides in the core of the Logos itself. Plato is confident that he can escape it by means of good rhetoric, but he soon hears within discourse the simian imitation of discourse.[5]

In commenting upon the *Gorgias* and the *Phaedrus,* Levinas insists that the problem of rhetoric is extreme, all pervasive, and, seemingly, inescapable. The most serious problem of rhetoric is not simply that it is an art of flattery or similar to a political art, nor is it rhetoric's amoral goal of winning an argument by whatever means. Rhetoric's real danger is that it imitates the real to such an extent that determining which is appearance and which reality may not be possible, even by "good rhetoric" or dialectic. Whereas Plato at times suggests that a separation between bad and good rhetoric, like distinguishing between appearance and reality, is possible within discourse, Levinas seems to question this. As he notes in another essay, with respect to Husserl, "It is probably difficult to separate language and rhetoric — which would constitute, for Husserl's quest for the absolute in the form of transcendental idealism, a major difficulty. Or does the philosophical genius consist precisely in the power of finding the first words, and do the great systems make up the foundation of our rhetoric? But the confrontation of the metaphorical with everyday language also reflects another concern: the protection of truth from eloquence."[6] This introduces a crisis in philosophy in its office as critique of ideology, a crisis that surpasses the mastery of dialectic and may even undermine the very discipline of philosophy. This "simian imitation of discourse," in which "ideology hides in the core of the Logos itself," means that rhetoric is not susceptible to immanent critique. Only a transcendence, what Levinas terms an "idealism," can offer a vantage point for the critique of rhetoric as ideology. Again, Levinas turns to Plato and the *Gorgias* for an example of such an idealism:

> Plato sets forth a *beyond* of institutional justice, like that of the dead judging the dead (*Gorgias* 523e), as if the justice of the living could not pass beyond the clothing of men, that is, could not penetrate the attributes that in others, offer themselves to knowing, to knowledge, as if that justice could not pass beyond the qualities that mask men; as if the justice of the living judging the living could not strip the judges of their nature, which they always have in common with those qualities that hide the judges; as if justice could not, consequently, come near people who were not people of rank and, in the proximity to others, reach out towards the absolutely other. In the myth of the *Gorgias*, Zeus, with extreme precision, accuses the "last judgment," which he intends to reform in the spirit worthy of a god, of remaining a tribunal where "fully dressed" men are judged by men equally fully dressed, by judges who "have placed in front of their own soul a veil made of their eyes and ears and their whole bodies." A veil made entirely of eyes and ears! Essential point: dressed up, others lack unity.[7]

The trope of clothing that obscures understanding of the "naked truth" is an ancient topos attached to the representation of rhetoric as a cosmetic art.[8] Like a veil, it hides and deceives. Is a judgment such as the one Zeus desires possible only after death, after the body which hides the soul and language that likewise obscures judgment have no place? Or is ethical judgment possible such that deception may be recognized and gotten beyond in this world, with a judgment anticipating the "final judgment"? At stake in this question is whether bad rhetoric and good rhetoric, that is, philosophy, can be clearly and in some critical sense finally separated — whether idealism can go beyond ideology. Levinas goes on in "Ideology and Idealism" to note that it is the social community that is represented by the "clothed beings" in Plato's myth at the end of the *Gorgias:* "In the social community, the community of clothed beings, the privileges of rank obstruct justice. The intuitive faculties, in which the whole body participates, are exactly what obstructs the view and separates like a screen the plasticity of the perceived, obscures the otherness of the other, the otherness precisely because of which the other is not an object under our control but a neighbour."[9] For Levinas—and he believes for Plato as well—the question of judgment concerns not only what is true but also an ethics not determined or undermined by the "community of clothed beings." Through this judgment that transcends the bodily and social, ideology critique does not lead to totality but to a recognition of the "otherness of the other." In Levinas's version of critique, it is not sameness that is the "naked truth" beneath the clothes of social hierarchy but, rather, irreducible difference and otherness. Indeed, it is only when this otherness is recognized that the ethical emerges, that the other is not object but neighbor:

> We must note that for Plato a relation may be possible between the one and the other, though they are "dead to the world," and lack, as a result, a shared other; that a relation might be possible without a common ground, that is to say, a relationship in difference; that the difference signifies a nonindifference; that this nonindifference might be developed by Plato as ultimate justice, and here, with all the approximations of myth, there is expressed in the *essence* of being an eccentricity, a dis-inter-*estedness*. . . . Ethics is not superimposed on essence as a second layer where an ideological gaze would hide, incapable of looking the real in the face. . . . The signification—each for the other—ethics, and the breaking of essence are the end of the illusions of its appearance. Plato speaks of a judgement bearing finally on merit. Would this merit be some real attribute underneath the apparent qualities, some preexisting attribute, which judgement could not do without, introducing in turn others by way of concepts and lacking any way of escape? Or, going from oneself to others, as if each of us were dead, the last judgement, is this not the manner in which a being puts himself in the place of another, contrary to any perseverance in being, to all *connatus essendi,* to all knowledge that receives from others only concepts? And what can be the meaning of the movement to put oneself in another's place, if not literally drawing nigh to the neighbour [*l'approche du prochain*]?[10]

Levinas reads Plato's apparently ontological myth as if it were an ethical one, shifting the temporality into the present, in which one puts oneself in the place of another "*as if* each of us were dead." This ethical eschatology functions "as if" one were facing final judgment. The connection of death, otherness, and temporality is a theme in much of Levinas's writing, from his essays in *Time and the Other* and *Totality and Infinity* to his *Otherwise Than Being, or Beyond Essence.*[11] It is the nonrecouperable otherness of death which signifies the impassible otherness of the other person. Unlike Heidegger, for whom (according to Levinas) the recognition of my finitude makes possible the emergence and project of *Dasein,* my recognition of the mortality of the *other* person obligates me ethically to her or him. It is ethics, not ontology, that is grounded in this eschatological insight.[12]

The problem with rhetoric, for Levinas, is that it is both embedded in and expressive of ideology. It is the masking and substitution of appearance for the real, the true. And within that ideological representation there is no self-critique possible. Only by going beyond ideology in what Levinas terms "Idealism" may rhetoric be undone. What is the character of this Idealism for Levinas? It is not a form of transcendence in which the God-term would be the perfection or fulfillment of what is. It would have to be both beyond and other than what it transcends, for Levinas, to be able to critique rhetoric and ideology. This "beyondness" is signified in Plato's myth at the close of the *Gorgias.* Eschatology rather than an ontology of creation opens the ethical relation and judgment. If ideology is grounded in and represents totality as unsurpassable, the transcendence of ethical idealism is, in Levinas's terms, "otherwise than being or beyond essence." Ethical judgment facing the finitude of the other person obligates one (or, as Levinas instructs, obligates *me*) excessively to the care of, responsibility for, the other. Again, unlike Heidegger, for whom the recognition of my finitude throws me into an unsurpassable being-toward-(my)-death understood and lived in ontological terms alone, Levinas's focusing on the other's finitude makes possible and requires my transcendence beyond ontology and totality to ethics and infinity. The logic of infinity moves forward ceaselessly toward the other person always before and yet beyond me. The logic of totality, on the other hand, proceeds from part to containing or comprehensive whole. The breaking of the finality of the grasp upon totality betokens an ethics oriented in terms of the infinite and the unsurpassable otherness of the other person. It is this ethics of alterity that makes the critique of rhetoric and ideology possible.

Rhetoric in Levinas's Later Writings

Although ethics makes possible a critique of ideology, Levinas's later works urge not the removal of rhetoric from language but of eloquence from rhetoric. "Eloquence," for example, is the term in Levinas's essay "Everyday Language and Rhetoric Without Eloquence" which bears the burden of "bad rhetoric." In this essay, Levinas draws on a commonplace distinction within the history of rhetoric itself, that between a rhetoric of persuasion and a rhetoric of figures and tropes, to problematize the relation of eloquence and rhetoric. Levinas, then, offers a way of thinking about rhetoric which in some measure rehabilitates it.

He begins the essay with the following characterization of rhetoric: "Rhetoric, as is well known, designates the art that is supposed to enable us to master language: whether it be, as Plato laments, to persuade the hearer by means of a discourse devoid of truth, showing the appearance of truth in verisimilitude, creating the illusion of truth; or whether it be, as Aristotle would have it, by seeking the conditions of a credible, persuasive discourse in the extension of the conditions of truth. Rhetoric thus includes the knowledge of certain 'figures' of the *said,* of the circumstances in which they are appropriate and the rules for their effective use."[13]

In this opening paragraph Levinas characterizes the art of rhetoric as the art of persuasion, either — with Plato — through mere appearance, falsehood, and deception or through the invention of enthymemes in the discovery of what Aristotle termed the "available or appropriate means of persuasion." In the Aristotelian version, rhetoric serves the public "extension of the condition of truth." In either case, however, the knowledge of the " 'figures' of the *said*" is part of the artful functioning of rhetoric inasmuch as it serves the purpose of persuasion. In the next paragraph, Levinas separates or "frees" the rhetoric of figures and tropes from its subordination to and governance by the end of public persuasion. And this focus on figures and tropes is also a "well-known," if later, view of rhetoric.[14] "But it is also possible to understand by the term rhetoric these figures of discourse themselves, the structure that belongs to language."[15] The view of a rhetoric of figures and tropes developed subsequently in this essay by Levinas resembles that of Paul Ricoeur more than that of Jacques Derrida.[16] Levinas notes:

> Already at the level of elementary analysis, discourse does not appear in the simplicity of a relation connecting, on a one-to-one basis, verbal signs and their corresponding realities. At the level of words, [there is] a distance between the "proper" meaning of the word and its "displaced" or metaphorical, figurative meaning. And it is as if this rhetorical movement of the "word in its literal sense" that carries it toward the figurative sense were not merely an effort to overcome an indigence of vocabulary and to designate a being or notion for which we have no words; it is as if the metaphor were necessary to the very signification it "produces" by its reaching beyond the literal meaning, which, in its own way, participates, lingering unforgettably, in the signification. . . . The function of language would appear to be not just to express — faithfully or unfaithfully — a prior, totally internal thought: its rhetoric seems a part of the intellectual act, and to be the very intrigue in which a *this-as-that* is assembled; a this-as-that at the heart of a *datum* that, according to Heidegger's usage, would already be world. . . . That hypothesis is all the more justified when we consider that, ultimately, words are always the beneficiaries of the meaning conferred upon them by their role in the semantic unit of the statement.[17]

The "proper" meaning that is transgressed is a language that Ricoeur uses in *The Rule of Metaphor* to describe the creative functioning of metaphor which puts in question the notion of literal meaning as correspondence to reality. Metaphor produces meaning, for Ricoeur, through and beyond the clash of its alternative significations. The meaning is not "behind" the word, phrase, or text but "before" (Levinas would say "beyond") it. For Ricoeur, reference is not archaeological but creative. The metaphor or text refers to the meaning it produces.

It is precisely these two elements, the notion of the "proper" (as *propre,* connected to my own, to property and self) and the transcendence of metaphorical reference, that Derrida questions. In this conflict Levinas can be seen as mediating between Ricoeur's and Derrida's positions. For while like Ricoeur, he preserves a language of transcendence, he agrees with Derrida's critique of the *propre* and the displacement of the self in favor—here, however, unlike Derrida—of the priority of the otherness of the other person. This difference has to do with Levinas's location of rhetoric and everyday speech in terms of ethical proximity as opposed to the flowery and distracting beauty of eloquence. This notion of ethical proximity depends in turn on Levinas's conception of everyday speech: "But if words literally have no proper meaning, they do possess a certain fixity of meaning within an order that, at first sight, can only be defined in a purely empirical manner: in daily life. Words at that level have a current meaning due to their usage surrounding interhuman relations based on custom and tradition and the everyday repetitions they entail. Those are the meanings of words according to usage, as if the language were nothing but a 'tool.' Indeed, but it is also a whole folklore of proverbial wisdom, thought and language being constituted in the proximity and familiarity of interlocutors who know each other."[18] The context of speech is the everyday communications within a familiar (perhaps even face-to-face) community which shares customs and traditions of word usage. The solution, however, is not to appeal to folklore or proverbial wisdom to replace poetic, logical, or rhetorical virtuosity with a sort of "vernacular truth." Philosophy plays an important role here. For "the confrontation of the metaphorical with everyday language also reflects another concern: the protection of truth from eloquence."[19] Philosophy is even more important now that the scene of persuasion has shifted from the public to the private realm. When subordinate to public persuasion, eloquence served a function that disciplined its seductive powers. But now that eloquence permeates the private domain without restriction, its danger is even greater. The truthfulness of everyday language must now be protected from eloquence as never before. Not only do figures of discourse structure thought, but the beauty of the words, of the expression itself, seduces apart from what the words convey. Truth no longer is crucial to persuasion by eloquence.

In order to liberate everyday speech from eloquence and its dominating effects, plain speaking is not enough. A kind of violent verbal debunking and unmasking has been undertaken in an attempt to counteract eloquence:

> We resort to everyday parlance to bring down and profane the heights of eloquence and the verbal sacredness it engenders. Even everyday speech is found to be not everyday enough, not straight enough. The decency of words, the noble cadence of oratorical speech, the respectability of books and libraries must be debunked. Bring in the filthy words, interjections, graffiti — make the walls of the city cry out. . . . But — and this may denote a strange powerlessness of language in its very power — the language directed against eloquence in turn becomes eloquence. Too beautiful to be true, does language not also become too horrible to reflect reality?[20]

If everyday speech inescapably has an element of eloquence, Levinas asks whether we can "speak of the *essence* of everyday speech, and what is the distinctive trait of that essence?"[21] Here, Levinas turns to philosophy to ask the prior question of "what the meaning of language is, such as we have viewed it up until now."[22] Philosophy responds that language does "the same work . . . as thought: to know and to reveal being."[23] This identification of the work of thought and language with one purpose, "to know and to reveal being," has been the project of philosophy, according to Levinas, from Plato to Heidegger.[24] But Levinas raises several questions that push to the limits of this philosophical tradition, opening up a distinction between the Saying and the Said through which prophetic speaking intervenes, relocating the ethical in everyday communication and, thus, the drawing near of one person to another:

> I wonder whether, in that whole tradition, language as *Said* has not been privileged, to the exclusion or minimizing of its dimension as *Saying*. There is, it is true, no *Saying* that is not the *Saying* of a *Said*. But does the *Saying* signify nothing but the *Said*? Should we not bring out, setting out from the *Saying*, an intrigue of meaning that is not reducible to the thematization and exposition of a *Said*, to that correlation in which the *Saying* would bring about the appearing of beings and being? . . . Beyond the thematization of the *Said* and of the content stated in the proposition, *apophansis* signifies as a modality of the approach to the other person. The proposition is proposed to the other person. The *Saying* is a drawing nigh to one's neighbor. And as long as the proposition is proposed to the other person, as long as the *Said* has not absorbed that approach, we are still within "everyday language." Or, more precisely, in everyday language we approach our fellow-man instead of forgetting him in the "enthusiasm" of eloquence.[25]

This approach to the other person is what breaks the spell of eloquence. If philosophy represents the disappearance of the Saying into the Said—the identification of the purpose of both thought and language with the knowing and revealing of being—then the separation of thought and language, Said and Saying, allows language to return to the speaking situation itself as the drawing near to the other person.

It is here that Levinas moves beyond philosophy to the prophetic, from the subordination and absorption of the Saying to and within the Said to the Saying as constitutive of the ethical. One might have thought, however, that given Levinas's earlier distinction between rhetoric and eloquence, he would here return not to a denigration of rhetoric but to one of eloquence and its identification with the Said as opposed to the prophetic. For the Saying seems to be an instance of the rhetorical dimension of discourse in which, as Ricoeur—like Levinas—says about discourse, "someone says something to someone."[26] But Levinas *does* seem to repeat his identification of all rhetoric with "bad rhetoric" in the conclusion of this essay:

> Doubtless the rhetoric of the *Said* can absorb the ethics of proximity; but it is to the degree that proximity is maintained in discourse that the circle within which the "life-world" signifies is drawn, within which *everyday exchanges* take place, and from which eloquence is excluded under penalty of provoking laughter. It is not by the degree of elevation achieved by the inevitable rhetoric of all speech that the essence of the "life-world" and "everyday language" can be defined; the latter are described by proximity to one's neighbor, which is stronger than that rhetoric, and in relation to which rhetoric's effects are to be measured. But it is also in the proximity to the neighbor, remaining *totally other* in that proximity, that—beyond the *distantiation* of rhetoric—the significance of a *transcendence* is born, going from one person to the other, to which metaphors capable of signifying infinity bear reference.[27]

Ethics here is posed as beyond both rhetoric and philosophy. Prophetic discourse as Saying "is not exhausted in the giving of meaning as it inscribes itself . . . in the Said":[28]

> It is communication not reducible to the phenomenon of the *truth-that-unites:* it is a non-indifference to the other person, capable of ethical significance to which the statement itself of the Said is subordinate. The proximity that declares itself in this way is not a simple failure of the coinciding of minds that truth would bring with it. It is all the surplus of sociality. Sociality that is also irreducible to *knowledge* of the other; it is delineated in language after an entirely different model than intentionality, despite all the importance given to the *Said* in language and that is further emphasized in a rhetoric already departing from the everyday logos.[29]

The prophetic relates to the everyday but opposes the rhetorical "already departing from the everyday logos." Here the prophetic is opposed to the rhetorical-philosophical. Each has a different relation to the everyday. The philosophical, like the rhetorical, is now understood to absorb the Saying in the Said. Only responsibility for the other person, not addressing her or him, makes the Saying prior, excessive, and beyond the Said. The surplus of sociality in proximity is the excessive responsibility of one for the other.

Toward a Re-Reading of Rhetoric in Levinas's Thought: The Prophetic

This surplus can also be the basis of another reading of the relation between rhetoric, the Saying, and prophetic speech.[30] I cannot here fully develop my rereading of Levinas in these terms, but I shall suggest a direction for thinking about the role of rhetoric, especially, in his later thought. Levinas's best treatment of critical transcendence and iconoclasm from within discourse is his development of the notion of the *Saying* and the *Said* in his later writings. And it is here that rhetoric can become — I argue both with and against Levinas — not simply the other of philosophy from which it can be clearly and finally distinguished. On the contrary, the critique of rhetoric as image (as plastic and as idol) remains for Levinas an unfinished, indeed infinite, task. It requires us continually to address and attend to another person, to make dynamic and temporal what has become static and frozen. This later Saying is also an unsaying of the Said. There is no Saying without a Said (except, it would seem, prophetic Saying), but without the continual Saying, the Said resembles a statue — a static image outside the ethical temporality of one for another. The Saying as both saying to another and the unsaying or breaking of the idolatrous Said is an always incomplete performance of an infinite demand. It is a discourse beyond or otherwise than both rhetoric and philosophy that, however (again I argue both with and against Levinas), participates in and draws upon both.

Indeed, Levinas seems to address this problem in his *Otherwise Than Being*. While prophetic discourse may depend upon philosophy's critique of rhetoric and — like rhetoric, only otherwise — draw near to the other person, it is still prophetic discourse which offers the peculiar transcendence toward the other that critiques both rhetoric and philosophy as two forms of totalizing speech. Prophetic witness is iconoclastic. It is a stance in relation to discourse that does not simply stand outside of it but infinitely points beyond itself to the temporality of the other person. It is because of this, I think, that Levinas at times characterizes the prophetic as the Saying of the Saying (without the Said). The very form and purpose of prophetic discourse is to witness to transcendence for the sake of the other person(s).

What, then, is the relation of rhetoric to prophetic discourse for Levinas? Is rhetoric simply the other of prophecy? Is rhetoric inexorably tied to immanence and idolatry? What is the role of philosophy in relation to rhetoric and prophecy? In order to address these questions, I shall turn briefly again to *Totality and Infinity* and then to Levinas's essay "God and Philosophy" and *Otherwise Than Being.*

In *Totality and Infinity,* Levinas ties the "prophetic word" to justice, not only to the face of the other person but to the "third party," that is justice to the other person(s) besides the other whose face I am responding to. Rather than a "self-sufficient 'I-Thou' forgetful of the universe . . . ,"

> the third party looks at me in the eyes of the Other—language is justice. It is not that there first would be the face, and then the being it manifests or expresses would concern himself with justice; the epiphany of the face qua face opens humanity. . . . The presence of the face, the infinity of the other, is a destituteness, a presence of the third party (that is, of the whole of humanity which looks at us), and a command that commands commanding. This is why the relation with the Other . . . is also sermon, exhortation, the prophetic word. By essence the prophetic word responds to the epiphany of the face, doubles all discourse not as a discourse about moral themes, but as an irreducible movement of a discourse which by essence is aroused by the epiphany of the face inasmuch as it attests the presence of the third party, the whole of humanity, in the eyes that look at me.[31]

Levinas is suspicious of the injustice produced when the I-Thou relation is understood as "clandestine," as just between you and me, excluding all others. Rather, the I-Thou is the infinite relation to the other person in which all of humanity is included. It must be this "prophetic word" of justice.

In Levinas's later writings, when he shifts to a discourse of Saying, Unsaying, and the Said, this relation to the "third party," to a critique of the Said, and to justice, seems to be in abeyance or even to disappear. Can this be the case? What would the prophetic word be without its critique of idolatry, without an Unsaying of the Said, and without a call to justice? How are we to read his later treatments of the prophetic?

In "God and Philosophy," Levinas writes of a Saying without the Said as preceding a Saying of the Said, as proximity, as witness to the *glory*, as prophetic testimony:

> This excess is *saying.* Sincerity is not an attribute which eventually receives the saying; it is by saying that sincerity—exposed without reserve—is first possi-

ble. Saying makes signs to the other, but in this sign signifies the very giving of signs. Saying opens me to the other before saying what is said, before the said uttered in this sincerity forms a screen between me and the other. This saying without a said is thus like silence. It is without words, but not with hands empty. If silence speaks, it is not through some inward mystery or some sort of ecstasy of intentionality, but through the hyperbolic passivity of giving, which is prior to all willing and thematization. Saying bears witness to the other of the Infinite which rends me, which in the saying awakens me. . . . Saying as testimony precedes all the said. Saying before setting forth a said is already the testimony of this responsibility — and even the saying of a said, as an approach to the other, is a responsibility for him. Saying is therefore a way of signifying prior to all experience. A pure testimony, it is a martyr's truth which does not depend on any disclosure or any "religious" experience; it is an obedience that precedes the hearing of any order. . . . The religious discourse that precedes all religious discourse is not dialogue. It is the "here I am" said to a neighbor to whom I am given over, by which I announce peace, that is, my responsibility for the other. "Creating language on their lips. . . . Peace, peace to him who is far and to him who is near, says the Eternal" [Isaiah 57:11].[32]

Ending with the quotation from Isaiah, this section immediately precedes a section entitled "Prophetic Signification," in which Levinas writes: "Prophesying is pure testimony, pure because prior to all disclosure. . . . It is in prophesying that the Infinite passes — and awakens."[33] The Saying of the Saying without (or prior to) the Said is the passing of the In-finite. It is a testimony to the *glory*, to transcendence. The prophetic is issued in the one who is commanded, who responds, like Abraham, "Here I am!" (*me voici!*). But this "Here I am!" is said to a neighbor, for whom I thereby announce my responsibility. It is in this sense, then, that the "saying opens me to the other before saying what is said" and is "the hyperbolic passivity of giving." This putting of oneself at the other's disposal, this proximity, is an enacting of both the witness to the In-finite and the *glory* as well as the prophetic command. This prophetic testimony, however, appears to come from the very one who is commanded to responsibility for the other, in the phrase "Here I am!" Is this prophetic word altogether the same as witness to the Infinite and testimony to the *glory?* Levinas writes, "One can call this plot of infinity, where I make myself the author of what I understand, *inspiration*. It constitutes, prior to the unity of apperception, the very psyche in the soul. In this inspiration, or prophesying, I am the go-between for what I set forth. 'God has spoken that you shall not prophesy,' says Amos [Amos 2:12], comparing the prophetic reaction to the passivity of the fear which takes hold of him who hears the roaring of wild beasts."[34] The connection of prophecy to in-spiration and the In-finite here emphasizes that the prophetic is not a word like other words but signifies as God (not human being) having spoken, even though this saying emerges from the one-to-the-other as a responsibility — a "Here I am!" — prior to the Said of speaking. The prophetic is radical proximity, the Saying of the Saying without the Said, because it is not only the ontology of the finite but the transcendence of the In-finite testifying as such. Does this mean that we no longer have, as in *Totality and Infinity,* concern for the "third party," for justice, for the problem of ideology and the Unsaying of the Said? How are we to understand this Saying of the Saying as proximity? Is this the rhetorical speech situation par excellence, demonstrating on Levinas's part a transvaluing of rhetoric, now in prophetic discourse?

In responding to these questions, I would like first to reemphasize Levinas's words, quoting again from a prophet, this time Amos, to the effect that it is important for prophetic saying to be understood as "God [having] spoken that you shall not prophesy." There is, it seems, lurking within the prophetic not only the emphasis on its divine *in-spiration* but a hint of the problem of false prophecy, a problem analogous to that "shadow" which haunts philosophy — rhetoric. It is, furthermore, the prophetic that cannot be contained within philosophy and which exposes the ideological character of philosophy itself even as philosophy critiques ideology in the ambiguity of the Said of prophetic speech.

> In our times — is this its very modernity? — a presumption of being an ideol
> ogy weighs on philosophy. This presumption cannot claim to be a part o
> philosophy, where the critical spirit cannot content itself with suspicions, bu
> owes it to itself that it bring forth proofs. This presumption, which is irrecus
> able, draws its force from elsewhere. It begins in a cry of ethical revolt
> bearing witness to responsibility; it begins in prophecy. . . . A meaning thu
> seems to bear witness to a beyond which would not be the no-man's-land o
> non-sense where opinions accumulate. . . . There is meaning testified to i
> interjections and outcries, before being disclosed in propositions, a meanin
> that signifies as a command, like an order that one signifies. Its manifestatio
> in a theme already devolves from its signifying as ordering; ethical significa
> tion signifies not *for* a consciousness which thematized, but *to* a subjectivity
> wholly an obedience, obeying with an obedience that precedes understand
> ing. Here is a passivity still more passive than that of receptivity in knowing
> the receptivity that assumes what affects it.[35]

These "interjections and outcries, before being disclosed in propositions [c philosophy]," are yet not "merely" opinion or the rhetorical other of philosc phy. They are, rather, the "cry of ethical revolt, bearing witness to responsibi ity; it begins in prophecy." This prophetic cry is prior to the philosophical i

that it is "obeying with an obedience that precedes understanding." And it is a "passivity still more passive than that of receptivity in knowing." It is the ethics of radical proximity and of testimony to the Infinite and transcendence. "Transcendence as signification, and signification as the signification of an order given to subjectivity before any statement, is the pure one-for-the-other."[36] It does not seem that Levinas has here abandoned his distinctions between rhetoric and philosophy and prophecy. The Saying of the Saying without the Said is neither rhetorical nor philosophical but ethically prior to them, that is, the prophetic. Does this mean that the prophetic resolves all the problems of idolatry and ideology that haunt rhetoric and philosophy? As my earlier allusion to the possibility of false prophecy indicates, I think that although prophecy *addresses* these problems, it cannot for Levinas be understood to solve them, despite his account of the prophetic Saying of the Saying without and prior to the Said as pure witness to transcendence.

To further address these issues, I turn to Levinas's discourse about prophecy in *Otherwise Than Being*. In the section on "witness and prophecy" in chapter 5 of his book, Levinas seems to suggest that one cannot simply move from rhetoric to philosophy to prophecy with ever increasing clarity such that one can be said to get beyond the problems of ideology and idolatry. The "Saying of the Saying without the Said" that characterizes the "Here I am!" of prophecy does not thereby mean that prophetic discourse escapes the ambiguity of ideology and idolatry.

> By reason of these ambiguities, prophecy is not the makeshift of a clumsy revelation. They belong to the glory of the Infinite. That prophecy could take on the appearances of information circulating among others, issued from the subject or from influences undergone by the subject . . . that is the enigma, the ambiguity, but also the order of transcendence, of the Infinite. . . . Transcendence owes it to itself to interrupt its own demonstration. . . . It is necessary that its pretension be exposed to derision and refutation, to the point of suspecting in the "here I am" that attests to it a cry or a slip of a sick subjectivity. But of a subjectivity responsible for the other! There is an enigmatic ambivalence, and an alternating of meaning in it.[37]

What reason for this ambiguity and its recognition is important enough to warrant the interruption of transcendence itself? Levinas does not wish transcendence to be understood, as in classical theologies, as a way of getting out of the mess of the everyday into a secured discourse in which one speaks "in the name of God." To anchor transcendence in a thematization of the name of God such that it becomes a shortcut out of the ambiguities of relation to other person(s) would be an understanding of transcendence to which Levinas is clearly opposed. The importance of remaining in proximity to the other(s) is the prophetic itself. As Levinas says, transcendence "needs the diachrony that breaks the unity of transcendental apperception, which does not succeed in assembling the time of modern humanity, in turn passing from prophecy to philology and transcending philology toward prophetic signification. For it is incapable of denying the fraternity of men."[38] Because the prophetic signifies, is enacted through and as proximity to the other person, its transcendence is for the other and is not a unity of transcendental apperception grounded in and for the self. Thus, the prophetic as the Saying of the Saying without the Said is not thereby a pure prophetic, transcendent moment. It is the "Here I am!" of putting the self at the disposal of the other; it is proximity or nearness to the other(s). For even the "Here I am!" can be an instance of deception, "a cry or a slip of a sick subjectivity." But — further ambiguating the prophetic — this slip of a sick subjectivity may be "a subjectivity responsible for the other!" The prophetic, like every discourse or relation (from rhetoric and philosophy to the testimony of inspiration) is subject to idolatry and ideology: "Thematization is then inevitable, so that signification itself show[s] itself, but does so in the sophism with which philosophy begins, in the betrayal which philosophy is called upon to reduce. This reduction always has to be attempted because of the trace of sincerity which the words themselves bear and which they owe to saying as witness, even when the said dissimulates the saying in the correlation set up between the saying and the said. Saying always seeks to unsay that dissimulation, and this is its very veracity."[39]

Philosophy is called upon to reduce the betrayal of a sophism within all words, including the prophetic. While the prophetic may be otherwise than Being, it is as subjectivity and word susceptible to deception. But deception itself is not only that; it may be a "subjectivity responsible for the other" that may resonate with the "inspiration or prophecy of all language": "In the play activating the cultural keyboard of language, sincerity or witness signifies by the very ambiguity of every said, where, in the midst of the information communicated to another there signifies also the sign that is given to him of this giving of signs. That is the resonance of every language 'in the name of God,' the inspiration or prophecy of all language."[40]

The sign that is given to him of this giving of signs is the "Saying of the Saying," that is, the prophetic. As it is a giving of signs, prophecy is not beyond language and is, thus, susceptible to ideology and the idolatrous. As a gifting of and through signs, however, it is a prophetic Saying. If philosophy is preserved in relation to the prophetic so as to critique — to reduce "the sophism with which philosophy begins" and that haunts the prophetic — where is rhetoric in all this? Is it merely aligned with sophism? In the only mention of rhetoric in this section of *Otherwise Than Being,* Levinas addresses this issue as follows:

In its saying, the said and being are stated, but also a witness, an inspiration of the same by the other, beyond essence, an overflowing of the said itself by a rhetoric which is not only a linguistic mirage, but a surplus of meaning of which consciousness all by itself would be incapable. Here there is a possibility both of ideology and of sacred delirium: ideology to be circumvented by linguistics, sociology and psychology, delirium to be reduced by philosophy, to be reduced to signification, the-one-for-the-other, a mission toward another in the glory of the Infinite. Transcendence, the beyond essence which is also being-in-the-world, requires ambiguity, a blinking of meaning which is not only a chance certainty, but a frontier both ineffaceable and finer than the tracing of an ideal line.[41]

The term "rhetoric" here bears the very ambiguity of the location of prophecy. It is "beyond essence," an "overflowing of the said itself by a rhetoric" which is *both* a linguistic mirage and a surplus of meaning. This surplus of meaning, furthermore, is that of which "consciousness all by itself would be incapable." What, then, is this surplus of meaning? Is it the "word of God," ideology, or sacred delirium? The latter two are, for Levinas, suspect. What he seems to suggest is that this surplus of meaning could be one or a mixture of any or all three of these meanings: prophecy, ideology, and sacred delirium. Rhetoric can bear (signify) any or all of these. It is, furthermore, the function of linguistics, sociology, and psychology to "circumvent" ideology, and the work of philosophy to "reduce" sacred delirium. Note that rhetoric itself does not serve a critical function but rather bears the ambiguity of discourse. Such ambiguity is required, however, if transcendence is not to deny the "fraternity of men" and if it is to be a "beyond essence which is also being-in-the-world," that is, proximity. Rhetoric as ambiguity is not merely negative. It serves an important function if prophecy is to be the one-for-the-other, a transcendence that is also radical proximity. But rhetoric is not the prophetic, for all that. It signifies the irreducibly ambiguous character of discourse, including prophetic saying. Importantly, rhetoric in this instance is not simply transcended and overcome by the prophetic—and here the tone of Levinas's remarks on rhetoric differ markedly from those in *Totality and Infinity*—but rhetoric may be necessary if the prophetic is to be in-spiration, that is, a transcendence which is not above or beyond but within proximity. This reenvisioning of the character, function, and location of rhetoric raises anew and in a different way the relation of rhetoric—through the prophetic—to justice.

Levinas's treatment of the relation of justice and the prophetic and the third" is clearly emphasized in his *Totality and Infinity*, as I have shown. These three terms are conjoined in his *Otherwise Than Being* as well, but only in one rather ambiguous passage: "It is in prophecy that the Infinite escapes the objectification of thematization and of dialogue, and signifies as *illeity*, in

the third person. This 'thirdness' is different from that of the third man, it is
the third party that interrupts the face to face of a welcome of the other man
interrupts the proximity or approach of the neighbor, it is the third man with
which justice begins."[42] Part of what is ambiguous in this passage is whether
the "third" is the third man or the third party. But what must be emphasized
here, I think, is that this prophetic signifying "as *illeity*, in the third person"
reintroduces the problem of justice interrupting proximity. While the problem
of justice is not further developed in this passage of *Otherwise Than Being*, i
still haunts Levinas's treatment of the prophetic in this text. How can we
further develop this relation of the prophetic, justice, and proximity in regard
to Levinas's later thought?

Prophecy and Justice:
On Reading Rhetoric and Philosophy Otherwise

Following this reevaluation of rhetoric in *Otherwise Than Being*,
claim—both with and contra Levinas—that prophetic discourse criticall
opens up the entanglement of and functioning between rhetoric and philoso
phy, appropriating the persuasive speech situation of the rhetor to her or his
interlocutor or audience as an instance of proximity, and recovering (albei
otherwise) the desire of philosophical discourse for the universal in propheti
discourse's concern with both justice and transcendence in the face of thi
proximity. The role of philosophy in critiquing ideology is thus maintained
but the relation of rhetoric and philosophy must itself be critiqued in light c
rhetoric's role in proximity. Is this a task that philosophy can undertake, c
does the ambiguity of rhetoric in relation to proximity become prominent i
and important for, especially, prophetic discourse?

I suggest that a detour through the prophetic and the question of justice an
proximity to other person(s) must be undertaken to make evident the injustic
done to rhetoric by philosophy.[43] Rhetoric as proximity, however, must not b
simply a return to the concentrated, claustrophobic closeness of the *il y a*
Rhetoric that is mere manipulation of closeness is such a terrible return. B
rhetoric as a surplus of meaning in which transcendence also "requires amb
guity, a blinking of meaning which is not only a chance certainty, but a frontie
both ineffaceable and finer than the tracing of an ideal line," is in the sam
location of the prophetic, that is, proximity, and the frontier between rhetor
and prophecy is nearly indistinguishable, yet ineffaceable. Rhetoric's proxim
ity to the prophetic presents both a danger and a possibility. The danger is th
return to ideology, sacred delirium, idolatry, and the *il y a*. The possibility
that of prophetic in-spiration. Although this entails an epistemological prob
lem that suggests an undecidability between rhetoric and the prophetic, it

not simply that. This ambiguity is important for the proximity of in-spiration. But critique and the question of justice remain to guard the prophetic from, as it were, mere or bad proximity. Thus, rhetoric and philosophy are both critiqued through the prophetic Saying, even as the problems of idolatry and ideology continue to haunt this very prophetic Saying.

In conclusion, I must again raise the problematic haunting of discourse by rhetoric and of ethics by ontology in Levinas's thought. This is a crucial question because Levinas's most central claim, as I have outlined, is that ethics is first philosophy. Every other aspect of his thought revolves around and depends upon this move. Does my revaluing of rhetoric (and philosophy) in relation to prophetic witness fatally contaminate this distinction, reintroducing ideology and idolatry into the moment of transcendence and the prophetic itself? With such a breach in the wall Levinas builds between rhetoric and philosophy and between rhetoric/philosophy and the prophetic, will the priority of ethics and ontology be reversed and the distinction between justice and injustice come tumbling down? This is a grave possibility. I cannot here, given constraints of space, sufficiently argue that ethics as first philosophy is secure in my rereading, although I do seek to preserve the ethical claim to priority. I can now only indicate that contrary to Levinas's insistent identification of justice with the "overcoming of rhetoric," I believe that at stake in the revaluing of the relationship between rhetoric and philosophy is the question of justice.

For rhetoric has been a maligned discourse, characterized in feminized terms that either efface or mark it as dangerous, reproducing and supporting hierarchies of gender difference based on stereotypes instituted from the very beginnings of philosophy as a discipline — indeed, with Plato.[44] The question of the justice of Levinas's treatment of woman, women, the female, and the feminine is an important one, and one that has been addressed by a range of critics, from Simone de Beauvoir to Luce Irigaray to Catherine Chalier to Tina Chanter. Elsewhere I engage more directly both these issues and critics.[45] Here, I conclude with a suggestion of the stakes of the question I have raised. Is to rehabilitate rhetoric to create injustice or to rectify a wrong? Will rereading and transvaluing rhetoric in Levinas's thought subvert the priority of ethics or will it further justify it, even in its own terms? I hope the latter will be the case. Only further explication and argument will clarify the consequences, the fate, of this way through the rhetorical and ethical impasses within Levinas's thought.

Notes

I would like to thank the Harvard Divinity School Women's Studies in Religion program for granting me a research fellowship, which enabled me to complete this essay in a

congenial and supportive context. In particular, I would like to thank as invaluable interlocutors David Tracy, Cornel West, Hent de Vries, and Robert Gibbs. I am also grateful to
Wendy Olmsted and Walter Jost for their helpful editorial insights and suggestions.

1. Emmanuel Levinas, *Totality and Infinity*, trans. Alphonso Lingis (Pittsburgh: Duquesne University Press, 1969), 70–72 [originally published in French as *Totalité et infini*
(The Hague, Netherlands: Martinus Nijhoff, 1961)]. In treating Levinas's early views of
rhetoric, I will focus primarily on *Totality and Infinity*, although I will also consider some
of his early essays. It is important here to note that the explication of Levinas's thought in
the opening of my essay follows the narrative emplotment of the relations between
ontology and ethics and between self and other in *Totality and Infinity*. In Levinas's later
writings, this narrativization is either downplayed or rendered absent in favor of a simul-
taneity or temporal reversal of these relations. In keeping with the focus of my essay, I will
not offer an overall account of Levinas's later thought but address how this shift affects
Levinas's explication of rhetoric.

2. Near the conclusion of his essay, "Reason as One for Another: Moral and Theoretical Argument in the Philosophy of Levinas," Steven G. Smith claims that "it is precisely
to the problematic appreciation of rhetoric that Levinas makes a great contribution, for
his entire philosophy is deliberately and self-consciously 'rhetorical'" ("Reason as One
For Another: Moral and Theoretical Argument in the Philosophy of Levinas," in *Face to
Face with Levinas*, ed. Richard A. Cohen [Albany: State University of New York Press,
1986], p. 68). This despite the fact that the term "rhetoric" in Levinas's writings is almost
always pejorative. Indeed, in the footnote to the sentence cited above, Smith notes Levinas's criticism of rhetoric in *Totality and Infinity* in the section entitled "Rhetoric and
Injustice" from which I quoted in the main body of this essay (see *Totality and Infinity*
70–77, especially 70–72). Smith's apologia, on the other hand, is brief: "Notwithstanding that in *Totality and Infinity* . . . Levinas takes 'rhetoric' to be manipulation of, rather
than sincere appeal to, the listener and on this basis endorses the traditional opposition of
true speech to mere rhetoric. But 'rhetoric' means 'public speech,' which is surely a
paradigm of true speech" ("Reason as One for Another," 71). This terse sentence hardly
explains, let alone justifies, the use of the term "rhetoric" to represent justice in contrast
to the explicitly opposed claims of Levinas's text. Smith's further explication of rhetoric
as "sweet reason" as opposed to the "hard necessity of coercive logic or evidence" is both
important and helpful, but it also requires further explication and development to overcome the apparent "evidence" of Levinas's text(s) against rhetoric. Smith's essay remains,
despite these qualifications, one of the most helpful readings of the rhetorical dimension
of, especially, Levinas's later writings. The association of the Saying with proximity and
of rhetoric and the Said with propositions, grammar, and logic is particularly helpful. As
will be made clear below, I agree with Smith's argument that in his later writings Levinas's
views of rhetoric shift. But this account should be justified not simply as a move from a *via
negativa* (in *Totality and Infinity*) to a *via eminentiae* (in Emmanuel Levinas, *Otherwise
Than Being, or Beyond Essence*, trans. Alphonso Lingis [henceforth *Otherwise Than
Being*] [The Hague, Netherlands: Martinus Nijhoff Publishers, 1981] [originally published as *Autrement qu'être ou au-dela de l'essence*, Phaenomenologica 54 (The Hague:
Martinus Nijhoff, 1974)]) but as a reevaluation of and response to the problem of idolatry in language. In these terms, the negative associations of "rhetoric" with deception

ideology, and idolatry are not denied or effaced but are systematically addressed, although not thereby overcome. To briefly anticipate my argument, the identification of rhetoric as ideology — and Levinas's texts equating rhetoric and injustice — become in his later writing the Said that is unsaid (but, of course, not finally unsaid) in the Saying of an ethical discourse that Levinas terms "prophecy." This Saying preserves and performs an iconoclastic function, questioning the previous dichotomous separation of "rhetoric" and "dialectic."

In *Fragments of Redemption,* Susan A. Handelman makes a similar but more nuanced and developed argument that Levinas's thought should be understood as "at bottom 'rhetorical'" (*Fragments of Redemption: Jewish Thought and Literary Theory in Benjamin, Scholem, and Levinas* [henceforth *Fragments*] [Bloomington: Indiana University Press, 1991], 237). She more directly notes that Levinas understands rhetoric in ways that make it part of the ethical problem. As she remarks, "Insofar as language is defined here as a relation to another, Levinas seems to propose an ultimately 'rhetorical' theory of language. He reiterates throughout his work, however, the ancient philosophical contempt for rhetoric, which he views as the approach to the neighbor through ruse, a mode of sophistic manipulation and violence rather than search for truth. Yet, Levinas's insistence on language as preeminently a call or command before it is an exchange of information is at bottom 'rhetorical'" (236–37). And as she further remarks, "Rhetoric was always grounded in the social concreteness of language as an address and effect on an audience, a personal other, but Levinas follows the ancient bias of Plato in viewing rhetoricians as sophists concerned not with pure truth but only with manipulation" (237). Handelman is aware that for Levinas "rhetoric" is at best an equivocal term. Further, she correctly cites Plato as his source for the pejorative view of rhetoric. However, Handelman's interest in her *Fragments* is both constructive and comparative (between the thought of Benjamin, Scholem, Rosenzweig, and Levinas). She does not closely work through the equivocal nature of rhetoric in Levinas's writings but rather introduces Chaim Perelman's "new rhetoric" as another, compatible way of conceiving of the relations between reason, ethics, and rhetoric in Levinas's thought. Although I find this "new rhetoric" and its reappropriation of Aristotle suggestive for contemporary philosophy and theology, I will not here follow this path. Indeed, it is a short cut through the thicket of Levinas's writings which I wish to resist in favor of a longer route.

3. See Handelman's treatment in *Fragments* of the *Saying* as "that 'rhetorical' aspect of language prior to philosophy — a primary appeal and relation with the other before any discourse can even begin" (248). As I discuss below, Levinas's treatment of the "prophetic" character of the Saying is a way of recovering this primary relation otherwise and beyond the opposition of philosophy and rhetoric. As such, it allows him to continue to critique and transcend rhetoric as the other of justice in discourse even as he seems, in his later writings, to include a more equivocal understanding of the relation between rhetoric and prophecy. This is a mostly disavowed recovery of rhetoric if it is, indeed, a return to rhetoric at all.

4. Handelman notes this as well on p. 237 of *Fragments.* Indeed, in the section of *Totality and Infinity* on "Rhetoric and Injustice," Levinas — in the parts I did not quote here — draws extensively upon Plato, especially from the *Phaedrus.* It is important to note, however, that Plato's view of rhetoric shifts among these texts, especially with the

affiliation of rhetoric and love in the *Phaedrus* as opposed to the problematic of the lack of ethical foundation or character in rhetoric in the *Gorgias*. The status of rhetoric in the *Republic* can be understood as analogous to that of poetics in that text. As with other issues in Plato's corpus, we must not only follow out the themes through his writing but distinguish between the dialogues, their problems, subjects, and purposes. Treating Plato as if he had a single, unvarying view on any subject risks collapsing them into a doctrinaire reading in which much of the critical resources within his writing becomes effaced. I do not develop a comparison of Plato's views of rhetoric here, but the characterizations that I make in what follows — based on these three texts of Plato, among others — must be understood as contextualized distinctly in each of the dialogues, to differing ends and with different consequences. I am here pulling out a major strand that has dominated the reception of Plato's understanding of rhetoric, including Levinas's.

5. Emmanuel Levinas, "Ideology and Idealism," in *The Levinas Reader,* ed. Sean Hand (Oxford: Basil Blackwell, 1989), 241.

6. Emmanuel Levinas, "Everyday Language and Rhetoric Without Eloquence," in *Outside The Subject,* trans. Michael B. Smith (Stanford: Stanford University Press, 1994), p. 138 [first published in French as "Le Quotidien et la philosophie," in *Philosophica* 40 (Bern: Verlag Paul Haupt, 1981)].

7. Levinas, "Ideology and Idealism," 243.

8. See my "Rhetoric as Ideology Critique: The Gadamer-Habermas Debate Reinvented," *Journal of the American Academy of Religion* 62, no. 1 (Spring 1994): 123–50, and my "A Matter of Discipline: Reading for Gender in Jewish Philosophy," in Miriam Peskowitz and Laura Levitt, eds., *Judaism Since Gender* (New York: Routledge, 1996), 158–73.

9. Levinas, "Ideology and Idealism," 243–44.

10. Ibid., 244.

11. Emmanuel Levinas, *Time and the Other,* trans. Richard A. Cohen (Pittsburgh: Duquesne University Press, 1987) [originally published in French as "Le Temps et l'autre," in J. Wahl, *Le Choix, le monde, l'éxistence* (Grenoble: Arthaud, 1947), and republished with a new preface by Levinas in 1979 as *Le Temps et l'autre* (St. Cement, France: Fata Morgana)].

12. This eschatological judgment in the present, according to Levinas, is also possible through prayer. Levinas describes prayer in his essay "Prayer Without Demand" (*Levinas Reader,* 232–33) in terms strikingly resonant with those of Plato's myth described above.

13. Levinas, "Everyday Language and Rhetoric Without Eloquence," 135.

14. For views of rhetoric that are especially pertinent to the French intellectual scene in which Levinas wrote this essay see, for example, Tzvetan Todorov, *Theories of the Symbol,* trans. Catherine Proter (Ithaca: Cornell University Press, 1982) [first published in French as *Théories du symbole* (Paris: Editions du Seuil, 1977)], and Gerard Genette, *Figures of Literary Discourse,* trans. Alan Sheridan (New York: Columbia University Press, 1982) [in French, essays 1, 2, 3, 9, and 10 first published in *Figures I* (Paris: Editions du Seuil, 1966) and essays 4, 5, 7, 8, and 11 first published in *Figures II* (Paris: Editions du Seuil, 1969)].

15. Levinas, "Everyday Language and Rhetoric Without Eloquence," 135.

16. Paul Ricoeur, "Creativity in Language" and "Metaphor and the Main Problem o

Hermeneutics," in *The Philosophy of Paul Ricoeur: An Anthology of His Work,* ed. Charles E. Reagan and David Stewart (Boston: Beacon, 1978), 120–33 and 134–48; Ricoeur, *The Rule of Metaphor: Multi-Disciplinary Studies of the Creation of Meaning in Language,* trans. Robert Czerny [henceforth *Rule of Metaphor*] (Toronto: University of Toronto Press, 1977) [originally published in French as *La Métaphore vivre* (Paris: Editions du Seuil, 1975)]; Jacques Derrida, "White Mythology: Metaphor in the Text of Philosophy," in *Margins of Philosophy,* trans. Alan Bass (Chicago: University of Chicago Press, 1982) [first published in French as *Marges de la philosophie* (Paris: Editions de Minuit, 1972)]. *The Rule of Metaphor* responds in many respects to Derrida's *Margins of Philosophy.*

17. Levinas, "Everyday Language and Rhetoric Without Eloquence," 135–36.

18. Ibid., 137. Levinas's argument here closely resembles that of Moses Mendelssohn's in *Jerusalem, or On Religious Power and Judaism,* trans. Alan Arkush (Hanover, N.H.: University Press of New England, 1983), 117–20 (see also pages 102–3).

19. Levinas, "Everyday Language and Rhetoric Without Eloquence," 138. At stake here is not only the problem of idolatry but, relatedly, the problem of an ultimate appeal to the *volkish* traditions as a sufficient form of legitimation of the everyday community and its speech.

20. Ibid., 139–40.

21. Ibid., 141.

22. Ibid.

23. Ibid.

24. Ibid.

25. Ibid., 141–42.

26. See note 2, above, for Susan Handelman's similar views on this matter.

27. Levinas, "Everyday Language and Rhetoric Without Eloquence," 142–43.

28. Ibid., 142.

29. Ibid.

30. Smith and Handelman, each in a different manner, point to such a way through the impasse of rhetoric in Levinas's thought. On rhetorical surplus bearing ambiguity, especially in his *Otherwise Than Being,* see my discussion below of Levinas's views of the relation to rhetoric and prophecy in terms of such a surplus.

31. Levinas, *Totality and Infinity,* 213.

32. Emmanuel Levinas, "God and Philosophy," in *Collected Philosophical Papers,* trans. Alphonso Lingis (Dordrecht, Netherlands: Martinus Nijhoff, 1987), 169–70. Only the first *Saying* is italicized in this text. Following the Lingis translation, I have quoted this text without further italicizing or underlining the terms *Saying, Said,* or *Unsaying.*" This essay was first published in French as "Dieu et la philosophie," *Le Nouveau Commerce,* 30–31 (1975): 97–128.

33. Levinas, "God and Philosophy," 171.

34. Ibid.

35. Ibid., 172.

36. Ibid., 173.

37. Levinas, *Otherwise Than Being,* 152.

38. Ibid.

39. Ibid., 151–52.

40. Ibid., 152.

41. Ibid.

42. Ibid., 150. It appears to be the "third party" to which Levinas here refers. This ambiguity is reduced somewhat, but not entirely, in the French original.

43. In my "Rhetoric as Ideology Critique," I suggest that a rhetorical reading of the relations between rhetoric and philosophy can make evident the "systematically distorted" character of their relation when read through the "canonical" reading of rhetoric by philosophy. See also *The Rhetoric Canon*, ed. Brenda Deen Schildgren (Detroit: Wayne State University Press, 1977), for a treatment of the problem of canonical readings of rhetoric and how it can be read otherwise.

44. See my "Rhetoric as Ideology Critique" and "A Matter of Discipline."

45. This essay is a part of a larger project, "Figures of Marginalization: Rhetoric, Gender, Judaism," in which these issues of ethics, rhetoric, and configurations of gender are addressed. My essays, "Rhetoric as Ideology Critique: The Gadamer-Habermas Debate Reinvented," "A Matter of Discipline: Reading for Gender in Jewish Philosophy," and "On Thinking Identity Otherwise," in Laurence Silbertstein, *Mapping Jewish Identity* (New York: New York University Press, 2000), also bear on this larger project.

13

Theological Reflections on the Hyperbolic Imagination

STEPHEN H. WEBB

The rhetoric of excess conjures up anarchy and deception, but it also shares certain features with religious transcendence and ethical demands and obligations. How do hyperbole, religion, and morality intersect? I shall try to unfold the various layers of rhetorical excess in an attempt to locate the peculiar logic of experiences and claims that suspend the ordinary and expected. The nonconformity of the trope of hyperbole can serve as a model for all discourses that seek the meaningful beyond the grammatical rules that limit the reach of meaning. Yet excess itself must have a context if it is not to be reduced to mere exaggeration, a linguistic discharge that achieves nothing lasting or permanent. I shall show that theological discourse renders excess meaningful and practical without reducing it to a useful strategy or figurative tool. More specifically, in the act of gift giving, hyperbolic rhetoric is translated into moral praxis, thus demonstrating how the "too much" of a good exaggeration can be "just right." The context that most helps to make sense of a giving that is at once unruly and beneficial is, I suggest, the Christian doctrine of the Trinity, where excess produces a community of givers that nonetheless does not dissipate the disruptive power of the gift.

For most of literary history and tradition, hyperbole has been treated as the bad boy of the tropes family,[1] a cunning attempt to manipulate the unsuspecting by claiming or demanding more than the situation permits. Ever since

Aristotle connected virtue and prudence, hyperbole has been considered in epistemological terms a naive form of deception and in moral terms a crass form of self-promotion. As Aristotle wrote, "Hyperboles are for young men to use; they show vehemence of character."[2] If a good metaphor is a sign of genius, a noble exercise in managing diversity, exaggerations are quintessentially democratic, a figurative anticipation of anarchy. Such unsublimated exclamations, as Aristotle insinuates, are symptomatic of an imbalanced and immature character. As an illegitimate trope with a questionable genealogy, hyperbole has rarely benefited from the subtle analyses that critics pay to tropes like irony and metaphor, perhaps because it lacks metaphor's poetry and irony's sophistication. Condemned for being both overly bold and simplistically transparent, one wonders that it is used at all. Frequently associated with unproductive polemics, insincere flattery, and stubborn fanaticism, the basic gesture of hyperbole is against qualification, decorum, and moderation. Unlike irony, which involves a hyperreflective awareness of the opposite of what is said or meant, hyperbole really means what it says, and unlike metaphor, which congenially negotiates the merger of two disparate images, hyperbole abruptly transgresses the ordinary and expected in order to separate rather than join. How could the hyperbolist not exist in a kind of Sartrean state of bad faith, refusing to admit that what is said is really "mere exaggeration"? Such insolence can be not only surprising but also terrifying. Given a hyperbolic claim, what reply can be given that would not look like litotes (understatement)? If nothing proportionate or adequate can be said in return, then how can anything be said at all? Perhaps, then, it is best to dismiss or ignore the hyperbolic altogether — unless it can be shown that hyperbole can say or do something significant that cannot otherwise be said or done.

Hyperbole is not always given such restricted treatment. If Aristotle's *Nicomachean Ethics* can be interpreted as one of the most careful and sustained attacks on hyperbole ever written (*phronesis* is the practice of measuring correct behavior by its middle ground between opposing extremes), then Longinus's *On the Sublime* (*Peri Hupsous*) can be read as one of the most moving defenses of this embattled trope. Here hyperbole is revealed as a powerfully seductive expression of noble passions that transport the reader into the realm of the incomparable. For Longinus the rhetoric of excess is a means of instilling the experience of the sublime, which in turn is an awestruck appreciation of the morally heroic. Hyperboles, then, should not be indiscriminate; to invest great emotion in the mundane would be ridiculous, not sublime.[3] Hyperbole must be measured by the event it is trying to capture. Longinus sets out to salvage hyperbole by making it do the work of celebrating the courageous deeds of a heroic morality. Nonetheless, he risks reducing hyperbole to a descriptive function that is appropriate and exact. In his hands, hyperbole becomes an instrument or tool for imitating and re-creating certain emotions that correspond to these moving events. Can a hyperbole that is both appropriate and useful still be called hyperbole? Longinus raises the question, which is becoming increasingly urgent among contemporary philosophers and theologians. Can hyperbole be more than a transitory release of passion? Can it express the violence of transgression while still staking a moral claim?

In our overworked culture, excess too often denotes the merely excessive, a sublime experience without any moral implications. Hyperbole spans the continuum from the frivolous, promiscuous, and prodigal to the luxurious, intoxicating, and ecstatic. Hyperbole, then, marks the irresponsibility of language, that moment when by means of profusion and exuberance, language is no longer bound to instrumentality and utility. Hyperbole can be defined in functional terms as an inherent temptation within language, the original sin, we could say, against the structures that make communication reasonable, ordered, and trustworthy. In this sense, hyperbole is nothing more than "hype," the weekend of the tropes, a release from the laborious demands of objectivity, clarity, and quantification. When hyperbole is given a purpose, a task, it is easy to see how hyperbole breeds cynicism. Longinus thought that hyperbole should be used carefully to substantiate the claims of greatness, but today we are all too aware of how hyperbole is overused to promote and magnify the value of various consumer goods, inflating the superficial to the point of banality.[4] Capitalist culture utilizes everything, even what breaks the boundaries of the useful, so that the most Dionysian expressions of surplus and exuberance are co-opted and marketed for the purposes of exchange and profit. With the impoverishment of religious excess comes the commodity as fetish, where extravagant acts are reduced to nothing more than desiccated quotations of rituals and dramas that have lost their original aura. Excess, then, becomes a sedative, a way of numbing the desires that exchange cannot satisfy. No wonder that many social critics have suggested that irony is the current trope of choice for intellectuals alienated from the glitter and pomp needed to magnify the value of the market.

Can hyperbole, excessive words and deeds that violate the expectations of the ordinary and the everyday, be both outlandish and valuable, both unrestrained and transformative? This is a question that is especially crucial for anyone interested in the shape and the future of religious discourse. Christianity, like every religion, points to something more—whether it be faith, hope, or love—than can be inferred from present circumstances. Since the Enlightenment, religious beliefs have been treated by modern, secular culture as crude hyperboles that denigrate reality through their illusory promises.

Secular culture sees religion as superfluous, as at worst a purposeless excess or at best a supplement that compensates for certain unfortunate deficiencies in modern life. Liberal theologians have often anxiously struggled to show that the exaggerations of Christianity, if properly downsized by prudence, really do make sense. They argue that religion represents or symbolizes (and thus exaggerates) what is universally true and implicitly an aspect of all human experience. By understating religion in order to make it seem reasonable, liberal theologians have inadvertently helped it become commonplace, something to be taken for granted, something that goes without saying.[5] Where religion retains some of its hyperbolic form, in fundamentalism, the hyperbole is oddly mixed with the literalism of science which, along with a deep resentment of modernity, makes these hyperboles sound more menacing than inviting.

From the immoderate courage of the Hebrew Prophets with their demands for justice, the fantastic parables of Jesus that insist on the absoluteness of the value of love, and the startling claims of christology that conceptualize the unthinkable, to eschatological visions filled with hope in the midst of despair and a defense of faith as a way of seeing what cannot be seen, Christianity is a religion of excess, not just in its dogmas, rituals, mystics, and saints but also in its everyday practices and beliefs. Christianity, through its doctrine of original sin, sees the world as it actually is, that is, governed by calculative self-interest, yet Christianity also imagines that the world is really what it apparently is not: full of love and grace. This imagination can be construed as following the contours of the trope hyperbole.

A trope is a word or phrase that turns its back on a habitual meaning in favor of something novel and surprising. Every trope models a conversion, demanding a change from one way of speaking (or living) to another.[6] Every trope is a little lie, asking us to see what could not be seen before, underwritten with a promise that is pledged only to those who are willing to inhabit the newly imagined space. Hyperbole is more than emphasis, which implies that what hyperbole emphasizes could be accurately understood without the help of ornamentation and embellishment. Hyperbole is the drive toward magnification and intensification that comprises all of rhetoric. Regardless of whether hyperbole is the Ur-trope, the trope of tropes, the basic shape of all troping, I do want to suggest that the survival of Christian theology depends upon a plausible articulation of a hyperbolic imagination.

For example, when Christians say that God is love (1 John 4:8), they mean that love is more present than anyone could possibly imagine, and that God can be named by the very human experience of love. "God is love" does not conceptually clarify what we already know, nor does it metaphorically marry the known with the unknown. Instead, the hyperbolic "is" denies the metaphorical "as if" in a compact condensation that fuses the vertical and the horizontal in a call for conversion, the demand to find love everywhere God is, with the consolation that in God is the love that is nowhere else to be found. Like the reasonable older brother in Jesus' story of the prodigal son, we are usually wondering why the father values the useless and the wasteful. Surely the merits of productivity and efficiency are what the father/God should reward. This story subverts, then, the ordinary expectations of patriarchal order. Indeed, the parables of Jesus embody a force that breaks open our myopic visions to a dimension where going too far in the name of the other is the right and only thing to do. Such illogical love demands that we do the impossible, making friends of enemies and giving a place to those who have no place. The farthest extension of this love is the impossible imperative of changing the past, of all that has been. In love there are no facts. Forgiveness enables us to forget what has been done to us, to change the harmful act into something we both accept and forget. Forgiveness irrationally transgresses the finality of time, and it gives without asking for something back. It turns every "it was" not into a Nietzschean "I willed it" but into a compassionate "so let it be."

Not only does the God of love offer a primary example of the necessity of hyperbole, but acts of evil also require a discourse that transcends the rational. Think, for example, of how the witnesses to the Holocaust were accused, at first, of exaggeration.[7] Even to themselves they thought that what they had been through could hardly be real. The Holocaust was and remains unbelievable owing both to its enormity and to the moral indifference that made it possible. Scholars today continue to debate whether the Holocaust was unique and what kind of language is appropriate for discussing it. Surely it is impossible to exaggerate such evil, but it is also important to say that the mode of excess is the only discourse even remotely proportionate to the event. We who were not there refuse to think that unthinkable acts are all too easy to commit. All evil, like the good itself, defies the calculations of rationality and the expectations of civility, a break with the ordinary that can only be exclaimed and shouted about. The courage required to confront and imagine the enormity of evil is not unrelated to our willingness to enter into the equally excessive dimension of love and grace. Evil makes God's love both necessary and impossible, thus requiring not a prose of the probable but a poetics of the fantastic.

Perhaps the most startling excess in Christianity is the one received from Judaism, the idea that the faithful have been chosen, not for some exclusive exemption from life's difficulties or for rewards and benefits denied to others, but for special responsibilities and obligations that include witnessing God's love for all people.[8] This excess does not arise from a pagan affirmation of the

fecundity of nature, a celebration of the eternity of the seasons and the holiness of the sense of place. It is also quite different from the phallic economy
of an excess that splurges and squanders on the basis of a sovereign self-
affirmation, without any thought to the purpose, goal, or return of such ex-
penditures. Instead, this excess emerges from the other, both the infinite and
the finite other, because in every finite other is an infinite demand for justice
and compassion. The ethics of this excess has little or nothing to do with the
rules of civility, prudence, and rational self-interest. Instead, ethics in the Jewish and Christian faiths is hyperbolized, so that the sublime is discovered
within the ethical realm itself.

Jewish theologians and philosophers are right to suggest that too frequently
Christian hyperboles are precipitate and premature. Christians too often want
to think that the Kingdom of God is already climactically realized in the
person of Jesus Christ, so that the worship of Jesus Christ can take the place of
ethical action. Judaism is correct to insist that the eschatological point when
the "too much" is "just right" is always "not yet." This is the great lesson that
Judaism continues to teach Christianity: that the coming (or return) of the
Messiah does not represent an escape from the world but must coincide with
the establishment of justice. This is why Christians should always mix a little
irony with their hyperbole. A hyperbole lucidly aware of itself, its limitations
and its foolishness, and yet still willing to speak without limit about the limit-
lessness of God's love — such would be an appropriate hyperbole for our age.

Can hyperbole embody a morality? Can the excessive really be ethical?
When is going too far really the right thing to do? The Jewish and Christian
traditions, in their privileging of the poor, sick, and homeless, imagine and
inhabit a hyperbole that is simultaneously ethical and excessive. This hyperbole can be defined as establishing a coincidence between the "too much" and
the "just enough." Most accounts of hyperbole occupy one side of this polar-
ity, arguing either that excess is always a dysfunctional surge that is therefore
irrelevant, wasteful, and dangerous or that excess is always a way of disguising
that which can be said otherwise, thus perpetuating the rule of the same. The
strange logic of religious hyperbole brings these two polarities together while
still preserving their tension. Is that convergence point an illusion? The question can be answered only by the wager of going too far in the name of the
other and thus testing whether the uncommon makes sense. Christianity enables us to solicit excess not as an intoxicating experience or as a means of
amplification but as a conjunction of style and action that imagines the impossible as necessary and the poetic as all too practical. Ethical excess is thus
simultaneously transgressive and appropriate, deceptive and true, ridiculous
and sublime. Love is the transition point where the tropology of religious

excess is translated into praxis. At this limit, action is vulnerable to the temptation of fanaticism, yet hyperbole allows us to imagine what we otherwise cannot even see, let alone say.

The philosopher who has done the most to articulate the excess of ethics and an ethics of excess is Emmanuel Levinas. In *Totality and Infinity* he argues that ethics is prior to metaphysics, by which he means that the question of what I am to do must be asked before trying to answer the question of what is, or what is really real.[9] If we begin by trying to determine the boundaries of reality, then we will inevitably marginalize or treat as a supplement that which is more than the really real. If we begin with a metaphysics of what is, then what could be, the demands of justice and compassion, will be found wanting as something less real than reality itself. Levinas, rooted in a profoundly Jewish understanding of the priority of the stranger,[10] argues that the other, by devaluing our stake in what counts for reality, is a "not" that is really something more than the real. This more, what Levinas calls the face of the other, is an infinity that disrupts all our attempts to create a totality of our existence. Levinas, however, is not interested in a more that is ecstatic, sublime, and sacred. The "uncontrollable surplus"[11] of the sacred merges people together in a festive and reckless enthusiasm, consequently annulling the distance between persons that is necessary for ethical responsibility. Levinas shows how we can accede to the infinite without the fear of being violently torn out of the profane. God's otherness is in the otherness of the neighbor, the stranger, the person in need; there is no other other. "To know God is to know what must be done."[12] Justice is the only path to God. There is no other name for God than what I am asked to do here and now.

Jacques Derrida has analyzed the theological dimension in Levinas's figurative strategy, "the superlative excess, the spatial literality of the metaphor. No matter how high it is, height is always accessible; the most high, however, is higher than height. No addition of more height will ever measure it. It does not belong to space, is not of this world."[13] Levinas uses the language of exteriority, asymmetry, and verticality to show how the other breaks the bonds of desire that enclose the self. Ordinarily, he admits, we try to grasp the other in terms of use, service, and function. "Labor remains economic; it comes from the home and returns to it, a movement of Odyssey where the adventure pursued in the world is but the accident of a return."[14] Authentic otherness surpasses this appropriation by violating the rules of economics, and thus the other becomes an (unpaid) teacher: "The calling in question of the I, coextensive with the manifestation of the Other in the face, we call language. The height from which language comes we designate with the term teaching."[15] The infinite face of the other is both extravagant and binding, a hyperbole that speaks both the impossible and the necessary. What the infinity of the face finally teaches is the demand that we not kill. "The being that presents himself in the face comes from a dimension of height, a dimension of transcendence whereby he can present himself as a stranger without opposing me as obstacle or enemy."[16] The inviolable other is the gift that denies our desire to profit from every relationship, creating a permanent debt that cannot be exchanged.

In Levinas's other great work, *Otherwise Than Being, or Beyond Essence,* the hyperbolic proclamation of otherness is impossibly intensified.[17] He equates the metaphysical quest for essence with "interest" in the fullest sense of that word, where "nothing is gratuitous" (5). In contrast to metaphysics, he defends what he calls "saying," a sensuous and disinterested reception of the other that precedes the thematization of the "said." The result is a "sacrifice without reserve" (15), "a hyperbolic passivity" (49) in which "the debt [to the other] increases in the measure that it is paid" (12). Subjectivity is comprised of radical vulnerability and exposure, "a passivity more passive still than the passivity of matter" (180). I must be willing to substitute myself for the other (to die the other's death, in contrast to Heidegger's position that my death is always and only my own), even to the point of giving the bread from out of my own mouth. The language of verticality continues in this book, even though Levinas now emphasizes horizontal proximity as well: "Height is heaven. The kingdom of heaven is ethical. This hyperbole, this excellence, is but the for-the-other in its interestedness" (183). For Levinas, the good literally does not count, in the sense that it does not calculate, and thus it is not valued by the interests of this world. "Freedom in the genuine sense can be only a contestation of this book-keeping by a gratuity" (125), "the gratuity of sacrifice" (120). The excess of the other is so much more than what is that the question of what it is cannot even be raised; this excess is not anything, a nothing (which is without essence) that defeats our attempts at understanding but demands our conversion, our turning away from the self and toward that which perpetually surprises and intrusively interrupts our frantic attempts to stake out and secure what it means to be.

In *Against Ethics,* John Caputo responded to the challenge of Levinas by pursuing the hyperbolization of ethics in his own way.[18] For Caputo, obligation is an event that just happens, in a multiplicity of fashions, so that we cannot have a theory of what obligation, in its singularity, really is. Obligation is a disaster to the self's attempts to establish itself, but it is impossible to trace obligation back to a metaphysical or theological origin. Obligations, in fact, occur before I arrive on the scene, so that my very agency is born from the emergency of being obligated. This means, however, that I am always too late to find out what happened at the site of the wreck of an obligation. For the self that seeks security, obligations are accidents waiting to happen, without any essence that can be mapped out in advance. If we knew what obligations were, we could make plans to avoid them, but their anarchic dispersal means that evasion is out of the question. Moreover, the sheer number of obligations that confront us is a catastrophe that can never be managed or resolved. We not only arrive too late on the scene of obligation, we also always leave something undone.

Although Caputo draws much of his ethical vocabulary from Levinas, contrasting an obligation that is "ugly, Jewish, Abrahamic" (12)[19] with the Greek bias toward harmony and completion, he also distances himself from the ambitious and elevated pitch of Levinas's work. He tries to minimize its religious overtones: how Levinas implicates the infinity of God in the infinity of the finite other. Calling himself a clerk, not a poet, of the infinite, he repeatedly states that "Levinas is too pious" (32). By focusing on the singularity of otherness, Levinas lapses into theology. "The problem with Levinas is that he has made ethics into a holy of holies, an inviolable inner sanctum, pure and uncontaminated" (125). Caputo recognizes that any account of otherness and ethics always contains metaphysical and self-interested assumptions, so he talks about the "jewgreek" even though his concern for the inassimilable orients him more to the Jew than to the Greek. Caputo wants a multiplicity of others and a variety of obligations, something that would not only dismantle the project of metaphysics but also shake the foundations of ethics.

What he most continues from Levinas is the language of hyperbole. "Obligations are our hyperbolic act of affirming infinite worth, of attaching hyperbolic significance to the least among us, of answering infinite moral demands, within the frail, finite, fragile bounds of our mortality" (246). Obligation is a hyperbolic interruption of ethics because the law, which generalizes from the principles of ethics in order to cover as many cases as possible, must highlight those features of a case that are abstract and similar. The law knows nothing of proper names, of individuals and their particular needs and demands. Individuals are always different, and perfect justice would be "a hypervalorization of everything singular and idiosyncratic, a hyperresponsiveness and responsibility, to the smallest and most singular" detail (89). The ethical act, then, must risk a transgression of reason and the law, of prudence, which is to say, of ethics itself. To act for the other "*is* excess. It wants to be as hyperbolic as possible" (121). The question is, how hyperbolic is that? What difference does Caputo's hyperbole make?

Indeed, for Caputo, as with Derrida, hyperbole is really just another name for difference. He accuses Levinas of treating hyperbole as a symbol, so that the face of the finite other hints at some otherness still more other than that.[20]

Hyperbole in Caputo's hands refers to an always absent singularity, an inescapable difference that fundamentally denies rational coherence even as it demands my most vigilant attention. The problem is that the rhetorical configuration of the play of differences is a kind of hyperbole that sacrifices excess to something else. For Derrida, for example, metaphysics—the desire to establish a totality on the basis of my own existence—always returns to preempt the transgressive gestures of ethics. In other words, irony circumvents hyperbole, so that the Jew and the Greek must be thought of together, simultaneously: what goes too far is determined by, and eventually becomes again, what already is.

By following Derrida rather than Levinas, Caputo in the end understates the power of hyperbole. By isolating it from any generalizable claims, he reduces it to the many obligations that assault me and that are impossible to organize. Hyperbole is the numbing recognition that there is always more for me to do, and that the most pressing tasks will never be finished. This hyperbole does not exaggerate anything; it does not intensify any demands made upon me or magnify the claims of an other. It merely underscores the fact that the self is implicated in an insuperable structure of differences that defies any single sign of identity, so that who I am is what others make of me. For Caputo and Derrida alike, difference itself takes a hyperbolic form—differences always exceed the economy of rationality—but hyperbolic actions toward the other always return to the self, so that the only difference hyperbole makes is in the form of an exaggerated irony.

Is it possible to break the bonds of economics by spending more for the other than what is returned? Are all other-oriented acts really profitable or at least compensated by some equivalent counter-gift? Christianity, through its doctrine of original sin, has been deeply suspicious of any claims on behalf of generosity or self-sacrifice. Nonetheless, Christianity also recognizes that through grace, which is itself a gift (as well as the power and sustenance of all giving), giving to others becomes a possible impossibility. Where Christianity most reflects on the extravagance of giving is in the discourse on the saints, who literally embody the rhetoric of excess. Saints go too far for a reason, but because they do this in spite of the usual claims of reason, they are held in suspicion and contempt. No one in the modern period has been more drawn to the quixotic features of sainthood than William James. In *The Varieties of Religious Experience*, he pursues those geniuses of the spirit who "have known no measure" because their reckless impulses paradoxically reveal what religion really is.[21] For them, "superabundance, over-pressure, stimulation" are essential (412). To borrow the language of Georges Bataille, they operate from a general rather than a restricted economy; their whole being is open to experi-

diture and loss rather than the recuperative calculation and profit of a self-enclosed and circular system.[22] They are able to endure the otherwise transient brilliance of humanity's most extravagant hopes and visions. In other words, they incarnate hyperbole.

For James saints are both extravagant and responsible. Holding these two adjectives together is not easy. One dominant path in postmodern thought, from Friedrich Nietzsche to Gilles Deleuze and Bataille (and, most recently, Mark C. Taylor), has articulated a notion of squandering as the most poignant expression of human freedom and sovereignty.[23] Borrowing from Neoplatonic theology, these thinkers imagine a human subjectivity that gives naturally and abundantly, not from any need or lack but from a superfluity that stems from self-affirmation. Generosity is an expression of strength and power. For Deleuze, for example, Nietzsche's will to power denotes a play of forces that is not engaged with any external considerations.[24] Giving that takes the other into account risks strife, resentment, or envy. The powerful will, on the other hand, is not reactive or oppositional but purely and playfully positive. Giving is born from a plenitude that naturally and effortlessly overflows. As Zarathustra proclaims, "I love him whose soul squanders itself, who wants no thanks and returns none: for he always gives away and does not want to preserve himself."[25] The overman does not give, in the sense of becoming involved in a give-and-take relationship of mutual and voluntary obligation, but instead creates, because what is given is a new and original event that does not respond to any prior gift.

Bataille takes this position to various fascinating extremes. Freedom is transgression for Bataille, not transcendence; generosity names every act that defies social convention in an expenditure that is at once erotic and mystical, full of danger and anguish. Bataille finds in the history of religion a movement toward a utilization of excess that is indistinguishable from the rise of morality. For primordial religions, the sacred is a region of self-dissolution that provides a break from the realm of labor and, through its power to overcome individuality and autonomy, makes possible human solidarity. Christianity, by contrast, tries to preserve the objectivity of the individual by anthropomorphizing and moralizing the sacred, in effect, separating sacrificial acts that preserve the self from acts that submerge the self in the social whole. What Bataille holds against Christianity is that it gives excess a purpose and thus comes dangerously close to reducing it to the world of productivity and rationality. For Bataille, the expenditure of excess is a jubilant and inebriated blurring of boundaries that dramatizes the last frontier of human freedom and is, in the end, indistinguishable from a ritualized confrontation with death. It is hard not to come to the conclusion that with Nietzsche, Deleuze, and Bataille generosity is a form of ecstasy that is not primarily concerned with the good of the other. Ironically, in an attempt to develop a model of subjectivity that overturns the illusion of a substantial and solid self, this variety of postmodernism ends by portraying a giving that is for itself and thus a self that gives only to itself. Such excess not only fails to challenge but also risks reinforcing the hegemony of exchange.

Edith Wyschogrod tries to mitigate the potentially anarchic and solipsistic consequences of postmodern philosophy by continuing James's fascination with the moral earnestness of saints. For Wyschogrod, saints serve as models of a desire that is disconnected from the exigencies of supply and demand. Saintly desire is not, however, squandered and wasted in acts of self-assertion. Instead, the saint is drawn to the good of the other. As Wyschogrod puts it, "The saintly desire for the Other is excessive and wild."[26] This desire is not based on need, because the saint sees through the illusion of a unified self. If the other were useful, fulfilling some deficiency or lack, then good works would emerge from resentment or envy, not bounty. The saint, in fact, puts deconstruction into practice by recognizing the primordial reality of difference. This metahagiography implies a secret relation between altruism and deviance; the freedom of the saints makes them seem like scoundrels, and their single-mindedness is a scandal to modern sensibilities. They indicate that morality is not connected to autonomy and rationality, and thus they exercise a critical solvency on the foundational certainties of moral theorizing. Morality can only be shown, not explained, in stories that embody a compelling insurgency for sacrificial action. Hagiography has an imperative and practical force.

Given the current consensus of cynicism on moral issues, Wyschogrod is right that we need saints now more than ever. Unfortunately, in her hurry to celebrate difference, she dehistoricizes and decontextualizes saints by disconnecting them from their religious beliefs and institutional environments. Saints exemplify a specific community's most intense moral demands, mediating what cannot otherwise be attained, yet Wyschogrod wants to abstract the essence of saints from their social situation.[27]

The result is an expression of excess that despite the retrieval of the ideas of narrative and moral example is thin, vague, and dubious. Wyschogrod has no choice but to isolate excess within the individual moral actor. Consequently, in spite of her acknowledgment that the Jewish and Christian traditions, in contrast to Nietzsche's promotion of excess-as-ecstasy-for-its-own-sake, channel excess into an obsessive (and even annoying, as with Simone Weil) concern for the other, she places excess in desire, in eros, in the self more than the other, thus rendering it idiosyncratic and idealistic. Can desire, even productive (rather than acquisitive) desire that is born from an attraction toward the good, ever escape the economic logic of appropriation and consumption? Is excessive desire alone a sufficient motivation for the moral life? Where does such desire come from, and how does it create relationships of mutuality, that is, how is the gift returned without thereby lapsing into exchange, not generosity?

Perhaps nowhere is the problem of articulating a hyperbolic imagination more relevant than in the current discussions of generosity and gift giving. Our culture is deeply suspicious about the possibilities of charity. Irony exercises an anorectic constriction of generosity by seeing in every gift only self-interest and self-promotion. Giving, we are taught to assume, is a way of disguising or deferring the desire to receive; generosity dramatizes or stylizes exchange, but the performance of excess does not alter the reality of reciprocity. The form of giving can vary widely across cultures, but the substance of exchange never changes. The ostensible recipient of the gift is merely the occasion for an expression of a will to power. Giving is thus reduced to economics, to an exchange based on the pursuit of profit instead of the good of the other.[28] There is something almost religious about modern scholarship's ascetic renunciation and disavowal of any positive meaning in donative acts. To admit that a gift really can be given would be to indulge in a desire that has been penuriously prohibited. This temptation would be a transgression against the rigorous authority (the operational requirements) of theory and critique. Nevertheless, it is too easy to reduce all interactions to the single model of exchange. Indeed, elevating exchange to a metaphysical principle can be reassuring because of the dominance of economic rationality in the modern Western world. To insinuate that all relationships are secretly controlled by exchange is to make our own presuppositions final and universal. Thinking the other of exchange becomes possible only by bracketing our own convenient expectations and conspiratorial prejudices.

If exchange is the dominant model for social interaction today, then authentic gift giving is in trouble. If the gift always rebounds to the giver, then how can it really be given in the first place? The circle is a powerful symbol for reciprocity, the coincidence of beginnings and endings, an economy where what is sent must necessarily return, but the geometry of the gift must be closer to a disjunctive loop if it is to trace the figure of generosity. Exchange is the process where the energy of the gift is exhausted or consumed, converting the gift into the commodity. Derrida pushes the aporia of the gift to its most illogical extreme: "For there to be a gift, it is necessary [*il faut*] that the donee not give back, amortize, reimburse, acquit himself, enter into a contract, and that he never have contracted a debt."[29] To receive the gift as a gift is to incur an obligation or debt, which must, in the appropriate fashion and at the right time, be repaid. Even the expression of gratitude, a return that is meant to not look like a return, is enough to annul the gift. The gift, then, if it is to be such, must completely disappear after it is given. It must be given at the moment of the effraction of the circle, in the fleeting present moment without thought of the past (debt) or the future (return). Such giving is like Kierkegaard's attempt to locate the madness of faith in the instant of a decision. The gift, then, like the present time that can never be captured, must be unintended, almost accidental — it must not be, or it must be nothing, in order for it to be given. A gift must always be more than it is, because once it is, it is no more.

There can be no law of giving if the very idea of a law is that it measures something proportionate and balanced. Derrida suggests that rationality itself is bound to the law of economy, to making that which is diverse equivalent and regular. How then can the gift be given if it cannot even be thought? Derrida intensifies the New Testament discourse (see Matt. 6:1–4) on the privacy of giving (as opposed to the Greek and Roman sense that generosity is the privilege of the wealthy and a well-rewarded duty for the maintenance of civil society). He can thus make the remarkable comment that "it is necessary to be forgiven for appearing to give."[30] Every gift that draws attention to itself needs the counter-gift of forgiveness (forgiveness, Derrida implies, for the appearance of giving), although he is not clear about how forgiveness itself can ever be given. Sacrifice must become spiritualized and inward, an act seen only by God. Yet Derrida also insists that religion merely belabors and thus profits from the difficulties of generosity, converting excess into an even higher form of exchange (thus hidden sacrifices are meant to buy a reward in the afterlife).[31] Derrida seems to strain after an ultimate excess that enters into relationships of mutuality without surrendering to exchange — and such an excess would be modeled on God's grace — but he also suspects religions of hiding exchange within the folds of grace.

The problem is that Derrida has defined excess as that which cannot be responded to or even recognized, so that he sees no way in which the gratuitous can be constructively connected to relationships of mutuality and reciprocity. Take, for example, his own response to the discourse on ultimate otherness in Levinas. Derrida doubts whether such otherness is purely unrelated to exchange. The other who forces us to reply (who creates our responsibility) already reduces the excess of the gift to the dynamic of exchange. "Finally, the overrunning of the circle by the gift, if there is any, does not lead to a simple, ineffable exteriority that would be transcendent and without relation. It is this exteriority that sets the circle going, it is this exteriority that puts the economy in motion."[32] The excessive other thus creates a dilemma: to return the gift is to violate the height of the transcendent face, yet not to show gratitude is to reject the gift altogether. Every gift has its wage, yet to return the gift is to wager against giving itself. Derrida instantiates this dilemma in his own belabored response to Levinas, writing in a double bind that shows both gratitude and ingratitude.[33] Indeed, all commentary results in betrayal; all gifts must be denied if they are to be properly returned. By writing about Levinas, Derrida is forced to interrupt the primacy and priority of the other; the best he can do is write in such a way as to invite other interruptions, disseminating what was given to him along a path that cannot be followed or mapped.

Perhaps, in the end, Derrida is closer to Levinas than he would like to admit. He accepts Levinas's notion of excess and then problematizes (exaggerates?) it. It is important, then, to rethink Levinas from the start. For Levinas the excess all lies on the side of the other, but it is an excess that is not blinding or paralyzing because it prompts my own excessive acts in the response of responsibility. Levinas is suspicious of the Christian language of love, which can too easily imply an intimacy and community that supersedes the demands of justice. The reciprocity of love, the closed society of the couple, leaves out the third party, which provides the opening of ethics. Love is too easy and natural, a way of expanding the ego to encompass the other. The proper response to otherness is a kind of insomnia, a vigilant wakefulness to the needs the other assigns to us. The other does not liberate us from the demands and anxieties of finitude; instead, the infinity of the other is a veto on the self's desire to expand without limits. To be is to be chosen, involuntarily elected in my singularity as a hostage for the other. The summons of responsibility is ancient, a more original burden than my attempts to establish my self-identity. This stark, even exaggerated account of asymmetry leaves no place for mutuality, for the give-and-take that is an aspect of every gift economy.

Levinas is against christology because every other, not just Jesus Christ, puts us into an infinite debt of obligation, and nobody can take our place, nobody can be our substitute and free us from this debt.[34] Every person we meet incarnates the face of God, and we are all called upon to be messiahs, substituting ourselves for others. Substitution, as the normative structure of all relationships, is a process that can never come to an end because the self never coincides with itself. God is not one of us, and we are not one with each other; instead, ethics precedes from an infinite distance that must be repeatedly crossed. Even admitting the fundamental differences between a Christian and a Levinasian account of incarnation, Levinas still provides an important corrective to those christological theories that establish an ontological sameness between God and humanity and thus replace ethics with worship and praise. A Christian theology that takes Levinas seriously would have to show how Jesus Christ constitutes the insomnia of God, God's eternal vigilance and wakefulness to God's others, that is, us. This theology would also have to show how

Christian messianism does not bring giving to a close. Instead, the gift of Jesus must be seen as obligating us to continue God's gifts by paying attention to all those others who are in need. Jesus Christ is not, then, the face of God upon which Christians can gaze for salvation. Instead, Jesus is the shape and definition of a gift of excessive otherness that liberates us to give and give again.[35]

For Christian theology, the gift of the other is liberating as well as obliging, so that Christianity holds together excess and exchange in a Chalcedonian manner, that is, without reducing one to the other. Christianity does not isolate the grace of giving from the corrupting demands of exchange, an impossible exercise in the pursuit of purity that would make the gift wonderful to experience but would render it private and therefore invisible and thus irrelevant to everyday practices. The gift is a love that empowers mutuality, not a demand that creates asymmetry. Christianity does this by providing a threefold structure of generosity that preserves the tension between the gift and exchange but also shows how they can be constructively connected. This structure is the Trinity, which is the idea that God is essentially relational, that is, that God not only gives but is constituted by a process of giving.[36]

First, then, God the Father points to the idea that giving is not incidental or secondary to who God is. The metaphysical quest to establish God as the highest being is bound to fail. If God is a being, then God's power over us is intrusive and God is subjected to the same forces of economizing that we are. The possibility of distinguishing excess and exchange seems dependent on the possibility of thinking the difference between God and beings, that is, the possibility of naming God otherwise than with the nomenclature of exchange. Theology asks what it means to give, not what it means to be. As Jean-Luc Marion writes, "If, to begin with, 'God is love,' then God loves before being, He only is as He embodies himself — in order to love more closely that which and those who, themselves, have first to be."[37] Giving is the being (or the beyond being, the *hyperousia*) of God. God is God in that God gives form to excess without dissipating generosity, thus embodying a creativity that does not monopolize the profit. God is the persuasive rhetoric of hyperbole, the way in which exaggerated demands and dreams make sense without becoming common and mundane.

Second, God the Son discloses that all giving occurs through acts of shared suffering, through wounds and even through catastrophe. For Christians, Jesus Christ is the specific shape of all of God's giving, showing that what God gives is ultimately God's own self. In a kenotic christology (based on Philippians 2:5–11), God becomes incarnate by giving up the rights and benefits that naturally accrue to the divinity. This christology, however, still assumes that God did not need to give, that it is God's choice to become involved in the precarious life of human flesh. God voluntarily abandons the divine power in order to share in human finitude, but God did not have to make this decision, and God could still be God without identifying with the fate of Jesus' life and the continuance of that life in the Holy Spirit. I am suggesting, from the perspective of the gift, that Jesus Christ represents God's intimate participation in the continuous circulation of the gift, its risky journey through space and time. In Jesus Christ, excess is exchanged, while remaining excessive. Indeed, in the condensed narrative of Jesus' life the whole history of God's giving is disclosed as a splendid squandering that rejuvenates and restores. Giving thus is not a fruitless self-denial aimed at some otherworldly reward, or an impotent and frustrated act of rebellion against the restraints of economic rationality, but a sacrificial affirmation of the restless movement that already constitutes who we are. The rhetoric of this giving is perfectly expressed in the parables, where the illogic of abundance is offered above and beyond the moderate and reasonable concerns of self-interest and self-preservation. Jesus shows that prodigality is the only way to return home.

Third, and finally, with God the Holy Spirit we have our participation in the return of the gift, the way it takes shape as it is passed along but not depleted. For Christian theology, gift giving is the ratification of grace, which is itself nothing more than pure excess, a gratuitous endowment of God's love. Grace is an excess that both consoles and provokes, joining the recipients together in a community that replenishes the gift by passing it along. Because the gift does not have to be, it can free us from the obsessive desire to secure our own existence at the cost of others, that is, to own ourselves before we give. The gift that is given up returns not as reward but as the condition for further giving. Only in a community that gives everything for the promotion of giving itself can excess take shape without merely repeating the dynamic of exchange. The church, then, is the name for the "community without unity" where the proliferation of giving creates both difference and solidarity.[38] Excess needs a form if it is not to be excessive in the pejorative sense (wasteful and irrelevant). In the church, giving begets further giving, so that the church is the form of that which is potentially formless and anarchic. The church is thus the structure of the event of the gift wherever it happens. The church brings the narrative of the gift of God full circle, but it is a circle that does not end where it began. The gifts of God disrupt the logic of pure origins by constructing a postmodern narrative that denies the traditional plot structure of beginning, middle, and ending. The Trinity tells us that the gift is always being given and that giving does not end with the establishment of the giver's identity but instead continues as a way of bringing together identity and community, so that God too comes to be through the infinite path of the gift. The love we give spirals back toward God in ever inclusive and disconnected loops, showing how grace gives birth to a mutuality that animates and vivifies exchange, so that the "more" of the gift really "is."

Love, then, is the proper name (given the namelessness of God) for the excess of excess, the law that makes excess what it is, which is above every law. Love is the wager that excess does have an ethics, an illegal wager made by the outlaw who is willing to transgress the unwritten rules of what is necessary and proper. Such giving transcends intentionality, occurring along the borders between persons, thus calling into question the idea of self-identity and the duality of self and other. Like the Holy Spirit, the gift is amorphous and fluid, a faceless profusion of energy that nonetheless draws individuals together in a community of givers, where God will be, as the gift continues to disseminate, all in all. As with the Trinity, the church represents the possibility of a society where individuals are who they are through extravagant acts of mutual generosity. In sum, Christian theology proclaims a blessed excess, locating hyperbole in a process, not just in the event of the other or in individual desire for the good. Excess is the self-perpetuating radiance of God's becoming for and through us. Excess is God's own unfolding life, how God comes to be God through the propulsion of excess. We too come to be ourselves by participating in the course of the gift, which moves in a spiraling loop toward the good that is beyond being, the community we anticipate when we put hyperbole into play and thereby render the exaggerations of religion true.

Notes

1. The image drawn from masculine adolescence is, in this case, appropriate, because hyperbole is often portrayed as an intrusive interruption or a sudden profusion in the midst of ordinary discourse. For a review of the rhetorical tradition, see Robert Evans, "Hyperbole," in the *Princeton Encyclopedia of Poetry and Poetics,* ed. Alex Preminger (Princeton: Princeton University Press, 1965). Also see Stephen H. Webb, *Blessed Excess, Religion and the Hyperbolic Imagination* (Albany: State University of New York Press, 1993).

2. Aristotle, *Rhetoric,* trans. Martin Otswald (Indianapolis: Bobbs-Merrill, 1962), 1413a29–30.

3. Notice the key phrase, "in the right place": "For I would make bold to say that nothing contributes to greatness as much as noble passion in the right place; it breathes the frenzied spirit of its inspiration upon the words and makes them, as it were, prophetic." Longinus, *On Great Writing,* trans. G. M. A. Grube (Indianapolis: Bobbs-Merrill, 1962), 11.

4. For more on this point, see Stephen H. Webb, "A Hyperbolic Imagination: Theology and the Rhetoric of Excess," *Theology Today* 50 (April 1993): 56–67.

5. Indeed, the power and the ambiguity of Protestantism lies precisely in the attempt

to moralize religious excess. The Protestant Reformers set out to liberate the grace of God from human control and manipulation, but Protestantism ended up rejecting all religious expressions that were not practical and useful. By trying to eliminate superstition, Protestantism turned religion over to utilitarianism. Suspicion of the social value of rituals of excess led Protestants to channel their spiritual energies either into a rigorous ethical code or into a cultivation of inward and therefore private spiritual states. Rarely have Protestant theologians been able to articulate a constructive theory of religious excess that avoids either arid moralism or subjective enthusiasm.

6. See David Dawson, *Literary Theory* (Minneapolis: Fortress, 1995), especially the following comment: "For the Christian reader, the troping of the Hebrew Bible so that it becomes the Christian Old Testament foreshadows (or, from another point of view, reflects) the reader's own turning toward the person of Christ" (1).

7. "Even if we were to tell it, we would not be believed." Primo Levi, *The Drowned and the Saved* (New York: Vintage, 1988), 12.

8. "Being chosen involves a surplus of obligation for which the 'I' of moral consciousness utters." Emmanuel Levinas, *Difficult Freedom, Essays on Judaism,* trans. Seán Hand (Baltimore: Johns Hopkins University Press, 1990), 177.

9. Emmanuel Levinas, *Totality and Infinity,* trans. Alphonso Lingis (Pittsburgh: Duquesne University Press, 1969).

10. See Susan A. Handelman, *Fragments of Redemption, Jewish Thought and Literary Theory in Benjamin, Scholem, and Levinas* (Bloomington: Indiana University Press, 1991).

11. Levinas, *Difficult Freedom,* 14.

12. Ibid., 17. Levinas criticizes every form of mysticism, including a mystical attachment to place: "The Jewish man discovers man before discovering landscapes and towns" (22). Freedom from sedentary forms of existence, a perpetual exile, becomes for Levinas a precondition for the vigilance of the ethical life. Judaism gives piety no other root — no idols of saints, local cults, sacred landscapes — than the epiphany of the face of the other.

13. Jacques Derrida, "Violence and Metaphysics," in *Writing and Difference,* trans. Alan Bass (Chicago: University of Chicago Press, 1978), 93. For another reading of Levinas's use of hyperbole in his conception of the height of the other, see Paul Ricoeur, *Oneself as Another,* trans. Kathleen Blamey (Chicago: University of Chicago Press, 1992), 335–41.

14. Levinas, *Totality and Infinity,* 176–77.

15. Ibid., 171.

16. Ibid., 215.

17. Emmanuel Levinas, *Otherwise Than Being, or Beyond Essence,* trans. Alphonso Lingis (The Hague: Matinus Nijhoff, 1981).

18. John D. Caputo, *Against Ethics* (Bloomington: Indiana University Press, 1993).

19. I am not endorsing Caputo's language here. For many postmodern philosophers, the Jew represents that which cannot be assimilated, that is, that which is permanently exiled, a particularity or contingency that defies conceptuality. These philosophers risk condemning Jews to the diaspora all over again by perpetuating the symbol (even if they give it positive meaning) of the wandering Jew who is the eternal other to Christianity. By essentializing the Jew, real Jews are made to disappear.

20. "Infinity for Derrida is not symbolic but hyperbolic infinity, as opposed to Levinas, for whom it is expressly something metaphysical and even theological, something ethico-theo-logical": John D. Caputo, *Demythologizing Heidegger* (Bloomington: Indiana University Press, 1993), 200.

21. William James, *The Varieties of Religious Experience* (New York: Vintage, 1990), 15. For more on James, see Stephen H. Webb, "The Rhetoric of and About Excess in William James's *The Varieties of Religious Experience*," in *Religion and Literature* 27 (Summer 1995): 27–45.

22. See Georges Bataille, *The Accursed Share: An Essay on General Economics*, vol. 1, trans. Robert Hurley (New York: Zone, 1989).

23. See Stephen H. Webb, *The Gifting God: A Trinitarian Ethics of Excess* (New York: Oxford University Press, 1996), chap. 2.

24. Gilles Deleuze, *Nietzsche and Philosophy*, trans. Hugh Tomlinson (New York: Columbia University Press, 1983).

25. Friedrich Nietzsche, *Thus Spoke Zarathustra*, trans. Walter Kaufmann (New York: Penguin, 1978), 15.

26. Edith Wyschogrod, *Saints and Postmodernism: Revisioning Moral Philosophy* (Chicago: University of Chicago Press, 1990), 255.

27. As David Matthew Matzko argues, "Any attempt to find a saint, a sage, or a prophet requires interpretive practices which shape the constitution of the community because the practice of naming saints is also a process of naming what social (moral and religious) practices are held to be constitutive of common life": "Postmodernism, Saints and Scoundrels," *Modern Theology* 9 (January 1993), 22. Moreover: "The saint is a self who is constituted by others; and in this sense, the saint has become the focal point for work that has been done, by both saints and supplicants, to create a network of relationships which can be called a community" (30).

28. Marx is the great skeptic of generosity. He celebrates the bourgeoisie for stripping away the embellishments of exchange. There is nothing kind or gentle about capitalism, according to Marx, but it is, nonetheless, honest and clear about the reality of exchange.

29. Jacques Derrida, *Given Time: 1. Counterfeit Money*, trans. Peggy Kamuf (Chicago: University of Chicago Press, 1992), 13.

30. Jacques Derrida, *Mémoires, for Paul de Man*, trans. Cecile Lindsay, Jonathan Culler, and Eduardo Cadava (New York: Columbia University Press, 1986), 149.

31. See Jacques Derrida, *The Gift of Death*, trans. David Wills (Chicago: University of Chicago Press, 1995): "But an infinite calculation supersedes the finite calculating that has been renounced. God the Father, who sees in secret, will pay back your salary, and on an infinitely greater scale" (107).

32. Derrida, *Given Time*, 30.

33. See Jacques Derrida, "At This Very Moment in This Work Here I Am," trans. Ruben Berezdiven, in *Re-Reading Levinas*, ed. Robert Bernasconi and Simon Critchley (Bloomington: Indiana University Press, 1991).

34. In *Otherwise Than Being*, Levinas generalizes the idea of incarnation to mean our sensible experience of the body in all its "maternity, vulnerability, apprehension" (76) Incarnation is epitomized in hunger, but it also means that I am capable of giving away the bread from my mouth. Levinas also helps to explain why the *idea* of sainthood (not

the existence of saints!) is not inherent in Judaism. The individual's relationship to God is mediated by the Torah, by the entire body of the people of Israel, and by a radically just relationship to all people, but not by other individuals who stand out in their intimacy with the divine and thus can alleviate some of my responsibility for that relationship.

35. In a discussion of Saint Paul's use of the phrase "how much more," Paul Ricoeur suggests, "It is in this way that the church, through the mouth of Paul, gives a *name*, the name of Jesus Christ, to the law of superabundance": *Figuring the Sacred: Religion, Narrative, and Imagination,* trans. David Pellauer, ed. Mark I. Wallace (Minneapolis: Fortress, 1995), 282. Notice, though, that when Ricoeur talks about hyperbole as an essential expression of Christianity, he subordinates it to metaphor, analogy, and other tropes and genres (233–34).

36. I am not saying that the phenomenon of giving is a vestige of the Trinity in Saint Augustine's sense; that argument would prematurely find the Trinity operative in sinful human acts. Instead, I am saying that the Trinity illuminates what gift giving can and therefore ought to be. The Trinity does not shed light on the ontological structure of generosity, precisely because giving, as an aspect of excess, is not a structure of being at all. Rather, the process of community-creating excess that is the Trinity points to what is not but also pressures us into moving toward what could come to be.

37. Jean-Luc Marion, *God Without Being,* trans. Thomas A. Carlson (Chicago: University of Chicago Press, 1991), p. xx.

38. I borrow this phrase from William Corlett, *Community Without Unity: A Politics of Derridian Extravagance* (Durham, N.C.: Duke University Press, 1989).

PART IV

Rhetoric and Community

The close connection between rhetoric and religion has profound consequences for the possibility of unity within social and religious communities.
Earlier Marjorie O'Rourke Boyle noted that the Renaissance humanists appreciated the "unitive power" of religion and rhetoric, "the bond of society,
the integration of self, and communion with God," drawing on the classical
orators for whom speech was a socializing and civilizing act. In a similar way,
Kathy Eden's thoughtful study links adages, commonly held formulations of
belief that unify both discursive practice and social relationships, to secular
and Christian conceptions and practices of friendship, love, and community.
She understands Plato's *Phaedrus,* for example, as integrating the "commonal-
ty of friendship into the praxis of erotic love" and the praxis of love "to
discursive practice." On the other hand she notes that Callicles, in Plato's
Gorgias, seeks a "natural justice" that promotes relations not of equality but
of advantage. Rhetorically proper relations of the part to the wholes and "the
particular instance to the general class" within egalitarian formulations of
community shape similar relations within political community.

In his chapter on religious images, Stephen Happel contrasts modern aesthetics and art writing, which are preoccupied with form abstracted from
function, moral purpose from daily life, with Renaissance and other contemporary rhetorical approaches to art. The latter, in particular — in the writings

of such theorists as Michael Baxandall, W. J. T. Mitchell, Svetlana Alpers, and others — reestablish possibilities for the unity of art and society, art and theology, religious truth and artistic truth, by relocating art within its numerous possible social contexts. By analyzing Carravagio's *The Conversion of St. Paul* within the context of the theological controversies of its own time, Happe applies the rhetorical insights of those contemporary aestheticians, himself illustrating how religious claims can be embodied in artistic, and rhetorically artistic, forms.

Mark Krupnick uses Kenneth Burke's notion of symbolic action to demonstrate how religious doctrine can be understood to shape "attitude and motive." According to Krupnick's argument, "religious doctrines . . . are seen by Burke as symbolic acts insofar as they are ways of 'naming' and 'sizing up' situations, especially situations marked by internal contradictions." Krupnick analyzes how religious discourse as symbolic action provided ways for individuals and groups to act responsively in "objective, real-life situations" and to cope with practical exigencies of their situations. He considers how such diverse figures as Saint Augustine, John Calvin, Oliver Cromwell, and Edmund Wilson appropriated and reformulated rhetoric about the Jews as a people of the Book, both to situate attitudes toward the Jews and to cope with the hardships of their own situations. Like many of the chapters in this volume, Krupnick's essay stresses the discursive formulations as strategies that people use to engage with historically contingent, particular problems.

The emphases on symbolic action and on community as central to rhetorical and religious discourse and practice easily lead to considerations of how traditional texts and worship provide antecedent meanings which precede any individual act of understanding, believing, or worshiping. For James Fodor and Stanley Hauerwas, religious experience is always articulated within a language: God is a performing God and human actions "truly and properly performed will be nothing short of, and nothing other than, 'a movement into our createdness.'" Worship itself, as performance, constitutes such a movement and "that Christians are saved in and for time, not from time, means that they are committed to cultivating the virtues that characterize good performers, accomplished improvisers, persuasively peaceable rhetoricians." Drawing on the rhetorical notion of *inventio,* Fodor and Hauerwas suggest that "all performances of God's called people . . . are repeat performances, at once emulating the one true performance of God in Christ but also an extension and variation — an improvisation, if you will — of that singularly defining performance

14

Koinonia *and the Friendship Between Rhetoric and Religion*

KATHY EDEN

A powerful advocate in the first half of the sixteenth century for a renewed friendship between rhetoric and religion was Desiderius Erasmus, who
opens his popular collection of ancient proverbs, the *Adages,* with an old saw
widely applied: "Between friends all is common" (Gr. *ta ton philon koina;* Lat.
amicorum communia omnia).[1] Hastening as usual through numerous Greek
and Roman references, including in this case Euripides, Aristotle, Theophras-
tus, Terence, and Cicero, Erasmus lingers momentarily over two authorities,
Pythagoras and Plato. Pythagoras, as we shall see, deserves this special attention as the reputed source of the saying. Plato also merits it, not only because as
the most ardent spokesman for Pythagorean doctrine he furnishes the fullest
brief for communal as against private property — the position rebutted, Erasmus reminds us, by Plato's own pupil Aristotle[2] — but also because in so doing,
he of all the ancients most nearly approaches Christ's thinking on this matter.

As Erasmus explains in a prefatory gloss on this adage, the founder of the
Academy, like the Redeemer, understood the deep and abiding relation be-
tween *koinonia* and *philia* — between commonality and love (LB, II, 6F–7A;
CWE, 31, 15):

> What other purpose has Plato in so many volumes except to urge a com-
> munity of living [*communitatem*], and the factor [*auctorem*] which creates

it, namely friendship [*amicitiam*]? . . . What other purpose had Christ, the prince of our religion? One precept and one alone He gave to the world, and that was love [*caritatis*]; on that alone, He taught, hang all the law and the prophets. Or what else does love teach us, except that all things should be common to all [*ut omnium omnia sint communia*]? In fact that united in friendship [*amicitia*] with Christ, glued to Him by the same binding force that holds Him fast to the Father, imitating so far as we may that complete communion [*communionem*] by which He and the Father are one, we should also be one with him, and, as Paul says, should become one spirit and one flesh with God, so that by the laws of friendship [*amicitiae jure*] all that is His is shared with us and all that is ours is shared with Him; and then that, linked one to another in the same bonds of friendship [*amicitiae vinculis*], as members of one Head and like one and the same body we may be filled with the same spirit, and weep and rejoice at the same things together.

As fundamental to Christian as to Platonic fellowship, Erasmus claims, this proverbial wisdom informs at least two of the most cherished practices of Christianity: the Eucharist and monasticism.

Also fittingly called "communion" (Gr. *koinonia;* Lat. *communio*), the Eucharist enacts the bond of friendship — unity from multiplicity — in the "mystic bread, brought together out of many grains into one flour, and the draught of wine fused into one liquid from many clusters of grapes" (*CWE,* 31, 15). Similarly, monasticism — and more precisely, cenobitic in contrast to eremitic monasticism — transforms many individuals into one community.[3] So Erasmus concludes his first adage on the commonality among friends with an etymology of *coenobium* (Gr. *koinobion*), the religious common life, crediting Pythagoras with the way of life that such friendship engenders (LB, II, 14F CWE, 31, 30):

> Not only was Pythagoras the author [*parentem*] of this saying [*sententiae*] but he also instituted a kind of sharing [*communionem*] of life and property in this way, the very thing Christ wants to happen among Christians. For all those who were admitted by Pythagoras into that well-known band who followed his instruction would give to the common fund whatever money and family property they possessed. This is called in Latin, in a word which expresses the facts, *coenobium,* clearly from community [*societate*] of life and fortunes.

Although Erasmus owes his genealogy of the monastic life here to a faulty edition of Aulus Gellius's *Noctes Atticae* (1.9.12), which reads *coenobium* for (the less familiar Roman legal formula) *ercto non cito,*[4] this misreading only serves to confirm the exalted status of *koinonia* or community in Christianity as Erasmus inherits it. For the humanist reformer *philosophia Christi* shares with the most profound Greek philosophies — Platonism and Pythagorean-ism — the commitment to *communitas* created, as he says above, by *amicitia*.

This first of the more than four thousand adages that finally constitute the *Adagaiorum chiliades,* in other words, initiates the reader into the ancient cult of friendship and community even while inviting her to consider their link to long-standing Christian practices. Inaugurating as it does a work so imposing and, on Erasmus's own account, so innovative in form and intention,[5] the first adage also sets in relief the effects of these fundamental concepts on, more specifically, literary or discursive practices. For like the common fund of the Pythagoreans, as the *Adages* repeatedly demonstrates, proverbs themselves belong to no single author but equally to all members of the larger cultural community.[6] Not least of the things that friends hold in common, proverbs unite into one statement the wisdom and experience of the many. With this first adage, then, Erasmus invests *koinonia* with the power to shape not only social and religious but also literary forms.

As we might expect from the author of the *Adages,* a project outspokenly designed to reappropriate the wisdom of the ancients, this investment is more properly a reinvestment. For *koinonia,* as a shaping principle, not only served the same ancients that Erasmus appropriates, but it did so in a variety of con-texts, including theological, political, and rhetorical. Taking direction from Erasmus's decision to pause momentarily over two of these ancients, I shall explore the role of *koinonia* in a few of the Platonic and Pythagorean texts — Christian as well as non-Christian — that have fostered the long-standing friendship between rhetoric and religion.

Curiously missing from the citations of Erasmus's first adage is Plato's *Phae-drus,* which ends with the proverbial affirmation regularly attributed to Py-thagoras that friends hold everything — including their prayers — in common (279C: *koina gar ta ton philon*). Indeed, this dialogue arguably takes *philia,* or friendship, especially in relation to *eros,* or erotic love, as a principal focus.[7] Lysias rests his argument in favor of the nonlover, as Phaedrus repeats it, on the assumption that the *erastes,* or lover, is incapable of *philia,* setting it and *eros* at odds. And Socrates, complying with his friend's request for a speech that rivals Lysias's, first challenges the sophist without challenging this assumption. Whereas friends hold all things in common, including property and other friends, lovers, by contrast, deprive their beloveds of both (239E–240A):

> It is evident to everyone, and especially to a lover, that he would pray above all that his beloved be bereft of those who are for him the most friendly, most well-intentioned, and most divine, for a lover would welcome his beloved's being deprived of father and mother, relatives, and friends [*philon*], since he believes they will cause difficulties and raise objections to his most delightful

relationship with his beloved. Moreover, he will believe that someone who has property, whether gold or other possessions, will not be as easily caught nor, when caught, as easily managed. As a result it is altogether inevitable that a lover will be jealous of the property his darling possesses and rejoice at its loss.[8]

Proving himself an inadequate *koinonos*, or associate (239C), the lover of Socrates' first speech behaves in a way strikingly opposed to the model of friendship epitomized by the dialogue's closing proverb. Instead of advancing the commonality and equality at the root of friendship, the so-called left-handed lover disdains the beloved's property as a threat to his continued inferiority. The lover of Socrates' palinode, in contrast, conforms to the behavior proverbially endorsed. Relinquishing all his own possessions, including family, friends, and property, for the company of the beloved (252AB), he gains in exchange a *philia* that both surpasses any he has ever experienced (255B) and endures throughout his life (256CE; see also 234A).

Integrating the commonality of friendship into the praxis of erotic love, Socrates predictably extends the same principle of integration to discursive practice. As much about logos as about *eros*, as readers frequently note, the *Phaedrus* not only situates its consideration of a better and worse kind of love within a consideration of a better and worse kind of rhetoric but sets a standard for loving that applies equally to speaking and to writing.[9] Just as the model for the relationship between lover and beloved is a commonality characteristic of *philia*, so the model for discourse is unity or oneness, memorably figured here, in anticipation of Erasmus's corporeal metaphor above, as a living organism whose parts are in a proper relation both to one another and to the whole (264C). This unity moreover, is logical as well as formal, pertaining not only to the proper relation between part and whole but to that between particularity and generality.[10] Enforcing this standard, Socrates evaluates the three speeches on love in large part according to how well they exemplify dialectical method, that process of collection grounded, like *philia* itself, in similarity or likeness (261E–262A, 266BC, 273DE).

For complementing the commonplace that friends hold all things in common is the related commonplace, also attributed to Pythagoras, that similarity or likeness begets friendship.[11] Twice Socrates alludes to this proverb, calling it a *palaios logos*, an old saying: first while arguing the case for the nonlover (240C) and then as part of his brief for the lover (255B). In so doing, he puts into practice what Aristotle soon afterward and Erasmus centuries later noticed in theory, namely, that proverbs constitute a common intellectual stock or property of culture preserved by tradition. Far from uniform in its applica tion, as both theorists will claim, this intellectual legacy in the possession of the orator serves argumentation on either side of the question.[12]

So Socrates challenges Phaedrus's highly rhetorical claim that he can only imperfectly re-create the main lines of Lysias's oration with another adage about *philia,* this one, like the others, also attributed to Pythagoras. Knowing full well that his friend has memorized Lysias's speech, Socrates exposes Phaedrus's ploy with a particularized version of the proverb that a friend is a second self *(ton philon heteron auton):* "If I don't know Phaedrus, I have forgotten myself" (228A). And so great is similarity in friendship that Phaedrus in turn counters Socrates' rhetorical coyness in refusing to challenge Lysias's speech by brandishing the same proverb (236C).[13]

In the *Phaedrus,* in other words, Plato constructs a homology between discursive and social praxis rooted in the concept of commonality and unity. If the paradigmatic social form of this practice is friendship, the paradigmatic discursive form is the proverb, giving more than incidental weight not only to the various adages about friendship repeated throughout this dialogue but also to its "summary judgment" that friends hold all things in common. Whereas the *Phaedrus* ends with a proverb, however, Plato's other dialogue explicitly concerned with rhetoric begins with one.

Plato opens the *Gorgias* with a brief skirmish between Callicles and Socrates on proverbial ground. In the first words, Socrates manages both to duck Callicles' attempted assault with a deadly commonplace — that Socrates has conveniently arrived, like the coward of the adage, too late for the battle — and to disarm his opponent by substituting another, less provocative saying: not too late for the fight but for the feast (447A).[14] Introducing both the agonistic and culinary analogies that will pervade Socrates' conversation with three different interlocutors in the course of this dialogue, Plato also introduces more particularly the context for his argument against Callicles, the third and last of the three. For fighting differs from feasting in that the former activity brings enemies together, the latter, friends. And friendship, here as in the *Phaedrus,* provides a framework for examining rhetoric.

Proclaiming himself an honorary member of the *koinonia sophias* or "wise guys' club" that Callicles and his friends have formed to debate matters of mutual interest (487B), Socrates seizes the opportunity to anchor his argument against Calliclean rhetoric in the notion of *koinonia.* For if it is the case, as Callicles puts it in his lengthy portrait of the man who neglects this art at great risk to himself (482C–486D), that "natural justice" promotes not equality but advantage, or *pleonexia* (483AE) — taking more than one's share — then what possibility is there for *koinonia* or community (490B–491A)? And if *pleonexia,* here as in the *Republic,* undermines political community, so does its counterpart, in the form of an improper relation of the part to the whole or the particular instance to the general class, undermine the formal and logical integrity of discourse. For not unlike other craftsmen in this regard, Socrates argues, the rhetorician must "arrange everything according to a certain order (*taxin*), and [force] one part to suit and fit with another [*prepon te einai kai harmottein*], until he has combined the whole [*to hapan*] into a regular [*tetagmenon*] and well-ordered [*kekosmemenon*] production" (503E504A; cf. 464C and *Phaedrus*, 236A, 264A).[15]

The crucial, unmistakably Pythagorean, qualities foregrounded here are *taxis* and *kosmos* (cf. 504AD), qualities no less essential to the psychology of the individual than to rhetorical production and political action. So, Socrates continues, someone lacking temperance and justice, like the thief, can neither formulate a well-ordered speech (see 503D) nor form part of a commonwealth (507E–508A):

> For neither to any of his fellowmen can such a one be dear [*prosphiles*], nor to God; since he cannot commune [*koinonein*] with any, and where there is no communion, there can be no friendship [*philia*]. And wise men tell us, Callicles, that heaven and earth and gods and men are held together by communion and friendship, by orderliness [*kosmioteta*], temperance, and justice; and that is the reason, my friend, why they call the whole [*to holon*] of this world by the name of order [*kosmon*], not of disorder or dissoluteness. Now you, as it seems to me, do not give proper attention to this, for all your cleverness, but have failed to observe the great power of geometrical equality [*he isotes he geometrike*] amongst both gods and men: you hold that self-advantage [*pleonexian*] is what one ought to practice, because you neglect geometry.[16]

To rebut Callicles, then, Socrates does more than summon the adage that ends the *Phaedrus*. He rests his case on the teachings of this other group of "wise guys," the Pythagoreans, who affirm that the universe itself—the cosmos—is held together by an attractive force that binds not only mortal creatures to one another but mortal to immortal in correspondence with the model of mathematics.[17] Callicles' misguided pursuit of rhetoric as popularly practiced, according to Socrates, like all wrong action follows from ignorance, here specifically ignorance of Pythagorean discipline, including mathematics.

Unschooled in the doctrines of Pythagoras, Callicles also misunderstands the relation between the rhetorician and his audience. For it too, Socrates claims, derives from an old Pythagorean saying: like to like (510B).[18] Only by really befriending (*eis philian*) the Athenian people—that is, only by becoming profoundly like them—can a rhetorician hope to persuade them (513B; see *Laws* 716B–717D). After much argumentation, in other words, Socrates returns to a claim advanced earlier in the dialogue against his first interlocutor

Far from being an art or *techne* grounded in knowledge of a subject matter, rhetoric is a kind of know-how, an *empeiria,* by which the ignorant gratify others like themselves. "So he who does not know," Socrates puts the case to Gorgias at the outset, "will be more convincing to those who do not know than he who knows" (459B).

Like the *Phaedrus,* then, and in stark contrast to the art both practiced and preached by such sophists as Lysias and Gorgias, the *Gorgias* characterizes its own rhetorical theory as founded on the principle of *koinonia,* with its attendant qualities of *taxis* and *kosmos.* In addition to incorporating elaborate myths of psychic migration, myths that boldly advertise Plato's pedigree in the earlier Italian school,[19] these two dialogues, more pointedly for this essay, betray their Pythagorean heritage in their reliance on proverbial statement, especially proverbs about friendship. In keeping with this legacy of myth and proverb, moreover, these dialogues also inherit the Pythagorean homology between politics, rhetoric, and theology, a homology rooted in a cosmic *philia,* which is rooted in turn in *koinonia.*

In spite of the strong Pythagorean element of these two dialogues on rhetoric, however, the continued accessibility and even force of the ideas in subsequent centuries is due less to Plato than to later students of the Platonic and Pythagorean traditions — students such as Aulus Gellius, Diogenes Laertius, and Iamblichus. The founder of a school near Antioch at Apamea in Syria, Iamblichus built his curriculum around the academic progress from Pythagoras to Plato, gradually shepherding his students through an ordered reading of ten Platonic dialogues, including the *Gorgias* and the *Phaedrus.*[20] Presumably his pedagogical approach to Pythagoras as a propaedeutic to Platonic study is reflected in his work on the Pythagorean way of life, the so-called *De vita Pythagorica.*

In this work Iamblichus paints the literary portrait of a man who is not only the first philosopher (58) but the founding father of *philia* — friendship of all for all (69–70, 229–30).[21] Included in this universal *koinonia* is the bond between immortals and mortals, body and soul, citizens with one another, men with women, adults with children, all humans with one another, and ultimately all living creatures: "All these may be summed up in that one word 'friendship,' and Pythagoras is the acknowledged founding father of it all. He handed on to his followers such a remarkable tradition of friendship that even now people say of those who show each other unusual goodwill, 'They belong to the Pythagoreans'" (230).

Philia, in other words, underlies the interrelated arenas of theology, psychology, politics, ethics, and even anthropology and zoology. These disciplines and the interrelation between them on the model of geometry form the core of

Pythagorean education, or *paideia* (see, for example, 37–40, 130, 201–3). Indeed, Pythagoras regards *paideia* itself, handed down from teacher to pupil, as common intellectual property, the *koine euphuia* of all members of the cultural community — the kind of property one does not lose by giving it away (43).[22] And this only apparently paradoxical nature of intellectual property finds its analogue in the most widely attested custom of the Pythagoreans, namely, their peculiar handling of material property.

For constituting a "commonwealth" in the radical sense, Pythagorean community holds all possessions in common (see, for example, 72, 81, 92) on the grounds that communalism, as Plato himself learned from Pythagoras, is a precondition of justice (167–68):

> The origin of justice . . . is community feeling and fairness, for all to share experience, approximating as closely as possible to one body and one soul, and for everyone to say "mine" and "someone else's" about the same thing (just as Plato also testifies, having learnt it from the Pythagoreans). Pythagoras established this best of all men, eradicating all selfishness of character and extending the sense of community to the very last possessions, the things which cause faction and disruption. Everything was in common and the same for all: no-one had any private property. One who liked community living used the common possessions in the most just way; one who did not took back his own property, and more than he had brought to the common store, and left. Thus he established justice, in the best possible way, from its first principle.

Eradicating *pleonexia* by eliminating its cause in the distinction between "yours" and "mine," Pythagorean society encouraged its citizens to spend their time in such communal activities as walking together, studying together, exercising together, collaborating on the solution to administrative and legal problems, dining together, reading together after dinner, and singing hymns together to the gods (95–100).[23]

Famous in late antiquity for instituting a common routine that bound initiates into a unified society, Pythagoras was equally famous for instituting a rhetorical praxis conducive to this kind of community, the so-called *Pythagorae symbola*. Among the most widely applied of these sayings were those about friendship. Weaving these well-worn adages into his literary portrait of the philosopher (see, for example, 84, 92), Iamblichus takes the time to explain their role in his philosophical agenda (103–5; see also 161–62, 227):

> But the most necessary form of teaching, for Pythagoras, was by symbols. Almost all Greeks were enthusiastic about this kind of teaching, because it is of very great antiquity; the Egyptians gave it its most subtle form and highest status. In the same way Pythagoras also valued it greatly, as may be seen by

those who can perceive the meaning and unspoken content of the Pythagorean symbols, and can realise how much rightness and truth is in them once they are freed from the concealment of their riddling form, and how well their simple and straightforward transmission [*paradosin*] suits the greatness, indeed the closeness to god which surpasses human understanding, of these philosophers. . . . Unless one can interpret the symbols, and understand them by careful exposition, what they say would strike the chance observer as absurd — old wives' tales, full of nonsense and idle talk. But once they are deciphered as symbols should be, and become clear and transparent instead of obscure to outsiders, they impress us like utterances of the gods or Delphic oracles, revealing an astounding intellect and having a supernatural influence on those lovers of learning who have understood them.

Deftly accommodating the psychology of their audience, the sayings of Pythagoras strike noninitiates as enigmatic or even commonplace, while disclosing a wealth of meaning to those who understand them.[24] And this much-admired rhetorical practice, complementing the social practice of a true Pythagorean commonwealth, is further aligned with a hermeneutical practice that becomes the trademark of Iamblichus's own *paideia*.

For Iamblichus not only sets the reading list for his students, including the order in which the prescribed works should be read, but he also teaches students how to understand these works, encouraging them to begin their exegeses by finding what he calls the *skopos*.[25] Like the Pythagorean proverb, or *symbolon*, in unifying the wisdom of the many into a single statement, the *skopos* of a literary text articulates its thematic unity in a single, brief formulation that through interpretation explains in turn the manifold complexities of that text. Once the reader identifies the *skopos*, which all parts of the text hold in common insofar as they belong to a unified whole, she can then go on to interpret the details in light of their commonality. Not surprisingly, Iamblichus takes his mandate for reading this way from Plato himself, and especially from Socrates' observations in the *Phaedrus* concerning the organic nature of skillfully crafted discourse, defined as discourse in which one part relates not only to all the other parts but to the whole (264C).

Philologically in error, then, the closing remarks of Erasmus's first adage on the origins of *coenobium* nevertheless hit the mark in a broader historical sense. For early Christianity does inherit the joint Pythagorean-Platonic legacy of a commonality that is at once social and discursive, religious and rhetorical. Among the earliest and most influential proponents of cenobitic monasticism, Saint Basil, for instance, advocates both withdrawal from promiscuous social intercourse (R.2, 344A–345B) and participation in the common life with like-minded believers (R.3, 345B–348A).[26] A student of so-called classical *paideia*, including Platonism and Pythagoreanism, long before his supposed encounter with Pachomian monasticism, Basil defends *koinos bios* not only in terms of the apostolic community featured in Acts (for example, 2:44, 4:32) but also in terms of organic wholeness familiar from the *Phaedrus*.[27] His defense, more-over, emphasizes the advantages that accrue to individual and community from holding intellectual rather than material property in common (346DE):

> Consequently, in the common life the private gift of each man becomes the common property of his fellows. . . . So that of necessity in the community life the working of the Holy Spirit in one man passes over to all the rest at once. Now all you who have read the Gospels know the great danger incurred by the man living alone, who has one gift perhaps, and makes it useless by idleness, digging a hole for it in himself. Whereas when a number live together a man enjoys his own gift, multiplying it by imparting it to others, and reaps the fruits of other men's gifts as if they were his own.

Like Basil (perhaps even to some extent following his lead), Saint Augustine too both practices and preaches *coenobium*.[28] And the commonality of the best way of life, for Augustine, corresponds to the commonality of the best kind of discourse.

In his own *Regula*, Augustine insists on community property, *omnia communia*: "Do not call anything your own; possess everything in common" (1.3);[29] and he structures *communitas* around both cooperative labor and, recalling the Pythagorean routine outlined by Iamblichus, the more leisurely "group activities" of walking, dining, talking, praying, reading, and singing hymns. Life in the monastery, in other words, resembles in some important details communal life for the first Pythagorean initiates at Croton.[30] Indeed, Augustine's dialogue in two books entitled *De ordine*, written during the experiment in monastic living at Cassiciacum, ends its exploration of the orderly arrangement of the universe, a topic explored by Socrates in the *Gorgias*,[31] by invoking the authority of Pythagoras. "And what has been disclosed almost to our very eyes by you today?" Augustine's lifelong friend Alypius asks him in *De ordine*, "Is it not that venerable and almost divine teaching which is rightly attributed to Pythagoras — in fact, proved to be his?" (2.20.53).[32]

Before concluding this dialogue with the explicit association of his own teachings on the matter with those of Pythagoras, moreover, Augustine weaves Pythagorean principles everywhere into the fabric of his argument, including not only the principle of commonality but also its rhetorical correlative, organically unified discourse, and its social correlative, friendship. "Therefore, both in analyzing [*discernendo*] and in synthesizing [*connectendo*]," he claims (2.18.48),

> It is oneness [*unum*] that I seek, it is oneness that I love. But when I analyze, I seek a homogenous unit [*purgatum*]; and when I synthesize, I look for an integral unit [*integrum*]. In the former case, foreign elements [*aliena*] are avoided; in the latter, proper elements [*propria*] are conjoined to form something united [*unum*] and perfect. . . . And what else do friends strive for, but to be one [*unum*]? And the more they are one, so much the more are they friends. A population forms a city, and dissension is full of danger for it: to dissent—what is that, but to think diversely [*quid est autem dissentire, nisi non unum sentire*]?

For Augustine, as for Pythagoras and Plato, friendship, politics, and the discursive reasoning that underlies all rhetorical production depend on the successful integration of the individual parts into a whole (see, for example, 1.7.18).

So in the *Confessions,* to take only the most widely known instance, Augustine characterizes both psychological and social order as the proper relation between multiplicity and unity, the parts and the whole (for example, 1.12.19, 2.1.1, 3.8.15, 10.29.40). And the ordered society, he reasons, takes friendship as its model. For it is *amicitia* that creates unity between many souls (2.5.10). For this reason, Augustine remembers, he feared his own disintegration at the early death of his unnamed friend, one whose intimacy with himself he expresses in terms of the Pythagorean proverbs of "a second self" and "one soul in two bodies" (4.6.11).

First in this and then in subsequent friendships, in other words, Augustine recalls experiencing the unifying force of such a social bond (4.8.13):

> There were other things which occupied my mind in the company of my friends: to make conversation, to share a joke, to perform mutual acts of kindness, to read together well-written books, to share in trifling and in serious matters, to disagree though without animosity—just as a person debates with himself—and in the very rarity of disagreement to find the salt of normal harmony, to teach each other something or to learn from one another, to long with impatience for those absent, to welcome them with gladness on their arrival. These and other signs come from the heart of those who love and are loved and are expressed through the mouth, through the tongue, through the eyes, and a thousand gestures of delight, acting as fuel to set our minds on fire and out of many to forge unity.

A unifying force before conversion, after conversion friendship continues to shape Augustine's social philosophy, even to the point of providing a conceptual framework for monastic community, including the failed experiment at Rome, the withdrawal to Cassiciacum, and eventually the retreat to the monastery at Thagaste.[33]

From their first failed beginnings, moreover, these religious communities took on the Pythagorean code of common property (6.14.24):

> Among our group of friends we had animated discussions of a project: talking with one another we expressed detestation for the storms and troubles of human life, and had almost decided on withdrawing from the crowds and living a life of contemplation. This contemplative leisure we proposed to organize in the following way: everything that we could raise we would put into a common treasury and from everyone's resources would create a single household chest. In sincere friendship nothing would be the private property of this or that individual, but out of the resources of all, one treasury would be formed; the whole would belong to each, and everything would belong to everybody.

And this Pythagorean ideal of commonality informs Augustine's thinking not only about monasticism as a social organization of friends holding things material and spiritual in common but also about discourse as one of those activities — perhaps even the central activity — that binds friends together. For it is in conversation, joke telling, and reading and even disputing together, as he clarifies in the quotation cited above, that individuals express their friendship and forge the bonds that unify a multiplicity.

For Augustine, moreover, as for Plato and Pythagoras, the best social praxis corresponds to the best rhetorical praxis. Like community, discourse depends on the proper relation of the parts to a whole.[34] Indeed, Augustine defines human in contrast to divine experience in terms of rhetorical discursiveness — the paradigm, to his way of thinking, of this relation. Whereas for God there is no beginning, middle, or end — the past, present, and future of narrative — but only the wholeness of eternity (see, for example, 4.10.15, 4.11.17, 9.10.24, 11.6.8, 11.11.13), for us temporality unfolds after the fashion of such rhetorical activities as storytelling (10.8.13, 11.18.23), recitation (11.28.38), and even conversation (9.10.24). So when Augustine labors to communicate the somewhat more-than-human communion with God and with each other that he and Monica experienced at Ostia, he articulates its cessation as a return to "the noise of our human speech where a sentence has both a beginning and an ending" (9.10.24).

Similarly, when he labors to account for the multiplicity of interpretations that Scripture engenders in such a way that these partial understandings may strengthen a spiritual commonwealth rather than erode it, he once again turns to the Pythagorean notion of commonality, a common store — here the common ownership of the truth rhetorically revealed in Scripture. Of those, in contrast, who would claim some individual right of possession, Augustine insists that (12.25.34) it cannot be merely their private property. If they respect an affirmation because it is true, then it is already both theirs and mine, shared by all lovers of the truth. But their contention that Moses did not mean what I say but what they say, I reject. I do not respect that. . . . for your truth does not belong to me nor to anyone else, but to us all whom you call to share it as a public possession. With terrifying words you warn against regarding it as a private possession, or we may lose it (Matt. 25:14–30). Anyone who claims for his own property what you offer for all to enjoy, and wishes to have exclusive rights to what belongs to everyone, is driven from the common truth to his own private ideas, that is from truth to a lie. For "he who speaks a lie" speaks "from his own" (John 8:44).

As an extended community of like-minded friends in God, in other words, the faithful share their spiritual or intellectual wealth. In this way, they bear a profound similarity to the paradigmatic Christians, the cenobitic monks, who, like the first initiates at Croton (as well as the first apostles), hold all things in common.

Fundamental to both social and rhetorical practices, this commonality, or *koinonia,* as I have tried to outline in brief scope, belongs to all who share in his rich and complex tradition. Their inheritance includes not only material but, even more significant, intellectual property. And this common intellectual store, as Erasmus so keenly noticed in the adage that introduces his own treasury of the collective wisdom of the ancients, marks a defining feature of the long-standing friendship between Pythagorean, Platonist, and Christian as well as between rhetoric and religion.

Notes

1. No. 94 of the *Adagiorum collectanea* of 1500, this adage was moved to first position in the *Adagiorum chiliades* of 1508, where it remained for all subsequent editions. In its earliest form, moreover, it was only six lines long and featured Terence rather than Plato. On the remarkable evolution of this adage and the collection as a whole see T. C. Appelt, *Studies in the Contents and Sources of Erasmus' Adagia* (Chicago, 1942), John C. Olin, "Erasmus' *Adagia* and More's *Utopia,*" *Miscellanea Moreana: Essays for Germain Marc'hadour,* ed. Clare M. Murphy, Henry Gibaud, Mario A. DiCesare (Binghamton, N.Y., 1989), 127–36, and Margaret Mann Phillips, *The Adages of Erasmus* (Cambridge, 1964). See also Daniel Kinney, "Erasmus' *Adagia:* Midwife to the Rebirth of Learning," *Journal of Medieval and Renaissance Studies* 11 (1981): 169–92.

For the Latin text of the *Adages* I have used *Opera Omnia,* ed. J. LeClerc (Leiden, 1703), vol. 2, hereafter LB; for the English, *The Collected Works of Erasmus* (Toronto, 1982), vols. 31–33, hereafter CWE.

2. See LB, II, 14CD; and Aristotle, *Politics,* 2.1, 1261a2, and 4.11, 1295b24. See also Luke T. Johnson, *Sharing Possessions: Mandate and Symbol of Faith* (Philadelphia,

1981), 121–25; Olin, "Erasmus' *Adagia*," 129–30; and cf. *Rhetoric* 1.5.7. In *Nicomachean Ethics*, 9.12.1, Aristotle states that *philia* is *koinonia*. And see A. W. Price, *Love and Friendship in Plato and Aristotle* (Oxford, 1986); and John M. Cooper, "Aristotle on Friendship," in *Essays on Aristotle's* Ethics, ed. Amélie Oksenberg Rorty (Berkeley, 1980), 301–40.

3. On the difference between cenobitic and eremitic monasticism see R. A. Markus, *The End of Ancient Christianity* (Cambridge, 1990), esp. 77–79 and 158–69. See also James E. Goehring, "The Origins of Monasticism," in *Eusebius: Christianity and Judaism*, ed. H. W. Aldridge and G. Hata (Detroit, 1992), 235–55; Brian Patrick McGuire, *Friendship and Community: The Monastic Experience* (Kalamazoo, Mich., 1988) and Rowan Greer, *Broken Lights and Mended Lives: Theology and Common Life in the Early Church* (University Park, Pa., 1986), esp. 162–83. For Erasmus on the relation between early monasticism and friendship, see the "Letter to Paul Volz," *CWE*, 6, 88–89; between the Eucharist and friendship, see *velut in cratere philotesio* (IV.iii.96), LB, II, 1024A, and *panem ne frangito* (I.i.2), LB, II, 23D; and for what monks could learn from Pythagoras, *quo transgressus* (III.x.11), LB, II, 935BF.

4. See *CWE*, 30, 31n43, and cf. Cicero, *De oratore*, 1.56.237. The passage in Aulus Gellius reads as follows (*The Attic Nights*, trans. J. C. Rolfe [Cambridge, Mass., 1927; rpt. 1984] 1.9.12): "But I must not omit this fact either—that all of them, as soon as they had been admitted by Pythagoras into that band of disciples, at once devoted to the common use whatever estate and property they had, and an inseparable fellowship [*societas inseparabilis*] was formed, like the old-time association which in Roman legal parlance was termed an 'undivided inheritance' [*ercto non cito*]."

5. See especially *Ep*. 126 to William Blount, Lord Mountjoy, *CWE*, 1, 259, where Erasmus claims that he is the first writer in Latin to attempt such a compendium of proverbs. On the relation of the *Adages* to Polydore Vergil's *Proverbiorum libellus* (Venice, 1498), see Appelt, *Studies in the Content and Sources of Erasmus'* Adagia, 68–77.

6. On the proverb as common property see the *Prolegomena* to the 1508 edition, LB, II, 1A–13F, *CWE*, 31, 3–28, esp. LB, II, 2B, *CWE*, 31, 4–5, and LB, II, 7DE, *CWE*, 31, 16. And see my " 'Between Friends All Is Common': The Erasmian Adage and Tradition," *Journal of the History of Ideas* 59 (1998): 405–19.

7. On the *Phaedrus* and especially its treatment of *philia*, see *Plato's Erotic Dialogues* trans. William S. Cobb (Albany, 1993), 169–70; Charles L. Griswold, *Self-Knowledge in Plato's* Phaedrus (New Haven, 1986); Jean-Claude Fraisse, *La Notion d'amitié dans la philosophic antique* (Paris, 1974), 158–67.

8. *Plato's Erotic Dialogues*, 98. See also Seth Benardete, *The Rhetoric of Morality and Philosophy: Plato's* Gorgias *and* Phaedrus (Chicago, 1991), 192–93.

9. See, for instance, G. R. F. Ferrari, *Listening to the Cicadas: A Study of Plato's* Phaedrus (Cambridge, 1987); Griswold, *Self-Knowledae in Plato's* Phaedrus, 138–201 and Paul Plass, "The Unity of the *Phaedrus*," *Symbolae Osloenses* 43 (1968): 7–38 reprinted in *Plato: True and Sophistic Rhetoric*, ed. Keith V. Erickson (Amsterdam 1979), 193–221.

10. For a clear statement of the role of *koinonia* in dialectical thinking see the *Statesman*, trans. Harold N. Fowler (Cambridge, Mass., 1925; rpt. 1975) 285AB: "Because people are not in the habit of considering things by dividing them into classes, they hastily